COMMON CORE GRAMMAR
HIGH SCHOOL EDITION

COYOTE CANYON PRESS
Claremont, California

Coyote Canyon Press
Claremont, California
www.coyotecanyonpress.com

Copyright © 2015 Thomas Fasano

National Governors Association Center for Best Practices, Council of Chief State School Officers, Common Core State Standards, English Language Arts Standards. Publisher: National Governors Association Center for Best Practices, Council of Chief State School Officers, Washington, DC. Copyright 2010. For more information, visit www.corestandards.org/ELA-Literacy.

Printed in the United States of America

ISBN 978-0-9890080-4-4

CONTENTS

Author's Note

This book was conceived and written by an English teacher. That's what I do. I teach high school English, and towards that end I make every effort to use the Common Core language standards in my daily work with students.

So why a grammar book aligned to the CCSS? And why one written by me? Simple: there was a need for one. I searched for a grammar book to put to good use in my classroom, one aligned to the Common Core, but the search went cold fast. The book I wanted and imagined did not exist. My next course of action was obvious: I was going to have to write it myself.

Previously, I published a book called *English Grammar in Review,* now sadly out of print—and not much use to me in the classroom since it was very much a pre-Common Core book. But a grand opportunity presented itself. I could rewrite, edit, and augment the lessons in that older book and thereby fashion a grammar book compliant with the Common Core high school standards.

The College Readiness Anchor Standards for Language 9–12 are the same for all high school students. The fundamental language skills don't vary, but the level at which students learn and can demonstrate those skills increases in complexity as they move along from one grade to the next.

It's this rise in difficulty that is the organizing principle of this book. Each lesson builds on previous lessons, coinciding with how the complexity of the standards changes across grade levels.

Anchor and language standards are referenced and cross-referenced on every page so that teachers and students know which standards are being taught and which objectives are being addressed. Teachers will have a convenient reminder of what the standards say, what they mean, and what effective language instruction looks like. Students will be confident in knowing that the instruction they're receiving falls within the larger context of the standards.

Each chapter contains detailed and complete lessons with thousands of example sentences that clarify core language skills. Accompanying exercises and writing prompts provide the necessary practice for students to learn, apply, and demonstrate these skills.

It is my hope that this book will prove to be a starting point for the study of English grammar—that is, a source of highly adaptable lessons for teachers to use as they create their own lessons, or realign older lessons from previous standards to be taught under the Common Core.

Thomas Fasano
Claremont, California

COMMON CORE GRAMMAR
HIGH SCHOOL EDITION

PART I:
PRIMARY CONCEPTS

CHAPTER

1

Nouns

ENGLISH LANGUAGE ARTS STANDARDS

☞ *CCSS.ELA-LITERACY.L.9–12.1:* *Demonstrate command of the conventions of standard English grammar and usage when writing or speaking.*

☞ *CCSS.ELA-LITERACY.L.9–12.2:* *Demonstrate command of the conventions of standard English capitalization, punctuation, and spelling when writing.*

☞ *CCSS.ELA-LITERACY.L.9–10.1.B:* *Use various types of phrases (noun, verb, adjectival, adverbial, participial, prepositional, absolute) and clauses (independent, dependent; noun, relative, adverbial) to convey specific meanings and add variety and interest to writing or presentations.*

☞ *CCSS.ELA-LITERACY.L.11–12.1.A:* *Apply the understanding that usage is a matter of convention, can change over time, and is sometimes contested.*

NOUNS

CCSS.L.9–12.1:
Demonstrate command of the conventions of standard English grammar and usage when writing or speaking.

A *Noun* is a word that names something. The something that a noun names may be:

- An animate or an inanimate thing with physical existence: as, *person, dog, plant, stone, winner, town.*

- An abstract or spiritual concept: as, *compassion, honor, hatred, honesty, love.*

- Some quality or property belonging to an object; as, *color, weight, thickness, density.*

- An action: as, *singing, exercising, dancing.*

Note. In the sentence, "Studying is necessary to pass the exam," *studying* is a noun (gerund) because it is the name of an act and is the subject of the verb *is;* but notice that in "He was studying all night," *studying* is not a noun: it is a part of the verb *was studying,* which tells what he was doing.

CLASSES OF NOUNS

CCSS.L.9–12.2:
Demonstrate command of the conventions of standard English capitalization, punctuation, and spelling when writing.

Nouns fall into two classes: Common Nouns and Proper Nouns.

A ***Common Noun*** is the name for all the members of a class of objects—that is, the name is common to all the members of the class: as, *state, country, man, bank, lake.*

A ***Proper Noun*** is the distinctive name of an individual member of a class: as, *Virginia* (a member of the class of *state*), *Germany* (*country*), *William* (*male*), *Erie* (*lake*).

The word "proper" traces its root through the word "property" and has the meaning of "one's own." In writing, proper nouns are capitalized. Such words as *Pepsi* (a can of Pepsi), the *French,* a *Canadian,* a *Moose* (a member of the Moose Lodge), *Democrats, Protestants,* etc., are also capitalized. Although these nouns are names common to all the members of a class, they are also the names of particular members of a class.

Special Classes

CCSS.L.9–12.2:
Demonstrate command of the conventions of standard English capitalization, punctuation, and spelling when writing.

The two classes—common and proper—cover all nouns, but included in these two are some special types.

An ***Abstract Noun*** names a cognitive or abstract concept: as, *benevolence, courtesy, trust, tranquility, strength, resilience.*

A ***Collective Noun*** is the name of a collection or group of similar objects: as, *mob, herd, club, team, company* (a commercial organization), *U.S. Navy, United Nations, Republican Party, Army Corps of Engineers.*

A ***Compound Noun*** is a combination of two or more existing nouns or other parts of speech: as, *grandmother, highway, businessman, commander-in-chief, brother-in-law, sales department, payroll, Marriott Hotel, Apple Computer.*

A ***Count Noun*** names something that can be counted and may be either physical or abstract: as, *pencil, pencils; mouse, mice; idea, ideas; dream, dreams.*

A ***Noncount Noun*** (also known as a ***Mass Noun***) is the name of something that cannot be counted and is used only in the singular; it may or may not be abstract: as, *clutter, wisdom, silence, satisfaction, music.*

PROPERTIES OF NOUNS

Nouns have Number, Gender, and Case.

Number

CCSS.L.9–12.2:
Demonstrate command of the conventions of standard English capitalization, punctuation, and spelling when writing.

Number is that aspect of a noun that designates whether one or more than one object is indicated.

The ***Singular Number*** indicates one object only: as, *cat, lake, woman.*

The ***Plural Number*** indicates two or more objects: as, *cats, lakes, women.*

The plural number in most instances is formed by adding *-s* or *-es* to the singular form: as *spoon, spoons; glass, glasses; house, houses; fax, faxes.*

Gender

CCSS.L.9–10.1.B:
Use various types of phrases (noun, verb, adjectival, adverbial, participial, prepositional, absolute) and clauses (independent, dependent; noun, relative, adverbial) to convey specific meanings and add variety and interest to writing or presentations.

Gender is that property of a noun that indicates the sex of an object. In English these distinctions are a matter of biology or custom, not actual grammatical gender, as it is in French, for example.

There are three genders: Masculine, Feminine, and Neuter.

The ***Masculine Gender*** indicates a being of the male sex: as, *man, son, nephew, bull, father, Anthony.*

The ***Feminine Gender*** indicates a being of the female sex: as, *woman, lady, sister, niece, hen, sow, Sophia.*

The ***Neuter Gender*** indicates an object of no sex: as, *tree, rock, carton, city, ground, clouds, tomatoes.*

In addition to these three genders, the term ***Common Gender*** refers to nouns that may be either masculine or feminine but don't designate any particular gender: as, *ancestor, baby, schoolmate, spouse, parent, teacher.*

Note. Some inanimate objects are often spoken of as if they were feminine. For example, ships are often spoken of as *she,* as are automobiles and trains; also the Catholic Church has traditionally been referred to as feminine. Sometimes, in poetry, celestial objects such as the moon are referred to as *she;* the sun, as *he.* These uses are chiefly historical or poetical. In ordinary prose, especially in science, these words are treated as neuter, with the possible exception of *ship,* which stubbornly retains its feminine reference.

Exercise 1.1: Classes of Nouns

Underline the nouns and write whether they are common or proper nouns, collective, abstract, or compound nouns.

WRITING PROMPT:
Write ten sentences with common, proper, collective, abstract, and compound nouns.

1. Each office was occupied by a team of engineers.

2. His two best friends from many years ago—a man and his wife—lived in Florida.

3. The famous conductor was my grandfather.

4. Americans are, I gather, friendly and hospitable.

WRITING PROMPT:
Write a paper about a trip or vacation you've taken. Describe the places you visited, and include common, proper, collective, abstract, and compound nouns.

5. The charity was supported by influential members of the community.

6. I worked for a shipping company that summer on a loading dock under the hot sun.

7. My father was my hero; he was also the man I feared the most.

8. The note from the officer was filled with ambiguity and needed clarification.

9. Vendors set up their booths of fresh fruits and vegetables.

10. No Republicans voted for the Affordable Care Act.

CCSS.L.9–12.2:
Demonstrate command of the conventions of standard English capitalization, punctuation, and spelling when writing.

11. Each house was occupied by a family of refugees.

12. His two children—a son and a daughter—are the benefactors of a good education.

13. Nature has no kindness, no hospitality, during a rain.

14. The conductor of the orchestra was the nephew of an Italian actress.

CCSS.L.9–10.1.B:
Use various types of phrases (noun, verb, adjectival, adverbial, participial, prepositional, absolute) and clauses (independent, dependent; noun, relative, adverbial) to convey specific meanings and add variety and interest to writing or presentations.

15. Seoul, Korea, is a bellwether of technology and modernization.

16. This society was supported by a group of influential alumnae.

17. We worked out of the Thames under canvas, with a North Sea pilot on board.

18. Among the trees the hunters saw three deer—a buck and two does.

19. Presently I ascended to the hurricane-deck and cast a longing glance toward the pilot-house.

20. The memorandum must first be translated into English.

21. He considered the weekend chores a drudgery.

Exercise 1.2: Using the Correct Gender of Nouns

Place each of the following words in its proper class and write the corresponding forms of the other genders. Consult a dictionary if necessary.

WRITING PROMPT:
Make a list containing thirty nouns, ten in each of the three genders. Use each in a sentence.

WRITING PROMPT:
Write sentences with the following words: *earl, abbess, schoolmaster, porter, hind, mare, ram, sire, witch, sultan, czar, widow, marquis, executor, salesman, tailor, hero, bride, songster, great-uncle, nephew, buck, horseman, bachelor, belle.*

	MASCULINE	FEMININE	COMMON
1. student	_____	_____	_____
2. child	_____	_____	_____
3. parent	_____	_____	_____
4. deer	_____	_____	_____
5. duck	_____	_____	_____
6. hen	_____	_____	_____
7. sheep	_____	_____	_____
8. cattle	_____	_____	_____
9. goose	_____	_____	_____
10. pig	_____	_____	_____

CCSS.L.9–10.1.B:
Use various types of phrases (noun, verb, adjectival, adverbial, participial, prepositional, absolute) and clauses (independent, dependent; noun, relative, adverbial) to convey specific meanings and add variety and interest to writing or presentations.

Write the corresponding masculine or feminine forms. Consult a dictionary if necessary.

11. landlord _____
12. duke _____
13. wife _____
14. stag _____
15. lion _____
16. shepherd _____
17. emperor _____
18. bachelor _____
19. hostess _____
20. ram _____
21. tiger _____
22. lad _____

CCSS.L.9–12.2:
Demonstrate command of the conventions of standard English capitalization, punctuation, and spelling when writing.

Case

CCSS.L.9–12.2:

Demonstrate command of the conventions of standard English capitalization, punctuation, and spelling when writing.

Case is that property of a noun or pronoun that indicates the relation of the noun or pronoun to the rest of the sentence. Some languages, like German and Russian, have fully developed systems of case. English does not. Traditional grammars taught that English nouns have three cases: *nominative, objective,* and *possessive*. But in English, the only distinction of case in nouns is between the **Common Case** (subject and object forms) and the possessive. The apostrophe indicates that a noun is in the possessive case.

The **Possessive Case** denotes possession.

This is the **gentleman's** hat.

FORMS OF NOUNS

CCSS.L.9–12.2:

Demonstrate command of the conventions of standard English capitalization, punctuation, and spelling when writing.

The three cases have the following forms:

	SINGULAR	PLURAL	SINGULAR	PLURAL
Nominative	boy	boys	lady	ladies
Objective	boy	boys	lady	ladies
Possessive	boy's	boys'	lady's	ladies'

The **Nominative** and **Objective Cases** of a noun have the same form. Thus, there can be no confusion in the use of them.

The **Possessive Case** of a noun is marked by the use of an apostrophe (').

The possessive case of a *singular noun* is regularly formed by adding an *'s* to the end of the noun: as, *woman's, mayor's, girl's*.

The possessive case of a *plural noun* is formed by adding an apostrophe to the simple plural when the plural ends in *-s*: as, *dogs'* (simple plural *dogs*), *girls'* (simple plural *girls*). The possessive case is also formed by adding *'s*, as in the singular, when the simple plural does not end in *-s*: as, *women's* (simple plural *women*), *children's* (simple plural *children*).

In compound nouns, titles, or names having a unit idea, an apostrophe (') or an apostrophe s (*'s*) is added: as, *mother-in-law's, the Prince of Wales', the Queen of England's*. Usage varies for some compounds: *attorney generals'* or *attorneys general's* (better to rephrase this with an *of*-genitive: as, *briefs of the attorneys general*).

CHAPTER 1

CCSS.L.9–12.1:
Demonstrate command of the conventions of standard English grammar and usage when writing or speaking.

Sometimes the possession is of a modified type. For example, in the expressions, "Einstein's theories" and "Wordsworth's poems," Einstein and Wordsworth are the possessors only in the sense that they are the theorists or creators. Compare the two kinds of possession indicated in the following sentence: "This is *David's* copy of *Wordsworth's* collected poems."

Some instances of possession indicate a lack of ownership entirely: a *day's* work, my *year's* salary, the *law's* delay. These phrases mean "the work *of a day*," "my salary *for a year*," "the delay *of the law*."

A noun in the possessive case is usually equivalent to a phrase beginning with *of*. For example, we may say either "*Hardy's* poems" or "the poems *of Hardy*"; "the *governor's* mansion" or "the mansion *of the governor*"; "the *President's* agenda" or "the agenda *of the President*." We would not, however, say "the car *of Johnny*" for "*Johnny's* car" or "the law *of Murphy*" for "*Murphy's* law." When making such distinctions in usage, the student must be guided by his or her ear for what sounds correct.

As a general rule the possessive case is not used with inanimate objects. A phrase with *of* is used instead: thus, "the cover *of the book*" (not "the *book's* cover"), "the branches *of the tree*" (not "the *tree's* branches"). There are, however, numerous exceptions to this rule: *time's delay, ship's mast, earth's surface, tree's fruit*, etc.

Exercise 1.3: Writing the Proper Possessive Case Forms

Write the possessive case forms, singular and plural, for the following nouns.

	SINGULAR	PLURAL
1. boy	_____	_____
2. child	_____	_____
3. army	_____	_____
4. mosquito	_____	_____
5. monkey	_____	_____
6. goose	_____	_____
7. ox	_____	_____
8. month	_____	_____
9. editor-in-chief	_____	_____
10. daughter-in-law	_____	_____
11. wife	_____	_____
12. lady	_____	_____
13. woman	_____	_____
14. mailman	_____	_____
15. Burroughs	_____	_____
16. notary public	_____	_____
17. hero	_____	_____
18. attorney general	_____	_____
19. elf	_____	_____
20. thief	_____	_____
21. mouse	_____	_____
22. tooth	_____	_____
23. albino	_____	_____
24. concerto	_____	_____
25. maestro	_____	_____

WRITING PROMPT:
Write ten sentences using singular and plural forms of words from this exercise.

CCSS.L.9–12.2:
Demonstrate command of the conventions of standard English capitalization, punctuation, and spelling when writing.

CCSS.L.9–10.1.B:
Use various types of phrases (noun, verb, adjectival, adverbial, participial, prepositional, absolute) and clauses (independent, dependent; noun, relative, adverbial) to convey specific meanings and add variety and interest to writing or presentations.

PRINCIPAL FUNCTIONS OF NOUNS

CCSS.L.9–12.1:
Demonstrate command of the conventions of standard English grammar and usage when writing or speaking.

The principal functions of a noun in a sentence are:

Subject of a Verb

Predicate Noun

Direct Object of a Verb

Indirect Object of a Verb

Object of a Preposition

Apposition

Objective Complement

Nominative Absolute

Direct Address

Subject of a Verb

CCSS.L.9–12.1:
Demonstrate command of the conventions of standard English grammar and usage when writing or speaking.

A noun may be used as a **_Subject of a Verb_**.

The **birds** flew away.

The **man** jumped off the bridge.

Here comes the **train**.

The subject names the person or thing that is the "doer" of the verbal action. In some sentences the subject follows the verb, as in the last example above.

Predicate Noun

LINKING VERBS:
Nouns can be used after these linking verbs: _be, become, remain, turn, prove, constitute, represent, comprise._

A noun may be used as a **_Predicate Noun_**.

Hitler became the **dictator** of Germany.

The president of Russia is **Vladimir Putin.**

My grandfather was a **clockmaker**.

The gangster turned **snitch**.

Normally a predicate noun follows a linking verb and answers the question _who?_ or _what?_ It also stands for the _same_ person or thing as the subject. For example, "Hitler became _what?_"—Answer, the _dictator_. "The president of Russia is _who?_"—Answer, _Vladimir Putin_. The _dictator_ is the same person as _Hitler_ (subject); _Vladimir Putin_ is the same person as the _president_ (subject).

Direct Object of a Verb

CCSS.L.9–10.1.B:

Use various types of phrases (noun, verb, adjectival, adverbial, participial, prepositional, absolute) and clauses (independent, dependent; noun, relative, adverbial) to convey specific meanings and add variety and interest to writing or presentations.

A noun may be used as the **_Direct Object of a Verb_**.

> The carpenter built a **house**.
>
> The soldier killed the **enemy**.

The direct object names the receiver of the action denoted by the verb; it answers the question _what?_ or _whom?_ and it stands for a person or thing _different_ from the subject. For example, "The carpenter built _what?_"—Answer, a _house_. "The soldier killed _whom?_" Answer, the _enemy_. The _house_ is not the same person or thing as the _carpenter_ (subject); the _enemy_ is not the same person or thing as the _soldier_ (subject).

Both the predicate noun and the direct object of a verb answer the same question, _what?_ or _who?_ (_whom?_). They are easily distinguished, however, by their relation to the subject: the predicate noun stands for the _same_ person or thing as the subject; the direct object stands for a _different_ person or thing. The only exception occurs in the use of a reflexive pronoun as the object of a verb.

The direct object occasionally precedes the subject of the verb.

> These **shoes** she bought in Paris.

Indirect Object of a Verb

CCSS.L.9–10.1.B:

Use various types of phrases (noun, verb, adjectival, adverbial, participial, prepositional, absolute) and clauses (independent, dependent; noun, relative, adverbial) to convey specific meanings and add variety and interest to writing or presentations.

A noun may be used as the **_Indirect Object of a Verb_**.

> The man gave his **wife** a gift.
>
> Mary paid the **bank** money.

The indirect object tells _to whom_ or _to what, for whom_ or _for what_ something is done. In the first sentence above, the direct object _gift_ tells _what_ the man gave, and the indirect object _wife_ tells _to whom_ he gave it; in the second sentence, the direct object _money_ tells _what_ Mary paid, and the indirect object _bank_ tells _to what_ she paid it.

A phrase beginning with the preposition _to_ or _for_ can be used in place of an indirect object. Thus, the first sentence would become "The man gave a gift _to his wife_"; the second sentence would become "Mary paid the money _to the bank_." With an indirect object, the _to_ or _for_ is never expressed in the sentence; when expressed, _to_ or _for_ is followed by an object of a preposition, not an indirect object.

The following verbs can take both a direct and indirect object: *give, pass, bring, lend, promise, provide, offer, owe, pay, tell, buy, cook, bake, pick, play, sing, ask, hand, teach, offer, send, award, feed, read, sell, serve, write, fetch, get, leave, pour, prepare, spare, begrudge, forward, grant, leave, loan, mail, show, sing, take, build, make, order, paint, reserve, save, take, allow.*

Object of a Preposition

CCSS.L.9–10.1.B:

Use various types of phrases (noun, verb, adjectival, adverbial, participial, prepositional, absolute) and clauses (independent, dependent; noun, relative, adverbial) to convey specific meanings and add variety and interest to writing or presentations.

A noun may be used as an *Object of a Preposition*.

> The barista served the coffee in a timely **manner**.
>
> King Lear and his fool walked across the **heath**.
>
> The plane arrived from **New York**.

Here *manner*, *heath*, and *New York* are the objects of the prepositions *in*, *across*, and *from*, respectively. (Prepositions are words like *to, from, under, through, during, between, above, by, over, before*, etc.)

The object of the preposition answers the question *what?* or *whom?* Thus, "He swam across the *lake*." Across *what?*—Answer, the *lake*.

In Apposition

CCSS.L.9–10.1.B:

Use various types of phrases (noun, verb, adjectival, adverbial, participial, prepositional, absolute) and clauses (independent, dependent; noun, relative, adverbial) to convey specific meanings and add variety and interest to writing or presentations.

A noun may be used in *Apposition* with another noun.

> My brother, the **taxi driver,** has his own blog.
>
> I heard my neighbor's dog, **Carson,** barking.
>
> We visited Richmond, the former **capital** of the Confederacy.

A noun in apposition stands for the same person or thing as some other noun: in other words, it is another name for the same person or thing. With two nouns in this sort of combination, the one that follows the first is said to be *in apposition* with the first, not the first with the second.

Note. A predicate noun and a noun in apposition with the subject of the sentence both stand for the same person or thing as the subject. What distinguishes them is that the predicate noun is connected to the subject by a verb.

> My neighbor is a **professor** (predicate noun).
>
> My neighbor, the **professor**, arrived at the party (apposition).

A noun in apposition may be separated from its related noun by several words if the relation between the two nouns is clear.

> A lone **man** walked across the desert, a solitary **figure** in the scorching landscape.

Objective Complement

CCSS.L.9–10.1.B:

Use various types of phrases (noun, verb, adjectival, adverbial, participial, prepositional, absolute) and clauses (independent, dependent; noun, relative, adverbial) to convey specific meanings and add variety and interest to writing or presentations.

A noun may be used as an *Objective Complement*.

> Americans elected Ronald Reagan **president**.

> They made my uncle **supervisor**.

The objective complement is added to the direct object in order to complete the meaning expressed by the verb ("complement" is something that completes). Thus, in the second example, they didn't make my *uncle*; they made my uncle *supervisor*. A simple test for an objective complement is to insert *to be* between the direct object and the noun that follows: for example, "They made my uncle *to be* supervisor." If *to be* can be inserted in this position without changing the meaning of the sentence, then the second noun is an objective complement.

The objective complement is commonly used with verbs expressing the idea of *choosing, making, electing, appointing, finding, considering, believing, judging, presuming, thinking, declaring*, etc.

> Concert-goers considered Mozart a **prodigy**.

> The police found the man a raving **lunatic**.

Nominative Absolute

CCSS.L.9–10.1.B:

Use various types of phrases (noun, verb, adjectival, adverbial, participial, prepositional, absolute) and clauses (independent, dependent; noun, relative, adverbial) to convey specific meanings and add variety and interest to writing or presentations.

A noun may be used with a participle to form what's known as a *Nominative Absolute* construction.

> The **curtain rising**, the audience anticipated the start of the play.

> The **book being** short, I read it in two hours.

> Her **mind frozen**, she couldn't think.

> The **memory seared** into my mind, I wasn't about to forget it.

The nominative absolute construction consists of a noun followed by a participle. A participle is a verb-form ending in -*ing*, -*ed*, or -*en*, such as *rising, being, baked, written*.

CCSS.L.9–12.2:

Demonstrate command of the conventions of standard English capitalization, punctuation, and spelling when writing.

When such a construction is placed at the beginning of the sentence, it must be carefully distinguished from a noun used as the subject of the verb.

For example, in the sentence, "The soldiers needing backup, helicopters soon arrived," *soldiers* is in the nominative absolute construction with the participle *needing*, and *helicopters* is the subject of the verb *arrived*. On the other hand, in "The soldiers, needing backup, radioed command for helicopters," *soldiers* is not in a nominative absolute construction: it is the subject of the sentence (subject of the verb *radioed*).

Note. The word absolute, as a grammatical concept, means "free" or "unconstrained." The noun in a nominative absolute construction is "free" from the traditional uses of a noun in a sentence, such as subjects or objects.

Direct Address

CCSS.L.9–12.2:

Demonstrate command of the conventions of standard English capitalization, punctuation, and spelling when writing.

A noun may be used in ***Direct Address***.

> **David**, I received your snail mail yesterday.
>
> My illness, dear **friend**, is worse than imagined.
>
> **Sandy**, come here.
>
> **Students**, listen up.

Here *David, friend, Sandy,* and *students* are the names or words by which the persons are addressed. These nouns do not function as the subjects of the verbs. The subject in the first sentence is *I*; in the second, *illness*; in the third and fourth, *you* understood (the subject is usually omitted in a direct command because it is always *you*). With reference to the third example, compare "Sandy comes here every day," in which *Sandy* is the subject.

CCSS.L.9–10.1.B:

Use various types of phrases (noun, verb, adjectival, adverbial, participial, prepositional, absolute) and clauses (independent, dependent; noun, relative, adverbial) to convey specific meanings and add variety and interest to writing or presentations.

Note. A word used in direct address is set off from the rest of the sentence by a comma or commas.

Any word can be used in one of the principal functions of a noun and thus may be used as a noun or noun-equivalent in the sentence.

> **Run** is a verb.
>
> He mispronounced **superfluous**.
>
> The **poor** pay more.

In the first sentence, *run*, which is normally a verb, is a noun-equivalent because it is the subject of the verb *is*. In the second sentence, *superfluous* is a noun-equivalent because it is the object of the verb *mispronounced*. In the third sentence, *poor* is a noun-equivalent because it is the subject of the verb *pay*.

Nouns Used as Other Parts of Speech

CCSS.L.9–10.1.B:
Use various types of phrases (noun, verb, adjectival, adverbial, participial, prepositional, absolute) and clauses (independent, dependent; noun, relative, adverbial) to convey specific meanings and add variety and interest to writing or presentations.

Some words that are usually nouns may be used:

- As *Adverbs* (adverb-equivalents), to denote *time, place, measure*, etc.

 We're going on vacation **tomorrow**.

 I went **home**.

 She ran ten **kilometers**.

These words are regularly used as nouns since they are the names of things; but in the above sentences they are used as adverbs. Any word that tells *when, where, how, how much*, or *how far* is an adverb.

- As *Adjectives* (adjective-equivalents)

 This is my **brother's** camera.

 The football game was **Sunday** night.

Exercise 1.4: Identifying Functions of Nouns

Underline and write the use of each noun (subject of a verb, object of a preposition, etc.).

WRITING PROMPT:
Write ten simple sentences, each containing one of the following: a direct object of a verb; an objective complement; a predicate nominative; a predicate adjective.

1. Voters are disgusted with Congress's inability to pass laws.

2. One of my favorite paintings is a Turner landscape.

3. My boss appointed me department supervisor.

4. During my tenure here, my dear colleagues, I've seen many changes and much progress.

5. The patrons gave the singer a round of applause.

6. The car's engine having stopped running, we need to get the car to the shop for repairs.

7. Yesterday, I received a raise at work.

CCSS.L.9–10.1.B:
Use various types of phrases (noun, verb, adjectival, adverbial, participial, prepositional, absolute) and clauses (independent, dependent; noun, relative, adverbial) to convey specific meanings and add variety and interest to writing or presentations.

8. You have to keep in mind, David, that we haven't had enough rain.

9. At the upcoming press conference, the governor will declare California to be in an official drought.

10. Rarely are these kinds of events ever reported in the newspaper.

11. Few voters will endorse the platform of the new party.

12. This picture is a reproduction of Reynolds' famous painting.

13. The next few months showed me strange things.

14. The president appointed Henry Adams secretary of the delegation.

15. During the past year, gentlemen, little progress has been made by the committee.

16. The morrow, being fairly fine, found Elizabeth-Jane again in the churchyard.

17. The audience gave the distinguished visitor a hearty welcome.

18. Man is priest, and scholar, and statesman, and producer, and soldier.

19. Our plan having failed, some new measure must be devised.

20. The movement of settlers toward Dakota became an exodus, a stampede.

Exercise 1.5: Identifying Predicate Nouns

Underline each predicate noun.

WRITING PROMPT:
Write ten sentences, each with a predicate noun.

1. One man's meat is another man's poison.

2. Cultivators of the earth are the most valuable citizens.

3. Plato's dialogues are the indispensable foundation of Western philosophy.

4. The errors and misfortunes of others should be a school for our own instruction.

5. Rats and mice and such small deer have been Tom's food for seven long year.

6. The golden rule in life is moderation in all things.

7. My mind to me a kingdom is.

CCSS.L.9–10.1.B:
Use various types of phrases (noun, verb, adjectival, adverbial, participial, prepositional, absolute) and clauses (independent, dependent; noun, relative, adverbial) to convey specific meanings and add variety and interest to writing or presentations.

8. Charity is the form, mover, mother, and root of all virtues.

9. Miserable comforters are ye all.

10. The comfort and ease which she never knew in her married life became the constant motive of her conduct.

11. Classical music is a category encompassing many forms of music throughout European history.

12. An honest man's the noblest work of God.

13. The biggest problem I have with Tolkien is his intentional use of vague language.

14. A whale ship was my Yale College and my Harvard.

15. Participants must have been members of the club for at least six months.

16. The English painter Joseph Turner became a huge influence on the development of modern art.

17. Has he always been an avid NFL fan?

18. Who is the newest member of our organization?

19. Robinson Crusoe remained a castaway on the island for twenty-eight years.

20. How could you have been such an idiot?

Exercise 1.6: Identifying Direct and Indirect Objects

Underline each direct object and write DO above it. Circle each indirect object and write IO above it.

WRITING PROMPT:
Write ten sentences, each with a Direct and Indirect Object.

1. He gave her all the shame and misery which a disagreeable partner for a couple of dances can give.

2. He held out his hand and Moss passed him the package.

3. Washington was overjoyed when a messenger brought him the word.

4. I don't want to lend you the money.

5. You did promise Powhatan what was yours should be his.

6. I dared not offer her the half-worn gloves.

7. Irwin paid them the amount they agreed upon.

8. We must not tell her what power she has.

9. Her boyfriend picked her a bunch of wildflowers.

10. He then played them a film about the Nazi regime to conclude the experiment.

11. I'm afraid you've been sold a bill of goods.

12. The professor taught his students great note-taking strategies.

13. The choir sang us a beautiful song.

14. An old friend told me a long and involved story.

15. The company offered me the job. John sent his grandmother a birthday card.

16. The bartender poured us another round of drinks.

17. The bank loaned my wife and me the money.

18. You need to reserve yourself a ticket for the event.

19. The teacher allowed us enough time to complete the assignment.

20. You must forward me the note.

21. The millionaire left his family a lot of money.

22. I can give your question a direct answer easily enough.

23. Aunt Isabella sent papa a beautiful lock of his hair.

Exercise 1.7: Identifying Direct Objects and Objective Complements

Underline each direct object and write DO above it. Circle each objective complement and write OC above it.

WRITING PROMPT:

Write ten sentences, each with a Direct Object and Objective Complement.

1. They did not, like me, make it the subject of long contemplation.

2. The newspaper called Saturday's developments in Parliament "an attempt at revenge, a blue-collar revolution in Parliament."

3. The deal makes Detroit the first cable market in the country to broadcast Bridges TV, a Muslim television network available on dish services.

4. Have the church elders named Mr. Henderson interim pastor?

5. The citizens of our town elected Stephen as mayor.

6. In his novel about religious apostasy, Thomas Hardy named his protagonist Jude Fawley.

7. The committee appointed Henderson head of the task force.

8. Many considered the man a fraud.

9. His neighbors branded him a thief.

10. The teacher wrote the parent an email.

11. The students gave the teacher their homework.

12. My wife cooked me my favorite Italian dish.

13. The carpenter built us a gazebo in the backyard.

14. The witness painted the police a picture of what happened.

15. I taught my students a grammar lesson.

16. The speaker threw a sop to the law-and-order crowd.

17. You picked yourself a winner this time.

18. They designated the procedures an unintelligible mess.

19. Elizabeth was crowned on 2 June 1953, and her privy and executive councils proclaimed her queen shortly afterwards.

Exercise 1.8: Writing with Subjects and Objects

Use the words indicated as subjects and objects to write sentences as directed.

CCSS.L.9–10.1.B:
Use various types of phrases (noun, verb, adjectival, adverbial, participial, prepositional, absolute) and clauses (independent, dependent; noun, relative, adverbial) to convey specific meanings and add variety and interest to writing or presentations.

1. (*telephone* as subject)

2. (*telephone* as direct object)

3. (*telephone* as indirect object)

4. (*telephone* as object of a preposition)

5. (*Molly* as subject).

6. (*Molly* as direct object)

7. (*Molly* as indirect object)

8. (*Molly* as object of a preposition)

9. (*cousin* as subject)

10. (*cousin* as direct object)

11. (*cousin* as indirect object)

12. (*cousin* as object of a preposition)

13. (*airplane* as subject)

14. (*airplane* as direct object).

15. (*airplane* as indirect object).

16. (*airplane* as object of a preposition)

17. (*honesty* as subject)

18. (*honesty* as direct object)

19. (*honesty* as indirect object)

20. (*honesty* as object of a preposition)

APOSTROPHES

CCSS.L.11–12.1.A:
Apply the understanding that usage is a matter of convention, can change over time, and is sometimes contested.

Apostrophes are critical to the understanding of nouns and are thus discussed in this chapter. (Most grammar books include apostrophes in a chapter on punctuation, but it is more helpful discussing them along with nouns.)

Apostrophes perform two main functions: they indicate possession, and they stand in for omitted letters and numbers.

In addition some style books allow the use of an apostrophe to form a plural when the lack of an apostrophe might cause confusion, such as the plurals of lowercase letters as in *cross your* t's *and dot your* i's.

With Most Singular Nouns

CCSS.L.9–12.2:
Demonstrate command of the conventions of standard English capitalization, punctuation, and spelling when writing.

Singular Nouns not ending in -s, including proper nouns, add 's even when the word ends in an s-sound, such as *x, z, ce, ch* or *sh*.

the **dog's** fur	the **killer's** gun	the **fox's** den
Max's money	the **place's** beauty	**Marx's** writings
the **latch's** strength	show **biz's** delight	**Xerox's** stock

For a singular common noun ending in -s, also add an apostrophe plus *s*.

the **waitress's** tips	the **princess's** beauty
congress's laziness	the **lass's** attitude

If the word that follows begins with an s, American newspapers add an apostrophe only.

the **hostess'** special dinner   the **witness'** story

With Singular Proper Nouns Ending in -S

CCSS.L.11–12.1.A:
Apply the understanding that usage is a matter of convention, can change over time, and is sometimes contested.

To form the possessive of a *Singular Proper Noun* ending in -s, add an apostrophe plus *s*.

Henry **James's** novels   **Jesus's** life

American newspapers add an apostrophe only.

Henry **James'** novels   **Jesus'** life

With Singular Proper Nouns Not Ending in -S

When forming the possessive of a ***Singular Proper Noun*** not ending in -*s*, add *'s*.

Bill's	That is **Bill's** car.
Marx's	We reject **Marx's** theories.
Lutz's	**Lutz's** land covers hundreds of acres.
Apple's	**Apple's** stock is at an all-time high.

With Plural Nouns Ending in -S

To form the possessive of a ***Plural Noun*** ending in *s*, add only an apostrophe, with a few exceptions detailed below.

CCSS.L.9–12.2:
Demonstrate command of the conventions of standard English capitalization, punctuation, and spelling when writing.

the **dogs'** rescue   my **grandmothers'** Christmas card

the **books'** popularity   the **ships'** redeployment

Add *'s* to form the possessive of an irregular plural noun not ending in s.

the **teeth's** decay   the **children's** opera

the **media's** fixation   the **nebula's** beauty

With Plurals of Family Names and Proper Nouns

CCSS.L.9–12.2:
Demonstrate command of the conventions of standard English capitalization, punctuation, and spelling when writing.

One must be careful when forming plurals and possessives of ***family names***. Last names adhere to the same rules detailed above, yet they account for many of the apostrophe errors in writing.

Common errors include *Merry Christmas from the Baker's, You're invited to the Smith's house for dinner,* and *the Harris's daughter is engaged to be married.*

Punctuating these constructions right is actually easy. Just keep in mind the basic rules of plurals and possessives. The errors can be avoided by pausing to identify whether you're referring to one or more persons—nothing more complicated than recognizing a singular or plural noun.

Mr. **Harris** and Mrs. **Harris** equal two **Harrises**.

John **Smith** plus Karen **Smith** are the **Smiths**.

Proper nouns that end in *-s* or an *s*-sound often form the plural by adding es, as is true for many common nouns: *one loss, two losses; one batch, two batches.*

one **Harris**, two **Harrises**

one **Welch**, two **Welches**

Franklin **Pierce** and Jane **Pierce** are the **Pierces.**

Brian **Williams** and Bernice **Williams** are the **Williamses**.

Once you understand that you have a singular noun like *Harris* or *Williams* or a plural like *Harrises* or *Williamses*, just apply the rules for forming possessives: add *'s* for a singular noun or only an apostrophe for a plural,

The **Harrises** run the **Harrises'** family business.

I enjoy Mrs. **Harris's** cooking.

Franklin **Pierce** and Jane **Pierce** live in the **Pierces'** house.

I'm visiting the **Welches** in Chicago, so I'll be staying at the **Welches'** house.

I've always loved Mrs. **Welch's** decorations.

Four **Williamses** live in the **Williamses'** house.

Apostrophe in It's

CCSS.L.9–12.2:
Demonstrate command of the conventions of standard English capitalization, punctuation, and spelling when writing.

Probably the most common punctuation error is confusing *it's* for *its*. The confusion stems from the assumption that *it's* is possessive because other possessive forms take *'s*. However, the correct possessive form is *its*, no apostrophe. The longer possessive pronouns—*hers, his, ours* and *theirs*—do not take an apostrophe, and neither does the possessive *its: The bird flapped its wings.*

The longer possessive personal pronouns never take an apostrophe and are used when no noun follows: *The money is hers; I don't want theirs; I'd rather have yours or mine.*

Exceptions to the Rules for Forming Possessives

A word that ends in *-s* and has the same form for the singular and plural, such as *economics,* forms the possessive by adding an apostrophe only, in both the singular and plural forms: *politics' victims, economics' shortcomings, a species' fossil record, these species' fossil record.*

CCSS.L.9–12.2:
Demonstrate command of the conventions of standard English capitalization, punctuation, and spelling when writing.

The same rule applies to the name of a place, an organization, or a publication that is a plural form ending in -s, even though the word may be singular: *the United States' landmarks*, *the National Academy of Sciences' revised policies*, Better Homes and Gardens' *articles*.

For . . . sake expressions with a singular noun ending in -s and followed by a word beginning with s form the possessive with an apostrophe alone.

for **goodness'** sake   for **righteousness'** sake

Also the possessive in *for . . . sake* expressions containing a singular noun ending in -ce or other letters forming an s sound followed by a word beginning with s takes an apostrophe only.

for **experience'** sake   for **appearance'** sake

But when the following word does not begin with an s, use 's.

the **experience's** cost   **conscience's** voice

Shared Versus Independent Possession

CCSS.L.9–12.2:
Demonstrate command of the conventions of standard English capitalization, punctuation, and spelling when writing.

When two or more nouns share possession, only the last one takes an apostrophe and an s.

Anthony and Bill's business

Anthony and Bill's associates (the associates belong to both Anthony and Bill.

When each noun possesses something independently—that is, when the possession is not shared—each takes an apostrophe and an s.

Anthony's and Bill's cars.

Anthony's and Bill's friends (Anthony and Bill have their own separate friends).

Double Possessive

CCSS.L.9–12.2:
Demonstrate command of the conventions of standard English capitalization, punctuation, and spelling when writing.

In a ***Double Possessive*** the idea of possession is expressed by both a prepositional phrase beginning with *of* and a noun or pronoun in the possessive case used as the object of the preposition.

She is a friend of **mine**.

Gardening is a pastime of my **wife's**.

Note. These types of constructions are called *double possessives* because the word *of* indicates possession along with the apostrophe plus -*s*. Some editors consider this type of expression redundant, but it is a well-established idiom, one that is allowed by editing styles in certain contexts.

CCSS.L.11–12.1.A:

Apply the understanding that usage is a matter of convention, can change over time, and is sometimes contested.

The Chicago Manual of Style allows for the double possessive if it meets two conditions: (1) the word after *of* must refer to something animate, such as a person, and (2) the word before *of* must refer to only a portion of the animate object's possession.

Several close friends of **Sophia's** were at the reception. (not all her friends)

All the friends of **Sophia** attended her wedding. (all her friends)

Double possessives occur quite naturally with personal pronouns.

He was a friend of **mine**.

It was a strategy of **hers**.

Exercise 1.9: Adding Necessary Apostrophes

Write sentences containing the possessive singular of the following.

WRITING PROMPT:
Describe something to your classmate so that they might guess at its identity. Use the pronouns *it* and *its* as well as the contraction *it's* in your writing.

1. Henry
2. James
3. Thomas
4. Mr. Fox
5. child
6. Charles Price

CCSS.L.9–12.2:
Demonstrate command of the conventions of standard English capitalization, punctuation, and spelling when writing.

7. Mrs. Gibbs
8. Edward
9. General Edwards
10. Hortense
11. Miss Bellows
12. commander-in-chief

Write sentences containing the possessive plural of the following.

WRITING PROMPT:
Write about the variety of student extracurricular activities at your school. Use both the singular and plural possessive forms of student.

13. Englishman
14. walrus
15. fox
16. sheep
17. horse
18. ox

CCSS.L.9–12.2:
Demonstrate command of the conventions of standard English capitalization, punctuation, and spelling when writing.

19. child
20. emperor
21. empress
22. Knight Templar
23. lady
24. heiress

Pronouns

ENGLISH LANGUAGE ARTS STANDARDS

☞ ***CCSS.ELA-LITERACY.L.9–12.1:*** *Demonstrate command of the conventions of standard English grammar and usage when writing or speaking.*

☞ ***CCSS.ELA-LITERACY.L.9–10.1.B:*** *Use various types of phrases (noun, verb, adjectival, adverbial, participial, prepositional, absolute) and clauses (independent, dependent; noun, relative, adverbial) to convey specific meanings and add variety and interest to writing or presentations.*

☞ ***CCSS.ELA-LITERACY.L.11–12.1.A:*** *Apply the understanding that usage is a matter of convention, can change over time, and is sometimes contested.*

☞ ***CCSS.ELA-LITERACY.L.6.1.D:*** *Recognize and correct vague pronouns (i.e., ones with unclear or ambiguous antecedents).*

PRONOUNS

CCSS.L.9–12.1:
Demonstrate command of the conventions of standard English grammar and usage when writing or speaking.

A ***Pronoun*** is a word used in place of a noun. It is commonly used as a substitute word to prevent the awkward repetition of a noun.

Take, for instance, "Michael asked *his* mother to send *him his* favorite sweatshirt, *which he* left behind in *his* closet." Without pronouns, we would have to say, "Michael asked *Michael's* mother to send *Michael Michael's* favorite sweatshirt, the *sweatshirt Michael* left behind in *Michael's* closet." The advantage of using pronouns is obvious.

Antecedent of a Pronoun

CCSS.L.9–10.1.B:
Use various types of phrases (noun, verb, adjectival, adverbial, participial, prepositional, absolute) and clauses (independent, dependent; noun, relative, adverbial) to convey specific meanings and add variety and interest to writing or presentations.

The noun for which the pronoun stands is called the *Antecedent* of the pronoun.

In the above example, *Michael* is the antecedent of *his, him, his, he,* and *his*; and *sweatshirt* is the antecedent of *which*.

A pronoun can have more than one antecedent.

Bring the **rake** and the **shovel** if **they** are in the shed.

A pronoun can also act as the antecedent of another pronoun.

He who is lazy will never succeed (**he** is the antecedent of **who**).

Everyone on the team always does **his** best (**everyone** is the antecedent of **his**).

Classes of Pronouns

CCSS.L.9–12.1:
Demonstrate command of the conventions of standard English grammar and usage when writing or speaking.

Pronouns are divided into the following classes.

- *Personal Pronouns:* "*He* wanted to spend time with *them*." "*She* sent *him* a text."

- *Relative Pronouns:* "George saw the man *who* was standing there." "I like the pasta sauce *that* my wife makes."

- *Interrogative Pronouns:* "*What* do you want?" "*Who* said that?"

- *Demonstrative Pronouns:* "*That* is my favorite book." "*These* are the best knives a chef can have."

- *Indefinite Pronouns:* "*Anything* would be better than *nothing*." "*Somebody* is responsible for this."

PROPERTIES AND USES OF PRONOUNS

CCSS.L.9–12.1:
Demonstrate command of the conventions of standard English grammar and usage when writing or speaking.

Pronouns have *Person, Number, Gender,* and *Case.* With a few exceptions, such as matters of form, what has been said about nouns applies to pronouns in that pronouns have the same functions as Nouns.

Personal Pronouns

The personal pronouns are *I, you, he, she,* and *it,* plus their various forms indicating the following properties.

	FIRST PERSON	SECOND PERSON	THIRD PERSON		
	MASC. OR FEM.	MASC. OR FEM.	MASC.	FEM.	NEUT.
		Singular Number			
Nominative	I	you	he	she	it
Possessive	my, mine	your, yours	his	her, hers	its
Objective	me	you	him	her	it
		Plural Number			
Nominative	we	you	they		
Possessive	our, ours	your, yours	their, theirs		
Objective	us	you	them		

The older second person forms—*thou* or *thee, thy* or *thine*—which were in common use centuries ago, are "solemn" in style and are rarely used today except in prayer and poetry. They are not used in ordinary speech, having been replaced by the forms *you, your* or *yours,* and *you.*

Person

CCSS.L.9–12.1:
Demonstrate command of the conventions of standard English grammar and usage when writing or speaking.

Personal pronouns are categorized into three grammatical "persons" based on the relation between the person who is speaking and the person to whom or the thing to which the pronoun refers.

The ***First Person*** indicates the *person speaking:* as, *I, me, we, us,* etc.

The ***Second Person*** indicates the *person or thing spoken to:* as, *you, your, yours.*

The ***Third Person*** indicates the *person or thing spoken of:* as, *he, she, it, him, her,* etc.

Number

CCSS.L.9–12.1:
Demonstrate command of the conventions of standard English grammar and usage when writing or speaking.

The ***First Person Pronouns*** in the singular number (*I, me, my, mine*) are used by the speaker when referring to himself or herself.

The first person plural pronouns (*we, our, ours, us*) are used by the speaker to refer to himself or herself and other persons with whom he or she is associated in a particular action: in other words, he or she is the speaker for the group.

The so-called "editorial *we*" used by op-ed writers ("*We* believe," "It is *our* opinion," instead of "*I* believe," "*I* think") is based on the idea that the writer is speaking for the entire editorial staff.

The **Second Person Pronouns** have the same forms for both the singular and plural numbers: *you, your, yours, you.*

Because *you* was originally a plural pronoun, the plural verb is always used when *you* is used as a subject, even when only one person is being addressed: thus, "*You* were lonely," never "*You* was lonely."

The **Third Person Pronouns** have the same form in the plural for all genders: *they, their* or *them, theirs.*

Gender

CCSS.L.9–12.1:
Demonstrate command of the conventions of standard English grammar and usage when writing or speaking.

In the **First** and **Second Persons** there is no change of form to indicate gender, and the pronouns *I, me, we, us, you,* etc., are of masculine or feminine gender according to whether the persons to whom they refer are male or female, respectively.

> **I** am William (masculine).
>
> **I** am Sandra (feminine).
>
> **You** are young men (masculine).
>
> **You** are young women (feminine).

In the **Third Person** there are different pronouns in the singular number for the different genders—*he, she,* and *it,* with their various forms being used to indicate when the person or thing spoken of is male, female, or neuter. In the plural number, the forms are the same no matter what the gender.

Note. It is often used to refer to animals or to infants, male or female.

Nonsexist Singular "They"

CCSS.L.11–12.1.A:
Apply the understanding that usage is a matter of convention, can change over time, and is sometimes contested.

In 2013 President Barack Obama praised a Supreme Court decision with the sentence "No American should ever live under a cloud of suspicion just because of what **they** look like." He could have said what **he** looks like, or what **he or she** looks like. Instead he chose the "singular" **they** to refer to a single person, male of female.

The first thing to realize about this usage is that it's been around for centuries, used by Chaucer, Shakespeare, the King James Bible, Swift, Byron, Shaw, Jane Austen, even *Fowler's Modern English Usage. They* and *their* help writers and speakers avoid using sexist language. *They* and *their* fill the need for a gender-neutral pronoun. *They* also helps us avoid cumbersome phrases and workarounds such as *it, one, he or she, s/he, his/her,* or invented pronouns like *hir, zhe,* or *thon.*

Case

CCSS.L.9–12.1:
Demonstrate command of the conventions of standard English grammar and usage when writing or speaking.

Most personal pronouns have different forms for the nominative, possessive, and objective cases.

NOMINATIVE	POSSESSIVE	OBJECTIVE
I	my, mine	me
we	our, ours	us
you	your, yours	you
he	his	him
she	her, hers	her
it	its	it
they	their, theirs	them

The appropriate form to use depends on the way the pronoun is used in the sentence (pronouns have the same general uses as nouns).

CCSS.L.9–10.1.B:
Use various types of phrases (noun, verb, adjectival, adverbial, participial, prepositional, absolute) and clauses (independent, dependent; noun, relative, adverbial) to convey specific meanings and add variety and interest to writing or presentations.

A **Nominative Case** form (*I, we, you, he, she, it, they*) is required when the pronoun is used:

- As the Subject of a Verb.

  He went out for a walk.

  They bought a new house.

- As a Predicate Pronoun (the same grammatical construction as a predicate noun).

  My sister is **she**.

  It is **I**.

  It was **they**.

The objective case in these constructions is considered by some incorrect, though in common use: as, "My sister is *her*" or "It is *me.*"

- In Apposition with the Subject of a Verb or with a Predicate Noun.

John F. Kennedy—**he** about whom many books have been written—was president during the Cuban Missile Crisis.

The candidate was John F. Kennedy—**he** who would become president.

- In the Nominative Absolute construction.

  They having reached a decision, the jury was ready to deliver its verdict.

- In Direct Address

  Okay, **you** guys, we need to get going.

An **Objective Case** form (*me, us, you, him, her, it, them*) is required when the pronoun is used:

- As the Direct Object of a Verb.

  The panhandler asked **us** for money.

  I saw **her** there.

- As the Indirect Object of a Verb.

  My wife made **me** dinner.

  I sent **him** a package.

- As the Object of a Preposition.

  I have several paintings by **him**.

  The soldiers shot at **them**.

  That's between **you** and **me** (not **I**).

- In Apposition with an Object of a Verb or a Preposition.

  They formed a neighborhood gang—**him** and his band of losers.

  The contract offered an increase in benefits for the workers—**them** and their families.

Note. A pronoun theoretically can be used as an objective complement: "Still grieving for their dead mother, the children made their step-mother her." However, in actual usage an objective complement is seldom a personal pronoun.

The **Possessive Case** of pronouns, like that of nouns, denotes possession.

The shorter possessive forms—*my, our, your, her,* and *their*—are used when a noun follows: as, "This is *my* car."

The longer forms — *mine, ours, yours, hers,* and *theirs* — are used when no noun follows: as, "This car is *mine*." (One still encounters in older English and in poetry the longer forms occurring before nouns: as, "*Mine* eyes have seen the glory of the coming of the Lord.")

Pronouns in the possessive case do not take an apostrophe: thus, *its, hers, theirs.* The form *it's* is not a possessive case pronoun; it is the contraction for *it is:* as, "*It's* a good idea." Compare, "The campaign lost *its* momentum" (possessive case).

Predicate Nominative

CCSS.L.11–12.1.A:
Apply the understanding that usage is a matter of convention, can change over time, and is sometimes contested.

If you ever say, "It is I," you've been influenced by Latin grammar.

Schoolmarms insisted for centuries that the old Latin model of the ***Predicate Nominative*** was applicable to English, that a pronoun serving as the complement of *be* must be in the nominative case (*I, he, she, we, they*) rather than the objective (*me, him, her, us, them*).

This concept works fine in Latin, but not in English. The fact is that the objective case is the default case in English and can be used anywhere, especially in spoken language. Thus, it is idiomatic to say something like *Who, me? What, me pay for it?,* and *You go first, me second.*

What's obvious is that the choice between *It is I* and *It is me* is one of formality versus informality. It has nothing to do with grammar.

Case after "Than" and "As"

CCSS.L.9–10.1.B:
Use various types of phrases (noun, verb, adjectival, adverbial, participial, prepositional, absolute) and clauses (independent, dependent; noun, relative, adverbial) to convey specific meanings and add variety and interest to writing or presentations.

The case of the pronoun in comparisons using ***than*** and ***as*** requires special attention. Should we say, for example, "He is taller than *I*" or "He is taller than *me*"; "He is as tall as *I*" or "He is as tall as *me*"? These are known as elliptical constructions, and the proper form of the pronoun can be easily determined by expanding the sentence to its fullest. For example, "He is taller than *I* (am)," "He is as tall as *I* (am)." Here it is easy to see that the proper form of the pronoun is *I* because it is the subject of the verb *am.*

Similarly, the sentence, "She likes Frank more than *me*," means "She likes Frank more than (she likes) *me*," in which case *me* is in the objective case because it is the object of the verb *likes.* In addition, the sentence, "She likes Frank more than *I*," means "She likes Frank more than *I* (do).

AGREEMENT OF PRONOUN AND ANTECEDENT

CCSS.L.9–10.1.B:
Use various types of phrases (noun, verb, adjectival, adverbial, participial, prepositional, absolute) and clauses (independent, dependent; noun, relative, adverbial) to convey specific meanings and add variety and interest to writing or presentations.

A pronoun must agree with its antecedent in person, number, and gender. In English, case is not a consideration in agreement of pronouns and antecedents.

Thus, if the antecedent is in the third person, singular number, masculine gender, the pronoun that refers to it must also be in the third person, singular number, masculine gender: for example, "The *boy* said that *he* was working on *his* homework." Compare, "The *girl* said that *she* was working on *her* homework" (third person, singular number, feminine gender).

ANTECEDENT	PRONOUNS
girl	she, her, hers, herself
boy	he, his, him, himself
house	it, its, itself
girls, boys, houses	they, their, theirs, them, themselves
(I—the speakers)	I, my, mine, me, myself
(you—the person spoken to)	you, your, yours, yourself, yourselves

The case of a pronoun is not determined by the case of the antecedent: the use of the pronoun in the sentence determines its case—subject of a verb, object of a verb, etc.

The antecedent of a personal pronoun may be in a sentence preceding the one with the pronoun.

Note. The pronouns *I* and *you* are regularly used with no expressed antecedent. *I* refers only to the speaker, and *you* refers to the person who is addressed. Therefore, it is possible not to have a clear antecedent in the sentence. In conversation, pronouns are often used with no clear antecedent when the context is clear: that is, when the person or thing referred to is made clear with a look, gesture, or some other means. "Consider him over there." "Give her back the book."

COMPOUND PERSONAL PRONOUNS

CCSS.L.9–12.1:
Demonstrate command of the conventions of standard English grammar and usage when writing or speaking.

The **Compound Personal Pronouns** are made by adding the suffix -*self* or -*selves* to the appropriate form of the simple pronouns.

May be copied for classroom use. Common Core Grammar by Thomas Fasano (Coyote Canyon Press: Claremont, CA); © 2015.

In the first and second persons, the suffix is added to the possessive case: *myself, ourselves, yourself, yourselves*. In the third person the suffix is added to the objective case: *himself, herself, itself, themselves*. Do not use the forms *hisself* and *theirselves*. They are considered illiterate.

Case

CCSS.L.9–10.1.B:
Use various types of phrases (noun, verb, adjectival, adverbial, participial, prepositional, absolute) and clauses (independent, dependent; noun, relative, adverbial) to convey specific meanings and add variety and interest to writing or presentations.

The *Case* of the simple pronoun to which the suffix is added does not correspond to the case of the resulting compound pronoun.

Although the suffix is added to the possessive case in the first and second persons, the resulting compound forms are not in the possessive case; they are in either the nominative or objective case, depending on their use in the sentence.

> I **myself** will be held responsible (nominative—in apposition with the subject **I**).
>
> I must have been kidding **myself** (objective—object of the verb).

Likewise, the third person forms, made from the objective case of the simple pronouns, are either nominative or objective, depending on their use in the sentence.

> She **herself** will arrange the meeting (nominative—in apposition with the subject).
>
> He made the desk for **himself** (objective—object of the preposition).

Reflexive Pronoun

CCSS.L.9–10.1.B:
Use various types of phrases (noun, verb, adjectival, adverbial, participial, prepositional, absolute) and clauses (independent, dependent; noun, relative, adverbial) to convey specific meanings and add variety and interest to writing or presentations.

In this use the action performed by the subject comes back to or is reflected back to the subject.

> He cut **himself** (direct object).
>
> They set aside some money for **themselves** (object of a preposition).
>
> She made **herself** a sandwich (indirect object).

When a *Reflexive Pronoun* is used as the direct object of a verb, we have the only exception to the rule that the direct object stands for a *different* person or thing than the subject. The test that the reflexive pronoun is the object of the verb is that it names the receiver of the action.

Note. In older English and in colloquial modern English the simple pronouns are used reflexively: as, "Now I lay me down to sleep." "I bought me a drink." "He got him a ticket to the concert." "I looked behind me." (In the last example, *me* is the accepted form.)

Emphatic Pronouns

CCSS.L.9–10.1.B: Use various types of phrases (noun, verb, adjectival, adverbial, participial, prepositional, absolute) and clauses (independent, dependent; noun, relative, adverbial) to convey specific meanings and add variety and interest to writing or presentations.

Compound pronouns can be used to add emphasis to a pronoun or noun.

> I **myself** will take care of it.

> They called a meeting with the supervisor **himself**.

Emphatic Pronouns are regularly in apposition with the preceding noun or pronoun; but not all emphatic uses of compound pronouns invoke apposition—although a note of apposition is retained in the following sentences:

> The decision, in and of **itself**, wasn't a bad one.

> She hasn't been **herself** lately.

> I worked on the project by **myself**.

Exercise 2.1: Indicating the Proper Case Forms of Pronouns

Underline each personal pronoun, and give the case of each.

WRITING PROMPT:
Write sentences in which the personal pronoun in the first person is used as a direct object, indirect object, predicate nominative; in the possessive singular with a noun; in the possessive singular without a noun.

1. Her loyalty made her reluctant to make staff changes.

2. He, being the oldest son, is more valuable to his father on the farm.

3. He being the oldest of the group, we nominated him to be club president.

4. That is she sitting to the left of her brother.

5. They have consulted with only two of their friends—you and me.

6. It was I who started it—not he.

7. You are at least ten years younger than she.

CCSS.L.9–12.1:
Demonstrate command of the conventions of standard English grammar and usage when writing or speaking.

8. Have you been told the latest about Harry and me?

9. John was surprised that the commission chose Fred rather than him.

10. Maria has as large a family as I.

11. A tour guide showed us around the city.

12. Her loyalty made her an invaluable friend.

13. He, being the most experienced of the group, was elected captain.

14. He might say something about it to her, hours later.

CCSS.L.9–10.1.B:
Use various types of phrases (noun, verb, adjectival, adverbial, participial, prepositional, absolute) and clauses (independent, dependent; noun, relative, adverbial) to convey specific meanings and add variety and interest to writing or presentations.

15. Their servants were kept out, but they themselves were admitted.

16. That is she sitting at the right of her father.

17. He asked me my opinion about them.

18. We wrapped ourselves in our blankets, and sat down by the fire.

19. It was I who found it—not he.

Exercise 2.2: Choosing the Proper Case Forms of Pronouns

Fill in the blanks with the proper case forms of the pronouns.

WRITING PROMPT:
Write two to three paragraphs describing a sports event you have watched. Use pronouns in place of any repetitive nouns.

1. The rough draft was corrected by the teacher and _____ (I, me).

2. The administrator and _____ should have arranged for the seminar (she, her).

3. He will give it to either Mark or _____ (I, me).

4. The group consisted of _____ six and the chaperon (we, us).

5. It astonished no one more than _____ (he, him).

CCSS.L.9–12.1:
Demonstrate command of the conventions of standard English grammar and usage when writing or speaking.

6. They met Danielle and _____ at the cafe (I, me).

7. If you were _____, why would you bother going? (she, her).

8. It was _____ who made us the offer (they, them).

9. You can golf as well as _____ (he, him).

10. _____ boys were all invited to the birthday party (we, us).

11. Each problem was checked by the instructor and _____ (I, me).

CCSS.L.9–10.1.B:
Use various types of phrases (noun, verb, adjectival, adverbial, participial, prepositional, absolute) and clauses (independent, dependent; noun, relative, adverbial) to convey specific meanings and add variety and interest to writing or presentations.

12. The superintendent and _____ should have arranged for the meeting (she, her).

Fill in the blanks with personal pronouns in the first or the third person.

13. He thought the burglars were _____.

14. He mistook the burglars for _____.

15. William is better at his lessons than _____.

16. Nobody volunteered except Edward and _____.

17. _____ boys have formed a debating club.

18. If I were _____ I would study art.

19. Arthur likes you better than _____.

20. Behind Maria and _____ came the guest of honor.

21. It was _____ that Joseph meant.

22. _____ two are always together.

23. Richard dislikes everybody, _____ most of all.

Exercise 2.3: Identifying Reflexive and Emphatic Pronouns

Identify the "self" pronouns in the following sentences as reflexive or emphatic.

WRITING PROMPT:
Write sentences in which *myself, yourself, ourselves, himself, herself, themselves* are used (1) intensively, (2) reflexively as direct object, (3) reflexively as indirect object.

1. The Archbishop himself preached the sermon.

2. I made this myself, but it was you yourself who gave me the idea.

3. Make yourself at home and help yourself to anything you fancy.

4. If you want a job well done, do it yourself.

5. The escaped convicts quarreled among themselves about where to hide.

6. He's a well-connected young man and thinks too highly of himself.

CCSS.L.9–12.1:
Demonstrate command of the conventions of standard English grammar and usage when writing or speaking.

7. Success in life depends largely on yourself.

8. The governor himself signed the letter.

9. He hasn't left himself anything to do when he gets old.

10. I decided to write the book myself.

11. I poured myself a drink.

12. My wife started the garden herself.

CCSS.L.9–10.1.B:
Use various types of phrases (noun, verb, adjectival, adverbial, participial, prepositional, absolute) and clauses (independent, dependent; noun, relative, adverbial) to convey specific meanings and add variety and interest to writing or presentations.

13. The police chief made the arrest himself.

14. She puts money aside every week for herself.

15. People harm themselves with bad diets.

16. I taught myself how to play the piano.

17. Lonely people have been known to mail packages to themselves.

18. She knows how to calm herself down after a panic attack.

19. I had to make dinner myself.

20. My brother found Sasquatch himself living in a swamp in Florida.

RELATIVE PRONOUNS

CCSS.L.9–10.1.B:
Use various types of phrases (noun, verb, adjectival, adverbial, participial, prepositional, absolute) and clauses (independent, dependent; noun, relative, adverbial) to convey specific meanings and add variety and interest to writing or presentations.

A ***Relative Pronoun*** acts as both a connective word and a reference word.

As a connective it introduces a clause—a group of words having a subject and a verb—and connects that clause to the antecedent of the pronoun. Relative pronouns introduce clauses with a nominal function in the sentence.

As a *reference word* a relative pronoun refers to and takes the place of its antecedent and thus makes the repetition of the antecedent unnecessary. The relative will then function as the subject of the verb in the clause it introduces or as one of the other uses of a noun in the clause.

For example, in "John found the wallet *that* he lost," the relative pronoun *that* connects the clause *that he lost* with the antecedent *wallet* and is used instead of *wallet* as the subject of the verb *lost*. In the sentence, "This is the woman *whom* you mentioned," the relative pronoun *whom* acts as both a connective and the object of the verb *mentioned*.

Note. Either *that* or *which* could be used in the above sentence, "John found the wallet *which* (*that*) he lost." However, *that* is most commonly used as a relative pronoun in restrictive clauses.

A relative pronoun is always part of its own clause with a subject and a verb and is separate from the main subject and verb of the sentence.

For example, the sentence, "She liked the wine *that* we drank last night" contains the main subject and verb, *She liked*, and also another subject and verb, *we drank*, which follows the relative pronoun *that*.

Classes of Relative Pronouns

CCSS.L.9–12.1:
Demonstrate command of the conventions of standard English grammar and usage when writing or speaking.

Relative Pronouns can be divided into two classes: Simple and Compound.

The ***Simple Relative Pronouns*** are *who, which,* and *that.*

The ***Compound Relative Pronouns*** are *what* and combinations made by adding *-ever* and *-soever* to *who, whose, whom, which,* and *what*: thus, *whoever, whosoever; whosever, whosesoever; whomever, whomsoever; whichever, whichsoever; whatever, whatsoever.* A distinguishing characteristic of compound relative pronouns is that they do not have an expressed antecedent.

Note. What is usually classified among the simple relative pronouns. Yet despite its simple form, it is like a compound relative pronoun because it does not have an expressed antecedent. Since function is more important than form, *what* is classified as a compound relative pronoun.

SIMPLE RELATIVE PRONOUNS

Antecedent

CCSS.L.9–10.1.B:
Use various types of phrases (noun, verb, adjectival, adverbial, participial, prepositional, absolute) and clauses (independent, dependent; noun, relative, adverbial) to convey specific meanings and add variety and interest to writing or presentations.

The three **Simple Relative Pronouns**, *who, which,* and *that,* frequently have an antecedent expressed in the sentence. This antecedent may be a noun or a pronoun.

> **He who** works hard will succeed.
>
> The **bear that** mauled the campers was killed by park rangers.
>
> The secretary will type the **report, which** is due next Tuesday.

Unlike a personal pronoun, a relative pronoun is most often in the same sentence as its antecedent, which usually comes immediately before the pronoun.

Note. Which can have an entire statement as an antecedent if the connection is clear: as, "The enemy position was uncertain, which made troop deployment all the more dangerous." Good writers often use this sort of construction, though its use is discouraged by many editors. In order to avoid this form of vague reference, a noun that sums up the whole statement can be substituted as the antecedent: "The enemy position was uncertain, a situation that (which) made troop deployment all the more dangerous."

CCSS.L.6.1.D:
Recognize and correct vague pronouns (i.e., ones with unclear or ambiguous antecedents).

Person, Number, and Gender

CCSS.L.9–12.1:
Demonstrate command of the conventions of standard English grammar and usage when writing or speaking.

A relative pronoun agrees with its antecedent in **Person, Number, and Gender**. Although the relative pronoun itself does not change form for these different properties, it is necessary to know the person and number of the relative in order to use the correct form of the verb. The form of the verb will be the same as would be used with the antecedent.

> I who **am** the oldest will retire first.
>
> They who **are** present will have to get the job done.

In the first sentence the antecedent is *I,* which is in the first person, singular number; the relative, therefore, is also in the first person, singular number, and requires the verb *am*. In the second sentence, the antecedent *they* is in the third person, plural number; consequently, the relative requires the verb *are*.

Gender has no effect on the use of the simple relative pronoun or the form of the verb.

Case and Use

CCSS.L.9–10.1.B:
Use various types of phrases (noun, verb, adjectival, adverbial, participial, prepositional, absolute) and clauses (independent, dependent; noun, relative, adverbial) to convey specific meanings and add variety and interest to writing or presentations.

The simple relative pronouns have the following **Case** forms, which are the same for both singular and plural numbers.

Nominative	who	which	that
Possessive	whose	(of which) (whose)	———
Objective	whom	which	that

Who is the only simple relative pronoun that changes form for the different cases.

Which has the same form for both the nominative and the objective cases. It has no regular form for the possessive case; the phrase *of which* is used instead. Sometimes *whose*, the possessive case of *who*, is employed as the possessive form of *which*. Thus, we may say, "South America has scores of indigenous tribes the languages *of which* have not been studied" or "South America has scores of indigenous tribes *whose* languages have not been studied."

That does not change form and has no possessive form.

The case of the relative pronoun does not depend upon the case of the antecedent; it is determined by the use of the pronoun in the clause it introduces.

> I met him **who** was just hired.
>
> I met him **whom** you mentioned.
>
> I met him **of whom** they spoke.
>
> I met him **whose** business folded.

In the above sentences, the personal pronoun *him* is in the objective case because it is the object of the verb *met*. In the first sentence, the relative pronoun *who* is in the nominative case because it is the subject of the verb *was* in its own clause. In the second and third sentences, *whom* is in the objective case because it is used as the object of the verb *mentioned* and the object of the preposition *of*, respectively. In the fourth sentence, *whose* is in the possessive case because it indicates possession of *business*, a word in its own clause.

The **Nominative Case** is used with the subject of a verb.

This is the student **who** failed my class.

I found my wallet, **which** was lost.

He got on the plane **that** was doomed to crash.

The *Objective Case* is used:

- With the Direct Object of a Verb.

    He is the guy **whom** they accused of stealing the money.

    Sandy mailed the Christmas cards, **which** she wrote the previous day.

    People are judged by the words **that** they use.

- With the Object of a Preposition.

    He had a meeting with the CIA agent from **whom** he bought the documents.

    This is the book to **which** they referred.

    She hit everything **that** she aimed at.

- The *Possessive Case* is used to denote possession.

    The pirates surrounded the ship, **whose** captain was furiously issuing orders.

Determining the Use of a Relative Pronoun

CCSS.L.9–10.1.B:
Use various types of phrases (noun, verb, adjectival, adverbial, participial, prepositional, absolute) and clauses (independent, dependent; noun, relative, adverbial) to convey specific meanings and add variety and interest to writing or presentations.

What is clear about a relative pronoun is that whatever its use in the sentence, it generally stands at the beginning of the clause it introduces. In English the usual order of elements in a sentence is *subject + verb + object + various other elements*. So if the relative pronoun is the subject of the verb, it stands in the usual position of the subject, that is, at the beginning of the clause. Its use can therefore be readily determined.

If the relative pronoun is not the subject, one can determine its use by rearranging the clause so that the subject comes first, then the verb, then the rest of the clause.

For example, take the sentence, "She is the woman *whom* you mentioned." Rearranged, the clause would read "you mentioned whom," in which *whom* can easily be seen as the object of the verb. Again, "This was the vacation *that* we dreamed about." Rearranged, the clause would read "we dreamed about *that*," in which *that* is clearly the object of the preposition *about*.

COMMON CORE GRAMMAR

When a relative pronoun is the object of a preposition, the preposition is often placed at the beginning of the clause before the pronoun: as, "She is the real estate agent *of whom* I spoke." Rearranged, the clause becomes "I spoke *of whom.*"

Careful attention must be given to the case of a relative pronoun in a clause that contains a parenthetical expression like *I thought, we believed, he said.* Compare the following sentences:

> He is the student **who** we believed would be a success.

> He is the student **whom** we believed you should tutor.

In the first sentence *who* is the subject of the verb phrase *would be* and is thus in the nominative case. In the second sentence *whom* is the object of the verb phrase *should tutor* and is thus in the objective case.

CCSS.L.11–12.1.A:
Apply the understanding that usage is a matter of convention, can change over time, and is sometimes contested.

Who and *whom* can cause problems. *Whom* is perceived as formal, and only a very formal speaker would say something like *Whom do you know?* But the biggest problem with *whom* is that it's often used incorrectly. In everyday use, it's appropriate in double questions like *Who's seeing whom?* and in fixed expression like *To whom it may concern.* Some language mavens believe *whom* will one day vanish from the language, but it continues to be used to make precise distinctions in case and usage.

Omission of a Relative Pronoun

Often the relative pronoun is not stated. In such instances it is said to be "understood."

> These are the keys ˆ you need (**that** is omitted before **you**).

> He is the candidate ˆ we voted for (**whom** is omitted).

Distinctions in the Use of "Who," "Whom," "Which," and "That"

CCSS.L.9–12.1:
Demonstrate command of the conventions of standard English grammar and usage when writing or speaking.

Who and *whom* are used with antecedents denoting persons.

> The soldier **who** was awarded the Purple Heart.

> The lawyer **whom** I retained.

Which is used with an antecedent denoting anything but a person.

> Our house, **which** sits at the end of a cul-de-sac.

Easter, **which** is in the springtime.

My car, **which** is in the shop.

Honesty, **which** is an admirable quality.

That is used with antecedents denoting persons or things.

The officer **that** wrote me a ticket.

The movie **that** won the Oscar.

COMPOUND RELATIVE PRONOUNS

The ***Compound Relative Pronouns*** are *whoever, whosoever; whosever, whose-soever; whomever, whomsoever; whichever, whichsoever; whatever, whatsoever; what.*

Antecedent

CCSS.L.9–10.1.B:
Use various types of phrases (noun, verb, adjectival, adverbial, participial, prepositional, absolute) and clauses (independent, dependent; noun, relative, adverbial) to convey specific meanings and add variety and interest to writing or presentations.

Compound relative pronouns most often have no ***Antecedent*** in the sentence. In a sense, they contain their own antecedent. *What, whichever,* and *whatever* (with the corresponding -*soever* forms) are equivalent to *that which* (plural, *those which*): that is, they are equivalent to the demonstrative pronoun *that* combined with the relative pronoun *which,* the demonstrative pronoun being the antecedent of the relative pronoun. Similarly, *whoever* is the equivalent of *he who* (plural, *they who*); the personal pronoun *he* is used as the antecedent of the relative pronoun *who.*

By way of example, the sentence, "Show me *what* you're talking about," may be expressed as "Show me *that which* you are talking about." The sentence, "Eat *whichever* you want," may become "Eat *that which* you want." "*Whoever* wants the bike can have it" is equivalent to "*He who* wants the bike can have it."

Note. In some sentences the antecedent is present. In the sentence, "Whoever turns the work in on time, he will receive credit," *he* is the antecedent of *whoever.*

Case and Use

Whoever and *whosoever* are the only compound relative pronouns that have different forms for all three cases.

Nominative	whoever	whosoever
Possessive	whosever	whosesoever
Objective	whomever	whomsoever

CCSS.L.9–10.1.B:
Use various types of phrases (noun, verb, adjectival, adverbial, participial, prepositional, absolute) and clauses (independent, dependent; noun, relative, adverbial) to convey specific meanings and add variety and interest to writing or presentations.

What, whichever, whichsoever, whatever, and *whatsoever* have the same forms for the nominative and objective cases and have no possessive forms.

The case of a compound relative pronoun, like a simple relative pronoun, is determined by how it is used in its own clause.

> He'll complain to **whoever** will listen.
>
> Make a good impression with **whomever** you meet.
>
> Associate with **whomever** you wish.
>
> I'll give the homeless man money, **whoever** he is.

In the first sentence, *whoever* is in the nominative case because it is the subject of the verb *will listen*; it is not the object of the preposition *to*. The whole clause, *whoever will listen,* is the object of the preposition.

In the second sentence, *whomever* is in the objective case because it is the object of the verb *meet*. It is not the object of the preposition *with*.

In the third sentence, *whomever* is in the objective case because it is the object of the preposition *with* "understood," not the preposition *with* expressed in the sentence: "Associate with *whomever* you wish (to associate *with*)."

In the last sentence, *whoever* is in the nominative case because it is a predicate pronoun. Note that the predicate pronoun precedes the subject instead of following the verb *is*.

Exercise 2.4: Identifying Relative Pronouns and Their Antecedents

Underline the relative pronouns, simple and compound; circle their antecedents.

WRITING PROMPT:
Write ten sentences with relative pronouns and antecedents.

1. This is my old friend, David Winkler, whom I have not seen in years.

2. Then he went across to his mother whilst I unbolted the door that gave on the corridor.

3. The room in which the boys were fed was a large stone hall.

4. Mr. Hunter, whose son has served in Iraq, argues that the current bill would endanger troops by interfering with the Pentagon's ability to share intelligence with battlefield commanders.

CCSS.L.9–12.1:
Demonstrate command of the conventions of standard English grammar and usage when writing or speaking.

5. Mary Cavendish was standing where the staircase branched, staring down into the hall in the direction in which he disappeared.

6. "You remember Branscom?" said Jaralson, treating his companion's wit with the inattention that it deserved.

7. There are many addicts who do not want to get off drugs, for whom the drug-induced high is the whole focus of living.

8. It is he who is to blame for the accident.

CCSS.L.9–10.1.B:
Use various types of phrases (noun, verb, adjectival, adverbial, participial, prepositional, absolute) and clauses (independent, dependent; noun, relative, adverbial) to convey specific meanings and add variety and interest to writing or presentations.

9. A reward will be given to whoever returns the purse.

10. Help is offered to whomever we consider worthy.

11. The man whom we honor today is your neighbor and mine.

12. She did not volunteer the reason which he seemed to hope for, and he wished her good night.

13. What they do will depend on future developments.

14. This was the woman who warned me so earnestly, and to whose warning I, alas, paid no heed!

15. For whosoever shall call upon the name of the Lord shall be saved.

Exercise 2.5: Indicating Case Forms of Relative Pronouns

Fill in the blanks with the proper case forms of the relative pronouns.

WRITING PROMPT:
Write ten sentences using the proper forms of *who* and *whom, whoever* and *whomever.*

1. The candidate _____ the Tea Party endorsed was defeated (who, whom).

2. They recognized him as an adversary _____ they must face sooner or later (who, whom).

3. A brochure will be mailed to anyone _____ asks for it (who, whom).

4. The commission will accept _____ the leaders appoint (whoever, whomever).

5. The convict _____ we thought the governor pardoned was still in prison (who, whom).

6. The president is the one _____ they believe is responsible for the war (who, whom).

7. The winner of the lottery, _____ he or she may be, won more money than anyone ever has (whoever, whomever).

CCSS.L.9–12.1:
Demonstrate command of the conventions of standard English grammar and usage when writing or speaking.

8. Give the paper to the woman _____ you see at the first desk (who, whom).

9. His case was tried before a judge _____ he and his lawyer thought was biased (who, whom).

10. Every participant _____ they looked for has been identified (who, whom).

CCSS.L.9–10.1.B:
Use various types of phrases (noun, verb, adjectival, adverbial, participial, prepositional, absolute) and clauses (independent, dependent; noun, relative, adverbial) to convey specific meanings and add variety and interest to writing or presentations.

11. The candidate _____ the president endorsed was defeated (who, whom).

12. They recognized him as an opponent _____ they must reckon with sooner or later (who, whom).

13. A prospectus will be sent to anyone _____ asks for it (who, whom).

14. The party will accept _____ the leaders appoint (whoever, whomever).

15. The prisoner _____ we thought the guards checked on last night actually escaped sometime before morning (who, whom).

Exercise 2.6: Distinguishing *Who, Which,* and *That*

Fill in the blanks with the proper relative pronouns—who, which, or that.

WRITING PROMPT:
Write ten sentences using
the proper forms of who or
whom; which, and *that.*

1. The term _____ he used is not even in Google.

2. Every citizen _____ believes in democracy should consider it an imperative to vote.

3. To the west is the Pacific, _____ nurtures the vineyards with rain and cool winds.

4. These are some of the words _____ you don't know.

5. The school _____ has the highest test scores will be awarded an achievement medal.

6. The bureaucrat _____ you asked about is not employed by the city.

7. She interviewed a voter _____ was similarly baffled.

CCSS.L.9–12.1:
Demonstrate command
of the conventions of
standard English grammar
and usage when writing or
speaking.

8. William Faulkner's first novel, *Soldier's Pay,* _____ was published in 1926, is a story about a returning WWI veteran.

9. The dinner was given in honor of our pastor, _____ was completing his tenth year at our church.

10. The storm _____ swept the city was the second worst in twenty years.

11. The name _____ he gave is not in the directory.

12. Every person _____ believes in democracy should go to the polls and vote.

CCSS.L.9–10.1.B:
Use various types of
phrases (noun, verb, adjectival, adverbial, participial,
prepositional, absolute)
and clauses (independent,
dependent; noun, relative,
adverbial) to convey specific meanings and add variety
and interest to writing or
presentations.

13. Mark Zuckerberg, _____ founded Facebook, is the chairman and chief executive of the company.

14. To the west are the Rockies, _____ protect the valley from the ocean winds.

15. These are some of the words _____ you mispronounce.

16. The city _____ has the fewest accidents will be awarded the safety medal.

17. The official _____ you inquired about is not in the city.

18. We have found only a few voters _____ are in favor of the proposed ordinance.

INTERROGATIVE PRONOUNS

The **Interrogative Pronouns** are used in asking questions. They are *who, whom, whose, which, what, when, where,* and *why.*

Antecedents

An interrogative pronoun does not have an **Antecedent** expressed in the sentence.

Case

CCSS.L.9–10.1.B:
Use various types of phrases (noun, verb, adjectival, adverbial, participial, prepositional, absolute) and clauses (independent, dependent; noun, relative, adverbial) to convey specific meanings and add variety and interest to writing or presentations.

Who has the following case forms.

Nominative	who
Possessive	whose
Objective	whom

Which and *what* retain the same form for both the nominative and objective cases and have no possessive forms.

Like other pronouns, the case of an interrogative pronoun is determined by its use in the sentence—subject of a verb, object of a verb, etc.

Who wants coffee? (Nominative case—subject of the verb).

Who was Charles Bukowski? (Nominative case—predicate pronoun).

Whose is that? (Possessive case—denoting possession).

Whom will you hire? (Objective case—object of the verb).

Whom did you collect money for? (Objective case—object of the preposition).

Position in the Sentence

CCSS.L.9–12.1:
Demonstrate command of the conventions of standard English grammar and usage when writing or speaking.

As a general rule, the interrogative pronoun is placed at the beginning of the sentence with an auxiliary verb placed before the subject in the main clause, an order which does not occur in subordinate clauses: "When *can* Sally *pay* us a visit?" "I wonder when Sally *can pay* us a visit." "Why *have* you *refused* to cooperate with the police?" "I don't understand why you *have refused* to cooperate with the police."

Interrogative Pronouns in Indirect Questions

CCSS.L.9–10.1.B:
Use various types of phrases (noun, verb, adjectival, adverbial, participial, prepositional, absolute) and clauses (independent, dependent; noun, relative, adverbial) to convey specific meanings and add variety and interest to writing or presentations.

Interrogative pronouns are used in both ***Direct*** and ***Indirect Questions***: "Tell me *whom* you met." "I asked her *why* she got the tattoo." In indirect questions the syntax of a direct question is expressed without an auxiliary verb.

Indirect questions most often follow verbs like *ask, tell, wonder,* etc. Thus, "Tell me *whom* you met" is the indirect form of the direct question, *"Whom did you meet?"* "I asked you *whose* party you attended" is the indirect form of *"Whose* party did you attend?" The question mark is omitted after an indirect question.

Distinction Between Interrogative and Relative Pronouns

CCSS.L.9–10.1.B:
Use various types of phrases (noun, verb, adjectival, adverbial, participial, prepositional, absolute) and clauses (independent, dependent; noun, relative, adverbial) to convey specific meanings and add variety and interest to writing or presentations.

There is a direct correspondence between ***Interrogative and Relative Pronouns.*** In fact, *who, whom, whose, which, when, where,* and *why* also act as relative pronouns. These come under the heading of ***wh*-words.**

Who	The woman **who** helped me.
Whom	The woman **whom** I helped.
Whose	The woman **whose** purse I stole.
Which	Thanksgiving, **which** I love.
When	The year **when** I began teaching.
Where	The city **where** I was born.
Why	The reason **why** the officer shot him.

Exercise 2.7: Identifying Interrogative Pronouns

Underline the interrogative pronouns and write the case of each.

WRITING PROMPT:

Write ten sentence with interrogative pronouns.

1. Whom did you ask for at the other house?

2. Tell me who was the last soul who touched your heart.

3. What were they doing when you saw them together?

4. Whom can we select that will help build our Lord's eternal kingdom?

5. I was wondering who won first prize in the International Piano Competition.

6. Whose book did you tell me about?

7. With whom did you say that you would like to go dancing?

CCSS.L.9–12.1:

Demonstrate command of the conventions of standard English grammar and usage when writing or speaking.

8. They would not tell us whom they use for this service.

9. Which of them will be most compatible with your particular frame of mind?

10. Can you guess who the next coach of the team will be?

11. Whom did you ask for at the office?

12. Who was the last person that was in the room?

13. What were they doing when you saw, them?

14. Whom can we select that will be acceptable to both factions?

15. Who won first prize in the Irish sweepstakes last month?

CCSS.L.9–10.1.B:

Use various types of phrases (noun, verb, adjectival, adverbial, participial, prepositional, absolute) and clauses (independent, dependent; noun, relative, adverbial) to convey specific meanings and add variety and interest to writing or presentations.

16. Whose book did you read first?

17. Whom did you say that you met in London?

18. They would not tell us whom they saw entering the garage.

19. You must decide for yourself which is the better bargain.

20. Can you guess who the next president will be?

21. The debate will be on the question of what this country should do in case of war.

22. Who among all these candidates is best suited for the position.

23. Who did they think was coming?

24. Tell me who you think should be chosen

25. Tell me whom you think you saw.

Exercise 2.8: Choosing Interrogative Pronouns

Fill in the blanks with the correct case forms of the interrogative pronouns.

WRITING PROMPT:
Write ten sentence with the interrogative pronouns *who* or *whom*.

1. _____ would you say made the best argument?

2. _____ should we have asked about this problem?

3. _____ can I ask for assistance with this problem?

4. Several times the investigators demanded to know _____ their co-conspirators were.

5. Tell me _____ your guest is.

6. There is some doubt as to _____ will be the Republican nominee.

7. I was telling them _____ I thought were in attendance last evening.

8. They would not tell me _____ they went bar-hopping with last evening.

9. The answer will depend upon _____ you ask.

CCSS.L.9–12.1:
Demonstrate command of the conventions of standard English grammar and usage when writing or speaking.

10. The success of your group's strategy will depend upon _____ your supervisor is.

11. I wanted to know _____ the layout is for a suite room.

12. Given the liturgical use of the piece was not likely or practical, _____ did you think would happen with it?

13. If it was not a mother's place to look after children, _____ on earth was it?

14. _____ was in the boxer's corner?

15. _____ was responsible for the mistake made in the audit?

16. The judge asked them _____ their accomplices were.

17. _____ should we have consulted about this matter?

18. _____ has England become very important as a manufacturing country?

19. _____ are the factors involved in determining overall overtime costs?

20. I looked at everyone and wondered _____ they came from, and _____ they were involved with, and _____ they were so happy to live in the city.

DEMONSTRATIVE PRONOUNS

The **Demonstrative Pronouns** are *this* and *that*, with their plurals *these* and *those* They are used to point out persons or things with definiteness or special emphasis.

Case

The demonstrative pronouns have the same form for the nominative and objective **Cases** and have no possessive form.

Antecedent

CCSS.L.9–10.1.B:
Use various types of phrases (noun, verb, adjectival, adverbial, participial, prepositional, absolute) and clauses (independent, dependent; noun, relative, adverbial) to convey specific meanings and add variety and interest to writing or presentations.

The **Antecedent** of the demonstrative pronoun may be:

- A single noun: as, "I recently reread *The Adventures of Huckleberry Finn*, and I believe *that* is the best of Mark Twain's novels."

- Two or more nouns referred to by a plural demonstrative pronoun: as, "I have spent many years reading Keats and Wordsworth. *These* are the most rewarding of the Romantic poets."

- A whole statement: as, "The Los Angeles Philharmonic charges a lot of money for tickets, and *that* keeps many people from attending their concerts." (In order to avoid ambiguity, this last type of reference is often avoided in formal writing.)

CCSS.L.6.1.D:
Recognize and correct vague pronouns (i.e., ones with unclear or ambiguous antecedents).

Often the demonstrative pronoun has no expressed antecedent. This is especially true in conversation, when persons or things referred to can be indicated with a gesture or a glance. A person seeing something of note has only to say, "Look at *that!*" or picking up a DVD, could say, "Have you seen *this* yet?"

This and *these* refer to objects comparatively near; *that* and *those*, to things comparatively farther away: as, "I like *this* as well as *that*." "I'll stick with *these* instead of *those*." *This* and *that* make reference to singular antecedents; *these* and *those*, to plural antecedents.

Distinction Between Relative and Demonstrative Pronouns

CCSS.L.9–10.1.B:

Use various types of phrases (noun, verb, adjectival, adverbial, participial, prepositional, absolute) and clauses (independent, dependent; noun, relative, adverbial) to convey specific meanings and add variety and interest to writing or presentations.

That can be either a **Relative** or a **Demonstrative Pronoun**. Compare the following sentences:

He opened the package **that** he ordered (relative).

He wanted to do **that**, time permitting (demonstrative).

The demonstrative *that* points out something as definitely as if one were pointing a finger at it. The relative *that* has none of this definite force. As a rule, the relative *that* is placed immediately after its antecedent and introduces a separate clause which modifies the antecedent. The demonstrative *that* can be at a considerable distance from its antecedent, even by a few sentences, and it does not introduce a separate clause.

INDEFINITE PRONOUNS

CCSS.L.9–10.1.B:

Use various types of phrases (noun, verb, adjectival, adverbial, participial, prepositional, absolute) and clauses (independent, dependent; noun, relative, adverbial) to convey specific meanings and add variety and interest to writing or presentations.

The **Indefinite Pronouns** take their name from the fact that they do not refer to definite persons or things.

Compare "*Somebody* will have to pick that up" (indefinite) with "*He* will pick that up" (definite).

The indefinite pronouns include a large number of words indicating various degrees of indefiniteness. The more common ones follow:

SPECIFIERS (SINGULAR)

another	no one	everyone	everything
anyone	nobody	somebody	
anybody	nothing	everybody	
anything	someone	something	

QUALIFIERS (PLURAL)

any	less	one	every
all	little	other	much
both	many	several	few
enough	more	some	either
each	most	such	neither

Case and Number

CCSS.L.9–12.1:

Demonstrate command of the conventions of standard English grammar and usage when writing or speaking.

The nominative and objective case forms of indefinite pronouns are the same, but some indefinite pronouns have a distinct possessive case form: as, *one's, other's, another's,* and the compound forms of *one* and *body* (*anyone's, everybody's*).

One and *other* also have plural forms: *ones* and *others*: as, "These are the *ones* I need." "The *others* aren't worth discussing."

Exercise 2.9: Identifying Demonstrative and Indefinite Pronouns

Underline the demonstrative and indefinite pronouns. Write D for demonstrative and I for indefinite.

WRITING PROMPT:
Write ten sentence with demonstrative and indefinite pronouns.

1. Bring us some of this and a few of those.

2. Each was jealous of the other's success.

3. He fears nothing except his own mortality, and that has always terrified him.

4. This is the time of year when something is always happening to one or the other of them.

CCSS.L.9–12.1:
Demonstrate command of the conventions of standard English grammar and usage when writing or speaking.

5. Many of them are completely uninterested in the opinions of others.

6. Anyone's guess is as good as mine.

7. Many have given money to help a few.

8. She opened a letter that someone sent her.

9. He had only a few friends, but these he knew intimately.

CCSS.L.9–10.1.B:
Use various types of phrases (noun, verb, adjectival, adverbial, participial, prepositional, absolute) and clauses (independent, dependent; noun, relative, adverbial) to convey specific meanings and add variety and interest to writing or presentations.

10. That was the message that someone laid on his desk.

11. Each was ambitious and wanted to outdo the other.

12. Southern enterprise and energy were all turned to planting.

13. He fears nothing except his own conscience, and that he always obeys.

14. Something bad happened to almost everything in the kitchen.

15. Each had a private feeling of bitterness about the other.

16. The face of another seemed to consist mainly of a huge nose.

17. Even these were fenced and guarded so that no one might come near to them.

18. I liked the way in which he told of his adventures, with a little frank boasting, enough to season but not to spoil the story.

19. Expanding rapidly in Japan are the so-called new religions, several of which are essentially Buddhist counterparts to Protestant fundamentalism.

Exercise 2.10: Identifying Indefinite Pronouns

Underline the indefinite pronouns, indicating whether it is a specifier or a quantifier.

WRITING PROMPT:
Write ten sentences with specifiers and quantifiers.

1. Even these were fenced and guarded so that no one might come near to them.

2. After three months of nothing, the two sides in the NFL lockout are at least talking to each other.

3. I liked the way in which he told of his adventures, with a little frank boasting, enough to season but not to spoil the story.

CCSS.L.9–12.1:
Demonstrate command of the conventions of standard English grammar and usage when writing or speaking.

4. No one could have heard this low droning of the gathering clans.

5. Some of the contents of the annex were reported this week by the *Washington Post* and the *Los Angeles Times*.

6. To prevent insurgents from discovering their identities, many lie to everyone, wives and family included, about their real jobs.

7. I promise you everything, and this is all I ask in return.

8. Something that did not belong to him dropped away, and he returned to a former state of being.

9. Not from Spy Rock nor from anywhere else can you see anything at Hilltop that is not honest and pure and loyal.

10. Neither had enough to say, but as they fumbled sheepishly and sleepily for words they were acknowledging that this encounter was a necessary step.

11. Either way, you killed them dead, sending them straight to Heaven or to nowhere.

12. Few of the friends he and his wife had in town sought them out anymore.

13. Someone once sank seashells in the wet cement of the patio.

14. Janet knew French as well as anyone who took six years of it in various respectable schools without ever speaking to a Frenchman.

15. They are both forgetful, she of errands she means to run and he of names.

16. He hated apartment living, especially the odors of other people's cooking seeping through the walls.

Exercise 2.11: Identifying Pronouns

Underline the pronouns and identify them by type.

WRITING PROMPT:
Write ten sentences with a variety of pronouns studied in this chapter.

1. They handed us some of the reports that were in the files.

2. The Scottish novelist whom you referred to is practically unknown to most of us in America.

3. Which of the two books do you consider more engaging?

4. Whatever good you do, it will be to your credit.

5. Whom should we choose for this work?

6. We ourselves have traveled to Europe a number of times.

CCSS.L.9–12.1:
Demonstrate command of the conventions of standard English grammar and usage when writing or speaking.

7. We have never loaned them money, for they are too proud to accept help of that sort.

8. That was the CEO himself whom you saw sitting behind the ornate desk.

9. He isn't interested in others' opinions.

10. They brought us some of the reports that were in the files.

11. The world was new to me, and I never saw anything like this at home.

12. What is the nature of the luxury which enervates and destroys nations?

13. Not many of those she looked at ever saw her again.

14. He, whoever he was, was trying to call me by name, but his voice was no more than a husky whisper.

15. He boasted that nobody could tell him anything new about chess.

16. There is nothing like knowledge that one has picked up or reasoned out for oneself.

17. Unfortunately my father did not see me as I saw myself.

18. Nobody could spread himself like Tom Sawyer in such a thing as that.

19. Who the man was the town authorities certainly did not know, neither could they apparently find out.

Chapter

3

Adjectives

ENGLISH LANGUAGE ARTS STANDARDS

☞ *CCSS.ELA-LITERACY.L.9–12.1:* Demonstrate command of the conventions of standard English grammar and usage when writing or speaking.

☞ *CCSS.ELA-LITERACY.L.9–12.2:* Demonstrate command of the conventions of standard English capitalization, punctuation, and spelling when writing.

☞ *CCSS.ELA-LITERACY.L.9–10.1.B:* Use various types of phrases (noun, verb, adjectival, adverbial, participial, prepositional, absolute) and clauses (independent, dependent; noun, relative, adverbial) to convey specific meanings and add variety and interest to writing or presentations.

☞ *CCSS.ELA-LITERACY.L.11–12.1.A:* Apply the understanding that usage is a matter of convention, can change over time, and is sometimes contested.

☞ *CCSS.ELA-LITERACY.L.11–12.2.B:* Spell correctly.

☞ *CCSS.ELA-LITERACY.L.9–10.2.C:* Spell correctly.

ADJECTIVES

CCSS.L.9–12.1:
Demonstrate command of the conventions of standard English grammar and usage when writing or speaking.

An ***Adjective*** is a word that describes a noun or modifies its meaning.

An adjective may:

- Describe a noun: as, *brilliant* scientist, *cold* coffee, *fast* car.

- Indicate which member or members of a group are denoted by the noun: as, *this* pen, *some* people, *any* woman, *three* books, *second* week.

Any word that describes or modifies a noun in this way is an adjective. Thus, we normally think of *weekend* as a noun, but in the sentence, "I enjoy *weekend* sports," the word is an adjective because it modifies the noun *sports*. Seen in this way, the possessive case of a noun can be classified as an adjective: as, *William's* desk, *Harry's* hat, the *lady's* dress.

DETERMINERS

CCSS.L.9–10.1.B:
Use various types of phrases (noun, verb, adjectival, adverbial, participial, prepositional, absolute) and clauses (independent, dependent; noun, relative, adverbial) to convey specific meanings and add variety and interest to writing or presentations.

Determiners, a large category, precede nouns and ***determine*** or limit their meaning. They are sometimes called "pronominal adjectives" in traditional grammar.

- ***Personal Pronouns:*** "This is *my* car." "He found *her* purse."

- ***Relative Pronouns:*** "The neighbor *whose* dog is barking came home." "*Whichever* wine you select, the dinner guests will probably like it."

- ***Interrogative Pronouns:*** "*Which* flavor do you want?" "*What* decision will the court make?"

- ***Demonstrative Pronouns:*** "*That* sort of thing is good to avoid." "*Those* apples are delicious."

- ***Indefinite Pronouns:*** "*Any* time off will be good." "*Some* situations are best avoided." "The *other* clerk was more helpful." "*Few* people care." "You don't have *much* time." "How *many* books do you own?" "The *few* friends he had are dead." The *little* money that he has will run out soon." "*Either* of these machines is suitable." "*Neither* of the participants is here." "*All* the money is gone." "*Every* person here knows the answer." "*Each* must do his best."

- ***Articles:*** definite (*the*), indefinite (*a, an*).

To decide whether or not a pronoun is used as a determiner, decide if it modifies a noun or functions as a noun.

DETERMINERS	PRONOUNS
That politician is corrupt.	**That** is a corrupt politician.
Which wine is better?	**Which** is better?
The **other** car is faster.	The **other** is faster.
This is **my** coat.	This coat is **mine**.

Predeterminers come before other determiners: multipliers (*double, twice, four/five times . . .*); fractions (*one-third, three-quarters*); words expressing quantity (*both, all*); intensifiers (*quite, rather, such*).

Exercise 3.1: Identifying Determiners

Underline the determiners, giving the type.

WRITING PROMPT:
Write ten sentences containing various determiners.

1. You just have to lower your expectations on the timetable on when they're going to get things done.

2. It was a tint rather than a shade, like ivory.

3. Tampa is expected to introduce him as its new football coach in the next few days.

4. Doctors cannot now tell, however, which women need the chemotherapy.

5. She had neither opportunity nor inclination to observe him closely during their interview in the vestibule.

6. The president's position on missile defense has been known for quite some time.

CCSS.L.9–10.1.B:
Use various types of phrases (noun, verb, adjectival, adverbial, participial, prepositional, absolute) and clauses (independent, dependent; noun, relative, adverbial) to convey specific meanings and add variety and interest to writing or presentations.

7. Austrians have dominated the first two days of training and will challenge for the podium in both races.

8. For us a truce means that two warring parties live side-by-side in peace and security for a certain period, and this period is eligible for renewal.

9. During his preparation for ministry, van Gogh admired Christ's humility as a common laborer and "man of sorrows" whose life he tried to imitate.

10. Fans will look at the box score and see eight players in double figures for only the second time in franchise history.

11. The science of medicine is the body of knowledge about body systems and diseases.

12. At all events Frank proposed it, and there was not a dissenting voice.

13. Medicine is a branch of health science concerned with restoring and maintaining health and wellness.

14. For more than half an hour he stayed there, struggling between life and death, dying in slow agony under our eyes.

15. A second category concerns a person who has a mixed track record.

16. But he was a tight-fisted hand at the grindstone, Scrooge, a squeezing, wrenching, grasping, scraping, clutching, covetous old 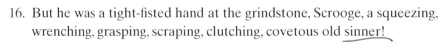sinner!

17. Holmes was silent, but his little darting glances showed me the interest which he took in our curious companion.

ARTICLES

CCSS.L.9–12.1:
Demonstrate command of the conventions of standard English grammar and usage when writing or speaking.

The adjectives *a, an,* and *the* are called **Articles**.

A and *an* are **Indefinite Articles**; *the* is a **Definite Article**. Their distinctive uses are shown in the following sentences.

> Hand me **a** pencil (any pencil).

> Hand me **the** pencil (a particular pencil).

Indefinite articles indicate a member of a class without designating which particular one; definite articles indicate a specific member or members of a class.

Uses of "A" and "An"

CCSS.L.9–12.1:
Demonstrate command of the conventions of standard English grammar and usage when writing or speaking.

The article *a* precedes a word beginning with a consonant sound; *an* precedes a word beginning with a vowel sound: *a* tree, *an* olive tree.

Note. Besides the common vowels of *a, e, i, o,* and *u,* in English a *y* can have the characteristics of either a vowel or a consonant. For example, an initial *y* is almost always a consonant (*yell, yard*); in the middle of a word, it is often a vowel (*analysis*).

The letter *u* can have either a vowel or a consonant sound. Before a word beginning with a *u* having a vowel sound, *an* is used: as, *an* understanding, *an* uncle; before a word beginning with a *u* having a consonant sound, *a* is used: as, *a* union (pronounced *yunion*), *a* uniform, *a* use.

Before a word beginning with *h, an* is used if the *h* is silent; *a* is used if the *h* is sounded: as, *an* honorable profession, *a* humid day, *a* house.

Adherence to the above rule is not universal. Some writers use *a* before a word beginning with *h* if the first syllable is accented and *an* if it is unaccented: as, *a* his´-tory; *an* his-tor´-ical event. However, this practice is not recommended.

POSITION OF ADJECTIVES

An adjective commonly precedes the noun it modifies.

> He was a **good** student.

Sometimes, for special emphasis, and in some special constructions, an adjective follows the noun.

He was a soldier, **strong** and **courageous**.

Predicate Adjective

CCSS.L.9–10.1.B:
Use various types of phrases (noun, verb, adjectival, adverbial, participial, prepositional, absolute) and clauses (independent, dependent; noun, relative, adverbial) to convey specific meanings and add variety and interest to writing or presentations.

An adjective modifying the subject frequently follows a verb, which in such cases is a linking verb: that is, a verb that links the adjective to the subject. An adjective used in this manner is called a ***Predicate Adjective***.

The cake was **huge** (huge cake).

The job will be **difficult** (difficult job).

The sky looks **ominous**.

The milk turned **sour**.

My father became **moody**.

A predicate adjective is used with the many forms of the verb *be* and such other linking verbs as *seem, appear, become, turn, feel, look, prove, smell, sound, taste, get, go, grow, keep, remain, stay*.

Sometimes, for special emphasis, the predicate adjective precedes the verb, and the subject follows.

Ominous was the sky.

Objective Complement

CCSS.L.9–10.1.B:
Use various types of phrases (noun, verb, adjectival, adverbial, participial, prepositional, absolute) and clauses (independent, dependent; noun, relative, adverbial) to convey specific meanings and add variety and interest to writing or presentations.

An adjective can follow a direct object of a verb, modifying the object and completing the meaning of the verb. An adjective thus used is called an ***Objective Complement***.

My uncle painted the barn **red**.

Heat turned the milk **sour**.

Sushi makes me **sick**. (Sushi doesn't make **me**—it makes me **sick**.)

The test for an objective complement—either an adjective or a noun—is to see whether *to be* can be inserted between the direct object and the complement without changing the meaning of the sentence. Compare:

I made the coffee (to be) **strong** (objective complement).

I poured a cup of coffee **strong** as acid (an adjective modifying the object).

The following verbs have objects that can take an adjective as an objective complement: *cut, drive, get, know, make, paint, pat, pick, plane, render, rub, send, shoot, sweep, turn, wipe, account, believe, consider, deem, find, hold, judge, presume, reckon, think, call, certify, declare, label, pronounce, brand, designate, proclaim, christen, dub, name, eat, leave, like, prefer, serve, show, want.*

COMPARISON OF ADJECTIVES

CCSS.L.9–10.1.B:
Use various types of phrases (noun, verb, adjectival, adverbial, participial, prepositional, absolute) and clauses (independent, dependent; noun, relative, adverbial) to convey specific meanings and add variety and interest to writing or presentations.

Adjectives have three forms of comparison: the ***Positive, Comparative,*** and ***Superlative***.

The ***Positive Degree*** is the simple form of the adjective that makes no comparison between objects: *soft, big, believable.*

The ***Comparative Degree*** is used to compare one object with another: that is, to compare two objects. To form the comparative degree, add -*er* to the simple form of the adjective, or use *more* (sometimes *less*) before it: *softer, bigger, more believable* (*less believable*).

The ***Superlative Degree*** is used to compare three or more objects. To form the superlative degree, add -*est* to the simple form of the adjective, or use *most* (sometimes *least*) before it: *softest, biggest, most believable* (*least believable*).

We therefore say:

The pillow is **soft** (positive degree).

The new pillow is **softer** than the old one (comparative degree).

The new pillow is the **softest** I've ever owned (superlative degree).

My wife is **beautiful**.

My wife is **more beautiful** than yours.

My wife is the **most beautiful** of all.

Occasionally the superlative degree indicates the greatest degree of a quality, without a definite comparison between objects.

CCSS.L.11–12.1.A:
Apply the understanding that usage is a matter of convention, can change over time, and is sometimes contested.

I took the **most perverse** pleasure in his misfortune.

She was a **most kind** woman.

There is no definite rule for determining whether the forms in -*er,* -*est,* or those in *more, most,* are correct for any particular adjective.

A few general rules follow:

- With adjectives of one syllable — and some with two syllables — the suffixes *-er* and *-est* are used: *thick, thicker, thickest; thrifty, thriftier, thriftiest.*

- With the majority of adjectives of three or more syllables — and many with two syllables — *more* and *most* are used: *beautiful, more beautiful, most beautiful; bizarre, more bizarre, most bizarre.*

- With some adjectives either *-er, -est,* or *more, most* may be used: *clever, cleverer* or *more clever, cleverest* or *most clever.*

When in doubt, be guided by the sound of the words or look them up in a good dictionary.

Irregular Comparison

CCSS.L.9–12.2:
Demonstrate command of the conventions of standard English capitalization, punctuation, and spelling when writing.

CCSS.L.11–12.2.B:
Spell correctly.

CCSS.L.9–10.2.C:
Spell correctly.

Several adjectives have irregular forms in the comparative and superlative degrees.

POSITIVE	COMPARATIVE	SUPERLATIVE
good	better	best
bad, ill	worse	worst
much, many	more	most
little	less, lesser	least
far	farther, further	farthest, furthest
old	older, elder	oldest, eldest
late	later, latter	latest, last
_____	inner	inmost, innermost
_____	outer	outmost, outermost
_____	utter	utmost, uttermost
_____	upper	uppermost
top	_____	topmost
bottom	_____	bottommost

Exercise 3.2: Writing with Adjectives

Use the indicated adjectives to write sentences, two adjectives in each sentence.

WRITING PROMPT:
Write sentences in which the indefinite article is directly followed by—
honorable, youthful, yew, ewe, euphonious, historical, history, hymn, humble, hilarious, university, express, horticultural, oratorio, automatic, heritage, harmonious.

1. (monstrous, enormous)

2. (gigantic, immense)

3. (gargantuan, colossal)

4. (minuscule, puny)

5. (infinitesimal, wee)

CCSS.L.9–10.1.B:
Use various types of phrases (noun, verb, adjectival, adverbial, participial, prepositional, absolute) and clauses (independent, dependent; noun, relative, adverbial) to convey specific meanings and add variety and interest to writing or presentations.

6. (lilliputian, petite)

7. (fiery, scalding)

8. (sweltering, torrid)

9. (frigid, icy)

10. (nippy, chilly)

11. (sensitive, touchy)

12. (leisurely, friendly)

Exercise 3.3: Degrees of Adjectives; Determiners

Underline the adjectives. Write the degree—positive, comparative, or superlative. Also, underline any determiners.

WRITING PROMPT:
Choose ten adjectives of your own, then write three sentences for each, using the positive, comparative, and superlative degrees.

WRITING PROMPT:
Compare the skills of two or more of your favorite athletes, actors, artists, etc. Use at least two degrees of comparison in your writing.

CCSS.L.9–10.1.B:
Use various types of phrases (noun, verb, adjectival, adverbial, participial, prepositional, absolute) and clauses (independent, dependent; noun, relative, adverbial) to convey specific meanings and add variety and interest to writing or presentations.

1. Their long ride made the passengers drowsy and ill-tempered.

2. I didn't spend much money on food.

3. The next three chapters were even better.

4. John's roommate went home for the long weekend.

5. Which Kindle book has sold the most copies this year?

6. Each country will have its foreign secretaries in attendance.

7. My wife ended up spending less money on the week's groceries than she expected to.

8. The searchers found the boys happy and hungry.

9. I haven't seen either movie, so I have no preference.

10. Only the last chapter was difficult to read.

11. Nature is good, but intellect is better.

12. He was a very gentlemanly person, good natured and superior.

13. Her long work hours made her tired and irritable.

14. In its latest report the committee called attention to the urgent need for more members.

15. The general furniture was profuse, comfortless, antique and tattered.

16. The test made our class alert for errors in grammar.

17. The longest way proved to be the quickest way.

18. What book has been the best seller during the past decade?

19. It was a stiff oak branch, sound as iron.

20. Meanwhile the lighthouse was growing steadily larger.

21. What's this crazy guy trying to tell me?

22. The stars are beautiful—Vega on a summer night, Sirius in winter.

23. The boy's bedroom overlooked a vacant lot where he often played with the other children of the neighborhood for an hour after school.

Exercise 3.4: Using Degrees of Adjectives

Fill in the blanks with the proper form of the adjective—comparative or superlative.

WRITING PROMPT:

Write sentences containing either the comparative or the superlative of the following words—*merry, uncomfortable, ill, joyfully, northern, old, far, in, out, early, little (adjective), little (adverb), badly, often, worthy, wonderful, accurate, far, nigh, top, much, severe.*

1. Of all the rooms in the house the master bedroom is the _____ (cooler, coolest).

2. I don't know whether your idea or mine is the _____ practical (more, most).

3. I could travel by car or by train, but I preferred the _____ because it was the _____ (latter, last) (faster, fastest).

4. Who writes the _____ emails—Angelica, Karen, or Sabrina (better, best)?

5. The result becomes _____ every day (doubtfuller, more doubtful).

6. He is the _____ man that I know (contrariest, most contrary).

7. This is the _____ thing that he ever did (foolishest, most foolish).

8. The money is _____ in the bank (safer, more safe).

9. The heat is _____ today (intenser, more intense).

10. From the list, they chose the _____ appropriate title (more, most).

11. He is _____ than his colleagues (radicaller, more radical).

12. He should be _____ with the children (patienter, more patient).

13. Which of the two girls do you think is the _____ (older, oldest)?

14. This arrangement is the _____ for us (suitablest, most suitable).

Exercise 3.5: Using Degrees of Adjectives

Give the comparative and superlative forms of these adjectives

WRITING PROMPT:
Choose five of the adjectives and write two sentences for each, one in the comparative and one in the superlative.

1. tall _____ _____

2. eager _____ _____

3. magnificent _____ _____

4. short _____ _____

5. delightful _____ _____

6. stupid _____ _____

7. silly _____ _____

CCSS.L.9–10.1.B:
Use various types of phrases (noun, verb, adjectival, adverbial, participial, prepositional, absolute) and clauses (independent, dependent; noun, relative, adverbial) to convey specific meanings and add variety and interest to writing or presentations.

8. brief _____ _____

9. well _____ _____

10. blue _____ _____

11. wicked _____ _____

12. tired _____ _____

13. victorious _____ _____

14. warm _____ _____

15. sudden _____ _____

CCSS.L.11–12.2.B:
Spell correctly.

16. famous _____ _____

17. sullen _____ _____

18. crisp _____ _____

CCSS.L.9–10.2.C:
Spell correctly.

19. much _____ _____

20. crude _____ _____

Chapter
4

Verbs

ENGLISH LANGUAGE ARTS STANDARDS

NOTE:
Some of the skills in this chapter were introduced at lower grade levels; yet, due to the recursiveness of the language standards, they require further attention at the high school level.

☞ ***CCSS.ELA-LITERACY.L.11–12.1.A:*** *Apply the understanding that usage is a matter of convention, can change over time, and is sometimes contested.*

☞ ***CCSS.ELA-LITERACY.L.11–12.1.B:*** *Resolve issues of complex or contested usage, consulting references* (e.g., Merriam–Webster's Dictionary of English Usage, Garner's Modern American Usage) *as needed.*

☞ ***CCSS.ELA-LITERACY.L.9–10.1.B:*** *Use various types of phrases (noun, verb, adjectival, adverbial, participial, prepositional, absolute) and clauses (independent, dependent; noun, relative, adverbial) to convey specific meanings and add variety and interest to writing or presentations.*

☞ ***CCSS.ELA-LITERACY.L.8.1.A:*** *Explain the function of verbals (gerunds, participles, infinitives) in general and their function in particular sentences.*

☞ ***CCSS.ELA-LITERACY.L.8.1.B:*** *Form and use verbs in the active and passive voice.*

☞ ***CCSS.ELA-LITERACY.L.8.1.C:*** *Form and use verbs in the indicative, imperative, interrogative, conditional, and subjunctive mood.*

☞ ***CCSS.ELA-LITERACY.L.7.1.A:*** *Explain the function of phrases and clauses in general and their function in specific sentences.*

VERBS

A *Verb* is a word that makes a statement about the subject. For a statement to be made about a subject, two elements are needed: something to make a statement

CHAPTER 4

COMMON CORE GRAMMAR

about and something to say about it. The first element is referred to as the subject of the sentence or clause; the second, as the verb.

A verb expresses one of two qualities:

- *Action:* as, "I *sing*." "He *eats*." "They *are attending* the meeting."

- *State* or *Condition:* as, "He *seems* quiet." "The milk *turned* sour." "We *are* happy."

Some verbs may express action in one sentence and a state or condition in another, depending on how they are used.

> He **went** to the movies.
>
> His luck **went** bad.

TRANSITIVE AND INTRANSITIVE VERBS

CCSS.L.8.1.C:
Form and use verbs in the indicative, imperative, interrogative, conditional, and subjunctive mood.

Verbs are either transitive or intransitive.

A *Transitive Verb* takes an object.

> We **saw** the dog.
>
> The woman **bought** a new dress.
>
> He **repaired** his car.

An *Intransitive Verb* does not take an object.

> The man **drove** fast.
>
> She **is running**.
>
> Dogs **bark**.

The word "transitive" stems from the same Latin root as "transit," meaning to "go over" or "pass over." Therefore, the action performed by the subject of a transitive verb passes from the verb to the object.

Some verbs can be either transitive or intransitive.

TRANSITIVE	INTRANSITIVE
The boy **shattered** the window.	The window **shattered**.
He **popped** the bottle open.	The bottle **popped**.

LINKING VERBS

CCSS.L.8.1.C:
Form and use verbs in the indicative, imperative, interrogative, conditional, and subjunctive mood.

A Linking Verb connects the subject with a predicate noun or predicate adjective.

> Mark **is** a sailor.
>
> He **will be** happy to hear that.

A Linking Verb is sometimes referred to as a **Copulative Verb**.

By far the most commonly used linking verb is *be* in its various conjugations: *am, is, was, were, will be, has been,* etc. In addition to *be,* any verb used to connect the subject with a predicate noun or predicate adjective is a linking verb: *look, become, appear, seem, wax, feel, grow, prove, remain, smell, sound, taste, turn.*

> He **looks** terrible.
>
> She **became** a doctor.
>
> He **waxed** nostalgic for times gone by.

As the above examples show, linking verbs do not have objects.

The verb *be* in its several forms is not always a linking verb, for it may be used as an intransitive verb meaning *to exist*: as, "The universe *is* a mystery." "The universe *is.*"

AUXILIARY VERBS

CCSS.L.9–10.1.B:
Use various types of phrases (noun, verb, adjectival, adverbial, participial, prepositional, absolute) and clauses (independent, dependent; noun, relative, adverbial) to convey specific meanings and add variety and interest to writing or presentations.

An **Auxiliary Verb** extends the meaning of another verb.

They are commonly referred to as **Helping Verbs**. For example, in *is running,* the auxiliary verb *is* helps to make a form of the main verb *run*; in *have drunk* and *will sing* the auxiliary verbs *have* and *will* help to make forms of the main verbs *drink* and *sing.*

Auxiliary verbs can be classified as **Principal Auxiliaries** (*do, have, be*), **Modal Auxiliaries** (*can, may, shall, will, could, might, should, would, must*), and **Marginal Modal Auxiliaries** (*ought, used to, need, dare*).

Be, have, do, and *will* are not always auxiliary verbs. They are often used as **Lexical Verbs**, that is, verbs with predicate meaning—in contrast to the purely grammatical meaning of auxiliaries: as, "She *is* here." "We *have* the money." "They *do* the heavy lifting." "I *willed* my numbers to come up."

When *be* and *have* occur in a verb phrase the order is *have + be*.

Note. *Be* and *have* are the most frequently used verbs in the English language, dating back to the Old English period. *Be* has the most irregular forms of any verb, being a combination of the two Old English verbs *beom* and *eom*.

Intervening words often come between an auxiliary verb and the main verb. In such cases, students must be careful when identifying the main verb in the sentence: as, "I *will* in the future *give* you instructions on what to do."

Exercise 4.1: Identifying Transitive, Intransitive, Linking, and Auxiliary Verbs

Underline the transitive and intransitive verbs, linking verbs, and auxiliary verbs; identify each function.

WRITING PROMPT:
Write several paragraphs about something you could have done better. Use auxiliary verbs to help you express your ideas.

1. The wind had triumphed, and swept all the clouds from heaven.

2. Surely this was his native village which he had left but the day before.

3. For nonconformity the world whips you with its displeasure.

4. This may seem singular, but it has nearly always been my experience.

5. Once a dripping servant brought him food, but he could not eat.

6. Then will justice reign and peace be in all the land.

7. Throughout the trial John remained a loyal friend of the prisoner.

8. He uncovered the vase, and threw the faded rose into the water which it contained.

CCSS.L.9–10.1.B:
Use various types of phrases (noun, verb, adjectival, adverbial, participial, prepositional, absolute) and clauses (independent, dependent; noun, relative, adverbial) to convey specific meanings and add variety and interest to writing or presentations.

9. His loyalty I have never questioned, but his judgment is often faulty.

10. Those young men whom he knew seemed uneasy when he was in the room.

11. The accident might not have occurred if he had been watching the road.

12. At last my hand came in contact with the knocker and I lifted it.

13. Sweet are the fruits of victory.

14. Did you find the author's name in the computer database?

15. A thin, gray fog hung over the city, and the streets were very cold, for summer was in England.

16. He appeared awkward and uncomfortable among these strangers.

CCSS.L.8.1.C:
Form and use verbs in the indicative, imperative, interrogative, conditional, and subjunctive mood.

17. He opened the volume, and took from its black letter pages a rose, or what was once a rose.

18. Have you, by any chance, ever considered the cause for this social unrest?

19. Judge Watson's successor will be in the city tomorrow.

20. The train will probably be late tonight.

Exercise 4.2: Using Transitive and Intransitive Verbs

The following verbs may be either transitive or intransitive. Fill in the blanks with a word or phrase that makes the verb transitive. Then write a sentence using the intransitive. Mark each sentence T (transitive) or I (intransitive). For example, "He shot a bear." (T); "He shot without taking aim." (I).

WRITING PROMPT:
Write fifteen sentences, each containing a transitive verb and its direct object. Write fifteen sentences containing an intransitive verb.

1. The man ran _____ .

2. They stole _____ .

3. She turned _____ .

4. I was reading _____ .

CCSS.L.8.1.C:
Form and use verbs in the indicative, imperative, interrogative, conditional, and subjunctive mood.

5. He called _____ .

6. The ushers rushed _____ .

7. The women fought _____ .

8. The girl can count _____ .

9. She acts _____ .

10. The soldier shot _____ .

11. Over the years my brother has changed _____ .

12. Complainers should stop _____ .

13. We will help _____ .

14. You efforts will improve _____ .

May be copied for classroom use. Common Core Grammar by Thomas Fasano (Coyote Canyon Press: Claremont, CA); © 2015.

PERSON AND NUMBER

CCSS.L.9–10.1.B:
Use various types of phrases (noun, verb, adjectival, adverbial, participial, prepositional, absolute) and clauses (independent, dependent; noun, relative, adverbial) to convey specific meanings and add variety and interest to writing or presentations.

A verb agrees with its subject in **Person** and **Number**.

> I **am** a teacher.
>
> She **is** a teacher.
>
> We **are** teachers.

In the first sentence, the subject *I* is in the first person, singular number. Therefore, the verb *am* is in the first person, singular number. In the second sentence, the verb *is* agrees with the subject *She*; they are both in the third person, singular number. In the third sentence, the verb *are* is in the first person, plural number, to agree with the subject *We*.

CHANGES IN FORM TO INDICATE PERSON AND NUMBER

The Verb "Be"

CCSS.L.8.1.C:
Form and use verbs in the indicative, imperative, interrogative, conditional, and subjunctive mood.

The verb *be* is the most irregular verb in the English language since it has the most forms.

In the present tense the verb *be* has distinct forms (*am* and *is*) for the first and third persons in the singular number; the other forms in the present tense are the same (*are*) for all persons.

The past tense has *was* in the first and third persons and *were* in the other forms.

PRESENT TENSE

SINGULAR	PLURAL
1. I am.	1. We are.
2. You are.	2. You are.
3. He (she, it) is.	3. They are.

PAST TENSE

1. I was.	1. We were.
2. You were.	2. You were.
3. He (she, it) was.	3. They were.

The Verb "Have"

CCSS.L.8.1.C:
Form and use verbs in the indicative, imperative, interrogative, conditional, and subjunctive mood.

In the present tense, the verb *have* takes the form *has* in the third person, singular number, and *have* in all the other forms.

SINGULAR
1. I have.
2. You have.
3. He (she, it) has.

PLURAL
1. We have.
2. You have.
3. They have.

All Other Verbs

CCSS.L.8.1.C:
Form and use verbs in the indicative, imperative, interrogative, conditional, and subjunctive mood.

In the present tense, all other verbs add *-s* in the third person, singular number.

SINGULAR
1. I talk.
2. You talk.
3. He (she, it) talks.

PLURAL
1. We talk.
2. You talk.
3. They talk.

These are the only changes ever made to an English verb to indicate person and number. English has a simplified system of conjugation as most verb-forms do not distinguish between person and number. To determine person and number it is necessary to refer to the subject.

The rule for person and number is consequently simple: In all verbs except *be* and *have*, the third person, singular number, present tense is indicated by adding an *-s*.

Note. In the "solemn" style of prayer, poetry, and older literature, the second person, singular number pronoun thou takes special verb-forms: *thou art, thou wast, thou hast been, thou speakest*, etc.

TENSE

CCSS.L.8.1.C:
Form and use verbs in the indicative, imperative, interrogative, conditional, and subjunctive mood.

Tense is the property of a verb that indicates time. There are six tenses—three simple and three perfect.

SIMPLE TENSES
Present
Past
Future

PERFECT TENSES
Present Perfect
Past Perfect
Future Perfect

The general uses of these forms are explained in the following sections, including progressive and emphatic forms.

Simple Tenses

CCSS.L.8.1.C:
Form and use verbs in the indicative, imperative, interrogative, conditional, and subjunctive mood.

The ***Present Tense*** usually indicates an action happening at the present time: as, "He *feels* the effect of it now."

The ***Past Tense*** usually indicates that an action happened sometime in the past: as, "He *felt* the effect of it yesterday."

The ***Future Tense*** usually indicates that an action will happen in the future: as, "He *will feel* the effect of it tomorrow."

Perfect Tenses

CCSS.L.8.1.C:
Form and use verbs in the indicative, imperative, interrogative, conditional, and subjunctive mood.

The three simple tenses cover all possible time: time *now*, time *gone by*, and time *to come*. Thus, the perfect tenses cannot indicate time not included in the simple tenses. The perfect tenses are used to call attention to the time of completion of an action and the continuation of its effect.

- The ***Present Perfect Tense*** indicates an action that began in the past and continues, or whose effect continues, in the present: as, "My mother *has sacrificed* much for her family."

- The ***Past Perfect Tense*** indicates an action that began in the past and continued, or whose effect continued, until later in the past: as, "When my favorite teacher retired, he *had taught* for over thirty years."

- The ***Future Perfect Tense*** indicates a future action that will be completed before another future action: as, "He *will have finished* his homework when I ask him about it later."

In Modern English the simple future tense is more likely to be used than the future perfect tense. Ordinarily, a person would say, "He *will finish* his homework by bedtime," instead of "He *will have finished*."

Forms of the Tenses

The forms of the tenses are as follows:

CCSS.L.8.1.C:
Form and use verbs in the indicative, imperative, interrogative, conditional, and subjunctive mood.

- The ***Present Tense*** is the base form of the verb: *talk, understand, think*.

- The ***Past Tense*** is usually formed:

  - by adding *-ed, -d,* or *-t* to the base form of the verb: *talk, talked; move, moved; deal, dealt*.

  - by changing the vowel in the base form without adding a suffix: *blow, blew; sink, sank; drink, drank; find, found*.

- The ***Future Tense*** consists of the auxiliary verb *will* or *shall* used with the base form of the verb: *will drink; shall understand*.

- The ***Present Perfect Tense*** consists of the auxiliary verb *have* or *has* used with the past participle: *have drunk; have understood*.

- The ***Past Perfect Tense*** consists of the auxiliary verb *had* used with the past participle: *had drunk; had understood*.

- The ***Future Perfect Tense*** consists of the auxiliary verbs *will have* or *shall have* used with the past participle: *will have drunk; shall have understood*.

Note. The grammatical category of the perfect tense is actually a type of ***Aspect***, which indicates that an event or state is seen as completed or continuing from a particular point in time. Both grammatical aspects discussed in this book (perfect and progressive) can be combined, as in *has been running* (perfect progressive). Because traditional grammar includes aspect as a quality of tense, I will maintain that categorization throughout this book.

PRINCIPAL PARTS OF A VERB

CCSS.L.8.1.C:
Form and use verbs in the indicative, imperative, interrogative, conditional, and subjunctive mood.

Three forms of a verb are essential and are therefore called the ***Principal Parts***. These forms are as follows:

- Present tense, singular number, first person.

- Past tense.

- Past participle.

PRESENT	PAST	PAST PARTICIPLE
talk	talked	talked
see	saw	seen
fly	flew	flown
break	broke	broken
sit	sat	sat

sing	sang	sung
lie	lay	lain
lay	laid	laid

These forms are important because every other verb-form is made by using one of these or a combination of them.

The future tense adds *will* or *shall* to the simple present.

The perfect tenses adds *have* or *has, had, will have,* or *shall have* to the past participle.

The present participle adds *-ing* to the present form: *talking, sitting.*

The present infinitive adds *to* to the base form: *to talk, to sit.*

"Shall" and "Will"

CCSS.L.11–12.1.B:
Resolve issues of complex or contested usage, consulting references (e.g., *Merriam–Webster's Dictionary of English Usage, Garner's Modern American Usage*) as needed.

Shall and *will* don't conform to any particular concrete rules of usage, although in England, *shall* is more likely to be used to express future time in the first person.

The usual lesson taught about these two modal auxiliaries is that in the first person use *shall* to express future time, but use *will* in the second and third. When expressing determination, it's the other way around.

The problem here is that this "rule" is not a rule at all. The editors of *Merriam-Webster's Dictionary of English Usage* researched the uses of these two words over the past six hundred years and concluded: "The traditional rules about *shall* and *will* do not appear to have described real usage of these words precisely at any time, although there is no question that they do describe the usage of some people some of the time and that they are more applicable in England than elsewhere."

TABLE OF FORMS

The following table gives the forms for the six tenses of the verbs *be, have,* and *talk* in different persons and numbers in the indicative mood, active voice.

The Verb "Be"

CCSS.L.8.1.C:
Form and use verbs in the indicative, imperative, interrogative, conditional, and subjunctive mood.

PRESENT TENSE

SINGULAR	PLURAL
1. I am.	1. We are.
2. You are.	2. You are.
3. He is.	3. They are.

PAST TENSE

1. I was.	1. We were.
2. You were.	2. You were.
3. He was.	3. They were.

FUTURE TENSE

1. I shall be.	1. We shall be.
2. You will be.	2. You will be.
3. He will be.	3. They will be.

PRESENT PERFECT TENSE

1. I have been.	1. We have been.
2. You have been.	2. You have been.
3. He has been.	3. They have been.

PAST PERFECT TENSE

1. I had been.	1. We had been.
2. You had been.	2. You had been.
3. He had been.	3. They had been.

FUTURE PERFECT TENSE

1. I shall have been.	1. We shall have been.
2. You will have been.	2. You will have been.
3. He will have been.	3. They will have been.

The Verb "Have"

CCSS.L.8.1.C:
Form and use verbs in the indicative, imperative, interrogative, conditional, and subjunctive mood.

PRESENT TENSE

1. I have.	1. We have.
2. You have.	2. You have.
3. He has.	3. They have.

PAST TENSE

1. I had.	1. We had.
2. You had.	2. You had.
3. He had.	3. They had.

FUTURE TENSE

1. I shall have.	1. We shall have.
2. You will have.	2. You will have.
3. He will have.	3. They will have.

PRESENT PERFECT TENSE

1. I have had.	1. We have had.
2. You have had.	2. You have had.
3. He has had.	3. They have had.

PAST PERFECT TENSE

1. I had had.	1. We had had.
2. You had had.	2. You had had.
3. He had had.	3. They had had.

FUTURE PERFECT TENSE

1. I shall have had.	1. We shall have had.
2. You will have had.	2. You will have had.
3. He will have had.	3. They will have had.

The Verb "Talk"

CCSS.L.8.1.C:
Form and use verbs in the indicative, imperative, interrogative, conditional, and subjunctive mood.

PRESENT TENSE

1. I talk.	1. We talk.
2. You talk.	2. You talk.
3. He talks.	3. They talk.

PAST TENSE

1. I talked.	1. We talked.
2. You talked.	2. You talked.
3. He talked.	3. They talked.

FUTURE TENSE

1. I shall talk.	1. We shall talk.
2. You will talk.	2. You will talk.
3. He will talk.	3. They will talk.

PRESENT PERFECT TENSE

1. I have talked.	1. We have talked.
2. You have talked.	2. You have talked.
3. He has talked.	3. They have talked.

PAST PERFECT TENSE

1. I had talked.	1. We had talked.
2. You had talked.	2. You had talked.
3. He had talked.	3. They had talked.

FUTURE PERFECT TENSE

1. I shall have talked.	1. We shall have talked.
2. You will have talked.	2. You will have talked.
3. He will have talked.	3. They will have talked.

SIMPLE, PROGRESSIVE, AND EMPHATIC TENSE FORMS

CCSS.L.8.1.C:
Form and use verbs in the indicative, imperative, interrogative, conditional, and subjunctive mood.

So far we have considered only the commonest forms of the verb in the different tenses. However, in addition to the simple form, there are two other forms that are used to express various tense relations: the **_Progressive_** and **_Emphatic_**.

- The **_Simple_** forms are those just given in the immediately preceding tables: I _run_, I _dream_, I _speak_, etc.

- The **_Progressive_** forms indicate that an event or state is in progress and can be seen as continuing or ongoing at the time indicated: I _am running_, I _was dreaming_, I _shall be speaking_, etc.

In general, this form expresses action more vividly then the simple or perfect forms. It consists of a form of the verb _be_ used as an auxiliary verb followed by the present participle of the main verb. (The present participle is formed by adding the suffix _-ing_ to the base form of a verb.)

- The **_Emphatic_** forms use a form of the verb _do_ (_do, does,_ or _did_) and give emphasis to the action of the verb: I _do care,_ You _don't say_.

For example, in response to a question, "Why don't you watch what you're saying?" one might respond, "I _watch_ what I'm saying" or "I _do watch_ what I'm saying." The latter statement shows more emphasis.

TABLE OF FORMS

CCSS.L.8.1.C:
Form and use verbs in the indicative, imperative, interrogative, conditional, and subjunctive mood.

The following table illustrates the simple, progressive, and emphatic forms in the present and past tenses (the plural form is not included).

	PRESENT TENSE	
SIMPLE	PROGRESSIVE	EMPHATIC
1. I talk.	1. I am talking.	1. I do talk.
2. You talk.	2. You are talking.	2. You do talk.
3. He talks.	3. He is talking.	3. He does talk.
	PAST TENSE	
1. I talked.	1. I was talking.	1. I did talk.
2. You talked.	2. You were talking.	2. You did talk.
3. He talked.	3. He was talking.	3. He did talk.

There are no emphatic forms for the future and perfect tenses.

FUTURE TENSE

SIMPLE	PROGRESSIVE
1. I shall talk.	1. I shall be talking.
2. You will talk.	2. You will be talking.
3. He will talk.	3. He will be talking.

PRESENT PERFECT TENSE

1. I have talked.	1. I have been talking.
2. You have talked.	2. You have been talking.
3. He has talked.	3. He has been talking.

PAST PERFECT TENSE

1. I had talked.	1. I had been talking.
2. You had talked.	2. You had been talking.
3. He had talked.	3. They had been talking.

FUTURE PERFECT TENSE

1. I shall have talked.	1. I shall have been talking.
2. You will have talked.	2. You will have been talking.
3. He will have talked.	3. They will have been talking.

QUESTIONS AND NEGATIVE STATEMENTS

CCSS.L.8.1.C:
Form and use verbs in the indicative, imperative, interrogative, conditional, and subjunctive mood.

In *Questions* and *Negative Statements,* do, does, and did are used, but not for emphasis. Instead, they are used in place of a missing auxiliary verb as a "stand-in auxiliary."

> I **love** pizza (affirmative).
>
> **Do** you **love** pizza? (question).
>
> I **do** not **love** pizza (negative).

When there is an auxiliary verb in an affirmative statement, *do, does,* or *did* is not required in questions and negative statements.

> He **will** stay.
>
> **Will** he stay?
>
> He **will** not **stay**.

Forms of the verb *be* (*is, am, are, was, were*) do not require an auxiliary.

> **Is** she home yet?
>
> They **are** not here.

Exercise 4.3: Using Verb Tenses

Write paragraphs using the following verbs. Add adverbs, such as not, only, *and* always, *if you wish.*

CCSS.L.8.1.C:
Form and use verbs in the indicative, imperative, interrogative, conditional, and subjunctive mood.

1. swear(s)	has sworn	will have sworn	will have been swearing
2. ride(s)	rode	has (have) ridden	has (have) been riding
3. freeze(s)	will freeze	will have frozen	has (have) frozen
4. drink(s)	drank	has (have) drunk	will have been drinking
5. break(s)	broke	has (have) broken	had been broken
6. blow(s)	blew	has (have) been blown	will have blown
7. hang(s)	hung	has (have) hung	had been hanging
8. run(s)	ran	has (have) been run	will run
9. hide(s)	hid	has (have) hidden	had been hidden
10. take(s)	took	has (have) taken	will have taken

Exercise 4.4: Identifying Progressive and Emphatic Forms

Underline the verbs and indicate whether they are progressive or emphatic forms.

WRITING PROMPT:
Choose ten of the sentences and rewrite them, changing the progressive to the emphatic and vice versa.

1. We did ride across the outskirts of town between rows of abandoned houses.

2. For the past few years he has been working as a photographer for the *Los Angeles Times*.

3. This bill does provide for a sweeping change in copyright laws.

4. The last of the autumn leaves were falling, and the air smelled of snow.

5. In this case we did feel that the penalty was too severe.

6. It has been months since we were traveling in Mexico.

7. When need arose, they did do their duty courageously.

CCSS.L.8.1.C:
Form and use verbs in the indicative, imperative, interrogative, conditional, and subjunctive mood.

8. Our visitors will be flying home in a few days.

9. They lay in the shade of the elm tree and were reminiscing about life years ago.

10. He did come in and drape his coat over the chair.

11. I did by that time hear a little more from him.

12. The war largely did obliterate fine distinctions.

13. The paper did not give complete details of the accident, but it did show that the driver of the car was negligent.

14. At present he is working in the copy room of the *Daily News*.

15. We are beginning our investigation on Monday and continuing it throughout the week.

16. For months this country knew nothing but war and desolation.

17. You will find many things there, but few that will amuse and stimulate you.

MOOD

CCSS.L.8.1.C:
Form and use verbs in the indicative, imperative, interrogative, conditional, and subjunctive mood.

Mood is that quality of a verb which indicates the manner in which a statement is made. Verbs have three possible moods: Indicative, Imperative, and Subjunctive.

- The *Indicative Mood* is most often used to make a positive statement of fact.

  I **arrived** at noon.

  The fence **was painted** white.

  He **is** a trusted friend.

  The verb in a direct question is also considered to be in the Indicative Mood because the question anticipates a positive statement.

  Will you **be** my partner?

  Has she **balanced** the books?

- The *Imperative Mood* is used to express a command or plea.

  Hand me the rope.

  Be careful with the knife.

  Let me entertain you.

  Let's get out of here.

- The *Subjunctive Mood* is used to express conditional statements, wishes, or to indicate doubt or uncertainty.

  If I **were** rich, I would buy a mansion.

  If music **be** the food of love, play on.

  Had I the courage, I would confront them.

  Oh, that it **were** so.

  I wish I **were** a better teacher.

Forms in the Different Moods

The *Indicative Mood* is used more often than the other moods. The forms that we have studied under the subject of Tenses are in the indicative mood.

CCSS.L.8.1.C:
Form and use verbs in the indicative, imperative, interrogative, conditional, and subjunctive mood.

The ***Imperative Mood*** takes the simplest form of the verb: as, *be* (Be careful); *come* (Come home); *work* (Work hard).

To make an emphatic or negative command, *do* is used with the regular imperative form.

Do call him and explain.

Do not **contact** him.

Note. The subject of a verb in the imperative mood is often not expressed. Because a command is addressed to a person, the subject is always understood to be *You*. Occasionally, though, for emphasis, the subject is stated: for example, "You do that" has more emphasis than "Do that."

The ***Subjunctive Mood*** has the same forms as the indicative mood as in the tables, with the following exceptions.

The Verb "Be" in the Subjunctive Mood

CCSS.L.8.1.C:
Form and use verbs in the indicative, imperative, interrogative, conditional, and subjunctive mood.

PRESENT TENSE

SINGULAR	PLURAL
1. (If) I be.	1. (If) we be.
2. (If) you be.	2. (If) you be.
3. (If) he be.	3. (If) they be.

PAST TENSE

1. (If) I were.	1. (If) we were.
2. (If) you were.	2. (If) you were.
3. (If) he were.	3. (If) they were.

The Verb "Have" in the Subjunctive Mood

CCSS.L.8.1.C:
Form and use verbs in the indicative, imperative, interrogative, conditional, and subjunctive mood.

PRESENT TENSE

1. (If) I have.	1. (If) we have.
2. (If) you have.	2. (If) you have.
3. (If) he have.	3. (If) they have.

All Other Verbs in the Subjunctive Mood

CCSS.L.8.1.C:
Form and use verbs in the indicative, imperative, interrogative, conditional, and subjunctive mood.

PRESENT TENSE

1. (If) I talk.	1. (If) we talk.
2. (If) you talk.	2. (If) you talk.
3. (If) he talk.	3. (If) they talk.

CCSS.L.7.1.A:

Explain the function of phrases and clauses in general and their function in specific sentences.

If is a conjunction, not a part of the verb. It is used in the foregoing tables because clauses in the subjunctive mood are often introduced by *If*.

In the subjunctive mood, the verb *be* has the form *be* throughout the different persons in both numbers of the present tense, and *were* throughout the past tense. Note that *were* is used in both the singular and plural number.

Compare the above forms of the subjunctive mood with those of the indicative mood: I *am*, you *are*, he *is*, we *are*, you *are*, they *are* (present); I *was*, you *were*, he *was*, we *were*, you *were*, they *were* (past).

The verb *have* has only one form in the subjunctive mood that is different from the indicative form: *have* instead of *has* in the third person, singular number, present tense: "If he *have* the money" (subjunctive); "He *has* the money" (indicative).

All other verbs have only one change in the subjunctive mood: the *-s* ending of the third person, singular number, present tense, indicative mood is omitted in the subjunctive: "(If) he *talk*" (subjunctive); "He *talks*" (indicative).

USES OF THE SUBJUNCTIVE MOOD

English formerly made extensive use of the subjunctive mood, and it is still found in poetry and some set expressions. In most prose and conversation, it has been replaced by modal auxiliaries and indicative forms. What follow are the most common uses of the subjunctive mood.

Present Tense

CCSS.L.8.1.C:

Form and use verbs in the indicative, imperative, interrogative, conditional, and subjunctive mood.

The present tense forms of the subjunctive mood are used:

- In expressing a present conditional statement, one that *may or may not be contrary to fact*.

    If it **be** true, then we're in trouble.

    If he **don't** care, then we won't either.

    Rain or **shine,** the event will take place.

Note. In these conditional clauses, most writers would prefer the indicative forms *is* and *doesn't* to the subjunctive forms *be* and *don't*, which sound old-fashioned and strange. In modern English, *the indicative mood has all but replaced the subjunctive* in these types of clauses.

CCSS.L.7.1.A:
Explain the function of phrases and clauses in general and their function in specific sentences.

Note The phrase *rain or shine* is an elliptical construction equivalent to "if it *rain* or if it *shine*."

- In expressing a concession after *though* or *although*.

> Although that **be** the case, they have already made up their minds.
>
> Though they **be** insufficient, we are stuck with them.

Note. The indicative forms (*is, are*) are more often used in these kinds of expressions.

- In certain parliamentary and set expressions.

> I move that the meeting **be** adjourned.
>
> She took care of herself lest she **become** ill.

- After verbs, nouns, or adjectives expressing command, necessity, and the like.

CCSS.L.11–12.1.A:
Apply the understanding that usage is a matter of convention, can change over time, and is sometimes contested.

> The contractor demanded that the building **be** up to code.
>
> The law requires that a prospective teacher **take** a test to qualify for a teaching credential (not **takes**).
>
> The judge's order was that the case **be** dismissed.
>
> It is imperative that she **do** this.

Note. Instead of the subjunctive forms, a verb phrase made with *shall* or *should* may be used instead: "The law requires that a prospective teacher *shall* take a test to qualify for a teaching credential." "It is imperative that she *should do* this."

Past Tense

CCSS.L.8.1.C:
Form and use verbs in the indicative, imperative, interrogative, conditional, and subjunctive mood.

The past tense of the subjunctive mood should be used:

- In clauses expressing a present condition that is *contrary to fact*.

> If he **were** alive, he would agree with us (not **was**).
>
> If I **were** in charge, I would fire everyone (not **was**).
>
> Suppose she **were** in charge—what would she do? (not **was**).
>
> If you **heard** him now, you would think of him as crazy.
>
> If he **knew** the reason, he would tell us.

These conditions are *contrary to fact*. In the first sentence, he is *not* alive; in the second, I am *not* in charge, etc. Compare these with "If he *was* at his desk, he must have been screening his calls when I phoned." This is *not a condition contrary to fact,* for he may or may not have been at his desk. The truth is not known. Therefore, the indicative form *was* is used instead of the subjunctive *were*.

- In wishes.

  I wish that she **were** more sympathetic (not **was**).

  I wish that I **were** not so absent minded (not **was**).

- After *as if* and *as though*.

  She acts as if she **were** very wealthy (not **was**).

  She trembled as though she **were** panicked (not **was**).

CCSS.L.7.1.A:

Explain the function of phrases and clauses in general and their function in specific sentences.

The past tense in the subjunctive mood does not indicate actual past time, despite being labeled the past tense. In English grammar the term *past tense* in the subjunctive mood serves only to designate the grammatical *form* of the verb: for example, *were* is the grammatical past tense of the subjunctive form of the verb *be*.

In conditional statements that are *contrary to fact*, the past subjunctive commonly indicates present time.

  If he **were** rich (now), he would buy us dinner.

  If I **were** in charge (now), I would fire you.

In *wishes* and after the conjunctions *as if* or *as though*, the past subjunctive indicates the same time as that of the main verb.

  I wish (now) that she **were** healthier (now).

  I wished (last year) that she **were** healthier (last year).

  He behaves (now) as if he **were** the boss (now).

  He behaved (yesterday) as if he **were** the boss (yesterday).

In the past tenses of all verbs, the only change in form between the indicative and the subjunctive moods comes in the first and third persons, singular number, of the verb *be*. For this verb the indicative is *was*, and the subjunctive is *were*. Attention to its different shades of meaning is necessary when using the subjunctive *were*.

The remaining past tense forms of the verb *be* and the past tense forms of all the other verbs are identical in both the indicative and subjunctive moods. For this reason the mood in a sentence must be determined from meaning and context. Should the conditional statement refer to present time and be *contrary to fact*, the verb is in the subjunctive mood. Should the conditional statement refer to past time and *may or may not be contrary to fact*, the verb is in the indicative mood.

> If he **understood** the question, he would not be so confused (present tense subjunctive—he does not understand the question).
>
> If he **understood** the question, he did not let on (past tense indicative—maybe he understood the question, maybe not).
>
> If he **were** rich, he would pay full price (he is **not** rich).
>
> If he **was** rich, why did he buy everything on sale? (maybe he was rich, maybe not).
>
> If she **knew** the answer, she would be able to help us.
>
> If she **knew** the answer, she showed no visible signs of it.

Past Perfect Tense

CCSS.L.8.1.C:
Form and use verbs in the indicative, imperative, interrogative, conditional, and subjunctive mood.

A condition *contrary to fact* in past time is indicated by the past perfect tense of the subjunctive mood.

> **If I had paid attention,** I would have understood the movie.
>
> **If I had stayed awake,** I might have enjoyed the movie.
>
> **Had I seen the movie,** I would have been able to talk about it.

Sentences like these, for the most part, present little chance for error because the subjunctive and indicative forms of the past perfect tense are identical in *all* verbs.

Exercise 4.5: Identifying Time in the Subjunctive Mood

Write the time indicated in the following subjunctive-mood sentences.

WRITING PROMPT:
Write twenty sentences, each containing a conditional clause. Tell whether each condition refers to present, past, or future time. Which of them are contrary to fact?.

1. If he is an alcoholic, his health will eventually be impaired.

2. If he were an alcoholic, his family would be fully aware of it.

3. If he was an alcoholic, then nobody knew about it.

4. If he had been an alcoholic, his liver would have eventually given out.

5. If that is true, you can go.

6. If that were true, you would not go.

7. If that was true, then why did you go?

8. If that had been true, you would not have gone.

9. If the air quality was good, we should have seen the mountains from my house.

CCSS.L.8.1.C:
Form and use verbs in the indicative, imperative, interrogative, conditional, and subjunctive mood.

10. If the air quality were good, we would see the mountains from my house.

11. If he is in trouble, he will write to you.

12. If he were in trouble, he would write to you.

13. If he was in trouble If, he should have written to you.

14. If he had been in trouble, he would have written to you.

15. If that is true, you can go.

CCSS.L.7.1.A:
Explain the function of phrases and clauses in general and their function in specific sentences.

16. If that be true, you can go.

17. If that were true, you could go.

18. If that had been true, you could have gone.

19. If the day was clear, we could see the mountains forty miles away.

20. If the day were clear, we could see the mountains forty miles away.

21. If he has been there, he knows the story.

22. If he had been there, he would know the story.

23. If they were not at home, they were at school.

24. If they were not at home, they would be at school.

May be copied for classroom use. Common Core Grammar by Thomas Fasano (Coyote Canyon Press: Claremont, CA); © 2015.

Exercise 4.6: Identifying the Mood of a Verb

Write the mood of each verb.

CCSS.L.8.1.C:

Form and use verbs in the indicative, imperative, interrogative, conditional, and subjunctive mood.

1. When the storm broke, the golfers were a mile from the clubhouse.

2. If he were a year older, he would be eligible to get a drivers license.

3. If he was present, he would know what transpired at the meeting.

4. When you have transcribed your notes, bring them to me.

5. The front office demands that everyone be in a seat by eight o'clock.

6. Has he told you about his adventures in Brazil?

7. I wish that Martha were more interested in listening to good music.

CCSS.L.7.1.A:

Explain the function of phrases and clauses in general and their function in specific sentences.

8. Several members moved that the new procedures be referred to a committee for approval.

9. Do tell us about your experiences in Germany.

10. If you are ready, we can start at once.

11. When the storm broke, the canoes were a mile from shore.

12. If he were a year older, he would be eligible for membership.

13. If he was present, he knows what was said at the meeting.

14. I felt as though I were moving in the midst of a novel.

15. Many modifications of this plan are now on trial.

16. Let us hope that the prophecy will be amply fulfilled.

17. Make that child's food, clothing, and education your personal affair.

18. I wish that Jane did take an interest in travel.

19. The evening meal was plain as the breakfast.

20. If there be anything farcical in such a life, the blame is not mine: let it lie at fate's and nature's door.

Exercise 4.7: Using the Proper Mood of a Verb

Fill in the blanks with the proper form of the verb be—indicative or subjunctive.

CCSS.L.8.1.C:
Form and use verbs in the indicative, imperative, interrogative, conditional, and subjunctive mood.

1. If the road _____ not so bumpy, he would drive faster.

2. The rules require that each ticket _____ individually punched.

3. If it _____ warmer this afternoon, we can go swimming.

4. If it _____ warmer, we could go swimming now.

5. The committee has demanded that the minutes of the meeting _____ emailed to all the members.

6. I wish that she _____ here this evening.

7. If that _____ true, then he is culpable.

CCSS.L.7.1.A:
Explain the function of phrases and clauses in general and their function in specific sentences.

8. It seemed as though the house _____ about to collapse.

9. If the attendees _____ more prompt, the meeting would have begun on time.

10. If he _____ late for class again this morning, he will be marked absent.

11. If the road _____ not so winding, he would drive faster.

12. The rules require that each ticket _____ individually signed.

13. Some members have asked that the minutes of the meeting _____ printed.

14. If that _____ true, he is responsible for the mistake.

15. He acts as if he _____ no longer interested.

16. If _____ you, I would refuse the penalty.

17. If he _____ ready, he should have notified us.

MODAL AUXILIARIES

CCSS.L.9–10.1.B:
Use various types of phrases (noun, verb, adjectival, adverbial, participial, prepositional, absolute) and clauses (independent, dependent; noun, relative, adverbial) to convey specific meanings and add variety and interest to writing or presentations.

Modal auxiliaries help other verbs express such meanings as ability, possibility, probability, permission, necessity, determination, obligation, condition, and futurity. The use of auxiliary verbs to express these different modalities is a feature of Germanic languages.

The Modal Auxiliaries are *can, may, shall, will, could, might, should, would,* and *must.* The following sentences give examples of their different moods (meanings).

> The guilty party **should** be punished (condition).
>
> We **will** finish on time (futurity).
>
> Most likely I **shall** close out the account (probability).
>
> I **will** see you later (futurity).
>
> You **may** borrow my car if you like (permission).
>
> The road **could** be blocked (possibility).
>
> I **can** play the piano (ability).
>
> He **must** get this right (necessity).
>
> They **might** be ready for us (possibility).
>
> We **could** arrive early if you wish (ability).
>
> He **would** eat too much if I didn't stop him (determination).
>
> You **should** do as he says (obligation).
>
> You **ought to** start at once (obligation).

Note. A few words are classified as *Marginal Auxiliaries: need, dare, used to,* and *ought.* Unique among the modals, *used* always takes the *to*-infinitive and occurs only in the past tense. It may take the *do* construction, in which case the spellings *didn't used to* and *didn't use to* both occur.

Verb Phrases Made with Modal Auxiliaries

Verb phrases made with Modal Auxiliaries have the following forms (modals have no future tenses).

Active Voice

CCSS.L.8.1.B:
Form and use verbs in the active and passive voice.

PRESENT TENSE

SINGULAR	PLURAL
1. I may see.	1. We may see.
2. You may see.	2. You may see.
3. He may see.	3. They may see.

PAST TENSE

1. I might see.	1. We might see.
2. You might see.	2. You might see.
3. He might see.	3. They might see.

PRESENT PERFECT TENSE

1. I may have seen, etc.	1. We may have seen, etc.

PAST PERFECT TENSE

1. I might have seen, etc.	1. We might have seen, etc.

Passive Voice

CCSS.L.8.1.B:
Form and use verbs in the active and passive voice.

PRESENT TENSE: I may be seen, etc.

PAST TENSE: I might be seen, etc.

PRESENT PERFECT TENSE: I may have been seen, etc.

PAST PERFECT TENSE: I might have been seen, etc.

For verb-forms made with the other auxiliaries, substitute in the preceding table *can* or *must* for *may* (*can see, must see*); *could, would,* or *should* for *might* (*could see, would have seen,* etc.).

Although *might* and *could* are the past tense forms of *may* and *can,* and *should* and *would* are the past tense forms of *shall* and *will,* they are often used in connection with present and occasionally future time.

The students **might** be ready to handle the lesson.

We **could** go shopping tomorrow.

Note. Although *shall* and *will* are used to form the future tense, they are present tense forms.

Progressive Forms

There are also progressive forms for the different tenses in the active voice: *may be seeing; might be seeing; may have been seeing; might have been seeing.*

VOICE

CCSS.L.8.1.B:
Form and use verbs in the active and passive voice.

Voice is the quality of a verb that indicates whether the subject of the verb is performing or receiving an action.

There are two grammatical voices: Active and Passive.

- A verb in the ***Active Voice*** shows the subject as acting.

  She **baked** the bread.

  The police **are investigating** the incident.

  We **have explained** the situation.

- A verb in the ***Passive Voice*** shows the subject as receiving the action.

  The police officer **was shot** in the line of duty.

  They **were caught** unawares by the tornado.

A transitive verb in the active voice takes a *direct object,* which names the receiver of the action; in the passive voice, the *subject* names the receiver. Therefore, any sentence with a transitive verb in the active voice can be transformed into a sentence having a verb in the passive voice—by using the object of the original active verb as the subject of the transformed sentence.

For example, the sentence, "The girl lost the *money*" (active), would become "The *money* was lost by the girl" (passive). In this type of transformation, the original subject, *girl,* becomes the object of the preposition *by* in the new sentence.

When a sentence in the active voice contains a noun used as an objective complement the noun is generally retained in the new sentence as a predicate noun.

  The American people elected Reagan **president** (active).

  Reagan was elected **president** by the American people (passive).

When an active verb has both a direct and an indirect object, either object may become the subject of the verb in the passive voice.

The stock paid my **aunt** a **dividend** (active).

My **aunt** was paid a **dividend** by the stock (passive).

A **dividend** was paid my **aunt** by the stock (passive).

Sometimes the object of a preposition that follows an intransitive verb is made the subject of the verb in the passive voice; the remaining preposition is used as an adverb.

The audience laughed at the **clown** (active).

The **clown** was laughed at by the audience (passive).

Forms of the Passive Voice

CCSS.L.8.1.B:
Form and use verbs in the active and passive voice.

The *Passive Voice* of any verb is made by using a combination of the past participle of the verb with the proper form of the verb *be*. This is true in all the various tenses and moods. Some form of the verb *be* is always used as an auxiliary verb in forming the passive voice.

The following table shows the passive voice of the verb *see* in the different tenses.

INDICATIVE MOOD FORMS

CCSS.L.8.1.B:
Form and use verbs in the active and passive voice.

PRESENT TENSE

SINGULAR	PLURAL
1. I am seen.	1. We are seen.
2. You are seen.	2. You are seen.
3. He is seen.	3. They are seen.

PAST TENSE

1. I was seen.	1. We were seen.
2. You were seen.	2. You were seen.
3. He was seen.	3. They were seen.

CCSS.L.8.1.C:
Form and use verbs in the indicative, imperative, interrogative, conditional, and subjunctive mood.

FUTURE TENSE

1. I shall be seen.	1. We shall be seen.
2. You will be seen.	2. You will be seen.
3. He will be seen.	3. They will be seen.

PRESENT PERFECT TENSE

1. I have been seen.	1. We have been seen.
2. You have been seen.	2. You have been seen.
3. He has been seen.	3. They have been seen.

PAST PERFECT TENSE

1. I had been seen.
2. You had been seen.
3. He had been seen.

1. We had been seen.
2. You had been seen.
3. They had been seen.

FUTURE PERFECT TENSE

1. I shall have been seen.
2. You will have been seen.
3. He will have been seen.

1. We shall have been seen.
2. You will have been seen.
3. They will have been seen.

SUBJUNCTIVE MOOD FORMS

CCSS.L.8.1.B:
Form and use verbs in the active and passive voice.

PRESENT TENSE

SINGULAR

1. (If) I be seen.
2. (If) you be seen.
3. (If) he be seen.

PLURAL

1. (If) we be seen.
2. (If) you be seen.
3. (If) they be seen.

CCSS.L.8.1.C:
Form and use verbs in the indicative, imperative, interrogative, conditional, and subjunctive mood.

PAST TENSE

1. (If) I were seen.
2. (If) you were seen.
3. (If) he were seen.

1. (If) we were seen.
2. (If) you were seen.
3. (If) they were seen.

Note. The other tenses in the subjunctive mood have the same forms as those in the indicative mood.

Exercise 4.8: Identifying the Active and Passive Voice

Write the voice of each verb.

WRITING PROMPT:
Write sentences in which the verb *teach* is used in the present progressive, past progressive, and future progressive tenses of the active voice.

1. The tents were grouped around an old oak tree.

2. We live in a house that was built by my great-grandfather.

3. The boats were crowded with refugees who were fleeing political oppression.

4. Does any reasonable person believe that legislation will curb drug abuse?

5. Throughout his life Nabokov collected butterflies.

6. The transcripts were officially sealed by the university's office of the registrar.

7. The Lusitania was sunk by a German U-boat.

CCSS.L.8.1.B:
Form and use verbs in the active and passive voice.

8. He is always sucking up to the boss.

9. A hurried survey revealed the wretched conditions under which the employees were working.

10. The low white tents of the hospital were grouped around an old schoolhouse.

11. This is the eternal question which confronts the artist and the thinker.

12. But the evil has come with the good, and much fine gold has been corroded.

13. Titles distinguish the mediocre, embarrass the superior, and are disgraced by the inferior.

14. Such a policy could not very well be advertised from the house-tops.

15. Here and there a soldier fell in the ranks, and the gap was filled in silence.

Exercise 4.9: Writing with the Active and Passive Voice

Rewrite the sentences, changing the verbs in the active voice to the passive—and the verbs in the passive voice to the active.

WRITING PROMPT:
Use each of the following verbs in both the active and the passive of the past, the future, and the perfect—*send, bring, teach, drink, get, set, lay, leave, find, forget.*

1. These phenomena have been investigated by scientists for many years.

2. The walls of the room were covered with priceless engravings from the Renaissance.

3. The new teaching standards were approved by the education secretary.

4. The natives brought the travelers gifts of jade and ivory.

5. *A Horse's Tale* was written by Mark Twain in his later years.

6. In the distance one could see the summit of Mt. Rainier.

7. Most of their spare time was spent gardening.

8. A new president will soon be elected by the voters.

CCSS.L.8.1.B:
Form and use verbs in the active and passive voice.

9. Scientists have been investigating these phenomena for many years.

10. A trade agreement with Canada has been approved by the Senate.

11. This book was written by Dickens in his later years.

12. I was brought up by my uncle.

13. That winter will never be forgotten by any of us.

14. The schooner was run down by the steamship.

15. The old man has opened a little antiques shop.

16. The hurricane has made great havoc along the Atlantic coast.

17. The children have been called home by their mother.

18. A policeman helped her over the crossing.

19. I was amused by your letter.

20. The tower was struck by lightning yesterday.

INFINITIVES

CCSS.L.8.1.A:

Explain the function of verbals (gerunds, participles, infinitives) in general and their function in particular sentences.

An infinitive consists of the base form of a verb preceded by the infinitive marker *to* and functions as a noun, an adjective, or an adverb: as, *to run, to drink, to sing, to dance, to help.*

The infinitive with its "to" marker should not be confused with a phrase consisting of the preposition *to* followed by a noun used as its object: compare *to run, to drink* (infinitives) with *to the house, to America* (prepositional phrases).

Uses of the Infinitive

CCSS.L.8.1.A:

Explain the function of verbals (gerunds, participles, infinitives) in general and their function in particular sentences.

An infinitive cannot *stand alone* as a verb: that is, it cannot be used with a subject to state a complete thought. For example, the phrases, "a plan *to balance* the budget" and "they *to pay* their taxes," are not complete sentences. A complete sentence must have a finite verb (a verb that can stand alone) in addition to the infinitive: "I *have* a plan to balance the budget." "They *are* to pay their taxes."

Infinitives are classified as **Nonfinite** verbs to distinguish them from **Finite** verbs, which can stand alone in a clause. The third person singular (*looks, sees*) is always **finite**, as are the past tense forms (*looked, saw*), whereas the present participle (*looking, seeing*), past participle (*looked, seen*), and infinitive (*to look, to see*) are **nonfinite**. The base form (*look, see*) can be either.

The following are nonfinite phrases:

> **To expect a miracle** is unrealistic.
>
> All he ever does is **complain**.
>
> **Having listened to you,** I think your attitude stinks.
>
> **Dazed and confused,** they realized they'd partied too much.

An infinitive may be used as a noun, an adjective, or an adverb modifying an adjective, adverb, or verb.

- As a Noun.

  > **To sing** is fun (subject of the verb).
  >
  > I want **to eat** (object of the verb—answers the question **what?**).
  >
  > **To sleep** is **to dream** (subject of the verb and predicate noun).

- As an Adjective.

Here is food **to eat** (modifies **food**).

She has a job **to complete** (modifies **job**).

- As an Adverb modifying an adjective, verb, or another adverb.

I am happy **to do it** (modifies the adjective **happy**).

The pizza is ready **to eat** (modifies the adjective **ready**).

We came **to talk** to you (modifies the verb **came**).

Most programs aren't funded enough **to make much difference** (modifies the adverb **enough**).

Note. Infinities answer journalistic questions. For example, an infinitive used as the object of a verb answers the question what? Infinitives used as adverbs answer the questions *when, where, how, how much, why,* etc.

Because infinitives are verb-forms, they can be modified by adverbs. They can also take direct and indirect objects, despite the fact that infinitives are often used as nouns, adjectives, or adverbs.

You want to arrive **early** (adverb modifying **to arrive**).

To arrive **at the concert early** was their intention (a prepositional phrase and an adverb).

He wanted to ask the **manager** (direct object of **to ask**).

I promised to give the **charity** a **donation** (indirect and direct objects).

The various *forms of the infinitive* are shown in the following table.

ACTIVE VOICE

	PRESENT TENSE	PERFECT TENSE
Simple	to go	to have gone
Progressive	to be going	to have been going
	PASSIVE VOICE	
Simple	to be gone	to have been gone

Tense and Voice

CCSS.L.8.1.A:

Explain the function of verbals (gerunds, participles, infinitives) in general and their function in particular sentences.

The infinitive has two tenses: the ***Present*** and the ***Perfect***.

- In the ***Active Voice***, the simple form of the present infinitive is formed by prefixing the "to" marker to the base form of the verb (*to drink*); the progressive form, by prefixing *to be* to the present participle (*to be drinking*).

CCSS.L.8.1.B:
Form and use verbs in the active and passive voice.

The simple form of the perfect infinitive is formed by prefixing *to have* to the past participle (*to have drunk*); the progressive form, by prefixing *to have been* to the present participle (*to have been drinking*).

- In the **Passive Voice**, the present infinitive is formed by prefixing *to be* to the past participle (*to be drunk*); the perfect infinitive, by prefixing *to have been* to the past participle (*to have been drunk*). Infinitives have no passive progressive forms.

Infinitives with the "to" Marker Omitted

CCSS.L.8.1.A:
Explain the function of verbals (gerunds, participles, infinitives) in general and their function in particular sentences.

The infinitive normally has the "to" marker; after certain verbs it is often omitted.

> You dare not **go** there (to go).
>
> I dare not **say** (to say).
>
> You need not **leave** so early (to leave).
>
> They saw him **fall** (to fall).
>
> I heard him **yell** (to yell).
>
> We felt the house **shake** (to shake).
>
> We let him **explain** (to explain).

Notice that in the last sentence, if *allowed* is substituted for *let*, the "to" marker is not omitted: "We allowed him *to explain.*" Also, in the third sentence, if the auxiliary *do* is used before *need*, the *to* is not omitted: "You do not need *to leave* so early."

Split Infinitives

CCSS.L.11–12.1.A:
Apply the understanding that usage is a matter of convention, can change over time, and is sometimes contested.

Split Infinitives are quite natural in the English language, although their usage is sometimes contested. This old usage rule is downright harmful to good writing. Many students have been brainwashed into thinking that splitting an infinitive is ungrammatical, so they end up with oddities such as *permanently to debate* or *want always to be first*, instead of *to permanently debate* or *want to always be first*.

There is no grammatical reason whatsoever *not* to split an infinitive. Great writers have done so for centuries. In fact, splitting an infinitive is quite natural when using certain adverbs of time and expressions such as *more than*: for example, *Prices are expected **to** more than **double**, The board voted **to** immediately **approve** the measure.*

Exercise 4.10: Identifying Infinitives

Underline the infinitives.

WRITING PROMPT:

Write sentences containing an infinitive used as subject, as predicate nominative, as appositive, as the object of a preposition, as an adjective; an infinitive used with *shall*, with *will*, with *must*.

1. To sign that contract would be a mistake.

2. The committee refused to make a recommendation.

3. To have known him would have been honor enough.

4. Their chief concern was to find the missing girl.

5. You need not care about her.

CCSS.L.8.1.A:

Explain the function of verbals (gerunds, participles, infinitives) in general and their function in particular sentences.

6. These pies are not good to eat.

7. The day was too hot to be pleasant.

8. To grant this claim would be a mistake.

9. The committee refused to comment on the court's decision.

10. He turned to walk home, meditating.

11. His dominant trait was to take all things into earnest consideration.

12. Many strangers came in the summertime to view the battlefield.

13. Not for some minutes did we have a chance to scrutinize our surroundings.

14. The first problem to be solved is a difficult one.

15. With a great deal of trouble we managed to get them down to the boat with us.

16. He has no desire to be known as a philanthropist.

Exercise 4.11: Infinitives

Fill in the blanks with the form of the infinitive indicated.

WRITING PROMPT:

Write sentences containing infinitive phrases used after verbs of *wishing, commanding, believing, declaring, perceiving.*

1. _____ her was a real honor. (Use (a) present active infinitive of *love;* (b) perfect active infinitive of *love.*)

2. He is pleased _____ for the job. (Use (a) present passive infinitive of *consider;* (b) perfect passive infinitive of *consider.*)

3. They want _____ early. (Use (a) present active infinitive of *arrive;* (b) present passive infinitive of *call.*)

4. The house is said _____. (Use (a) present active progressive infinitive of *burn;* (b) perfect passive infinitive of *destroy.*)

5. Her ambition is _____ Rose Bowl Queen. (Use (a) present active infinitive of *be;* (b) present passive infinitive of *choose.*)

CCSS.L.8.1.A:

Explain the function of verbals (gerunds, participles, infinitives) in general and their function in particular sentences.

6. I am sorry _____ so much confusion. (Use the perfect active progressive infinitive of *cause.*)

Use the infinitives as indicated (a separate sentence for each).

7. *To work* for the city—as (a) direct object of a verb; (b) predicate noun; (c) adjective.

8. *To travel* in England—as (a) subject of a verb; (b) adverb; (c) adjective.

9. *To send* the email—as (a) subject of a verb; (b) predicate noun; (c) direct object of a verb; (d) adjective; (e) adverb modifying a verb; (f) adverb modifying an adjective.

May be copied for classroom use. Common Core Grammar by Thomas Fasano (Coyote Canyon Press: Claremont, CA); © 2015.

PARTICIPLES

A **Participle** is a verbal adjective: in other words, it is a verb-form used as an adjective to modify a noun or pronoun.

Forms of the Participle

CCSS.L.8.1.A:
Explain the function of verbals (gerunds, participles, infinitives) in general and their function in particular sentences.

The Participle has three principal forms: the **Present Participle,** the **Past Participle,** and the **Perfect Participle**.

PRESENT PARTICIPLE	PAST PARTICIPLE	PERFECT PARTICIPLE
walking	walked	having walked
dancing	danced	having danced
drinking	drunk	having drunk
speaking	spoken	having spoken
shopping	shopped	having shopped
biting	bitten	having bitten

CCSS.L.8.1.B:
Form and use verbs in the active and passive voice.

In the **Passive Voice** the Participle also has the following forms:

Present Passive Participle: being hidden, being written.

Perfect Passive Participle: having been hidden, having been written.

In the **Active Voice** the Participle also has the following form:

PERFECT ACTIVE PROGRESSIVE PARTICIPLE: having been hiding.

- The **Present Participle** has an -ing suffix attached to the simple form of the verb: as, *walking, dancing, dreaming*. When the simple form of the verb ends in -e, the final letter is regularly dropped before adding -ing: as, *make, making; dance, dancing*. Verbs ending in -ee, -ye, and oe do not drop the final -e: as, *free, freeing; dye, dyeing; hoe, hoeing*.

- The **Past Participle** is formed by adding -ed, -d, -t, -en, or -n to the simple form of the verb: as, *talked, faced, crept, beaten, driven;* or by changing the vowel, with or without the addition of a suffix: as, *clung*—for the verb *cling; bound*—for the verb *bind; woken*—for the verb *wake*.

- The **Perfect Participle** consists of more than one word and is made by using the word *having* with the past participle: as, *having run, having talked, having spoken*.

Uses of the Participle

CCSS.L.8.1.A:

Explain the function of verbals (gerunds, participles, infinitives) in general and their function in particular sentences.

A participle modifies a noun or pronoun and is therefore an adjective.

The **swaying** trees signaled a storm.

A glass **filled** with wine can be inviting.

The dog **hit** by the car will survive.

In the first sentence, *swaying* describes trees; in the second and third, *filled* and *hit* tell which glass and which dog are referred to.

A Participle has four specific uses:

- As a Predicate Adjective.

    The movie is **entertaining**.

    The shoes were **ripped** and **soiled**.

- As an Objective Complement.

    I found the book **interesting**.

    She made our trip **rewarding**.

- In a Nominative Absolute construction.

    The car **having stalled,** we were stuck in the road.

    The meal **being finished,** we washed the dishes.

    He rose suddenly, his fists **clenched**.

    The boxer circled the ring, his eyes **fixed** on his opponent.

    The game was over, time **having run out**.

- As part of a Verb.

    I **am reading**.

    She **is working**.

A participle is a form of a verb but cannot be used *by itself* as a verb. When used with auxiliary verbs, the combination makes a whole verb: *is working, will be arriving, has been reading* (auxiliary verb(s) used with a present participle); *have danced, had seen, will have come, was hit, will be heard* (auxiliary verb(s) used with a past participle).

In verb phrases with *be* as an auxiliary, the participle has the power of a predicate adjective following a linking verb. For example, in the sentence, "The ship is *sinking!*" The participle *sinking* describes the subject *ship* (the sinking ship) in the way that in the sentence, "The ship is *huge*," the adjective *huge* describes the subject *ship* (the huge ship).

It is important to be able to distinguish between a participle used as a predicate adjective and a participle used as part of a verb.

> The book is **boring** (predicate adjective).
>
> The book **is boring** me to tears (part of a verb).

Since participles are forms of verbs, they can be modified by adverbs and may have objects.

> Thinking **quickly,** he evaded his pursuers.
>
> The woman sitting **there** is my wife.
>
> The man reciting the **lines** is an actor (direct object of **reciting**).
>
> Giving the **panhandler** a **dollar,** I drove away (indirect object and direct object).

GERUNDS

CCSS.L.8.1.A:

Explain the function of verbals (gerunds, participles, infinitives) in general and their function in particular sentences.

Students must not make the mistake of thinking that every "verb + ing" is a participle. A "verb + ing" is a participle only when used as an adjective; it is a *Gerund* when used as a noun: that is, as the subject of a verb, object of a verb, etc.

Compare the following sentences:

> The boy **playing** in the sandbox tripped and fell (participle—modifies **boy**).
>
> **Playing** in the sandbox is fun (gerund—subject of the verb).
>
> The boy enjoys **playing** in the sandbox (gerund—object of the verb).
>
> The best fun is **playing** in the sandbox (gerund—predicate noun).
>
> He lived for **playing** in the sandbox (object of the preposition **for**).

A gerund may have a direct object or both a direct and an indirect object.

> Paying your **employees** a decent **wage** is the right thing to do.

Possessive with Gerunds

CCSS.L.8.1.A:

Explain the function of verbals (gerunds, participles, infinitives) in general and their function in particular sentences.

Knowing whether to use an apostrophe in a sentence like *Sam's losing the tickets ruined our evening* or *Sam losing the tickets ruined our evening* is not always easy.

A noun or pronoun followed by a gerund takes the possessive form in some contexts. *The Chicago Manual of Style* requires it for proper names, proper nouns, and personal pronouns, especially when the gerund rather than the noun preceding it is the subject of the clause.

> Our **grandmother's** cooking for us on Thanksgiving was always a joy.

> We knew that my **brother's** dropping out of college was a big mistake.

When the noun or pronoun follows a preposition, the possessive case form is optional, according to *The Chicago Manual of Style*.

> She was concerned about her **husband** (or **husband's**) working late.

> I won't stand for **him** (or **his**) being picked on.

> The issue of **volunteers** (or **volunteers'**) pitching in this holiday season is crucial.

CCSS.L.11–12.1.B:

Resolve issues of complex or contested usage, consulting references (e.g., *Merriam–Webster's Dictionary of English Usage*, *Garner's Modern American Usage*) as needed.

Bryan Garner discusses the use of a ***fused participle*** in his *Garner's Modern American Usage*. A fused participle is a gerund "preceded by a noun or pronoun not in the possessive case." He gives the examples of ***Me*** *going home made her sad* as opposed to ***My*** *going home made her sad*; and *Shareholders worried about the **company** reorganizing* as opposed to *Shareholders worried about the **company's** reorganizing*.

Garner ends his discussion by quoting the grammarian Paul Roberts, who said it's a "niggling point but one on which many people niggle."

Exercise 4.12: Using Participles and Gerunds

WRITING PROMPT:

Write sentences containing a participle used as an adjective; a participle used as a predicate adjective; a participle modified adverbially; a participle taking an object.

Underline the participles and gerunds and label them.

1. Russia is a large country abounding in natural resources.

2. Walking in crowded Dublin was a new and absorbing experience for him.

3. This is a full and complete list of all the registered voters living in the precinct.

WRITING PROMPT:

Write sentences in which (1) a gerund and (2) a present participle are formed from—*run, hunt, leap, swim, strike, find, speak, sing, shout, play, skate, blow, spend, listen, eat, move, translate, recite, murmur, whisper, read, talk, complain, paint, build, give, breathe, teach, flow, shine.*

4. Making an online purchase in the morning should result in its arriving at your doorstep the next day.

5. Research for his dissertation meant spending long hours in the library sitting at a computer.

6. He fantasized about being stranded on a desert island and living the rest of his life there.

7. We heard a woman screaming for help.

8. He lay in the shade, his head resting on a mossy log.

9. The coming of darkness prevented us from finishing our round of golf.

10. Waking in a cheap hotel and scarfing up a hasty breakfast did not seem appealing to him.

11. It is a small country abounding in mineral resources.

CCSS.L.8.1.A:

Explain the function of verbals (gerunds, participles, infinitives) in general and their function in particular sentences.

12. The forest behind the house needed cutting back.

13. Frequently he must content himself with devouring his evening meal uncooked.

14. Every voter living in the precinct should register on Tuesday.

15. This does not mean refraining from doing what we want to do.

16. A letter mailed in the morning will be received the following day.

17. The long, low clouds seemed rather threatening.

18. The Earl was surrounded by his shouting and gesticulating followers.

STRONG AND WEAK VERBS

CCSS.L.8.1.C:
Form and use verbs in the indicative, imperative, interrogative, conditional, and subjunctive mood.

Verbs can be divided into two classes—Strong Verbs and Weak Verbs, depending on their past tense and past participle forms.

A **Strong Verb** forms its past tense by changing the vowel sound in its base (an *ablaut* or *vowel gradation*) with or without the addition of an *-en*, *-n*, or *-t* suffix. Some strong verbs make no changes whatsoever (no verb gradation and no suffix).

PRESENT TENSE	PAST TENSE	PAST PARTICIPLE
begin	began	begun
eat	ate	eaten
sing	sang	sung
deal	dealt	dealt
hit	hit	hit

WRITING PROMPT:
Write sentences containing the past participles of six weak verbs; of six strong verbs.

A **Weak Verb** forms its past tense and past participle by adding *-ed* or *-d* to the base form. This weak formation is the norm for English regular verbs. Newly introduced verbs enter the language as regular verbs: for example, *telephoned, televised, faxed, emailed, texted, tweeted*.

PRESENT TENSE	PAST TENSE	PAST PARTICIPLE
talk	talked	talked
fan	fanned	fanned
save	saved	saved
bake	baked	baked

DEFECTIVE VERBS

CCSS.L.8.1.C:
Form and use verbs in the indicative, imperative, interrogative, conditional, and subjunctive mood.

A **Defective Verb** lacks one or more forms. These are *may, can, will, shall, must,* and *ought. May, can, will,* and *shall* have a past tense form—*might, could, would,* and *should*—in addition to the present tense, but have no future or perfect tenses, and no infinitive or participle forms. *Must* and *ought* have only one form. These verbs are used primarily as auxiliary verbs.

Chapter

Adverbs

5

ENGLISH LANGUAGE ARTS STANDARDS

☞ **CCSS.ELA-LITERACY.L.11–12.1.A:** *Apply the understanding that usage is a matter of convention, can change over time, and is sometimes contested.*

☞ **CCSS.ELA-LITERACY.L.11–12.1.B:** *Resolve issues of complex or contested usage, consulting references* (e.g., Merriam–Webster's Dictionary of English Usage, Garner's Modern American Usage) *as needed.*

☞ **CCSS.ELA-LITERACY.L.9–10.1.B:** *Use various types of phrases (noun, verb, adjectival, adverbial, participial, prepositional, absolute) and clauses (independent, dependent; noun, relative, adverbial) to convey specific meanings and add variety and interest to writing or presentations.*

☞ **CCSS.ELA-LITERACY.L.11–12.2.B:** *Spell correctly.*

☞ **CCSS.ELA-LITERACY.L.9–12.2:** *Demonstrate command of the conventions of standard English capitalization, punctuation, and spelling when writing.*

ADVERBS

An *Adverb* is a word that modifies a verb, adjective, or another adverb.

He talks **slowly** (modifies the verb **talks**).

She was **almost** hysterical (modifies the adjective **hysterical**).

She plays the piano **very** fluidly (**very** modifies the adverb **fluidly**, which in turn modifies the verb **plays**).

CLASSES OF ADVERBS

CCSS.L.9–10.1.B:
Use various types of phrases (noun, verb, adjectival, adverbial, participial, prepositional, absolute) and clauses (independent, dependent; noun, relative, adverbial) to convey specific meanings and add variety and interest to writing or presentations.

The main classes of adverbs are:

- *Adverbs of Manner:* "She sings *beautifully.*" "He works *hard.*"

  Adverbs of manner answer the question *how?* Question, She sings *how?* Answer, *beautifully.*

- *Adverbs of Place:* "They went *there.*" "He drove *home.*" "I traveled *abroad.*"

  Adverbs of place answer the question *where?* Question, He traveled *where?* Answer, *abroad.*

- *Adverbs of Time:* "Their daughter will arrive *soon.*" "He saw the movie *yesterday.*" "I worked on this book *daily.*"

  Adverbs of time answer the question *when?* Question, He saw the movie *when?* Answer, *yesterday.*

- *Adverbs of Degree:* "He was *very* bright." "She spoke *most* persuasively." "They were *completely* unaware."

  Adverbs of degree answer the questions *how much?* or *how little?* but with a meaning different from that of adverbs of manner. Adverbs of degree always express the idea of amount, extent, or degree. The negative *not* is considered an adverb of degree expressing the greatest possible degree of restriction.

Note. These four classes cover most uses of single-word adverbs; other adverbial relations are expressed by phrases and clauses.

FORMS OF ADVERBS

CCSS.L.9–12.2:
Demonstrate command of the conventions of standard English capitalization, punctuation, and spelling when writing.

Adverbs are regularly formed by adding *-ly* to an adjective; as, *bad, quick,* and *certain.* Thus, we would say, "He is a *bad* boy" (adjective); but "He behaves *badly*" (adverb). Not all adverbs, however, end in *-ly.* For example, *very, fast, almost, early, late, hard, here, there, little, much,* and *often* are all adverbs. When an adverb of this kind is identical to its corresponding adjective form, the two are distin-

CCSS.L.11–12.1.A:
Apply the understanding that usage is a matter of convention, can change over time, and is sometimes contested.

guished only by their use in the sentence: "The train is *late*" (adjective) and "The train is running *late*" (adverb). They are known as "flat adverbs."

One should note that not all words ending in *-ly* are adverbs; such words may indeed be adjectives: as, a *lovely* gesture, a *godly* man, a *lively* speaker, a *comely* woman.

Nouns are often used as adverbs, especially as adverbs of *time* and *place*.

We go back to work next **Monday**.

She went **home**.

COMPARISON OF ADVERBS

CCSS.L.9–12.2:
Demonstrate command of the conventions of standard English capitalization, punctuation, and spelling when writing.

Like adjectives, adverbs have three degrees of comparison: the ***Positive, Comparative,*** and ***Superlative***. Unlike adjectives, only a few adverbs form their comparative and superlative degrees by adding *-er* and *-est* to the positive form: as, *often, oftener, oftenest; late, later, latest; soon, sooner, soonest*.

Most adverbs form their comparative and superlative degrees by using *more* and *most* or *less* and *least*: as, *beautifully, more beautifully, most beautifully; quickly, more quickly, most quickly; strenuously, less strenuously, least strenuously; securely, less securely, least securely*.

Some adverbs use either method of comparison: as, *often; oftener* or *more often; oftenest* or *most often*.

The following adverbs have an irregular comparison.

POSITIVE	COMPARATIVE	SUPERLATIVE
far	farther, further	farthest, furthest
near	nearer	nearest, next
well	better	best
little	less	least
much	more	most
ill, badly	worse	worst
late	later	latest, last
nigh	nigher	nighest, next

Some adverbs cannot be compared: as, *now, then, here, there, today, yesterday, yonder, twice*.

ADJECTIVES AND ADVERBS

CCSS.L.11–12.1.A:

Apply the understanding that usage is a matter of convention, can change over time, and is sometimes contested.

Flat adverbs are identical to their adjective counterparts. You can *drive fast* (adverb) or *drive a fast car* (adjective); *hit your head hard* (adverb) or *have a hard head* (adjective).

Some language mavens decry that the distinction between adjectives and adverbs is vanishing from the language. But the historical trend is the other way around. Standard English formerly had many more flat adverbs, such as *violent hot* (Daniel Defoe), *monstrous fine* (Jonathan Swift), and *exceeding good memory* (Benjamin Franklin).

CCSS.L.11–12.1.B:

Resolve issues of complex or contested usage, consulting references (e.g., *Merriam–Webster's Dictionary of English Usage, Garner's Modern American Usage*) as needed.

The following uses of flat adverbs make "perfect" good sense: *drive safe, go slow, you sure fooled me, they spelled my name wrong, the sun is shining bright.*

Here is a list of flat adverbs:

alike	all right	fine	first	just
kindly	off-hand	only	solo	still
alone	clean	deep	direct	even
extra	far	fast	free	freelance
full	full-time	further	hard	high
jolly	last	late	little	long
loud	low	next	non-stop	outright
overall	part-time	past	pretty	quick
right	slow	straight	tight	well
wide	wrong			

Exercise 5.1: Writing with Adverbs

Use the indicated adverbs to write sentences. Consult a dictionary if necessary.

WRITING PROMPT:
Write ten sentences using flat adverbs from the list on the previous page.

1. (monstrously, enormously)

2. (hugely, immensely)

WRITING PROMPT:
Think of something you know how to make or do well. Write directions on what to do, using precise adverbs to clarify your directions.

3. (colossally, widely)

4. (microscopically, minutely)

5. (infinitesimally, diminutively)

CCSS.L.9–10.1.B:
Use various types of phrases (noun, verb, adjective, adverbial, participial, prepositional, absolute) and clauses (independent, dependent; noun, relative, adverbial) to convey specific meanings and add variety and interest to writing or presentations.

6. (heatedly, torridly)

7. (feverishly, hotly)

8. (frigidly, icily)

9. (frostily, chillingly)

CCSS.L.9–12.1:
Demonstrate command of the conventions of standard English grammar and usage when writing or speaking.

10. (inconsequentially, oddly)

11. (subtly, elusively)

12. (surreptitiously, obscurely)

Exercise 5.2: Using the Correct Comparison of Adverbs

Underline the adverbs. Name the degree—positive, comparative, or superlative.

WRITING PROMPT:
Choose ten of the adverbs in this exercise and write three sentences for each—in the positive, comparative, and superlative.

1. Members of the audience were now listening more attentively.

2. He laughs best who laughs last.

3. They realized each spring that they planted way too many radishes.

4. I do not want them to be here tomorrow.

5. I never saw him so utterly confused as he was today.

6. They searched far and wide for a more suitable house to buy.

7. The enemy struck sooner than the generals expected.

CCSS.L.9–12.1:
Demonstrate command of the conventions of standard English grammar and usage when writing or speaking.

8. Polite patrons never speak loudly in the public library.

9. It was already late in the day, and the sun had almost disappeared.

10. Go now, and come back later.

11. The audience were now listening more intently.

12. The wind slowly died away.

CCSS.L.9–12.2:
Demonstrate command of the conventions of standard English capitalization, punctuation, and spelling when writing.

13. I shortly heard the raindrops falling on deck thick and fast.

14. Not many persons were immediately aware of the severity of the storm.

15. Then he sat down in the sun at one of the windows and silently smoked.

16. His rage ebbed away now altogether.

17. One of the islands formerly called the Two Sisters is gone entirely.

18. Spring usually comes somewhat later here in this northern country.

CCSS.L.11–12.2.B:
Spell correctly.

19. The young man felt suddenly quite homesick.

20. On these occasions we moved from our chairs, not gently but discourteously.

21. Living conditions were undoubtedly more comfortable in western Spain.

Chapter 6

Prepositions

ENGLISH LANGUAGE ARTS STANDARDS

NOTE:
Some of the skills in this chapter were introduced at lower grade levels; yet, due to the recursiveness of the language standards, they require further attention at the high school level.

☞ **CCSS.ELA-LITERACY.L.9–12.1:** *Demonstrate command of the conventions of standard English grammar and usage when writing or speaking.*

☞ **CCSS.ELA-LITERACY.L.11–12.1.A:** *Apply the understanding that usage is a matter of convention, can change over time, and is sometimes contested.*

☞ **CCSS.ELA-LITERACY.L.9–10.1.B:** *Use various types of phrases (noun, verb, adjectival, adverbial, participial, prepositional, absolute) and clauses (independent, dependent; noun, relative, adverbial) to convey specific meanings and add variety and interest to writing or presentations.*

☞ **CCSS.ELA-LITERACY.L.8.1.A:** *Explain the function of verbals (gerunds, participles, infinitives) in general and their function in particular sentences.*

☞ **CCSS.ELA-LITERACY.L.7.1.A:** *Explain the function of phrases and clauses in general and their function in specific sentences.*

PREPOSITIONS

CCSS.L.9–12.1:
Demonstrate command of the conventions of standard English grammar and usage when writing or speaking.

A ***Preposition*** is a word that appears before a noun, pronoun, or nominal, called the ***Object of the Preposition,*** to show a relationship between the object and some other word in the sentence. Thus, in the sentence, "The dog jumped *on* the couch," the preposition *on* shows the relation of the noun *couch* to the verb *jumped*—the dog jumped *on*, not *over*, the couch.

CCSS.L.9–10.1.B:

Use various types of phrases (noun, verb, adjectival, adverbial, participial, prepositional, absolute) and clauses (independent, dependent; noun, relative, adverbial) to convey specific meanings and add variety and interest to writing or presentations.

Prepositions express a broad range of meanings: *about, above, before, behind, down, for, from, in, of, out, over, through, to, with.*

The combination of a preposition, its object, and any modifiers of the object is called a ***Prepositional Phrase***. The following are some of the most common relationships that these words signal:

LOCATION:	The book is **on the desk**.
DIRECTION:	We flew **to Europe**.
TIME:	The job will be done **by Friday**.
ACCOMPANIMENT:	Mary went **with Bob**.
SOURCE:	The email is **from our boss**.
INSTRUMENTAL:	He was treated **with medication**.
PURPOSE:	I have a big dog **for protection**.
ATTACHMENT:	The edges **of the pages** are yellowed.

PARTICIPLES USED AS PREPOSITIONS:

concerning, during, following, considering, barring, excluding, failing, given, granted, including, owing regarding.

What follows is a list of common prepositions. Notice that some prepositions can be more than one word and are thus ***compound-prepositions***.

aboard	about	above	across	after
against	ahead	all	along	alongside
amidst	among	around	astride	at
away	because of	before	behind	below
beneath	beside	between	beyond	but
by	close	despite	down	except
for	from	front	in	in front of
in spite of	inside	instead of	into	like
near	next	of	off	on
onto	opposite	out	outside	over
past	round	since	through	throughou
to	top	toward	towards	under
underneath	until	up	up to	upon
with	with regard to	with respect to	within	without

OBJECT OF A PREPOSITION

Most often a preposition is followed by a noun or pronoun called an Object of a ***Preposition***. A preposition with its object is called a *prepositional phrase*

Yesterday I lay around the **house**.

I received an email from my **brother**.

CCSS.L.9–10.1.B:
Use various types of phrases (noun, verb, adjectival, adverbial, participial, prepositional, absolute) and clauses (independent, dependent; noun, relative, adverbial) to convey specific meanings and add variety and interest to writing or presentations.

In some ***Idiomatic Expressions***, an adverb or an adjective is used as the object, thereby functioning as a noun-equivalent.

- Adverb.

  I wasn't aware of it until **now**.

  I'd never heard it before **then**.

  Put it over **there**.

  I can see the whole thing from **here**.

- Adjective.

  Our work was in **vain**.

  Our Lord on **high!**

Sometimes the object is placed before the preposition.

  We searched the world **over** (**over** the world).

  He read the report **through** (**through** the report).

Words Used as Prepositions and as Adverbs

CCSS.L.9–10.1.B:
Use various types of phrases (noun, verb, adjectival, adverbial, participial, prepositional, absolute) and clauses (independent, dependent; noun, relative, adverbial) to convey specific meanings and add variety and interest to writing or presentations.

Some words considered prepositions may also be used as adverbs. When taking an object, they are prepositions; without an object, they are adverbs.

PREPOSITIONS	ADVERBS
She put it **in the box**.	Come **in**!
The boy ran **around the corner**.	He came **around**.
He walked **on the sidewalk**.	We need to move **on**.
She fell **down the stairs**.	She fell **down**.

OTHER PARTS OF SPEECH USED AS PREPOSITIONS

Like is used as a preposition in such sentences as these:

  You look **like** my sister.

  In many respects, you are just **like** my mother.

In the first sentence, *like* is an adverb; in the second, *like* is an adjective. In each instance *like* takes an object as though it were a regular preposition. These sentences may be seen as the result of ellipsis with *unto* omitted: "You look like (unto) my sister."

CCSS.L.11–12.1.A:
Apply the understanding that usage is a matter of convention, can change over time, and is sometimes contested.

Like is a preposition. Many prepositions, such as *after* and *before,* can take a clausal complement: after *I tell you,* before *you go. Like* has been used with clauses for six hundred years. Great writers have all used the word this way: Shakespeare, Dickens, Twain, Wells, and Faulkner. But this particular usage has been so vehemently attacked by language mavens that careful writers should avoid using the word as a conjunction to introduce a clause: "He looks *like* he hasn't slept" (incorrect). Here the proper conjunction is *as if* or *as though:* "He looks *as if* (*as though*) he hasn't slept." To avoid this "error," keep in mind that *like* should be followed by an object and not a clause.

Another bogus rule concerning *like* is that it may not be used to introduce examples, as in *Many new terms come from the digital world, like "crowdsourcing" and "selfie."* Language grumps would change this to *such as "crowdsourcing" and "selfie."*

CONSTRUCTIONS USED AS OBJECTS OF PREPOSITIONS

CCSS.L.8.1.A:
Explain the function of verbals (gerunds, participles, infinitives) in general and their function in particular sentences.

The object of a preposition is commonly a noun or pronoun in the objective case.

> She plays in the **backyard**.
>
> You need to give the money to **him**.

Other constructions, when used as the object, may be considered noun-equivalents.

- A Noun or Pronoun in the Possessive Case.

  > You can find fresh peaches at your **grocer's**.
  >
  > I prefer your work habits to **his**.

CCSS.L.7.1.A:
Explain the function of phrases and clauses in general and their function in specific sentences.

These constructions are the result of ellipsis, the actual object being an omitted noun which can be easily understood from context: "at your grocer's *store,*" "to his *work habits.*" The form "at your grocer" should not be used. It is an unidiomatic usage arising from an attempt to reduce the possessive case of the object to the objective case.

- An Adjective.

  > The movie is suitable for **young** and **old**.

This is an elliptical construction meaning "for young and old *people.*"

CCSS.L.9–12.1:
Demonstrate command of the conventions of standard English grammar and usage when writing or speaking.

- An Adverb.

  They should have been here by **now**.

  They received a letter from **home**.

- A Gerund or Gerundive Phrase.

  She's not very good at **singing**.

  He gave me advice about **buying a car**.

- An Infinitive or Infinitive Phrase.

  We weren't allowed to do anything but **sit**.

  I really have no option but **to bribe them**.

  They intended for us **to meet them there**.

- A Prepositional Phrase.

  He took a box from **beneath his desk**.

  The prisoner was beaten to **within an inch of his life**.

- A Clause.

  I'm focused on **whatever interests me at the moment**.

  Our boss will give bonuses to **whomever he likes**.

  It's hard not to draw conclusions from **what people say**.

SPECIAL USES OF PREPOSITIONS

CCSS.L.9–10.1.B:
Use various types of phrases (noun, verb, adjectival, adverbial, participial, prepositional, absolute) and clauses (independent, dependent; noun, relative, adverbial) to convey specific meanings and add variety and interest to writing or presentations.

A preposition with no object may be used as a modifier after a noun.

  He was on vacation the week **before**.

  I went on vacation the week **after**.

  They live in the apartment **above**.

  The room **below** is empty.

  Spiritualists are obsessed with life **beyond**.

  We felt our way **around** in the dark.

These are elliptical constructions equivalent to "the apartment *above mine*," "life *beyond this one*," etc.

A preposition without an object is regularly used to modify a verb: "He ran *along*."

A PREPOSITION AT THE END OF A SENTENCE

CCSS.L.11–12.1.A: Apply the understanding that usage is a matter of convention, can change over time, and is sometimes contested.

The old rule that a preposition should never come at the end of a sentence is based on a faulty comparison of English with Latin. In American schools the rule is a vestige of an outdated pedagogy. Students should regard it as a rule they have never heard *of*. Truth is, the construction cannot be avoided, especially in short questions, without sacrificing the natural cadence and syntax of English. Thus, "Who is this *for?*" is more natural than the stilted, "For whom is this?" Other examples are numerous.

> Where did she come **from?**
>
> Which person did you give it **to?**
>
> What does his complaint amount **to?**
>
> Which smartphone are you interested **in?**

Exercise 6.1: Identifying Prepositions and Their Objects

Underline the prepositions and their objects.

WRITING PROMPT:
Write ten prepositional phrases of your own and write sentences for them.

1. The students walked down the sidewalk and across the park to their school.

2. The coach began practice early because of the heat advisory.

3. From now until the end of May, their father will be out of town.

4. One by one the students walked in and took their seats in the auditorium.

WRITING PROMPT:
Describe the things you have done to occupy your time when you are bored at home. Use as many prepositional phrases as you can.

5. Because of his various obsessions, he did not nurture close relationships.

6. Poverty has always existed the world over.

7. Australia is as far as from here to Russia.

8. The cable-cars glided to all points of the compass.

9. They walked down the main street and across the park to their hotel.

10. Without exception all the windows were wide open and filled with spectators.

11. In spite of himself, the captain could not regain his neutrality of feeling toward his orderly.

12. The smoke kept coming out through imperceptible crevices.

13. The sight of that plain sheet of paper recalled the past with a painful vividness.

CCSS.L.7.1.A:
Explain the function of phrases and clauses in general and their function in specific sentences.

14. Against the blackness of the pines the windows of the old office above the express office stood out strongly bright.

15. The period was one of suffering and anxiety to the colonists.

16. The same conditions exist the world over.

17. There was not another building within several leagues of the place.

18. It is at least as far as from here to Chicago.

Exercise 6.2: Identifying Prepositional Phrases

Circle all the prepositional phrases.

WRITING PROMPT:
Choose ten prepositional phrases from this exercise and write sentences for them.

1. When I came to Florida, I thought stories about the swamp ape were ridiculous, but now I think there might be something to it.

2. It consisted of a bedroom, a kitchen and a scullery.

3. We know absolutely nothing concerning the Force we call God; and, assuming such an intelligent ruling force to be in existence.

4. I would love to win the lottery soon, instead of persisting in this horrible life of poverty I slipped into several years ago.

5. Three days later Fairfax received a letter from the officer charged with dispersing the group.

CCSS.L.9–10.1.B:
Use various types of phrases (noun, verb, adjectival, adverbial, participial, prepositional, absolute) and clauses (independent, dependent; noun, relative, adverbial) to convey specific meanings and add variety and interest to writing or presentations.

6. As traditional stores J.C. Penney, Barnes & Noble, Sears, and Macy's struggle in today's online shopping market.

7. Even Amazon is feeling pressure from startups like Jet, the hot discount shopping site from a former employee.

8. This kind of technology would enable women in villages to use their time efficiently and profitably during periods when they did not need to work in the fields.

9. Perhaps it is more accurate to say that the focus of the liberation theologies widened to include, in addition to all oppressed human beings, all oppressed creatures as well as planet earth.

10. I didn't know that there could be literature of that kind, with such subversive qualities, because up to that point I believed what those in charge said about us.

CCSS.L.7.1.A:
Explain the function of phrases and clauses in general and their function in specific sentences.

11. He said this treatment was not only counterproductive to gaining information from high-ranking prisoners, but might also violate the Geneva Convention's protections for treating prisoners with regard to rank and stature.

12. I will follow thee to the last gasp with truth and loyalty.

13. My crown is in my heart, not on my head, not decked with diamonds and Indian stones.

14. He escaped out of their hand and went away again beyond Jordan.

Chapter

7

Conjunctions

ENGLISH LANGUAGE ARTS STANDARDS

☞ **CCSS.ELA-LITERACY.L.11–12.1.A:** *Apply the understanding that usage is a matter of convention, can change over time, and is sometimes contested.*

☞ **CCSS.ELA-LITERACY.L.9–10.1.B:** *Use various types of phrases (noun, verb, adjectival, adverbial, participial, prepositional, absolute) and clauses (independent, dependent; noun, relative, adverbial) to convey specific meanings and add variety and interest to writing or presentations.*

☞ **CCSS.ELA-LITERACY.L.7.1.A:** *Explain the function of phrases and clauses in general and their function in specific sentences.*

☞ **CCSS.ELA-LITERACY.L.7.1.B:** *Choose among simple, compound, complex, and compound–complex sentences to signal differing relationships among ideas.*

CONJUNCTIONS

CCSS.L.7.1.A:
Explain the function of phrases and clauses in general and their function in specific sentences.

A *Conjunction* is a word used to connect words or groups of words.

Henry **and** William were famous (**and** connects the nouns **Henry** and **William**).

Troubles came **and** went (**and** connects the verbs **came** and **went**).

Give it to him **or** to me (**or** connects the phrases **to him** and **to me**).

The day was quiet, **but** I felt uneasy (**but** connects the clauses **the day was quiet** and **I felt uneasy**).

I attend weddings **when** I'm invited (**when** connects the clauses **I attend weddings** and **I'm invited**).

CLASSES OF CONJUNCTIONS

There are two classes of conjunctions—coordinate and subordinate.

Coordinate Conjunctions

CCSS.L.7.1.A:
Explain the function of phrases and clauses in general and their function in specific sentences.

A *Coordinate Conjunction* connects words and groups of words of similar grammatical value, as nouns with nouns, verbs with verbs, adjectives with adjectives, phrases with phrases, clauses with clauses, etc.

It was a dark **and** stormy night (**and** connects the adjectives **dark** and **stormy**).

CCSS.L.7.1.B:
Choose among simple, compound, complex, and compound–complex sentences to signal differing relationships among ideas.

I'll listen to Mozart **or** Beethoven (**or** connects the nouns **Mozart** and **Beethoven**).

She laughed **but** I cried (**but** connects the two main clauses **she laughed** and **I cried**).

The principal coordinate conjunctions are *for, and, nor, but, or, yet,* and *so* (these words are known to many students as FANBOYS).

Correlative Conjunctions

CCSS.L.7.1.A:
Explain the function of phrases and clauses in general and their function in specific sentences.

The following constructions are called *Correlative Conjunctions: both—and, not only—but (also), either—or, neither—nor.* Correlatives connect things in a sentence with emphasis and clarity.

Both my mother **and** my father were from New York.

Neither a borrower **nor** a lender be.

Subordinate Conjunctions

A *Subordinate Conjunction* connects a subordinate clause with another clause on which it is dependent.

I talked to him **when** I was angry.

CCSS.L.7.1.A:

Explain the function of phrases and clauses in general and their function in specific sentences.

She will pay our way **if** I ask her to.

I ate the pizza **because** I was hungry.

He drove **while** drunk.

I've worked at the warehouse **since** I got out of school.

My wife and I saved for decades **so that** we might retire.

A subordinate clause can be placed at the beginning of the sentence. Thus, the second sentence above might read, "If I ask her to, she will pay our way." Grammatically, the subordinate conjunction in such a sentence still connects the two clauses although it no longer comes between them.

CCSS.L.7.1.B:

Choose among simple, compound, complex, and compound–complex sentences to signal differing relationships among ideas.

The more common subordinate conjunctions are *if, because, although, though, when, while, until, since, as.*

BEGINNING A SENTENCE WITH A CONJUNCTION

CCSS.L.11–12.1.A:

Apply the understanding that usage is a matter of convention, can change over time, and is sometimes contested.

This is an area of dispute among English teachers, but not professional writers.

Many teachers instruct their students never to begin a sentence with a conjunction. But this is just bad advice. There is nothing wrong with beginning a sentence with a conjunction, such as *and, because, but, or, so,* etc. Conjunctions are among the commonest coherence markers, and they are used by many writers to begin a sentence whenever long and complicated clauses can't fit comfortably into a single long sentence.

DISTINGUISHING PREPOSITIONS FROM CONJUNCTIONS

CCSS.L.7.1.A:

Explain the function of phrases and clauses in general and their function in specific sentences.

Some general guidelines can be given for distinguishing between prepositions and conjunctions, both of which are connecting words.

- *And, but, or,* and *nor* and the corresponding correlatives formed from them are almost always conjunctions. An exception would be the use of *but* in the sense of *except* as a preposition, as in "Everyone agreed *but* me," in which case *but* is a preposition with the object *me.*

- Most conjunctions commonly introduce clauses: that is, they are followed by a subject and a verb, whereas prepositions are followed only by objects (nouns or pronouns), not by a subject and a verb, although a clause can serve as the object of a preposition.

Words Used as Prepositions or as Conjunctions

CCSS.L.7.1.A:
Explain the function of phrases and clauses in general and their function in specific sentences.

Some connectives can be used as either prepositions or conjunctions, depending solely on their use in the sentence.

PREPOSITIONS (FOLLOWED BY AN OBJECT)

I left **after** you.

He stood **before** you.

CONJUNCTIONS (FOLLOWED BY A SUBJECT AND A VERB)

I left **after** the food ran out.

He stood **before** the starter fired the pistol.

Exercise 7.1: Identifying Miscellaneous Conjunctions

Underline the coordinate, subordinate, and correlative conjunctions.

CCSS.L.7.1.A:
Explain the function of phrases and clauses in general and their function in specific sentences.

1. He is called the Dead Wolf as long as he lives, which is not long, as a rule.

2. Christianity sometimes suggests that craving for spiritual goods is desirable, but it gives no support to craving for unneeded material possessions and consumption.

3. If neither Hawkins not Ferentz emerges, the company will most probably sift through a hodgepodge of candidates, none of whom would make the splash that the CEO is looking for.

4. There are millions of people who are illegally in the United States, and it's unfortunate that there is still no coherent immigration policy.

5. One day, however, as he was lying half asleep in the warm water somewhere off the island of Juan Fernandez, he felt faint and lazy all over.

6. We want to make sure that whatever decision is taken is one that is going to benefit our own security.

7. I grew uncomfortable, meanwhile, for the afternoon wore fast away, and the man whom I sent off returned from his errand.

CCSS.L.9–10.1.B:
Use various types of phrases (noun, verb, adjectival, adverbial, participial, prepositional, absolute) and clauses (independent, dependent; noun, relative, adverbial) to convey specific meanings and add variety and interest to writing or presentations.

8. Federal officials encouraged people to call, but now cite the deluge of calls to explain why they were unable to give accurate answers.

9. I live in California, whereas my twin brother lives in Florida.

10. While you were sleeping, there was an earthquake.

11. You do things your way, and I'll do them mine.

12. She spent a lot of money on her hair, not that it made any difference.

13. Much as I like you, you're still a pain.

14. The old professor wanted to retire, except that he had no savings.

15. Almost three months have passed since the players made their last proposal and we have yet to receive a counter-offer from the league.

16. Bears are dangerous in the wild even if you have a gun with you.

17. I wanted to travel to Ireland this summer, but I didn't have the money.

Exercise 7.2: Using Conjunctions

Use the following conjunctions in sentences.

WRITING PROMPT:
Construct sentences containing *either* and *or*, *neither* and *nor*, *whether* and *or*, *not only* and *but also*, *both* and *and*, *though*, *if*, *because*. Construct six sentences with coordinate conjunctions; six with subordinate conjunctions; six with relative adverbs.

CCSS.L.7.1.A:
Explain the function of phrases and clauses in general and their function in specific sentences.

CCSS.L.9–10.1.B:
Use various types of phrases (noun, verb, adjectival, adverbial, participial, prepositional, absolute) and clauses (independent, dependent; noun, relative, adverbial) to convey specific meanings and add variety and interest to writing or presentations.

1. (nor)

2. (both . . . and)

3. (either . . . or)

4. (neither . . . nor)

5. (not only . . . but also)

6. (yet)

7. (whereas)

8. (provided)

9. (even though)

10. (for)

Exercise 7.3: Identifying Prepositions and Conjunctions

Underline the prepositions and conjunctions; circle the objects of the prepositions.

WRITING PROMPT:

Write sentences in which the following words are used as indicated—*for* (preposition, conjunction), *since* (preposition, adverb), *notwithstanding* (preposition, conjunction), *since* (preposition, adverb, conjunction), *until* (preposition, conjunction), *as* (conjunction), *that* (conjunction, relative pronoun), *but* (preposition, conjunction).

1. The car disappeared around a bend in the road.

2. They trudged through the woods until they came to a cabin beside a small lake.

3. The sun was shining, but the wind had a touch of autumn in it.

4. The police waited anxiously for the signal, for they knew that the bank robbers were armed and in a panic to escape.

5. He would not return before the end of the summer, unless he was needed at home.

6. The room was large and neatly furnished, but not homelike.

7. They cut down the old oak tree because it shut off their view of the mountain.

8. It seemed as though we were forgotten by the world.

CCSS.L.7.1.A:

Explain the function of phrases and clauses in general and their function in specific sentences.

9. There is no fire in the forecastle, and we cannot dry clothes at the galley.

10. His father, as well as his uncle and paternal grandfather, were teachers at private schools.

11. Before he left that evening, Spode made an alarming discovery.

12. You must start at once, or you will be late for work.

CCSS.L.9–10.1.B:

Use various types of phrases (noun, verb, adjectival, adverbial, participial, prepositional, absolute) and clauses (independent, dependent; noun, relative, adverbial) to convey specific meanings and add variety and interest to writing or presentations.

13. We found that someone destroyed both the original and the copy of the letter.

14. All this the young man noticed, but it neither quickened his pulse nor hastened his hand.

15. It was years since he himself coasted the China seas.

16. If you are tired, you should either take a nap or go for a walk.

17. The copy should be in on Thursday in order that we may finish the printing by Saturday.

18. Neither a borrower nor a lender be.

Chapter 8

Phrases

ENGLISH LANGUAGE ARTS STANDARDS

NOTE:
Some of the skills in this chapter were introduced at lower grade levels; yet, due to the recursiveness of the language standards, they require further attention at the high school level.

☞ *CCSS.ELA-LITERACY.L.9–10.1.B: Use various types of phrases (noun, verb, adjectival, adverbial, participial, prepositional, absolute) and clauses (independent, dependent; noun, relative, adverbial) to convey specific meanings and add variety and interest to writing or presentations.*

☞ *CCSS.ELA-LITERACY.L.8.1.A: Explain the function of verbals (gerunds, participles, infinitives) in general and their function in particular sentences.*

☞ *CCSS.ELA-LITERACY.L.7.1.A: Explain the function of phrases and clauses in general and their function in specific sentences.*

PHRASES

CCSS.L.9–10.1.B:
Use various types of phrases (noun, verb, adjectival, adverbial, participial, prepositional, absolute) and clauses (independent, dependent; noun, relative, adverbial) to convey specific meanings and add variety and interest to writing or presentations.

A *Phrase* is a group of related words without a subject and a verb. In broad terms, a phrase can include any group of related words without a subject and a verb: as, *a fast car, boiling rapidly*. Most often, however, the term "phrase" is reserved for certain groups of words containing a particular type of defining word.

Phrases can be classified into four classes according to the nature of their introductory words.

- PREPOSITIONAL PHRASES: "We flew **over the mountain**."

- INFINITIVE PHRASES: "He wanted **to sing the song**."

- PARTICIPIAL PHRASES: "I saw him **parking the car**."

• GERUNDIVE PHRASES: "**Reading novels** is a passion of mine."

The preceding phrases are introduced by prepositions, participles, infinitives, and gerunds, respectively.

Prepositional Phrases

CCSS.L.7.1.A:

Explain the function of phrases and clauses in general and their function in specific sentences.

A **Prepositional Phrase** consists of a preposition and its object along with any modifiers. Thus, the phrase, *along a very lonely highway*, consists of the preposition *along*, the object *highway*, and the adverb *very* modifying the adjective *lonely*.

Infinitive, Participial, and Gerundive Phrases

CCSS.L.8.1.A:

Explain the function of verbals (gerunds, participles, infinitives) in general and their function in particular sentences.

Infinitive, Participial, and **Gerundive Phrases** consist of infinitives, participles, and gerunds followed by objects or complements or adjuncts. **Adjuncts** are words or phrases of secondary importance to the phrase—including adjectives and adverbs and their respective phrases—and serve only to expand the essential parts of the phrase. For example, the infinitive phrase, *to explain the complex answer clearly*, consists of the infinitive *to explain*; its object *answer*; the adverb *clearly*, which modifies the infinitive; the article *the;* and the adjective *complex*, which modifies the noun *answer*.

ADJUNCTS USED IN FORMING PHRASES

CCSS.L.8.1.A:

Explain the function of verbals (gerunds, participles, infinitives) in general and their function in particular sentences.

Infinitives, participles, and gerunds are derived from verbs and retain some of the functionality of the original verbs. That is, they form phrases that may contain any of the verbal adjuncts, such as objects, predicate nouns and adjectives, and various adverbs. For example, gerunds are used as nouns; but unlike nouns, they take the **Adjuncts** of a verb since the verbal qualities have been retained.

CCSS.L.7.1.A:

Explain the function of phrases and clauses in general and their function in specific sentences.

The principal adjuncts used with infinitives, participles, and gerunds to form phrases are as follows (the phrases are set off by vertical lines; the adjuncts, by italics).

• Direct Object.

I needed | to finish the **report**.

The woman | driving the **truck** | got a ticket.

Grading **papers** | occupied most of my weekend.

- Indirect Object.

    To make **him** the supervisor | required a vote.

    The woman | baking **us** a cake | is my wife.

    Buying **everybody** gifts | wasn't easy.

- Predicate Adjective.

    To be **useful** | is my goal.

    Being **sick,** | she stayed home.

    Being **lonely** | is no fun.

- Predicate Noun.

    I wanted | to be a good **teacher**.

    Being a **perfectionist,** | she was never happy.

    Being a **smoker** | is unhealthy.

- Adverb.

    I expected | to be fired **immediately**.

    Swimming **effortlessly,** | she made it across the lake.

    Watching **intently** | is the way to enjoy movies.

- Prepositional Phrase.

    To perform **in the concert hall** | is a joy.

    Writing **with a pen,** | I developed writer's cramp.

    Swimming **across the lake** | was exhausting.

- Adverbial Clause.

    To read **when you're tired** | is difficult.

    Falling down **because he was drunk,** | the man broke his arm.

    Eating healthy food **although you hate it** | will still benefit you.

FUNCTIONS OF PHRASES

Phrases function as individual parts of speech: as nouns, adjectives, or adverbs.

CCSS.L.7.1.A:
Explain the function of
phrases and clauses in
general and their function
in specific sentences.

- As a Noun.

  Subject of a Verb:

  To sing the song was a joy.

  Paying off debt takes time.

  Predicate Noun:

  His intention was **to exonerate his client**.

  The trickiest part is **roasting the beans**.

  Direct Object of a Verb:

  I hope **to be there in time**.

  I enjoy **listening to piano music**.

  Object of a Preposition:

  I would love for **you to go with me**.

  She calmed the baby by **singing a lullaby**.

  In Apposition:

  His stated purpose—**to help us out**—was a ruse.

  His unstated goal—**eliminating our jobs**—was obvious.

CCSS.L.8.1.A:
Explain the function of verbals (gerunds, participles,
infinitives) in general and
their function in particular
sentences.

- As an Adjective.

  I met a girl **from Ipanema**.

  They allowed us permission **to enter the park**.

  The car **coughing blue smoke** is an old clunker.

- As an Adverb.

  I went **to see the football game**.

  The girl, **seeing her mother,** started to run.

  We saw the movie **in the evening**.

Adverbial phrases are like adverbial clauses in that they express time, place, manner, degree, purpose, cause, concession, and condition.

Infinitive Phrases, unlike other types of phrases, regularly perform the functions of the aforementioned three parts of speech. A gerundive phrase is used as a noun; a participial phrase is used as an adjective or as an adverb in a dual relation; and a prepositional phrase is used chiefly as an adjective or adverb.

Some ***Participial Phrases*** have an unusual ***Dual Relation:*** the participle that introduces the phrase is an adjective that modifies a noun, but the entire phrase is an adverb that modifies a verb. For example, in the sentence, "William, *seeing his predicament,* decided on another course of action," the participle *seeing* modifies *William,* but the entire phrase modifies *decided*—that is, it is an adverb telling *why* he decided.

A ***Gerundive Phrase*** has the same appearance as a participial phrase, but the two are distinguished by their use—a gerundive phrase is used as a noun, and a participial phrase is used as an adjective or as an adverb in a dual relation.

Exercise 8.1: Identifying Infinitive Phrases

Underline the infinitive phrases, and indicate whether they act as nouns, adjectives, or adverbs.

WRITING PROMPT:
Write ten sentences of your own, using infinitive phrases as nouns, adjectives, and adverbs.

1. /Saddam Hussein appeared in a Baghdad courtroom to hear the charges he would face when he went to trial as a war criminal.

2. I don't think it possible for me to get home now without a guide.

3. I warn you to refrain from provoking me, or I'll ask your abduction as a special favour.

4. His first intention was to hire a horse there and ride home forthwith, for to walk many miles without a gun in his hand and along an ordinary road, was as much out of the question to him as to other spirited young men of his kind.

CCSS.L.8.1.A:
Explain the function of verbals (gerunds, participles, infinitives) in general and their function in particular sentences.

5. Too stupefied to be curious myself, I fastened my door and glanced round for the bed.

6. His growing reputation was enhanced by the prominent role he was said to have played at the Second Vatican Council called by Pope John XXIII in 1962 to formulate doctrines for the church in the modern world.

7. If she was to forsake him it was surely for her to take leave.

8. The Red Cross committee was considering whether to bring more senior officials to Washington and whether to make public its criticisms.

CCSS.L.9–10.1.B:
Use various types of phrases (noun, verb, adjectival, adverbial, participial, prepositional, absolute) and clauses (independent, dependent; noun, relative, adverbial) to convey specific meanings and add variety and interest to writing or presentations.

9. According to Christ, to love God with all the heart, soul, mind, and strength is the greatest commandment.

10. I come to bury Caesar.

11. Oftentimes, to win us to our harm, the instruments of darkness tell us truths.

12. He has erected a multitude of new offices and sent hither swarms of officers to harass our people and eat out their substance.

13. Our fathers fled from the rage of religious tyranny and persecution, and came into this land to enjoy liberty of conscience.

14. After 1741, Handel abandoned opera to dedicate himself to the composition of oratorios.

Exercise 8.2: Identifying Participial Phrases

Underline the participial phrases.

WRITING PROMPT:
Write ten sentences,, using
participial phrases.

1. Every kingdom divided against itself is brought to desolation.

2. The weeds growing rankly by the roadside showed it in blots and splashes on their big, broad leaves.

3. As in Paradise, God walks in the Holy Scriptures, seeking man.

4. That faith was then new to me, and all Moxon's expounding failed to make me a convert.

5. Truth, crushed to earth, shall rise again.

CCSS.L.8.1.A:
Explain the function of verbals (gerunds, participles,
infinitives) in general and
their function in particular
sentences.

6. None of woman born shall harm Macbeth.

7. When imparting shocking intelligence to the sick he was affable enough.

8. My subject in fiction is the action of grace in territory held by the Devil.

9. The Second-Lieutenant was a brave and efficient officer, young and comparatively inexperienced as he was in the business of killing his fellow-men.

10. At the fountainhead of Western literature is the epic, the story of a hero struggling against the constraints of the human condition.

11. Congress shall make no law respecting an establishment of religion or prohibiting the free exercise thereof.

12. We could hear the rooks cawing from the trees beyond.

13. The creation, groaning with pain, suffers as a result of man's sin and folly.

14. The doctor nodded civilly, half thinking that the stranger's uncommon greeting was perhaps in deference to the historic surroundings.

15. The horses, shaking their harness, brought their driver's attention back to the present.

Exercise 8.3: Identifying Gerundive Phrases

Underline the gerundive phrases.

WRITING PROMPT:
Write ten sentences, using gerundive phrases.

1. Learning a foreign language gives many people a better understanding of their own.

2. Writing a full-length biography about a historical figure is hard work.

3. You can obtain some good information for your research paper by using the Internet wisely.

CCSS.L.9–10.1.B:
Use various types of phrases (noun, verb, adjectival, adverbial, participial, prepositional, absolute) and clauses (independent, dependent; noun, relative, adverbial) to convey specific meanings and add variety and interest to writing or presentations.

4. She enjoyed thinking about being famous someday.

5. Becoming a novelist requires working hard at your craft.

6. The twelfth amendment to the Constitution outlines procedures for electing the president and vice-president.

7. Scanning poetry can be a useful exercise for understanding a poet's style.

8. The proper purpose of the criminal justice system is the protection of the innocent by punishing the guilty.

9. Gardening is an enjoyable pastime for many people living in this area.

CCSS.L.8.1.A:
Explain the function of verbals (gerunds, participles, infinitives) in general and their function in particular sentences.

10. The young couple enjoyed walking along the beach together.

11. Watching your growing plants will give you a sense of pride.

12. Seeing those constellations will necessitate a telescope with a much higher magnitude.

13. Emily Dickinson began writing poetry at an early age.

CCSS.L.7.1.A:
Explain the function of phrases and clauses in general and their function in specific sentences.

14. Surely one of the primary tasks of the deacon must be helping the poor and sick of the congregation.

15. How much will replacing the water heater cost?

16. Reading literature in its original language will give you a better knowledge of its exact meaning.

17. She began lowering gingerbread treats in a basket to children waiting below her upper window.

18. He's a recluse but remains in touch with the outside world by communicating with family and friends through email and social media.

19. Ditching school is no way to advance yourself as a student.

NOMINATIVE ABSOLUTE PHRASE

CCSS.L.9–10.1.B:
Use various types of phrases (noun, verb, adjectival, adverbial, participial, prepositional, absolute) and clauses (independent, dependent; noun, relative, adverbial) to convey specific meanings and add variety and interest to writing or presentations.

This construction consists of a noun and a present or past participle.

> **The alarm having sounded,** the work day began.
>
> **My golf ball having landed on the green,** I grabbed my putter.
>
> **Dinner being ready,** we gathered in the dining room.
>
> **His emotions getting the better of him,** he started to cry.
>
> **Present company excluded,** nobody did anything.

A Nominative Absolute Phrase generally begins a sentence, but it can stand anywhere in the sentence.

> The car wouldn't start, **the battery having discharged completely**.
>
> He swung the ax, **his fingers clasped tightly on the handle**.

The *Nominative Absolute Phrase* regularly functions as an adverb indicating reason or time, but also concession, condition, or manner.

Occasionally the participle is left out of the absolute phrase when it is clear what the participle would be.

> **Game over,** we walked off the field.

INFINITIVE PHRASE WITH A SUBJECT

CCSS.L.9–10.1.B:
Use various types of phrases (noun, verb, adjectival, adverbial, participial, prepositional, absolute) and clauses (independent, dependent; noun, relative, adverbial) to convey specific meanings and add variety and interest to writing or presentations.

An infinitive is sometimes used with a noun or pronoun that stands in the same relation to the infinitive as the subject of a verb stands to that verb.

> I knew **Frank to be truthful**.
>
> We believed **her to be a troublemaker**.
>
> My parents expected **me to go to college**.

In these sentences the infinitive phrase takes a subject in the objective case because the infinitive phrase itself is the object of the transitive verb. Thus, the infinitive phrase is equivalent to a noun clause. For example, "I knew *him to be truthful*" is equivalent to "I knew *that he was truthful.*" The infinitive *to be* takes the place of the verb *was*, and *him* replaces *he*, the subject of *was*. *Him* is considered the subject of the infinitive.

Occasionally *to*, the infinitive marker, is omitted.

I saw her **dance** in the ballet.

The following sentences show a somewhat different relationship between the infinitive and its subject.

She asked **the guy to look for it**.

He told **her to open the window**.

In the above sentences, the infinitive can be viewed as the direct object of the verb, and the noun or pronoun as the indirect object. Thus, in "He told her to open the window," the infinitive *to open the window* tells *what* he said (direct object) and *her* shows *to whom* he said it (indirect object). Traditional grammar regards the infinitive phrase in these instances—the infinitive with its subject—as the direct object of the verb.

An infinitive with a subject is occasionally used as the object of the preposition *for*. The resulting prepositional phrase may be the subject of a verb, a predicate noun, or the object of a verb.

For you to say that would take courage (subject).

The best thing is **for him to remain quiet** (predicate noun).

I didn't intend **for you to get upset** (object).

The ***Subject of an Infinitive*** is always in the objective case, unlike the subject of a verb, which is always in the nominative case.

My employer considers **me** to be an asset.

I found **him** to be boring.

A ***Predicate Noun or Pronoun*** following an infinitive (subject in the objective case) is in the same case to agree with the subject.

I confused the two and thought him to be **her**.

The police believed the two suspects to be **them**.

Careful writers should keep in mind that when the infinitive is changed to a finite verb, both the subject and predicate pronoun are in the nominative case: "I confused the two and thought *he* was *she*."

Exercise 8.4: Identifying Classes of Phrases

Underline the prepositional, infinitive, participial, and gerundive phrases—and identify them.

CCSS.L.9–10.1.B:

Use various types of phrases (noun, verb, adjectival, adverbial, participial, prepositional, absolute) and clauses (independent, dependent; noun, relative, adverbial) to convey specific meanings and add variety and interest to writing or presentations.

1. No one wanted to accept Dracula's invitation to the castle.

2. A desire to leave a legacy brought him back to his hometown.

3. To become wealthy is not the primary objective in life.

4. Having money does not always result in having friends.

5. Knowing the alphabet is essential for a child who is learning to read.

6. To change business plans now would be to admit failure.

7. While they were visiting Coventry Cathedral, the tour members enjoyed hearing about the symbolism of reconciliation.

8. Considering her options carefully, Cindy chose the safest course.

9. Aristotle, who established the basic theory of tragedy, used Greek plays to illustrate his points.

CCSS.L.8.1.A:

Explain the function of verbals (gerunds, participles, infinitives) in general and their function in particular sentences.

10. He enjoys reading horror novels and books of travel.

11. At the table sat a wizened little man playing solitaire.

12. Everyone was eager to hear about the new coach in order to determine the team's chances of success.

13. Then lifting the tent door, he emerged into the open air.

14. The bridge spanning the creek was washed away by the flood.

15. To be responsible for a pet, you must not just take care of the animal but spend a lot of time with it.

16. The ancient Romans believed in building structures to improve the comforts of everyday life.

17. Tony has worked hard at improving his golf game.

18. The consul advised us to report at once to the British embassy.

19. Drinking too much at dinner can lead to taking a long nap.

20. To understand the changes in their son's behavior, his parents tried to ask him a series of questions.

21. Making a peanut butter and tuna sandwich, Alice managed to gross out her friends.

May be copied for classroom use. Common Core Grammar by Thomas Fasano (Coyote Canyon Press: Claremont, CA); © 2015.

Exercise 8.5: Writing with Participial Phrases

Write sentences with the following participial phrases.

CCSS.L.8.1.A:
Explain the function of verbals (gerunds, participles, infinitives) in general and their function in particular sentences.

1. (taking a bath)

2. (taken by surprise)

3. (injured on the ice)

4. (fallen out of favor)

5. (considering the consequences)

6. (selling all the tickets)

CCSS.L.7.1.A:
Explain the function of phrases and clauses in general and their function in specific sentences.

7. (studied thoroughly)

8. (excelling at all things)

9. (sensing our discomfort)

10. (pining away with love)

11. (pleasing to all)

12. (hoping for a treat)

13. (unnoticed by everyone)

14. (set for dinner)

15. (kept away secretly)

Exercise 8.6: Writing with Nominative Absolute Phrases

Write sentences with the following nominative absolute phrases.

CCSS.L.9–10.1.B:
Use various types of phrases (noun, verb, adjectival, adverbial, participial, prepositional, absolute) and clauses (independent, dependent; noun, relative, adverbial) to convey specific meanings and add variety and interest to writing or presentations.

1. (all things being equal)

2. (I being the best)

3. (no one else having my good qualities)

4. (my professor knowing high quality)

5. (everyone singing my praises)

6. (my talents being natural)

7. (my boss discerning true quality)

8. (my parents having seen my abilities)

9. (my classmates being impressed with my astuteness)

10. (all things considered)

Exercise 8.7: Writing with Infinitive Phrases

Use the following infinitive verbal phrases as subject, direct object, adjective, adverb, or subjective complement, as indicated.

CCSS.L.8.1.A:
Explain the function of verbals (gerunds, participles, infinitives) in general and their function in particular sentences.

1. to tell the story well (as subject)

2. to tell the story well (as subject)

3. to be happy (as direct object)

4. to be happy (as adverb)

5. to be happy (as adjective)

6. to be happy (as predicate adjective)

7. to want a house (as subject)

CCSS.L.7.1.A:
Explain the function of phrases and clauses in general and their function in specific sentences.

8. to want a horse (as subject)

9. to want a dog (as direct object)

10. to want a computer (as adjective or adverb)

11. to bake a cake (as subject)

12. to bake a cake (as subject)

13. to bake a cake (as direct object)

14. to bake a cake (as predicate adjective)

15. to bake a cake (as adjective)

16. to bake a cake (as adverb)

17. to gladden her heart (as subject)

18. to gladden her heart (as direct object)

19. to gladden her heart (as predicate adjective)

20. to gladden her heart (as adverb)

Exercise 8.8: Writing with Infinitive Phrases

Write paragraphs using the following infinitive verbal phrases. You may have more than one infinitive verbal phrase in a sentence, but you don't need an infinitive verbal phrase in each sentence.

CCSS.L.8.1.A:
Explain the function of verbals (gerunds, participles, infinitives) in general and their function in particular sentences.

1. to be rich, to have lots of friends, to buy happiness, to feel secure, to need wealth

2. to lift weights, to jog for miles, to swim in the pool, to hike in the mountains, to row for hours

3. to read a good book, to see action movies, to walk in the park, to loll on the beach, to watch television

4. to hear good music, to attend the ballet, to appreciate opera, to read literature, to see plays

5. to get married, to have children, to own a house, to find a good career, to take vacations

6. to throw a party, to invite my best friends, to eat and drink, to dance the tango, to talk with interesting people

CCSS.L.7.1.A:
Explain the function of phrases and clauses in general and their function in specific sentences.

7. to work on Wall Street, to know important people, to attend important meetings, to earn and spend millions, to have power

8. to raise children, to see them learn, to take them with me, to tell them stories, to watch them grow up

9. to be busy, to feel harried, to run late, to rush through everything, to have insomnia

10. to vacuum the carpets, to dust the shelves, to clean the bathrooms, to mop the kitchen floor, to change the beds

May be copied for classroom use. Common Core Grammar by Thomas Fasano (Coyote Canyon Press: Claremont, CA); © 2015.

Exercise 8.9: Writing with Gerundive Phrases

Write sentences with the following gerundive phrases.

CCSS.L.8.1.A:

Explain the function of verbals (gerunds, participles, infinitives) in general and their function in particular sentences.

1. (walking the dog)

2. (considering the weather)

3. (enjoying the flowers)

4. (announcing the event)

5. (raising the curtain)

6. (cheating on the exam)

7. (keeping fit)

8. (looking for trouble)

9. (furnishing an apartment)

CCSS.L.7.1.A:

Explain the function of phrases and clauses in general and their function in specific sentences.

10. (eating the cake)

11. (selling all my assets)

12. (breaking up the fight)

13. (being from California)

14. (pleasing my parents)

15. (being an athlete)

16. (stopping smoking)

17. (throwing the ball)

18. (seeking refuge)

19. (devoting my life)

20. (collecting the rent)

Exercise 8.10: Writing with Various Phrases

Write sentences using the following phrases as indicated (a separate sentence for each use).

CCSS.L.9–10.1.B:
Use various types of phrases (noun, verb, adjectival, adverbial, participial, prepositional, absolute) and clauses (independent, dependent; noun, relative, adverbial) to convey specific meanings and add variety and interest to writing or presentations.

1. *Baking the cake*—as (a) adjective; (b) gerund—subject of a verb; (c) gerund—direct object of a verb; (d) gerund—predicate noun.

2. *Smoking a pipe*—as (a) direct object of a verb; (b) object of a preposition.

3. *Renting the apartment*—as object of the prepositions *from*, *about*, and *because of*.

4. *To get the answer*—as (a) subject of a verb; (b) predicate noun; (c) direct object of a verb.

5. *To see the movie*—as (a) adjective; (b) adverb.

CCSS.L.8.1.A:
Explain the function of verbals (gerunds, participles, infinitives) in general and their function in particular sentences.

Change the infinitive phrases to gerundive phrases.

1. He likes to read comic books.

2. To mow the yard was his first task this weekend.

CCSS.L.7.1.A:
Explain the function of phrases and clauses in general and their function in specific sentences.

3. One of his jobs was to paint the old shed.

4. The best time to hunt deer is early in the morning.

5. They have found a way to mitigate the pain.

Clauses

ENGLISH LANGUAGE ARTS STANDARDS

NOTE:
Some of the skills in this chapter were introduced at lower grade levels; yet, due to the recursiveness of the language standards, they require further attention at the high school level.

☞ **CCSS.ELA-LITERACY.L.9–10.1.A:** *Use parallel structure.*

☞ **CCSS.ELA-LITERACY.L.9–10.1.B:** *Use various types of phrases (noun, verb, adjectival, adverbial, participial, prepositional, absolute) and clauses (independent, dependent; noun, relative, adverbial) to convey specific meanings and add variety and interest to writing or presentations.*

☞ **CCSS.ELA-LITERACY.L.7.1.A:** *Explain the function of phrases and clauses in general and their function in specific sentences.*

☞ **CCSS.ELA-LITERACY.L.7.1.B:** *Choose among simple, compound, complex, and compound–complex sentences to signal differing relationships among ideas.*

CLAUSES

A *Clause* is a group of related words containing a subject and a verb and forming part of the sentence. What distinguishes a clause from a phrase is that a clause has a subject and a verb, whereas a phrase does not.

Thus I *was a senior in high school when I got my scholarship* consists of a **Main Clause** (*I was a senior in high school*) and a **Subordinate Clause** (*when I got my scholarship*).

Some modern grammars consider the clause, not the sentence, as the basis of structural analysis, so that clauses and sentences have the same grammatical boundaries.

CCSS.L.9–10.1.B:
Use various types of phrases (noun, verb, adjectival, adverbial, participial, prepositional, absolute) and clauses (independent, dependent; noun, relative, adverbial) to convey specific meanings and add variety and interest to writing or presentations.

Clauses can be divided into two classes: Main and Subordinate. Main Clauses are sometimes called Independent Clauses. Subordinate Clauses are also known as Dependent Clauses.

A *Main Clause* is the principal part of the sentence, containing both a noun and verb phrase. Without this structure, there would be no complete thought and therefore no sentence.

A *Subordinate Clause* is dependent on the main clause and is used as a single part of speech in the sentence—that is, as a noun, adjective, or adverb.

Thus, in the sentence, "I poured the coffee when it was ready," the main clause, *I poured the coffee,* makes the principal statement and could stand alone as a sentence itself; the subordinate clause, *when it was ready,* is used as an adverb to modify the verb *poured*—it tells when I poured it.

MAIN CLAUSES

CCSS.L.7.1.B:
Choose among simple, compound, complex, and compound–complex sentences to signal differing relationships among ideas.

A *Main Clause* makes the principal statement in the sentence.

The simplest form of the sentence (a single clause with only one group of words containing a subject and a verb—for example, "They asked me out to lunch") is not customarily referred to as a clause, such a term being reserved for *a part of a sentence.* Nonetheless, this group of words is a main clause, albeit the only clause in the sentence.

Any sentence with two or more clauses must have at least one main clause. The other clauses can be either main or subordinate.

RELATIONSHIP BETWEEN MAIN CLAUSES

CCSS.L.9–10.1.A:
Use parallel structure.

When a sentence has two or more main clauses, there must be a logical relationship between them. The four logical relationships are as follows:

- Harmony or Agreement.

- Contrast or Opposition.

- Alternation or Choice.

  • Consequence or Inference.

The most frequently used conjunctions for these four classes are *and, but, or,* and *therefore.*

Harmony or Agreement in Thought

CCSS.L.9–10.1.B:

Use various types of phrases (noun, verb, adjectival, adverbial, participial, prepositional, absolute) and clauses (independent, dependent; noun, relative, adverbial) to convey specific meanings and add variety and interest to writing or presentations.

In this group the second clause makes a statement that naturally follows and carries forward the meaning of the first clause, sets forth another step in a series of thoughts, or adds another detail.

> The buzzer sounded, **and** the cake was done.
>
> I looked out the window, **and** across the street I saw the mailman.
>
> He never paid me back; **moreover,** he had no intention of doing so.
>
> I don't like cake; **besides,** I never eat dessert.

The principal conjunctions for this group are *and, moreover, furthermore, likewise, plus, in like manner,* and *besides.*

This general class has two special subclasses.

General Statement and Specific Example

CCSS.L.9–10.1.B:

Use various types of phrases (noun, verb, adjectival, adverbial, participial, prepositional, absolute) and clauses (independent, dependent; noun, relative, adverbial) to convey specific meanings and add variety and interest to writing or presentations.

The second clause gives an example illustrating the general statement in the first clause.

> There are a number of old ideas in this book: **for example,** the author states that Schubert died of syphilis.
>
> In many ways the boy is a horrible student: **for instance,** he never has his book and never takes notes.

The principal conjunctions for this group are *for example, for instance,* and *thus.*

General Statement and Specific Explanation

The second clause explains the idea in the first clause in more specific terms.

> He is a talented musician: he learns different instruments quickly and with very little study.

She is a great cook: **that is,** she cooks a variety of delicious meals.

Clauses in this relation are often joined without conjunctions. When employed, these connections principally are *that is* and *in other words*.

Contrast or Opposition in Thought

CCSS.L.9–10.1.B:
Use various types of phrases (noun, verb, adjectival, adverbial, participial, prepositional, absolute) and clauses (independent, dependent; noun, relative, adverbial) to convey specific meanings and add variety and interest to writing or presentations.

The thought in the second clause contrasts with that in the first.

Jim wants to be famous, **but** he has no talent.

The president spoke in favor of the bill; **nevertheless,** the Republicans were against it.

He has been in the job only one year; **however,** he has already had a big impact.

The principal conjunctions for this group are *but, however, nonetheless, on the other hand, yet,* and *on the contrary*.

Alternation or Choice

CCSS.L.9–10.1.B:
Use various types of phrases (noun, verb, adjectival, adverbial, participial, prepositional, absolute) and clauses (independent, dependent; noun, relative, adverbial) to convey specific meanings and add variety and interest to writing or presentations.

The second clause presents an alternative to the first clause.

You must have a receipt, **or** you will not get a refund.

I must have been daydreaming; **otherwise,** I fell asleep.

Put a log on the fire; **else** it will go out.

The principal conjunctions for this group are *or, nor, either—or, neither—nor, otherwise,* and *else*.

Consequence or Inference

CCSS.L.9–10.1.B:
Use various types of phrases (noun, verb, adjectival, adverbial, participial, prepositional, absolute) and clauses (independent, dependent; noun, relative, adverbial) to convey specific meanings and add variety and interest to writing or presentations.

The second clause states a fact that is a consequence of the fact stated in the first clause or an inference from it.

He observed crows in the field for decades after his undergraduate days; **consequently,** he was able to write a book about them.

The woman was petite with little upper-body strength; **consequently,** she was unable to lift the heavy boxes.

The child vanished without a clue, **so that** now the police believe she was kidnapped.

In each of the first two sentences, the second clause states a fact that is a direct consequence of the first statement. In the third sentence, the second clause is an inference from the first clause.

The principal conjunctions for this group are *but, or, yet, therefore, consequently, hence, accordingly, so, as a result, for this reason,* and *so that.*

CONJUNCTIONS USED WITH MAIN CLAUSES

CCSS.L.7.1.B:
Choose among simple, compound, complex, and compound–complex sentences to signal differing relationships among ideas.

The principal conjunctions used with main clauses have already been listed under the preceding different classes of relation. *And, but, or* and *yet* are the key coordinate conjunctions for the four classes; that is, they are the ones most frequently used. The others are used for the sake of variety and emphasis.

Sometimes a key conjunction is used in combination with another conjunction in its group.

And likewise, and moreover, and furthermore; but nevertheless, but yet, but however (rare); *or else, or otherwise* (rare)

And is frequently combined with conjunctions expressing consequence: *and therefore, and consequently, and so,* etc. *And* by itself does not express consequence and should not be used alone to express this relationship.

Position of the Conjunction

CCSS.L.7.1.B:
Choose among simple, compound, complex, and compound–complex sentences to signal differing relationships among ideas.

And, but, or, and *nor* stand at the beginning of the clause. Other conjunctions stand either at the beginning of a clause or somewhere within it.

He was drunk, **and** it showed on his face.

He was drunk; **furthermore,** it showed on his face.

He was drunk; **and furthermore,** it showed on his face.

He was drunk, **and** it was noticeable in his speech; **moreover,** it showed on his face and posture.

He stumbled and fell; his drunkenness, **therefore,** showed in his every movement.

Omission of the Conjunction

CCSS.L.7.1.B:
Choose among simple, compound, complex, and compound–complex sentences to signal differing relationships among ideas.

A conjunction is sometimes dropped if easily understood, and the connection between clauses is smooth.

> I am a teacher; ∧ my brother is a cab driver (**and** is omitted).

> People of humble origins can rise to positions of authority; ∧ Barack Obama was raised by a single mother and became president of the United States (**for example** is omitted).

> His coworkers think highly of him; ∧ his family thinks otherwise (**but** is omitted).

With three or more main clauses in a sentence, the conjunctions are often omitted between the clauses except the final two.

> Our bags were packed, the car was running, **and** we were ready to take off.

Sometimes conjunctions are placed between all the clauses.

> The trees swayed, **and** the wind blew, **and** the rain came through the windows.

Exercise 9.1: Identifying Main Clauses

Underline the main clauses.

WRITING PROMPT:
Write ten sentences, each
with two main clauses.

WRITING PROMPT:
Write about something
that you were late for
or missed. Write with
compound sentences,
using different relationships
between main clauses.

CCSS.L.9–10.1.B:
Use various types of
phrases (noun, verb, adjectival, adverbial, participial,
prepositional, absolute)
and clauses (independent,
dependent; noun, relative,
adverbial) to convey specific meanings and add variety
and interest to writing or
presentations.

CCSS.L.7.1.B:
Choose among simple,
compound, complex, and
compound–complex sen-
tences to signal differing
relationships among ideas.

1. I had little money back then; therefore, I ate poorly.

2. On Sundays we attended church, or we visited family.

3. Keep in mind a simple caveat: the salespeople want only your money.

4. The defense team got off to a rocky start; nevertheless, they felt confident of seeing their client acquitted.

5. All the payments have been made; moreover, they have been made on time.

6. John Updike was a man of many talents: he was a novelist, poet, artist, critic, and intellectual.

7. It was a dark, rainy evening, and there was no sound in the house.

8. There were many curious volumes in the library, but I had no time to look at them.

9. He had no money; moreover, he seemed little interested in earning any.

10. My native country was full of youthful promise; Europe was rich in the accumulated treasures of age.

11. She was undeniably tired; yet she all she did all day was loiter away the day.

12. On Saturdays we climbed the steep mountain trails, or we visited our friends in the valley below.

13. There were two other routes from Fort Laramie; but both of these were less interesting, and neither was free from danger.

14. Only one caution is necessary: that is, all holders of reserved tickets should be in their seats by eight o'clock.

15. We could not see those on deck; nor could we imagine what caused the delay.

16. There might be some difficulty at first; nevertheless, he felt sure of winning his case.

17. All the installments have been paid; moreover, they have been paid on time.

18. Benjamin Franklin was a man of many interests: he was printer, publisher, author, diplomat, and philosopher.

Exercise 9.2: Understanding Relationships between Main Clauses

Complete the sentences by adding a main clause that shows the relationship indicated. Use different conjunctions for the sentences.

CCSS.L.7.1.B:
Choose among simple, compound, complex, and compound–complex sentences to signal differing relationships among ideas.

1. There was a riot in the city center _____ (harmony or agreement).

2. He lost money in his IRA during the recession _____ (harmony or agreement).

3. For a year the navy searched for the missing plane _____ (contrast or opposition).

4. The candidate had the overwhelming backing of the members of his party_____ (contrast or opposition).

CCSS.L.7.1.B:
Choose among simple, compound, complex, and compound–complex sentences to signal differing relationships among ideas.

5. He studied for a year in a German university _____ (consequence or inference).

6. There was only one rational way to resolve the dispute _____ (specific explanation).

7. We have made a number of improvements to our house _____ (specific example).

8. California must have rain soon _____ (alternation or choice).

9. The mountain road was narrow and had many zigzags _____ (a) consequence; (b) harmony or agreement; (c) contrast or opposition. (*Make a separate sentence for each.*)

Exercise 9.3: Understanding Relationships between Main Clauses

Underline the noun clauses and write how each one is used.

CCSS.L.7.1.B:
Choose among simple, compound, complex, and compound–complex sentences to signal differing relationships among ideas.

1. The owner passed away, and the property passed into the hands of his family.

2. You must bring your ticket, or you won't be allowed inside.

3. The society is only two years old; however, it has already raised a lot of money for various charities.

4. We went to the door, and there we found the UPS guy with a package.

5. He never paid the fine; furthermore, he had no intention of paying it.

6. The house is modern; moreover, it is conveniently located.

7. He made a thorough study of the subject; consequently, he was very knowledgeable and could answer all our questions.

8. William is intelligent, but he lacks initiative.

CCSS.L.7.1.B:
Choose among simple, compound, complex, and compound–complex sentences to signal differing relationships among ideas.

9. There are a number of mistakes in the article: for example, the first paragraph uses the word "principal" for "principle" twice.

10. The boy was small for his age and somewhat frail; hence he was unable to defend himself against bullies.

11. In many respects the witness was hostile: for instance, he evaded key questions and could not recall essential details.

12. Donald Trump is a very wealthy man: his property and assets are conservatively valued at over ten billion dollars.

13. He practiced the golden rule: that is, he treated others as he wished to be treated.

14. Obama spoke eloquently in favor of gun control; nevertheless, his words fell on deaf ears.

15. Either my eyes deceive me, or the train is on time.

16. He hasn't paid back any of the money in a year; therefore we probably will never see that money again.

17. He was angry, and he could not conceal it from anyone.

18. His father is the president of the company, and his uncle used to be the operations manager.

SUBORDINATE CLAUSES

CCSS.L.9–10.1.B:
Use various types of phrases (noun, verb, adjectival, adverbial, participial, prepositional, absolute) and clauses (independent, dependent; noun, relative, adverbial) to convey specific meanings and add variety and interest to writing or presentations.

A ***Subordinate Clause*** is a group of words with a subject and a verb; it is used as a single part of speech in a sentence.

Subordinate Clauses function as nouns, adjectives, or adverbs, and are called noun clauses, adjective clauses, and adverb clauses.

Note. A special class of *wh*-words introduces a variety of subordinate clauses: *what, which, who, whom, whose, when, where, why,* and *how*. Wh-words can be intensified by adding *ever:* as, *whatever, wherever, why ever* (separate word after *why*).

Uses of Noun Clauses

CCSS.L.9–10.1.B:
Use various types of phrases (noun, verb, adjectival, adverbial, participial, prepositional, absolute) and clauses (independent, dependent; noun, relative, adverbial) to convey specific meanings and add variety and interest to writing or presentations.

Noun Clauses can be classified by their introductory word: *that*-clauses, *wh*-clauses, *if/whether* clauses, *to-infinitive* clauses, and *ing*-clauses. The principal uses of Noun Clauses are:

- As the Subject of a Verb.

    That the plane crashed is all we know.

    How well the book will sell depends on its targeted market.

    For a bridge to collapse like that is amazing.

    Whether it rains should not be a factor.

    Telling lies is wrong.

- As a Predicate Noun.

    The reason is **that we forgot**.

    To leave a legacy is **why I became a teacher**.

    My wish is **to be wealthy**.

    His favorite pastime is **playing the piano**.

- As the Direct Object of a Verb.

    She said **that she had experience**.

    The police do not know **how the prisoner escaped**.

    I don't care **if it rains**.

    He likes **everyone to be happy**.

No one enjoys **having vertigo**.

- As the Indirect Object of a Verb.

  They gave **whoever arrived first** a door prize.

- As the Object of a Preposition.

  I was concerned by **what happened**.

  Vote for **whichever candidate you like**.

  The bloodhounds ran closer to **where the escapee was hiding**.

  I am tired of **being treated like a child**.

- In Apposition with a Noun.

  The idea **that all men are created equal** is part of America's history.

  His ambition, **to be an actor,** was never fulfilled.

- As an Objective Complement.

  We will make him **whatever we want him to be**. (Compare, "We will make him a **superstar**.")

  You can call me **what you like**.

- In Direct Address.

  Whoever wants this, come here.

- In a Nominative Absolute Construction.

  That they loved each other being obvious, their marriage was stable.

Uses of Adjective Clauses

CCSS.L.9–10.1.B:
Use various types of phrases (noun, verb, adjectival, adverbial, participial, prepositional, absolute) and clauses (independent, dependent; noun, relative, adverbial) to convey specific meanings and add variety and interest to writing or presentations.

Adjective Clauses modify nouns and pronouns.

> I bought a used car **that I could afford**.
> The teachers **who work at my school** are paid well.
> I did not know the time **when it began**.
> The neighborhood **where we lived** went downhill.

Most adjective clauses follow the nouns they modify and are introduced by relative pronouns. *Relative Adverbs* can also introduce adjective clauses: see *when* and *where* in the last two examples. Relative adverbs are connective words similar to relative pronouns, but they always modify the adverbs in their respective clauses. For example, in "where we lived," *where* introduces a clause that modifies *lived*. The principal relative adverbs are *when, where,* and *why.*

Exercise 9.4: Identifying Noun Clauses

Underline each noun clause and indicate if it is used as a subject, predicate noun, direct object, or object of a preposition.

WRITING PROMPT:
Write ten sentences with noun clauses, using them as subjects, predicate nouns, direct objects, and objects of prepositions.

CCSS.L.9–10.1.B:
Use various types of phrases (noun, verb, adjectival, adverbial, participial, prepositional, absolute) and clauses (independent, dependent; noun, relative, adverbial) to convey specific meanings and add variety and interest to writing or presentations.

1. Indeed it is not certain whether the board members would agree to participate in such a forum with such vocal opponents

2. To begin with, whoever else might benefit by Mrs. Paterson's death, her husband would benefit the most.

3. The farmer explained that he was too old to work, and his only son was killed in Vietnam, so now there was nothing for him to do but sit and wait for the bank.

4. He said he wanted everyone to know how important their support was in his final battle.

5. Reflect on what you read, paragraph by paragraph.

6. That the report of the flood was exaggerated is now generally admitted.

7. That patent monopoly has occasionally been used to the detriment of society, few would deny.

8. We want to make sure that whatever decision is taken is one that is going to benefit our own security.

9. The fact that Pontiac was born the son of a chief would in no degree account for the extent of his power.

10. The research shows the emotional impacts are huge, whether they're separated from parents on this side or on the other side of the border.

11. The Democrats emerged after the election in a stronger position.

12. Mr. Hunter, whose son served in Iraq, argues that the current bill would endanger troops by interfering with the Pentagon's ability to share intelligence with battlefield commanders.

13. The settlers took comfort in the thought that winter would soon be past.

14. Those on the right of the party opposed power sharing on the basis that it was undemocratic and that the government was surreptitiously setting this agenda.

15. I told father that in the Bible itself maxims can be found by which we may test our convictions to see whether they are reasonable and just.

CHAPTER 9

Exercise 9.5: Identifying Adjective Clauses

Underline the adjective clauses and circle the nouns they modify.

WRITING PROMPT:
Write ten sentences, each with at least one adjective clause.

CCSS.L.9–10.1.B:
Use various types of phrases (noun, verb, adjectival, adverbial, participial, prepositional, absolute) and clauses (independent, dependent; noun, relative, adverbial) to convey specific meanings and add variety and interest to writing or presentations.

1. All the Germans whom we met seemed affluent and satisfied.

2. He was a man I knew years before in Florida.

3. This is the book to which the speaker referred several times in his lecture.

4. They chose an hour when the bars were still open.

5. The neighborhood reminds me of the place where we lived back east.

6. Then I went down into the streets, which are long and flat and without end.

7. The days that make us happy make us wise.

8. At present it is the farmer who pays most dearly for the luxury of high prices.

9. Places where people work are particularly fascinating after the bustle is over.

10. The old sexton, whom I frequently saw in the churchyard, lives in the Carlyle house.

11. Like all people whose minds are very active, Einstein hated to attend to little details like this.

12. A friend who lives in Australia friended me on Facebook.

13. A man who has a lot of money is a man who has a lot of money.

14. The wind which was driving hard from the north was freezing.

15. People who are friendly by nature, of course, have a lot of friends.

16. They chose an hour when the streets were almost deserted.

17. This place is the first German city I have visited.

18. Other men are lenses through which we read our own minds.

19. All men are afraid of books, who have not handled them from childhood.

20. I could not find the Bible passage which the priest quoted.

21. The statement that the man gave to the police was made up.

22. He's never visited the city where he grew up.

23. I enjoyed reading the novel, which was on bestsellers for several weeks.

May be copied for classroom use. Common Core Grammar by Thomas Fasano (Coyote Canyon Press: Claremont, CA); © 2015.

USES OF ADVERBIAL CLAUSES

CCSS.L.9–10.1.B:
Use various types of phrases (noun, verb, adjectival, adverbial, participial, prepositional, absolute) and clauses (independent, dependent; noun, relative, adverbial) to convey specific meanings and add variety and interest to writing or presentations.

Adverbial clauses mostly modify verbs, occasionally adjectives or adverbs.

Adverbial clauses can be grouped into nine general classes, according to the kind of relationship expressed.

- Clauses of Time.

  Keats wrote the sonnet **when he was twenty-one years old**.

  They drove off **before they knew their destination**.

  Whenever you arrive, someone will greet you.

Adverbial Clauses of Time answer the question, *When?*

- Clauses of Place.

  I planted the tree **where you wanted it**.

  Wherever she is, I hope she's happy.

Adverbial Clauses of place answer the question, *Where?*

- Clauses of Manner.

  The president campaigned **as if he were bored**.

  He did his job **as he was directed**.

Adverbial Clauses of Manner answer the question, *How?*

- Clauses of Degree.

  He has taken more food **than he can eat**.

  She is older **than she looks**.

  You can be as happy **as you want to be**.

  He tries as hard **as you do**.

  She swam faster **than the others did**.

  She was so uninformed **that she hadn't a clue**.

  The gash was so deep **that it required stitches**.

Adverbial Clauses of Degree answer the questions, *How much? How little? How far?* etc.

Included under Clauses of Degree are clauses that express the idea of (a) *Comparison,* see the fourth and fifth sentences above; and (b) *Result,* see the last two.

For example, in the fourth sentence a comparison is made between how *he* tries and how *you* try; in the last sentence the result of the depth of the gash was *that it required stitches.* These clauses also indicate degree and are therefore classified under this heading.

- Clauses of Cause or Reason.

    I became a teacher **because I thought it would be rewarding**.

    As he was intoxicated, I refused to let him drive.

    You should go to this website, **for it has the information you need**.

CCSS.L.7.1.A:

Explain the function of phrases and clauses in general and their function in specific sentences.

Adverbial Clauses of Cause or Reason answer the question, *Why?*

- Clauses of Purpose.

    We lived in an apartment **in order that we might save money**.

    I kept careful notes **so that I could remember the details**.

    Some people live **that they may eat**.

Adverbial Clauses of Purpose—like clauses of Cause or Reason—answer the question, *Why?* What distinguishes them from each other is that a purpose clause carries the idea that the action was *definitely planned beforehand* with a goal in mind.

- Clauses of Condition.

    We can finish the job **provided that everyone pitches in**.

    Should you want to go later, you will need to call.

    He won't tell you **unless asked**.

CCSS.L.7.1.B:

Choose among simple, compound, complex, and compound–complex sentences to signal differing relationships among ideas.

Adverbial Clauses of Condition are frequently introduced by *if,* sometimes *should* or *unless. Provided* and *provided that* are occasionally used. These clauses state the condition or circumstance under which something will happen or be possible.

- Clauses of Concession.

    Although the car was new, it already had mechanical problems.

    I was not discouraged **though my first attempt was awful**.

    His ideas are sound **even though they often lead him astray**.

An Adverbial Clause of Concession is frequently introduced by *although,* sometimes *though* and *even though.* It concedes that the statement it makes is in apposition to that of the main clause, but asserts that the main clause is nonetheless correct.

The compound relative pronouns *whatever, whichever, whoever* and expressions like *no matter what, whatever, however much* are sometimes used in place of *although* at the beginning of clauses of concession.

> **However much** you try, nothing works.
>
> **No matter what** he said, no one believed him.
>
> **Whatever** the rift between you two, you need to get over it.

The first sentence is equivalent to "Although you try hard, nothing works."

- Complementary Clauses Modifying Adjectives

  > I'm sure **that he stole it**.
  >
  > She was happy **that we went shopping**.
  >
  > We are aware **that his work history is spotty**.
  >
  > He was careful **that no one saw him**.

This group consists of clauses used after certain adjectives, such as *sure, careful, confident, afraid, happy,* which complete the meaning of the adjectives. A few of these clauses approximate the meaning of the eight types of clauses explained above. For example, in the sentence, "She was happy *that we went shopping,*" the adverbial clause has a meaning similar to that of "She was happy *because we went shopping*" (clause of reason).

Position of Adverbial Clauses

CCSS.L.7.1.A:
Explain the function of phrases and clauses in general and their function in specific sentences.

Adverbial Clauses may:

- Follow the main clause: "I will take up painting *when I retire.*"

- Precede the main clause: "*While you slept,* the phone rang."

- Come between the subject and the verb of the main clause: "My strategy, *if it works,* will result in higher profits."

Exercise 9.6: Identifying Adverbial Clauses

Underline the adverbial clauses.

WRITING PROMPT:
Write ten sentences with
adverbial clauses.

1. Although some repairs have been made, the property still needs a lot of work.

2. She can set up a spreadsheet in Excel as quickly as she can type a document in Word.

3. He was glad that the job was done.

4. He was a man who talked as if he saw too much of life.

5. The reader, if he likes, will have to supply the missing details of this disgusting story.

6. She was sure that her purse would be found.

7. They cannot finish the job by Friday even if they work harder.

CCSS.L.9–10.1.B:
Use various types of
phrases (noun, verb, adjectival, adverbial, participial,
prepositional, absolute)
and clauses (independent,
dependent; noun, relative,
adverbial) to convey specific meanings and add variety
and interest to writing or
presentations.

8. Wherever he goes, he is welcomed, for he is an interesting raconteur.

9. I am pleased that you called on your aunt while you were here in New York.

10. Geography would be more interesting if it were taught with the help of lantern slides.

11. Although some repairs have been made, the property is still in bad condition.

12. The Captain turned on the electric stove in his cabin, for the night was cold.

13. The deck looks as though no one has been on it for years.

14. The clouds now covered the whole sky so that one could see nothing on the forecastle-head.

CCSS.L.7.1.A:
Explain the function of
phrases and clauses in
general and their function
in specific sentences.

15. She can type a letter as fast as he can dictate.

16. He was glad that the work was finished so that he could take a break from his labors.

17. If nature was comfortable, man would never have invented architecture.

18. The characters in the story are convincing, because they are the people we meet and talk to every day.

Exercise 9.7: Identifying Adverbial Clauses

Underline the adverbial clauses and indicate what part of the sentence (verb, adjective, adverb) they modify.

CCSS.L.9–10.1.B:

Use various types of phrases (noun, verb, adjectival, adverbial, participial, prepositional, absolute) and clauses (independent, dependent; noun, relative, adverbial) to convey specific meanings and add variety and interest to writing or presentations.

1. When a thief is hanged, this is not for his own amendment but for the sake of others.

2. English has changed so significantly over the years that Old English looks like a foreign language.

3. Firstly, political history and culture are seen as important in that if the ideological gap between the sharing parties is narrow, chances of a successful partnership are high.

4. Thus, as soon as this view of the world is adopted and the other discarded, a demand for a Carthaginian peace is inevitable, to the full extent of the momentary power to impose it.

5. A man's life is always more forcible than his speech.

6. My days are swifter than a weaver's shuttle.

7. The faculty meeting lasted longer than it usually does.

CCSS.L.7.1.A:

Explain the function of phrases and clauses in general and their function in specific sentences.

8. The skipper presented an unmoved breadth of back: it was the renegade's trick to appear pointedly unaware of your existence unless it suited his purpose to turn at you with a devouring glare before he let loose a torrent of foamy, abusive jargon that came like a gush from a sewer.

9. There were no major civilizations in Europe until the Minoans established themselves in the Aegean.

10. Pick out your targets carefully lest we waste our ammunition.

11. There was a joke during the Nazi period that Hitler walked on water because he could not swim.

12. The science of medicine is the body of knowledge about body systems and diseases, while the profession of medicine refers to the social structure of the group of people formally trained to apply that knowledge to treat disease.

13. Although the work was hard, the continuous breeze kept us cool throughout the day.

14. While fighting in Italy in World War II, my uncle was captured by the Germans.

15. As a result of this new medication, our son now breathes much more easily than he did before.

SUBORDINATE CONNECTIVES

CCSS.L.9–10.1.B:
Use various types of phrases (noun, verb, adjectival, adverbial, participial, prepositional, absolute) and clauses (independent, dependent; noun, relative, adverbial) to convey specific meanings and add variety and interest to writing or presentations.

A **Subordinate Clause** can be introduced by (a) a Subordinate Conjunction, (b) a Conjunctive Adverb, or (c) a Relative or an Interrogative Pronoun.

A **Subordinate Conjunction** is an introductory or connective word that introduces a subordinate clause while also connecting it to the main clause.

> The car wouldn't start **because** it was out of gas.

> **If** the car has gas it will start.

When an adverbial clause comes before the main clause, the conjunction is a connecting word despite its position at the front of the sentence.

Sometimes, as when a noun clause is used as a subject of a verb, the conjunction is purely an introductory word with little if any of the function of a connective: as, "*That* you are sick is obvious."

CCSS.L.7.1.B:
Choose among simple, compound, complex, and compound–complex sentences to signal differing relationships among ideas.

A **Conjunctive Adverb** is not a true conjunction in the way that a subordinate or coordinate conjunction is. It is an adverb that shows the logical relationship between two independent clauses. Most writers use semicolons before them. They show *comparison, cause-and-effect, contrast, sequence,* but they do so with adverbial emphasis. Common conjunctive adverbs are *also, furthermore, namely, however, instead, therefore, meanwhile, likewise, still, accordingly, consequently, hence, thus, similarly, afterwards, subsequently.*

> I felt sick and feverish; **moreover,** my dizziness was getting worse.

> Nancy didn't think the experiment proved anything; **however,** she agreed with us that it provided compelling data.

> His graduate students looked to him for guidance; **instead,** he ignored them and only met with them when required.

A **Relative or Interrogative Pronoun** performs the function of both a connective and a noun: it connects the subordinate clause to the main clause while also acting in the subordinate clause as the subject or object of the verb, an object of a preposition, or a predicate noun.

A relative pronoun functioning as a determiner is both a connective and an adjective; as, "I know *which* smartphone I prefer."

Connective Omitted before Subordinate Clause

CCSS.L.7.1.B:
Choose among simple, compound, complex, and compound–complex sentences to signal differing relationships among ideas.

Sometimes the connective is omitted before a subordinate clause if the missing word can be easily understood. This type of usage is more common in speaking than in writing.

You said ∧ you would fix it (**that** omitted).

I selected the candidate ∧ I wanted (**whom** or **that** omitted).

Be that as it may, we will proceed as usual (**though** omitted—"**though** it be as it may").

Exercise 9.8: Writing with Adverbial Clauses

Use the following adverb dependent clauses in sentences of your own.

CCSS.L.9–10.1.B:
Use various types of phrases (noun, verb, adjectival, adverbial, participial, prepositional, absolute) and clauses (independent, dependent; noun, relative, adverbial) to convey specific meanings and add variety and interest to writing or presentations.

1. (although I don't want to)

2. (as soon as you called)

3. (as if you didn't know)

4. (even though I told you)

5. (given that you knew my plans)

6. (in order that I have enough time)

7. (on condition that you try)

CCSS.L.7.1.A:
Explain the function of phrases and clauses in general and their function in specific sentences.

8. (so that it doesn't happen again)

9. (unless you help me)

10. (until I have time)

11. (wherever I want to go)

12. (provided that you come, too)

13. (since you couldn't care less)

14. (as I don't really care)

15. (after I made plans)

16. (as I am very busy)

17. (before you make a decision)

18. (if I were you)

19. (whenever I make an attempt)

20. (while I still have time)

Exercise 9.9: Identifying Independent and Dependent Clauses

Underline the clauses and identify them as independent or dependent.

CCSS.L.9–10.1.B:

Use various types of phrases (noun, verb, adjectival, adverbial, participial, prepositional, absolute) and clauses (independent, dependent; noun, relative, adverbial) to convey specific meanings and add variety and interest to writing or presentations.

1. I am free to confess that I had a realizing sense of the fact that my hospital bed was not a bed of roses just then.

2. I knew that there was a range still farther back; but except from one place near the very top of my own mountain, no part of it was visible.

3. But when I peeped into the dusky street lined with what I at first innocently called market carts, now unloading their sad freight at our door, I recalled sundry reminiscences I heard from nurses of longer standing.

4. I progressed by slow stages up stairs and down, till the main hall was reached, and I paused to take breath and a survey.

5. There was no one in the whole world who had the slightest idea what he was talking about, save those who were themselves as nutty as he was.

CCSS.L.7.1.A:

Explain the function of phrases and clauses in general and their function in specific sentences.

6. He thought it odd, and with a little perfunctory shiver, as if in deference to a seasonal presumption that the night was chill, he lay down again and went to sleep.

7. And then, in answer to my asking why this should be so, he gave me a long story of which with my imperfect knowledge of the language I could make out nothing whatever, except that it was a very heinous offence.

8. Their children had the social and educational opportunities of their time and place, and responded to good associations and instruction with agreeable manners and cultivated minds.

9. Alice started to her feet, for it flashed across her mind that she never before saw a rabbit with either a waist-coat pocket or a watch to take out of it.

10. The dust in the road was laid; trees were adrip with moisture; birds sat silent in their coverts; the morning light was wan and ghastly, with neither color nor fire.

Chapter

Sentences

10

ENGLISH LANGUAGE ARTS STANDARDS

NOTE:
Some of the skills in this chapter were introduced at lower grade levels; yet, due to the recursiveness of the language standards, they require further attention at the high school level.

☞ *CCSS.ELA-LITERACY.L.9–12.1:* Demonstrate command of the conventions of standard English grammar and usage when writing or speaking.

☞ *CCSS.ELA-LITERACY.L.9–10.1.B:* Use various types of phrases (noun, verb, adjectival, adverbial, participial, prepositional, absolute) and clauses (independent, dependent; noun, relative, adverbial) to convey specific meanings and add variety and interest to writing or presentations.

☞ *CCSS.ELA-LITERACY.L.7.1.B:* Choose among simple, compound, complex, and compound–complex sentences to signal differing relationships among ideas.

SENTENCES

CCSS.L.7.1.B:
Choose among simple, compound, complex, and compound–complex sentences to signal differing relationships among ideas.

A *sentence* is a group of words that expresses a complete thought and can stand alone.

The sentence elements previously covered—parts of speech, phrases, and clauses—are *parts of sentences*. Used alone, they don't make a complete thought or statement (at least, not in formal writing). To make a complete thought, they must be used with other parts of a sentence.

Sentences can be divided into three classifications: (1) Simple, (2) Complex, (3) Compound, and (4) Compound-Complex. These classifications are based on the number and types of clauses used in a sentence.

SIMPLE SENTENCES

CCSS.L.7.1.B:
Choose among simple, compound, complex, and compound–complex sentences to signal differing relationships among ideas.

A *Simple Sentence* is a sentence with only one group of words having a subject and a predicate. Thus, the simple sentence has only one subject and one predicate. The subject and the predicate can be either simple or compound.

> **Bob went** to work (simple subject, simple predicate).
>
> The **family traveled** to Europe and **stayed** two weeks (simple subject, compound predicate).
>
> The **man** and his **dog walked** through the park (compound subject, simple predicate).
>
> The **lawyer** and his **client stood** before the court and **pleaded** for mercy (compound subject, compound predicate).

The subject may have two or more nouns or pronouns; and the predicate, two or more verbs. But the nouns and pronouns will form one part of the sentence; and the verbs, another part.

In compound and complex sentences, which have more than one clause, each clause has a separate subject and a separate predicate.

COMPLEX SENTENCES

CCSS.L.7.1.B:
Choose among simple, compound, complex, and compound–complex sentences to signal differing relationships among ideas.

A *Complex Sentence* is a sentence with one main clause and one or more subordinate clauses.

> These idiots believe **that the earth is flat**.
>
> The book, **which was written by Herman Melville,** is an American classic.
>
> **Although the car is old,** it still runs **as if it were new**.

Sentences with a noun clause as the subject of the main clause have an unusual form for a complex sentence. Unlike most complex sentences, they do not have two *separate, complete* clauses, for the noun clause is the subject of the main clause, the latter comprising the entire sentence. They are, nonetheless, classified as complex sentences.

> **That the project is a failure** is obvious.
>
> **Whatever you decide** will be fine.

COMPOUND SENTENCES

CCSS.L.7.1.B:
Choose among simple, compound, complex, and compound–complex sentences to signal differing relationships among ideas.

A **Compound Sentence** is a sentence with two or more main clauses.

> **The alarm sounded,** |and| **everyone filed out of the building**.

> **The fire was lit,** | **the burgers were sizzling,** |and| **the aroma of cooking meat soon filled the air**.

A compound sentence can also have one or more subordinate clauses in addition to the main clauses.

> I bought a ticket **after I stood in line for ten minutes,** and then I gave it to a person **who ripped it in half and handed me back the stub**.

From a structural standpoint, a compound sentence consists of two or more simple or complex sentences combined to form a single sentence.

COMPOUND-COMPLEX SENTENCES

CCSS.L.7.1.B:
Choose among simple, compound, complex, and compound–complex sentences to signal differing relationships among ideas.

A **Compound-Complex Sentence** contains at least two main clauses (making it compound) and at least one subordinate clause (making it complex).

> While I was waiting for the bus, a man who was reading next to me on the bench told me that the last time he rode the bus he was robbed, so now he carries little money and no valuables.

A man told me is the main clause.

While I was waiting for the bus is an adverbial clause modifying the verb *told*.

Who was reading next to me on the bench is an adjective clause modifying the subject *man*.

That the last time he rode the bus he was robbed is a noun clause used as the direct object of the verb *told*.

Now he carries little money and no valuables is a main clause.

> The fire that burned over a thousand acres is said to have been started by kids setting off fireworks while a Fourth of July celebration was taking place; but if this is true, the investigators who are looking into the start of the fire cannot understand why no one saw them take the fireworks or set them off.

CCSS.L.9–12.1:
Demonstrate command of the conventions of standard English grammar and usage when writing or speaking.

The fire is said to have been started by kids setting off fireworks is the first main clause.

The investigators cannot understand why no one saw them take the fireworks or set them off is the second main clause.

That burned over a thousand acres is an adjective clause modifying the noun *fire.*

While a Fourth of July celebration was taking place is an adverbial clause modifying the infinitive *to have been started.*

If this is true is an adverbial clause modifying the verb *cannot understand.*

Who are looking into the start of the fire is an adjective clause modifying the noun *investigators.*

Why no one saw them take the fireworks or set them off is a noun clause used as the object of the verb *cannot understand.*

(Notice that the conjunction *but* does not connect the two adverbial clauses *while the Fourth of July . . .* and *if this . . . .* It connects the two main clauses, *the fire is said to have been started by kids setting off fireworks* and *the investigators cannot understand why no one saw them take the fireworks or set them off.*)

DECLARATIVE, INTERROGATIVE, IMPERATIVE, AND EXCLAMATORY SENTENCES

CCSS.L.9–10.1.B:
Use various types of phrases (noun, verb, adjectival, adverbial, participial, prepositional, absolute) and clauses (independent, dependent; noun, relative, adverbial) to convey specific meanings and add variety and interest to writing or presentations.

Sentences are commonly divided into four categories according to the manner in which the thought of the sentence is expressed: (1) Declarative, (2) Interrogative, (3) Imperative, and (4) Exclamatory.

A ***Declarative Sentence*** states something as fact. It is punctuated with a period.

> The package was delivered yesterday.
>
> He wants to be able to go.

An ***Interrogative Sentence*** asks a question. It is punctuated with a question mark.

> What are you doing?
>
> Where did he go?

An **Imperative Sentence** expresses a command or entreaty. It is punctuated with a period.

> Be there on time.
>
> We need to get going.

An **Exclamatory Sentence** expresses strong feeling or emotion, as joy, fear, anger. It is punctuated with an exclamation mark.

> How wonderful the party is!
>
> What a mess this is!

Variations in Form

CCSS.L.9–12.1:
Demonstrate command of the conventions of standard English grammar and usage when writing or speaking.

The examples above show the typical forms of sentences that state a fact, ask a question, give a command, and express strong emotion, respectively. However, there are some variations of these forms.

A **Question** might have the word order of a declarative sentence, but the interrogative meaning is understood through intonation and the use of a question mark.

> You're following this? (instead of "Are you following this?")
>
> You don't want to do this, you say?

A **Command** may be expressed:

- In the form of a question.

> Will you please hold the door for me?

Sentences of this type clearly state a command or strong request, not a question, but a question mark is sometimes used.

- In the form of a declarative sentence.

> You will have to move to the end of the line.

- In the form of a combined command and question.

> Do it for me, okay?

These forms are used when the speaker wishes to soften a command or express it more politely than typical commands permit.

An **Exclamation** may be expressed:

- In the form of a question.

  Who would have ever believed that!

  Now, why would you say that!

- In the form of a declarative sentence.

  I'm sick of this!

  Your behavior is atrocious!

- In the form of a command.

  Don't delay! Buy at once!

  Help!

In the above sentences the strong feeling is indicated by the speaker's intonation and by the exclamation mark.

Exercise 10.1: Identifying Types of Sentences

Write whether the sentences are simple, compound, complex, or compound-complex.

WRITING PROMPT:

Write ten sentences—simple, compound, complex, and compound-complex.

WRITING PROMPT:

Write about a friend's or relative's visit to your home. Use a variety of sentence patterns to make the writing interesting. Try to vary sentence lengths.

CCSS.L.9–10.1.B:

Use various types of phrases (noun, verb, adjectival, adverbial, participial, prepositional, absolute) and clauses (independent, dependent; noun, relative, adverbial) to convey specific meanings and add variety and interest to writing or presentations.

CCSS.L.7.1.B:

Choose among simple, compound, complex, and compound–complex sentences to signal differing relationships among ideas.

1. The actor was happy that he got a part in a movie although the part was a small one.

2. Some students like to study after dinner.

3. We may not have a certain composer's experience, but we can recognize his or her attitude and relate it to our own.

4. He said he was not in attendance yesterday; however, many people saw him there.

5. He is a man now; he must, therefore, stop acting childishly.

6. I hope to live in Italy eventually because it is my favorite country.

7. One dark night in midsummer a man waking from a dreamless sleep in a forest lifted his head from the earth, and staring a few moments into the blackness, said: "Catharine Larue."

8. In spite of all our anxiety, we enjoyed this search for work.

9. The night was dark, and a stiff wind was blowing from the north, as we neared the mouth of the harbor.

10. Father Brown's friend and companion was a young man with a stream of ideas and stories, an enthusiastic young man named Fiennes, with eager blue eyes and blond hair.

11. Character is what we are; reputation is what men say we are.

12. He had two alternatives; he could take the evening train, or he could go by plane the next morning.

13. He saw thatched and timbered cottages, and half-a-dozen inns with creaking signs.

14. She again opened the storm-door, and this time joined the three men and the one woman waiting for her in the big two-seated buggy.

15. He liked the other employees, he was interested in the work, but sometimes he felt the futility of it all.

16. He was well connected; yet there was something wrong with his luck, and he never got on.

Exercise 10.2: Writing Different Types of Sentences

Rewrite the compound sentences as complex and, if possible, simple.

WRITING PROMPT:

Write ten interrogative sentences about the following topics. Reply in declarative sentences: (1) The American Revolution, (2) the Pilgrim Fathers, (3) the history of your own state, (4) the government of the United States, (5) Twitter, (6) writing essays.

WRITING PROMPT:

Compare and contrast two of your teachers. Use compound sentences in your writing.

CCSS.L.9–10.1.B:

Use various types of phrases (noun, verb, adjectival, adverbial, participial, prepositional, absolute) and clauses (independent, dependent; noun, relative, adverbial) to convey specific meanings and add variety and interest to writing or presentations.

CCSS.L.7.1.B:

Choose among simple, compound, complex, and compound–complex sentences to signal differing relationships among ideas.

1. He couldn't go home, for he had no place to go.

2. I took a taxi, and she drove home.

3. Men were gathered in groups in the town square, and they seemed agitated about something.

4. He didn't want help, and he didn't ask for any.

5. I wanted to go late, but she wanted to go early.

6. Dinner was finished, so we went downtown to the opera.

7. She cooked dinner for us every night, or we went out for food.

8. She owned a car, yet she didn't drive very much.

9. The work was hard, but we enjoyed doing it.

10. Mayor Gifford had the support of the machine, and he was re-elected by a large majority.

11. He had no ticket, and therefore he was not admitted.

12. There was no moon, but we had little difficulty in keeping to the trail.

13. He has been working on the problem for over a year, and during that time he has made some striking discoveries.

14. Men were gathered in groups on the avenue, and they seemed excited over something.

15. You must return the book, or you will have to pay a fine.

16. Give them three days more, and they will have the house ready for you.

17. I met a friend at the club, and he invited me to play a game of golf with him.

18. He wants to keep his credit clear; consequently he always pays his bills promptly.

19. The soldiers marched across the field outside the village, and with their rifles at the ready they appeared to be on the verge of violence.

20. He was always talking about getting ahead and being successful, yet no one could discern exactly what it was he did for a living.

Chapter

11

Subject and Predicate

ENGLISH LANGUAGE ARTS STANDARDS

NOTE: Some of the skills in this chapter were introduced at lower grade levels; yet, due to the recursiveness of the language standards, they require further attention at the high school level.

☞ *CCSS.ELA-LITERACY.L.11–12.1.B: Resolve issues of complex or contested usage, consulting references (e.g., Merriam–Webster's Dictionary of English Usage, Garner's Modern American Usage) as needed.*

☞ *CCSS.ELA-LITERACY.L.9–10.1.B: Use various types of phrases (noun, verb, adjectival, adverbial, participial, prepositional, absolute) and clauses (independent, dependent; noun, relative, adverbial) to convey specific meanings and add variety and interest to writing or presentations.*

☞ *CCSS.ELA-LITERACY.L.7.1.A: Explain the function of phrases and clauses in general and their function in specific sentences.*

☞ *CCSS.ELA-LITERACY.L.7.1.B: Choose among simple, compound, complex, and compound–complex sentences to signal differing relationships among ideas.*

THE SUBJECT

CCSS.L.7.1.B: Choose among simple, compound, complex, and compound–complex sentences to signal differing relationships among ideas.

The first requirement of a sentence is a **Subject;** the second, a **Predicate**. Every complete sentence, therefore, must have a subject and a predicate.

The subject of a sentence is either simple or compound. Typically, the subject is the first noun or pronoun in the sentence, and it represents what the rest of the sentence is "about," although this isn't always true. In a sentence containing more than one clause, each clause has its own subject.

Simple Subject

CCSS.L.9–10.1.B:
Use various types of phrases (noun, verb, adjectival, adverbial, participial, prepositional, absolute) and clauses (independent, dependent; noun, relative, adverbial) to convey specific meanings and add variety and interest to writing or presentations.

The **Simple Subject** often consists of a single noun or pronoun. Any modifiers or adjuncts are not a part of the Simple Subject.

For example, in the sentence, "*Cats* are curious animals," the simple subject is *cats;* in the sentence, "The new *professor* from Denmark is teaching the class," the simple subject is *professor*.

Instead of a noun or pronoun, any of the following constructions can be used as the simple subject.

- An Adjective: "The *poor* pay more."

- A Gerund: "*Swimming* is great exercise."

- An Infinitive: "*To win* is fun."

- A Phrase: "*Playing the piano* is a joy."

- A Clause: "*That it's going to rain* seems certain."

- A word used as a *word* and not understood as functioning as a part of speech: "*Layman* is an interesting word."

Note. Just the simplest part of a phrase or clause, without any modifiers, is the simple subject: as, "*To play* a round of *golf* in the rain | is not much fun." "*That most* of my *students* will not major in English | is a given." (The simple subjects are italicized.)

Compound Subject

CCSS.L.7.1.A:
Explain the function of phrases and clauses in general and their function in specific sentences.

A **Compound Subject** consists of two or more simple subjects. Frequently, these simple subjects are connected by conjunctions, but not always.

The **books** and the **shelves** were sold.

Complete Subject

Both the simple and the compound subject can be modified by various adjuncts. The combined group is called the **Complete Subject**.

Athletes who have the most talent do not always rise to the top in their sport.

CCSS.L.9–10.1.B:
Use various types of phrases (noun, verb, adjectival, adverbial, participial, prepositional, absolute) and clauses (independent, dependent; noun, relative, adverbial) to convey specific meanings and add variety and interest to writing or presentations.

The principal adjuncts used to modify subjects are:

- An Adjective: "The *huge* yard | stretched to the lake."

- A Noun in Apposition: "My wife, *Sandy,* | is a beautiful woman.

- A Noun in the Possessive Case: "*Shakespeare's* plays | are immortal."

- A Phrase: "The hood *of the car* | is warped." "The man *carrying the gun* | is dangerous."

- A Clause: "The student *who sells the most tickets* | will receive a cash prize."

- Any adjunct modifying the above adjuncts.

For example, an adjective modifying the simple subject may also be modified by an adverb—"A *frighteningly* angry dog was snarling"; a participle modifying the simple subject may be modified by an adverbial phrase or clause—"A man living *how he wants to* will be happy"; or a noun used as an adjunct of the simple subject may take any of the adjuncts of a noun—"My wife, *the fetching* Mrs. Fasano, is a charming woman."

Exercise 11.1: Identifying Simple, Compound, and Complete Subjects

Underline the simple, compound, and complete subjects; identify the adjuncts that complete the subjects.

WRITING PROMPT:
Describe what you and your classmates do during class that's completely off task. Use complete sentences.

CCSS.L.9–10.1.B:
Use various types of phrases (noun, verb, adjectival, adverbial, participial, prepositional, absolute) and clauses (independent, dependent; noun, relative, adverbial) to convey specific meanings and add variety and interest to writing or presentations.

1. Citizens of a democracy have a unique responsibility.

2. After many experiments, tomatoes, peas, corn, and other vegetables were found to grow abundantly.

3. Jerry Brown, the governor of California, who was to have been the chief speaker, was unable to come to the meeting.

4. The day and the hour came, and a cold rain fell.

5. Citizens of a free country are indeed fortunate.

6. Men and women in white, doctors and nurses, turned the soil, planted seedlings, sprayed bugs, spread fertilizer.

7. The freshness of the summer morning inspired and braced him as he stood.

8. Watching a coast as it slips by the ship is like thinking about an enigma.

9. After many experiments, peaches, oranges, grapes, and other fruits were found to grow luxuriantly.

10. The sealed and sullen sunset behind the dark dome of St. Paul's had in it smoky and sinister colors.

11. More than a century ago, Captain Scott and his team set out on a doomed race to be the first humans to reach the South Pole.

12. By this time it was night again, and though the child felt cold, being but poorly clad, her anxious thoughts were far removed from her own suffering or uneasiness, and busily engaged in endeavoring to devise some scheme for their joint subsistence.

13. A huge mist, capped with black clouds, came driving towards us.

14. Before Greg understood what was happening, one of the men in line at the bank pulled out a gun and began yelling for everyone to get down.

15. On Gramps' bureau was his will, smeared, dog-eared, perforated and blotched with hundreds of additions, deletions, accusations, conditions, warnings, advice and homely philosophy.

16. By dwelling near a church a person soon contracts an attachment for the edifice.

THE PREDICATE

CCSS.L.7.1.A:
Explain the function of phrases and clauses in general and their function in specific sentences.

Typically, the part of the sentence that is not the subject is the **Predicate,** which contains the verb and any verb phrases.

The heart of the predicate is a verb. The predicate is either simple or compound.

Simple Predicate

CCSS.L.7.1.A:
Explain the function of phrases and clauses in general and their function in specific sentences.

The **Simple Predicate** consists of a single verb, like *drink*, or a single verb phrase, like *have drunk*.

> I **drink** a lot of water.

> I **have drunk** a lot of water.

Compound Predicate

CCSS.L.7.1.A:
Explain the function of phrases and clauses in general and their function in specific sentences.

The **Compound Predicate** consists of two or more verbs, frequently connected by conjunctions.

> The girls **sing** and **dance**.

> I **went** to the post office and **mailed** a package.

Complete Predicate.

CCSS.L.7.1.A:
Explain the function of phrases and clauses in general and their function in specific sentences.

The simple or compound predicate may be modified by various adjuncts. The predicate with its adjuncts is called the **Complete Predicate**.

The principal adjuncts of the predicate are:

- A Predicate Noun or Adjective: "The woman | is a *doctor*." "My neighbor | is *crazy*."

Note. A predicate noun or a predicate adjective modifies the subject; but since it is contained within the predicate, it is considered part of the predicate.

- A Noun or Pronoun used as a Direct Object: "Miles Davis | played the *trumpet.*"

- A Noun or Pronoun used as an Indirect Object: "She | baked *us* a pie."

May be copied for classroom use. Common Core Grammar by Thomas Fasano (Coyote Canyon Press: Claremont, CA); © 2015.

- An Objective Complement, either a noun or an adjective: "They | consider him an *embarrassment.*" "He | painted the house *white.*"

- A Noun in Apposition: "We met Bill Clinton, the former *president.*"

- An Adverb: "She cried *silently.*"

- An Adverbial or Noun Phrase: "The plane flew *across the Pacific.*" "William stands *to make a lot of money.*" "I want *to pay for your vacation.*"

- An Adverbial or Noun Clause: "He took the job *because it pays well.*" "His mother said *that she would drive him.*"

- Any adjunct of the preceding adjuncts. These may include just about any part of speech.

Exercise 11.2: Identifying The Predicate

Indicate the simple, compound, and complete predicates; identify the adjuncts that complete the predicates.

CCSS.L.7.1.A:

Explain the function of phrases and clauses in general and their function in specific sentences.

1. His dream of success has become a sad fantasy.

2. The smoke alarm jarred him from his nap.

3. As he watched the thugs approaching from behind the trees, a feeling of terror overcame him.

4. The two prisoners dressed as service personnel advanced cautiously toward the gate, for they knew that the guards were armed.

5. An Alaskan rescue plane dropped a package of emergency rations for a stranded party of hikers.

6. A fire truck drove through a clearing in the forest under a stormy sky.

7. His dream was now a reality.

8. The ringing of the telephone aroused him from his reverie.

9. Activity is the only road to knowledge.

10. A few ragged crows flapped by over the naked fields.

11. The captain spun around on his heel and fronted us.

12. As he watched the shadows among the trees, a strange feeling of unreality came over him.

13. Then I unhooked and closed the door, and even pushed the bolt.

14. The two men carrying heavy oak staves advanced cautiously, for they knew that the guards were armed.

15. Elizabeth, that silent, observing woman, often noted how he was rising in favor among the townspeople.

16. The party of explorers were carefully following an ill-defined trail through the jungle.

17. He shrugged his shoulders, shook his head, cast up his eyes, but said nothing.

18. Had he no friends possessed of even slight intelligence?

19. Through a clearing in the forest, we could see a lone cabin.

POSITION OF THE SUBJECT AND PREDICATE

Normal Position

CCSS.L.7.1.A:

Explain the function of phrases and clauses in general and their function in specific sentences.

The normal arrangement of an English sentence is fairly set: the subject and its adjuncts come first; the predicate and its adjuncts come next. A line can be drawn down the middle of a sentence to separate its two parts. For example:

The house that my wife and I bought | sits at the end of a cul-de-sac.

Variations from the Normal Arrangements

CCSS.L.11–12.1.B:

Resolve issues of complex or contested usage, consulting references (e.g., *Merriam–Webster's Dictionary of English Usage, Garner's Modern American Usage*) as needed.

Sometimes—for emphasis, variety, or stylistic reasons—the normal arrangement of a sentence is changed, principally by reversing the order of the subject and predicate or by giving a position of emphasis to some of the adjuncts.

- The predicate with its adjuncts precedes the subject.

  Here comes trouble!

  Quietly and quickly scampers the mouse.

- The object precedes the subject.

  Cigarette smoking, you must avoid.

  What he was up to, nobody knew.

- An adverbial construction modifying a verb is placed at the beginning of the sentence; the adverbial can be a single adverb, phrase, or clause.

  Noisily they complained.

  At noon the meeting began.

  When the dog began to bark, the intruder took off running.

In questions, the verb or part of the verb phrase precedes the subject.

  Are you happy?

  Will you **accept** this?

Introductory "It" and "There"

CCSS.L.11–12.1.B:
Resolve issues of complex or contested usage, consulting references (e.g., *Merriam–Webster's Dictionary of English Usage, Garner's Modern American Usage*) as needed.

Sometimes a sentence can be split into what is called a ***Cleft Sentence***, in which the resulting sentence with an introductory *it* or *there* has two clauses with the emphasis on the second.

> It was welcomed news **that he won**.

> It was wonderful **to see such a large turnout**.

> There will be a special **guest** here tonight.

The subjects of the above cleft sentences can easily be recognized in the following original arrangements of them, in which the *it* and *there* are absent with no alteration in meaning.

> **That he won** was welcomed news.

> **To see such a large turnout** was wonderful.

> A special **guest** will be here tonight.

In the first group of sentences, the *it* and *there* are empty grammatical elements that allow for the placement of the subject after the verbs. In these kinds of cleft sentences, *it* and *there* are ***Expletives***—meaning "fillers"—introductory words.

As an expletive, *it* is used with a form of the verb *be* with a relative clause or a *to*-infinitive phrase. Cleft sentences with *it* place the emphasis of the sentence on the word or phrase immediately following the verb *be*.

> It was **Frank** who wrecked his motorcycle in Las Vegas last summer.

> It was **his motorcycle** that Frank wrecked in Las Vegas last summer.

> It was **in Las Vegas** that Frank wrecked his motorcycle last summer.

> It was **last summer** that Frank wrecked his motorcycle in Las Vegas.

It always takes a singular verb. *There* may be followed by a singular or plural verb, depending on the number of the subject.

> It **is** time **to get busy** (single phrase subject).

> It **is** inevitable **that an asteroid will hit the earth** (single clause subject).

> It **is** true **that Beethoven went deaf and that he continued to compose** (two clauses as subject).

> There **is** one **piece** of pizza left (singular subject).

> There **are** two **pieces** of pizza left (plural subject).

May be copied for classroom use. Common Core Grammar by Thomas Fasano (Coyote Canyon Press: Claremont, CA); © 2015.

Exercise 11.3: Understanding the Position of the Subject and Predicate

Underline the subjects and predicates—simple, compound, and complete; name the adjuncts that complete each subject and predicate; identify their position.

CCSS.L.11–12.1.B:

Resolve issues of complex or contested usage, consulting references (e.g., *Merriam–Webster's Dictionary of English Usage, Garner's Modern American Usage*) as needed.

1. Safeguards have already been put in place to prevent a repetition of the accident.

2. To withdraw the money from the account was their next step.

3. For the past two years they have lived an ascetic life, he and his wife.

4. There were the deacons and other eminently pious members of his church.

5. Simon Wiesenthal, the famed hunter of Nazis, many of whom escaped to South America after the war, committed his life to tracking them down.

6. It was not easy to state the logic in simple terms although he knew the subject inside out.

7. It is almost certain that the House of Representative will resist the president's recommendation.

8. Just then a distant whistle sounded, and there was a shuffling of feet on the platform.

9. Whatever we do about it, it will probably be futile.

10. To flip the omelet carefully was the next step in preparing a delightful breakfast.

11. There were many interesting people in attendance, but I had very little to say to them.

12. The smoke of the invisible fire was coming up again.

13. Precautions have already been taken to prevent a repetition of the accident.

14. From a single chimney smoke rose in columns.

15. Never did mortal suffer what this man suffered.

16. To get the money from the bank was their next step.

17. Now they lived a very simple life, he and his mother.

18. Down the stairs and into the courtyard streamed the frenzied mob.

19. There was a huge crowd in attendance at the movie theater, but I was determined not the let that take away from my enjoyment.

Chapter

12

Elliptical and Independent Elements

ENGLISH LANGUAGE ARTS STANDARDS

NOTE:
Some of the skills in this chapter were introduced at lower grade levels; yet, due to the recursiveness of the language standards, they require further attention at the high school level.

☞ ***CCSS.ELA-LITERACY.L.9–10.1.B:*** *Use various types of phrases (noun, verb, adjectival, adverbial, participial, prepositional, absolute) and clauses (independent, dependent; noun, relative, adverbial) to convey specific meanings and add variety and interest to writing or presentations.*

☞ ***CCSS.ELA-LITERACY.L.7.1.A:*** *Explain the function of phrases and clauses in general and their function in specific sentences.*

☞ ***CCSS.ELA-LITERACY.L.7.1.B:*** *Choose among simple, compound, complex, and compound–complex sentences to signal differing relationships among ideas.*

ELLIPTICAL ELEMENTS

CCSS.L.9–10.1.B:
Use various types of phrases (noun, verb, adjectival, adverbial, participial, prepositional, absolute) and clauses (independent, dependent; noun, relative, adverbial) to convey specific meanings and add variety and interest to writing or presentations.

An ***Elliptical Sentence*** is missing a grammatical part and is thus incomplete.

These kinds of sentences are most often used in dialogue and conversation when the omitted parts can be readily supplied from context.

Because of the ellipsis, a sentence may have an amended subject or verb. Often a short phrase or a single word may carry the meaning of an entire sentence.

Ellipsis principally occurs in a simple sentence, in a main or subordinate clause, or a phrase. The following examples are general occurrences.

Simple Sentences

- Exclamations.

    How dare you! (How dare you say I do that!)

    Welcome to our home! (You are welcome to our home.)

    God be with you! (I wish for God to be with you.)

    God bless! (May God bless you.)

    Sucks! (This really sucks.)

- Commands or Requests.

    Quiet, please. (Let's be quiet, please.)

    Come here. (You come here.)

    Some more coffee, please. (Give me some more coffee, please.)

- Questions.

    Ready? (Are you ready?)

    Why the hurry? (Why are you in a hurry?)

    Why even try? (Why do you even try?)

    You want? (Do you want this?)

    You said something. **What?** (What did you say?)

    He quit his job. **Why?** (Why did he quit his job?)

    Do you see the guy running? **Which one?** (Which one do you mean?)

- Statements in Answer to a Question.

    Who bought the doughnuts? **John**. (John bought the doughnuts.)

    When did you see the movie? **Last week**. (I saw the movie last week.)

    Did you study for the test? **Of course**. (Of course, I studied for the test.)

Main Clauses in Compound and Complex Sentences

CCSS.L.7.1.B:
Choose among simple, compound, complex, and compound–complex sentences to signal differing relationships among ideas.

One more hour, and it's quitting time. (One more hour will pass.)

Mr. Smith is a politician; **his son, an engineer**. (His son is an engineer.)

What if they won't pay? (What will we do?)

If you would only listen! (If you would only listen, things would be fine.)

Subordinate Clauses

CCSS.L.7.1.B:
Choose among simple, compound, complex, and compound–complex sentences to signal differing relationships among ideas.

If necessary, you will get stitches (if it is necessary).

When last heard from, she sounded happy (when she was last heard from).

While flying a kite, he was struck by lightning (while he was flying a kite).

The report is detailed, **yet to the point** (though it is to the point).

He behaved better **than usual** (than it was usual for him to behave).

He is as old **as the hills** (as the hills are old).

I like you better **than her** (than I like her).

You can tell that to **whomever you wish** (whomever you wish to tell that to).

The graduation ceremony will commence, **rain or shine** (*if it rain or if it shine*—subjunctive verb-form).

I thought you said something (the conjunction **that** is omitted).

You're the guy they wanted (the relative pronoun **whom** (or **that**) is omitted).

Phrases

CCSS.L.7.1.B:
Choose among simple, compound, complex, and compound–complex sentences to signal differing relationships among ideas.

The participle is occasionally omitted in *Nominative Absolute Constructions*.

Game over, we left the stadium (the game being over).

The preposition is sometimes omitted.

The cat stared at the bird, **all its senses on high alert** (with all its senses on high alert).

Note. The above sentence can be viewed as omitting a participle instead of a preposition: "keeping all its senses on high alert."

The object of a preposition is occasionally omitted following a noun or pronoun in the possessive case.

He is staying **at his mother's** (at his mother's house).

I'd like to switch coats **with yours** (with your coat).

Note. A similar omission of a noun occurs when a possessive case noun or pronoun is the subject of a sentence: "Mine is the fastest car around" (My car is the fastest car around).

INDEPENDENT ELEMENTS

CCSS.L.7.1.A:
Explain the function of phrases and clauses in general and their function in specific sentences.

An ***Independent Element*** has no grammatical connection to the rest of the sentence. These elements are related in thought to the context of the sentence, but there is no grammatical connection.

The main kinds of independent elements are ***Interjections, Parenthetical Expressions,*** and ***Independent Adverbs.***

Interjections

CCSS.L.9–10.1.B:
Use various types of phrases (noun, verb, adjectival, adverbial, participial, prepositional, absolute) and clauses (independent, dependent; noun, relative, adverbial) to convey specific meanings and add variety and interest to writing or presentations.

These principally express surprise or some other strong emotion.

Hmm, interesting.

Oh, no you don't!

Hell! I will.

Alas, it's time to go home.

Mmm, delicious.

Ah, I see.

Parenthetical Expressions

CCSS.L.9–10.1.B:
Use various types of phrases (noun, verb, adjectival, adverbial, participial, prepositional, absolute) and clauses (independent, dependent; noun, relative, adverbial) to convey specific meanings and add variety and interest to writing or presentations.

These have a wide range from a short phrase with a close connection to the rest of the sentence to a complete statement thrown into the sentence almost as an afterthought.

This class, **in my estimate,** is not useful.

To be fair, I have to evaluate his work properly.

My book, **in case you didn't notice,** is a bestseller.

Your assertion, **it seems to me,** is based on prejudice.

That woman—**I don't care if you tell her this**—is a bitch.

A lot of money—**about a thousand dollars**—must be raised for the school trip.

Independent Adverbs

CCSS.L.9–10.1.B:

Use various types of phrases (noun, verb, adjectival, adverbial, participial, prepositional, absolute) and clauses (independent, dependent; noun, relative, adverbial) to convey specific meanings and add variety and interest to writing or presentations.

These sentence adverbials modify an entire sentence, not any particular word in it, and also function as a slight connective with the preceding sentence.

> **Basically,** we were tired of taking orders from him.

> **Ultimately,** my goal is to find another line of work.

These can be positioned within the sentence.

> Eight years was **indeed** a long period of time.

> He **actually** dared to stand up for himself.

Note. Sometimes the word *speaking* is used with an ***Independent Adverb***, as, "We are all, *broadly speaking,* middle class." Independent Adverbs are sometimes hyphenated with *-wise*, as, "I do not know what I want to do *work-wise.*"

Exercise 12.1: Identifying Elliptical Constructions

Underline the elliptical constructions and expand them.

WRITING PROMPT:
Write ten sentences with elliptical constructions and independent elements.

1. Millions for defense, but not one cent for tribute.

2. That done, he decided to move on.

3. Well, what if he did do it?

4. Why go today when so pressed for time?

5. The oldest was eighteen years old; the youngest, only three.

6. You will find her at the doctor's.

7. Though exhausted and disinterested, he pushed onward through rain and wind.

CCSS.L.9–10.1.B:
Use various types of phrases (noun, verb, adjectival, adverbial, participial, prepositional, absolute) and clauses (independent, dependent; noun, relative, adverbial) to convey specific meanings and add variety and interest to writing or presentations.

8. Good! But a little faster, please.

9. Your story, if not believed, will be your undoing.

10. So far, so good.

11. Books are the best of things, well used; abused, among the worst.

12. He was a failing man, no doubt of that.

13. Nine o'clock at last, and the drudging toil of the day was ended.

14. Colet moved as if to ask the critic a question.

15. Strange to say, his fame vanished almost as quickly as it came.

16. "What sort of job?" asked her father suspiciously.

17. We had to hold on while on deck, and cling to our bunks when below.

18. A gray-haired woman was sitting in a rocking-chair, her hands in her lap.

19. The story, if true, is a frightening revelation of African political corruption.

20. "Please, Your Honor," answered the drum-major, whose rubicund visage had lost all its color, "the fault is none of mine."

Review of Just About Everything So Far

Use the following words in sentences of your own, using each of the indicated parts of speech.

CCSS.L.9–12.1:
Demonstrate command of the conventions of standard English grammar and usage when writing or speaking.

1. Sleep (noun, verb)

2. Dry (adjective, verb, noun)

3. Very (adverb, adjective)

4. Express (noun, verb, adjective)

5. Bellow (verb, noun)

6. American (adjective, noun)

7. Future (adjective, noun)

CCSS.L.9–12.2:
Demonstrate command of the conventions of standard English capitalization, punctuation, and spelling when writing.

8. Tomorrow (noun, adverb)

9. Flower (noun, verb)

10. Sovereign (noun, adjective)

11. Summer (noun, verb, adjective)

12. Double (adjective, adverb, verb)

13. Well (adjective, adverb)

CCSS.L.9–10.1.B:
Use various types of phrases (noun, verb, adjectival, adverbial, participial, prepositional, absolute) and clauses (independent, dependent; noun, relative, adverbial) to convey specific meanings and add variety and interest to writing or presentations.

14. Fast (adjective, adverb, noun)

15. Content (noun, adjective, verb)

16. Last (adjective, adverb, verb, noun)

17. Down (adverb, preposition)

18. For (preposition, conjunction)

19. Home (noun, adjective, adverb)

20. Lower (adjective, adverb, verb)

21. Off (adverb, preposition, adjective)

22. Up (adverb, preposition)

23. High (adjective, adverb, noun)

24. Except (verb, preposition)

25. What (adjective, pronoun, interjection)

26. While (noun, verb)

PART II:
ADVANCED CONCEPTS

Chapter

Nouns and Pronouns

13

ENGLISH LANGUAGE ARTS STANDARDS

NOTE:
Some of the skills in this chapter were introduced at lower grade levels; yet, due to the recursiveness of the language standards, they require further attention at the high school level.

☞ **CCSS.ELA-LITERACY.L.9–12.1:** *Demonstrate command of the conventions of standard English grammar and usage when writing or speaking.*

☞ **CCSS.ELA-LITERACY.L.11–12.1.A:** *Apply the understanding that usage is a matter of convention, can change over time, and is sometimes contested.*

☞ **CCSS.ELA-LITERACY.L.9–10.1.B:** *Use various types of phrases (noun, verb, adjectival, adverbial, participial, prepositional, absolute) and clauses (independent, dependent; noun, relative, adverbial) to convey specific meanings and add variety and interest to writing or presentations.*

☞ **CCSS.ELA-LITERACY.L.9–12.2:** *Demonstrate command of the conventions of standard English capitalization, punctuation, and spelling when writing.*

☞ **CCSS.ELA-LITERACY.L.8.1.A:** *Explain the function of verbals (gerunds, participles, infinitives) in general and their function in particular sentences.*

☞ **CCSS.ELA-LITERACY.L.7.1.A:** *Explain the function of phrases and clauses in general and their function in specific sentences.*

NOMINALS

CCSS.L.7.1.A:
Explain the function of phrases and clauses in general and their function in specific sentences.

A ***Nominal*** is a word, phrase, or clause that is nounlike because it functions as a noun, a noun phrase, or a noun clause in the sentence. The term is more comprehensive than the word *noun* since nouns and pronouns and other parts of speech can be nominals.

The principal functions of nominals are:

Subject of a Verb	Objective Complement
Predicate Noun	Direct Address
Direct Object of a Verb	Nominative Absolute
Indirect Object of a Verb	Apposition

This chapter details some special uses.

COGNATE OBJECT

CCSS.L.7.1.A:
Explain the function of phrases and clauses in general and their function in specific sentences.

Some verbs that are usually intransitive may take a special kind of object known as a ***Cognate Object,*** which expresses an idea similar to that of the verb.

He died a horrible **death**.

Sally lives a charmed **life**.

Frank smiled an uneasy **smile**.

RETAINED OBJECT

CCSS.L.7.1.A:
Explain the function of phrases and clauses in general and their function in specific sentences.

A verb in the passive voice may be followed by a retained object.

The charity was given a **donation** by a benefactor.

A donation was given the **charity** by a benefactor.

The student was awarded a **scholarship** by the foundation.

A scholarship was awarded the **student** by the foundation.

Either a direct or an indirect object of a verb in the active voice can be retained as the direct object in the passive voice. Thus, the sentence, "The gallery gave the golfer a round of applause," which is in the active voice, can be changed into the passive voice in the following ways.

The golfer was given a **round** of applause by the gallery (the direct object is retained as the direct object).

A round of applause was given the **golfer** by the gallery (the indirect object is retained as the direct object).

A clause or an infinitive phrase can function as a retained object.

> They were told by the electric company **that the power would be restored soon**.

> I was instructed by my boss **to deliver the message**.

In the active voice, the above sentences would read:

> The electric company told us **that the power would be restored soon**.

> My boss instructed me **to deliver the message**.

RECIPROCAL PRONOUNS

CCSS.L.7.1.A:
Explain the function of phrases and clauses in general and their function in specific sentences.

Each other and *one another* are called ***Reciprocal Pronouns***. *Each other* refers to two people; *one another* refers to three or more.

> We hated **each other**.

> We did business with **one another**.

These constructions employ a peculiar arrangement of subject and object. For example, in the first sentence, *we* appears to be the subject of the verb, and *each other* appears to be the direct object. Grammatically, *we* includes both *each* and *other;* seen this way, *each* is the subject and *other* is the object; *we* is a kind of "filler" word. The sentence can thus be revised as, "*Each* hated the *other*."

SPECIAL FORMS OF APPOSITION

Introduced by "Namely," etc.

CCSS.L.7.1.A:
Explain the function of phrases and clauses in general and their function in specific sentences.

A noun in apposition can be introduced by several words or phrases: *namely, that is, or, for example,* and *such as*.

> Two administrators—**namely, the principal and the assistant principal—** were arrested.

> The commander-in-chief, **that is, the president,** will have to decide.

> One must avoid excessive sodium, **or common table salt,** in order to control one's blood pressure.

> Some states, **for example, Texas,** have the death penalty.

Certain prices, **such as that for audio CDs,** remain stubbornly high.

A noun introduced by *for example* and *such as* is not a complete appositive because it represents only part of the meaning of the preceding noun: thus, in the second to last sentence, *Texas* is only one of the *states*.

A Noun Introduced by "As"

CCSS.L.7.1.A:
Explain the function of phrases and clauses in general and their function in specific sentences.

As is used to introduce a certain kind of appositive with some of the meaning of an adverb.

I have never respected him **as a musician**.

Grammar, **as a subject,** is interesting.

You, **as a homeowner,** have many responsibilities.

In the first sentence *musician* is in apposition with *him*, but *as a musician* also acts as a kind of adverb: it indicates in what manner I respect him. In the third sentence, *as a homeowner* carries some of the idea of reason ("You have responsibilities *because you are a homeowner*.")

A variation of this construction occurs when the second noun to be in apposition with another noun or pronoun in the possessive case

David's reputation as a **teacher** is sound.

Two nouns in apposition are frequently in the same case; therefore, a more usual construction would be "the reputation of David as a teacher." Nevertheless, the above construction is an acceptable idiom.

Note. Expressions like "my wife Sandy's car," which has different case forms for the nouns in apposition, are regarded as idiomatic.

Introduced by "Of"

CCSS.L.7.1.A:
Explain the function of phrases and clauses in general and their function in specific sentences.

Some nouns show apposition by the use of the preposition *of*, the appositive being the object of the preposition.

City of Los Angeles, state of California, county of Los Angeles, District of Columbia, island of Barbados, title of supervisor, firm of Goldberg and Hammer.

A Clause or a Phrase

CCSS.L.7.1.A:
Explain the function of phrases and clauses in general and their function in specific sentences.

A noun may be used in apposition with a clause.

> The overdue fines at the library are excessive, **a situation** that I need to avoid in the future.

Here the central idea of the main clause is summed up in one word, *situation*, which furnishes an antecedent for the following relative clause. This kind of construction is used in order to avoid a loose reference between a relative pronoun and a clause as an antecedent.

A noun clause or phrase may be used in apposition with a noun.

> The idea **that the fire started spontaneously** proved to be wrong.

> My initial response, **to call the police,** was the right thing to do.

> I love my job, **teaching high school English**.

Separated from Its Noun

CCSS.L.7.1.A:
Explain the function of phrases and clauses in general and their function in specific sentences.

A noun in apposition does not always immediately follow the noun with which it is in apposition.

> The old **textbooks** were piled on the shelf, a **reminder** of my college days (**reminder** is in apposition with **textbooks**).

> **He** handled the saw with authority, a journeyman **carpenter** with many years of experience (**carpenter** is in apposition with **He**).

OBJECTIVE COMPLEMENT

CCSS.L.7.1.A:
Explain the function of phrases and clauses in general and their function in specific sentences.

A Pronoun may be used as an *Objective Complement*.

> He did consider you **that**.
> You deemed him **what?**

A phrase or a clause may be used as an objective complement.

> They take me **for a fool**.
> You can consider me **whatever you want**.

Sometimes the word *as* introduces an objective complement.

> They judged him **as the winner**.
>
> He kept her **as a prisoner** in his cellar.
>
> I chose a Doberman **as a watchdog**.

In these constructions *as* is nothing more than an introductory word the main function of which is to create a smooth transition to the objective complement.

An objective complement with an introductory *as* occasionally carries the meaning of an adverbial element.

> They saw him **as** a nice **person**.

In this sentence, the expression *as a nice person* has some of the meaning of an adverbial phrase of manner, indicating *how* they considered him; compared with "they *considered* him *a nice person*," its relation to an objective complement is obvious.

Note. In "They considered him to be a nice person," the infinitive phrase may be regarded as an objective complement introduced by *to be.* Or the whole expression "him to be a nice person" may be regarded as an infinitive phrase with the subject *him,* the phrase itself being used as the direct object of the verb *considered.* When nouns and pronouns are objective complements, *to be* can serve as a test for the construction.

"THAT," "WHICH," "WHO," AND "WHOM"

CCSS.L.11–12.1.A:
Apply the understanding that usage is a matter of convention, can change over time, and is sometimes contested.

That is used solely in restrictive relative clauses; *who* and *which* are used in either restrictive or nonrestrictive clauses.

Contrary to what is often taught, there is nothing wrong with using *which* to introduce a restrictive relative clause, as in *The camera **which** cost me over five hundred dollars takes great pictures.* In fact, with some restrictive clauses, *which* is the only option, such as *That which doesn't kill you makes you stronger* and *The basket in which I put the flowers is made of wicker.* Even when not strictly called for, the word is often used to great effect, as in the Book of Matthew's "Render therefore unto Caesar the things **which** are Caesar's" and Franklin Roosevelt's "a day **which** will live in infamy."

Who is preferred to *that* when the antecedent is personal (people *who* visit me); but *that* is preferred to *who(m)* when it is an object in order to avoid the *who/whom* choice (the people *that* I visit).

A *Restrictive Clause* explains which person or thing you are talking about; that is, it restricts the comment to that particular person or thing. Without its inclusion, the meaning of the sentence would be altered (see the first six example sentences below).

A **Nonrestrictive Clause** gives further information that is not needed to identify the person, place, or thing that is spoken of. The nonrestrictive clause, which is set off with commas, may be omitted without changing the essential meaning of the sentence (see the last four example sentences below). *Which* should follow a comma or a preposition. Careful writers are mindful of this distinction; bad writers are not.

> The woman **who** (or **that**) hired me now works for another company (restrictive).
>
> We need to understand the things **that** are important to people.
>
> The gentleman **that** (or **who**(**m**)) we met last week is here tonight.
>
> The table **that** we bought last year collapsed.
>
> The boy **that** (or **towards whom**) the dog ran (**towards**) is our neighbor.
>
> The tree **that** (or **behind which**) the boy hid (**behind**) is ours.
>
> Apple, **which** (not **that**) employs thousands of people worldwide, is a good investment (nonrestrictive).
>
> The house, (**in**) **which** my wife and I have lived (**in**) for over ten years, is worth twice its former market price.
>
> My father, **who** (not **that**) was an engineer, retired to Florida.
>
> My twin brother, (**to**) **who**(**m**) I correspond (**with**) often, is coming to visit next week.

When the antecedent is long and complex, *wh*-pronouns are preferred.

> I have many interests outside my teaching career **which** give me great joy.
>
> I have a son attending college back east **who** never calls.

If the relative pronoun is not the subject of the relative clause, the pronoun can be deleted: the clause will then have an "understood" relative pronoun.

> The gentleman we met last week is here tonight.
>
> The table we bought last year collapsed.
>
> The boy the dog ran towards is our neighbor's.
>
> The tree the boy hid behind is ours.

When the verb in the relative clause is *be*, the pronoun must be *that* or "zero": for example, "The president is not the man *that* he was when first elected." "The president is not the man he was when first elected."

NOUNS USED AS ADJECTIVES AND AS ADVERBS

CCSS.L.9–12.1:
Demonstrate command of the conventions of standard English grammar and usage when writing or speaking.

A noun with the value of a prepositional phrase can be used as an adjective in elliptical constructions in which the preposition is omitted.

The pond is the **color** of mud (of a mud color).

The boots are a **size** too small (of a size) .

The rope is just the right **length** (of just the right length).

A noun used as an adverb can modify an adjective or an adverb.

You are ten **pounds** heavier.

She commutes five **miles** farther.

School starts a **month** earlier.

My old Mac is worth five hundred **dollars** (**worth** is an adjective)

The tomato plant is a **foot** taller.

In a year he's grown six **inches** taller.

Exercise 13.1: Identifying Special Function of Nominals

Underline the cognate objects, retained objects, reciprocal pronouns, special forms of apposition, objective complements, and nouns used as adverbs and adjectives.

WRITING PROMPT:
Write about a famous person who has inspired you. Use different forms of apposition to help you combine sentences.

CCSS.L.9–12.1:
Demonstrate command of the conventions of standard English grammar and usage when writing or speaking.

1. Each of the employees was allotted his share of the bonus.

2. A community organizer by the name of Obama was making himself a leader in the Chicago political scene.

3. Prime Minister James Callaghan was the loser of a parliamentary vote of confidence.

4. The reputation of Milton as a writer of political and religious prose is eclipsed by his fame as a poet.

5. They disliked each other intensely, but for no particular reason.

6. He had what they all dreamed of having—a family, a home, a career, money, and the respect of colleagues.

7. He has several hobbies, such as collecting old typewriters and playing the piano.

8. Advances in medicine succeed one another.

9. The river crested a yard higher than yesterday.

10. Scientific inventions succeeded one another.

11. Each of the crew was allotted his share of the booty.

12. A country lawyer by the name of Lincoln was making himself a leader in the anti-slavery campaign.

13. For it all came to this: I was nearly thirty-three years of age.

14. Then first did I know myself for a sun-worshiper.

15. The prime minister was given a vote of confidence by the House.

16. It revelled all through my head till sunrise again, a frantic and tireless nightmare.

17. The continent, however, was not so limited. It stretched nearly three thousand miles farther.

COMMON CORE GRAMMAR

Exercise 13.2: Understanding Relative Clauses

Provide the correct relative pronoun, labeling the clause as restrictive or nonrestrictive.

CCSS.L.9–12.1:

Demonstrate command of the conventions of standard English grammar and usage when writing or speaking.

1. This is the man _____ I recommended.

2. The man _____ I recommended is from California.

3. The man _____ brought the portfolio is not the one _____ I recommended.

4. I told Wilma, _____ I knew would keep my secret.

5. I told Wilma, _____ I knew I could trust.

6. I told Wilma, _____ I knew to be trustworthy.

7. I told Wilma _____ I knew for a long time.

8. No one _____ you know lives on this street.

9. All _____ I can say is, I am sorry.

10. Give me the same drink _____ I ordered yesterday.

11. A dog, _____ showed his teeth and growled, blocked the way.

12. Choose the partner _____ you like best.

13. The policeman was leading a little child _____ was separated from her mother.

14. Take the measures _____ seem to you necessary.

15. My shirt is the same size _____ yours is.

16. This is the picture _____ I am so proud of.

17. This is the picture of _____ I am so proud.

18. The man _____ is talking to Henry is the one _____ owns this house.

19. The guy standing outside the bank is the one _____ the police have been watching for several days.

20. The guy standing outside the bank is the one _____ the police believe robbed several banks in the area.

21. The robber is person about _____ the newspapers have been writing.

MISCELLANEOUS NOMINALS

CCSS.L.9–12.1:
Demonstrate command of the conventions of standard English grammar and usage when writing or speaking.

Various constructions are used as substitutes for nouns and pronouns.

Gerund and Gerundive Phrase: "I love *cooking.*" "He confessed to *embezzling funds.*"

Infinitive and Infinitive Phrase: "She wanted *to write.*" "*To meet the deadline* will require hard work."

Clause: "*What you wish for* might come true." "I know *that they were lying.*"

Adjective: "The *neediest* are usually the *most appreciative.*"

Adverb: "How do we get out of *here?*"

Any word used as a word that names itself: "*Sneaked* (not *snuck*) is the proper past tense of *sneak.*"

"As"

CCSS.L.9–12.1:
Demonstrate command of the conventions of standard English grammar and usage when writing or speaking.

As may be part of a phrase acting as a relative pronoun with *such* and *same.*

Such of the movies **as** I've seen this summer are boring ("Those of the movies **that** I've seen.")

Such funding **as** is needed will be allocated.

Such a performance **as** this will not be forgotten.

He gave the **same** excuse **as** you did.

After *same,* the relative pronoun *that* is regularly used instead of *as.*

Obama swore on the same Bible **that** Lincoln did.

I am in the same situation **that** I was in last year. ("I am in the same position **as** I was in last year.")

As has a special use as a relative pronoun, shown in the following sentences, in which the relative clause is unessential and thus parenthetical.

The phone no longer works properly, **as she began to demonstrate**.

I am, **as you know,** not happy about the outcome.

His prediction was correct, **as later events proved**.

As everyone knows, we are living in a digital age.

As expected, he was reelected (elliptical—"as was expected").

In constructions such as these, *as* generally refers to the entire statement and not to a definite antecedent, in the same manner that *which* is used by some writers to refer to a whole clause. Thus, the first sentence above is equivalent to "The phone no longer works properly, *which* (*a fact which*) the speaker began to demonstrate." The second sentence might read, "I am not happy about the outcome, *which* (*a fact which*) you know."

"But"

CCSS.L.9–12.1:
Demonstrate command of the conventions of standard English grammar and usage when writing or speaking.

But can be regarded as a relative pronoun equivalent to *that—not, which—not,* or *who—not,* as shown in the following sentence.

> There is not a wife in the west country/**But** has heard of the well of St. Keyne. (Robert Southey.)

But in this type of construction can be viewed as a conjunction introducing a clause whose subject is not expressed: thus, "There is not a wife in the west country *but* (who) has (not) heard of the well of St. Keyne."

"How" Plus an Infinitive

CCSS.L.8.1.A:
Explain the function of verbals (gerunds, participles, infinitives) in general and their function in particular sentences.

How, when, where, whether, what, or *who,* when followed by an infinitive, is used as a noun equivalent.

> She did not know **what to talk about** (object of the verb).
>
> I have yet to decide **whether to accept the offer.**
>
> The problem of **how to repair the bridge** was addressed by our finest engineers (object of the preposition **of**).
>
> **Where to go on vacation** is fun to decide (subject of the verb).

"For" Plus an Infinitive

CCSS.L.8.1.A:
Explain the function of verbals (gerunds, participles, infinitives) in general and their function in particular sentences.

A construction with the preposition *for* followed by an infinitive with a subject can be used as a noun-equivalent.

> **For you to think so** would be unwise (subject of the verb).
>
> She said **for you to bring home milk** (object of the verb).

May be copied for classroom use. Common Core Grammar by Thomas Fasano (Coyote Canyon Press: Claremont, CA); © 2015.

Exercise 13.3: Identifying Miscellaneous Nominals

Underline the less common words, phrases, and clauses used as nominals.

CCSS.L.9–12.1:

Demonstrate command of the conventions of standard English grammar and usage when writing or speaking.

1. In those early days, crossing the desert was a long and grueling undertaking.

2. We took only such articles of clothing as could be packed in our carry-on luggage.

3. For him to coordinate all these details without much assistance is distinctly noteworthy.

4. Instead of writing a letter to the editor, he left a comment on their webpage detailing every nuance of his opinion.

5. He asked for me to mail him the book.

6. The best plan for our retirement is to spend the winter in Lakeland, Florida.

7. If the trees around his house were on fire, as he supposed, he would have a hard time getting out.

8. We waited for such a time as was expedient.

9. He is the same age that his cousin is.

10. He was, as we later learned, the representative of a Turkish trader.

11. In those early days crossing the Great American Desert was a long and arduous undertaking.

12. We took only such articles as could be packed in a handbag.

13. They told us that our best plan now was to keep to the northward.

14. This afternoon Hannibal was fortunate in having an end seat.

15. To read well, that is, to read true books in a true spirit, is a noble exercise.

16. It seems he knows how to speak to his contemporaries.

17. For him to handle all this detail without help is manifestly impossible.

18. Instead of writing a letter to the auditors, he sent a cablegram asking them to meet him in New York.

GENDER

CCSS.L.9–12.1:
Demonstrate command of the conventions of standard English grammar and usage when writing or speaking.

The Masculine and Feminine Genders are distinguished:

By the use of male and female nouns: as, *bachelor, spinster; father, mother; uncle, aunt; monk, nun; brother, sister; nephew, niece.*

By the use of suffixes.

- Common suffixes added to masculine nouns to mark them as feminine gender are *-ess, ix, ine, e*: as, *prince, princess; count, countess, waiter, waitress; tiger, tigress; lion, lioness; god, goddess; host, hostess; millionaire, millionairess; poet, poetess; executor, executrix; dominator, dominatrix; hero, heroine; fiancé, fiancée.*

- A few feminine words are marked with a masculine suffix: as, *bride, bridegroom; widow, widower.*

Several words borrowed from foreign languages retain their original masculine and feminine endings: *alumnus, alumna* (plural, *alumni, alumnae*); *stimulus, stimuli; corpus, corpora; genus, genera; curriculum, curricula; bacterium, bacteria; criterion, criteria; index, indices.*

By the placement of a gender-specific word (masculine or feminine) either before or after another word: as, *manservant, maidservant; he-goat, she-goat; billy-goat, nanny-goat; chairman, chairwoman; foreman, forewoman; landlord, landlady.*

Some words have specific masculine and feminine forms: as, *king, queen; earl, countess; bachelor, spinster; fox, vixen; drake, duck; buck, doe; bull, cow; boar, sow; ram, ewe; stallion, mare; gander, goose; cock, hen; dog, bitch; stag, hind; colt, filly.*

For some words, the masculine form is preferred for the common gender: that is, for referring to both males and females: thus *usher* (masculine form) is commonly used to indicate both men and women (despite the existence of the feminine *usherette*); *alumnus* and *poet* are preferred to *alumna* and *poetess.*

FORMS FOR THE PLURAL NUMBER

CCSS.L.9–12.2:
Demonstrate command of the conventions of standard English capitalization, punctuation, and spelling when writing.

Most nouns form the plural by adding *-s* or *-es* to the singular: as, *day, days; month, months; church, churches.*

Some nouns ending in *f* or *fe* change the *f* to *v* before adding *-es* or *-s* for the plural: as, *elf, elves; knife, knives; loaf, loaves; thief, thieves.* Other nouns ending in *f* or *fe* take a regular plural form; as, *belief, beliefs; chief, chiefs; cliff, cliffs; roof, roofs*.

Nouns ending in *y* preceded by a consonant change the *y* to *i* and add -*es*: as, *sky, skies; lady, ladies; penny, pennies*. (The *y* is not changed to *i* after a vowel: as, *toy, toys; way, ways*.) The exception is for nouns ending in -*quy*: as *soliloquy, soliloquies; colloquy, colloquies*.

Words ending in -*o* preceded by a vowel add -*s*: *cameos, radios, duos, ratios, folios, studios*. Most words ending in -*o* preceded by a consonant add -*s*: *albinos, burros, armadillos, cantos, banjos, casinos*. Exceptions include *echoes, potatoes, cargoes, mottoes*. Words ending in -*oo* add -*s*: *kangaroos, cuckoos, tattoos, coos*.

Words ending in particular sounds (*ch, sh, j, s, x,* or *z*) form the plural in -*es*: *churches, aliases, boxes, ages, cases, mazes, edges, losses*.

Proper nouns ending in *y* form the plural by retaining the *y*: the two former *Germanys*; all the *Tom, Dick, and Harrys* of the world.

PLURAL MEANINGS:
Some words have two forms for the plural, each with a different meaning: *staff, die, cherub, index, stamen, pea, cloth, seraph, brother, penny, genius.*

Three nouns take -*en*: as, *brother, brethren* (in a religious sense); *child, children; ox, oxen*.

Seven nouns form the plural by changing the vowel: as, *man, men; foot, feet; goose, geese; mouse, mice; woman, women; tooth, teeth; louse, lice*.

Some foreign nouns absorbed into English retain their original plural forms: as, *millennium, millennia; medium, media; ultimatum, ultimata; bacillus, bacilli; locus, loci; larva, larvae; nebula, nebulae; index, indices; appendix, appendices; matrix, matrices; analysis, analyses; parenthesis, parentheses; corrigendum, corrigenda; addendum, addenda; analysis, analyses*. Many nouns in this class also take a regular plural form: as, *cacti, cactuses; aquaria, aquariums; vortices, vortexes; concerti, concertos*.

For compound nouns, the sign of the plural is suffixed to either the first or last member of the compound, as, *close-ups; spoonfuls; forget-me-nots; notaries public; passersby; drive-bys; court-martials* or *courts-martial; attorney generals* or *attorneys general; Knights-Templar* or *Knights-Templars; battles royal; poets laureate*.

The plural of letters, numerals, and abbreviations add *'s*: dot your *i's* and cross your *t's*; in the *1890's* (or, increasingly, *1890s*); two *Ph.D.'s* (or, increasingly, *Ph.D.s*).

Some nouns have the same form for the singular and the plural: as, *corps, deer, dozen, fish, heathen, Chinese, Japanese, Portuguese, salmon, sheep, swine, trout, trousers, breeches, knickers, pants, pajamas, shorts, drawers, clothes, bison, moose, salmon, swine, pickerel, shad, grouse, reindeer, sheep*.

Exercise 13.4: Knowing Correct Forms of the Plural

Give the plural form for the following nouns.

WRITING PROMPT:
Write sentences in which the following words are used in the singular number: strata, phenomena, alumnae, alumni, candelabra, species, cherubim, errata, bacteria, Japanese, beaux, vertebrae, Messers., theses, oases.

1. wharf
2. gulf
3. self
4. knife
5. staff
6. thief
7. chief
8. dwarf
9. scarf
10. calf
11. piano
12. volcano
13. solo
14. lily
15. monkey
16. potato
17. louse
18. 8
19. w
20. and
21. two
22. curriculum
23. stratum
24. fungus
25. nebula
26. axis
27. German

28. radius
29. lens
30. moose
31. wharf
32. index
33. piano
34. thesis
35. 4
36. 500
37. p
38. q
39. and
40. syllabus
41. staff
42. die
43. s
44. t
45. seraph
46. hero
47. stimulus
48. crisis
49. elf
50. heathen
51. brother-in-law
52. July
53. spoonful
54. memorandum

CASE

CCSS.L.9–12.1:
Demonstrate command of the conventions of standard English grammar and usage when writing or speaking.

The principal uses of cases with nouns and pronouns are:

The **Nominative Case** is used for a Subject of a Verb, a Predicate Noun, a word in Direct Address, and a noun in a Nominative Absolute construction.

The **Objective Case** is used for a Direct or Indirect Object of a Verb, an Object of a Preposition, and a noun used as an Objective Compliment.

A noun in Apposition has the same case as the noun with which it is in apposition.

The **Possessive Case** denotes possession.

Special uses of cases are given below.

Subject of an Infinitive

CCSS.L.8.1.A:
Explain the function of verbals (gerunds, participles, infinitives) in general and their function in particular sentences.

The **Subject of an Infinitive** is in the objective case.

> I know **him** to be honest.
>
> I heard **her** sing.
>
> Let **me** leave.

After some verbs, as in the last two examples, the *to*-marker of the infinitive is omitted. These two sentences are equivalent to "I heard her (to) sing," "Let me (to) leave." The last sentence can be compared to "Allow me *to* leave."

The idiomatic expression *let's* in expressions like "*Let's* go to the park" is a contraction of *Let us*, in which *us* serves as the subject of the following infinitive. In "*Let's you and me* clean the house," *you* and *me* are in apposition with *us* ("Let *us*, *you* and *me*, clean the house.") The pronouns are in the objective case to agree with the case of *us*. "Let's you and *I*...," though common, is incorrect.

Predicate Noun after an Infinitive

CCSS.L.8.1.A:
Explain the function of verbals (gerunds, participles, infinitives) in general and their function in particular sentences.

A Predicate Noun after an Infinitive is in the objective case, therefore agreeing with the subject of the infinitive.

> I wanted him to be **her**.
>
> The police believed the suspect to be **him**, the alleged killer.

In Exclamations

CCSS.L.9–12.1:
Demonstrate command of the conventions of standard English grammar and usage when writing or speaking.

The nominative, objective, and possessive cases are all used in *Exclamations*.

> **We!** We couldn't care less!
>
> Excuse **me!**
>
> **My!** How sorry you are!

Elliptical Constructions

CCSS.L.9–12.1:
Demonstrate command of the conventions of standard English grammar and usage when writing or speaking.

The possessive case of a noun or pronoun can give the appearance of being used—instead of the nominative or objective case—for the subject of a verb, a predicate noun, an object of a verb, or an object of a preposition.

> **Alan's** is the better boat (Alan's boat is the better one).
>
> That car is my **wife's** (my wife's car).
>
> My phone died, so William lent me **his** (his phone).
>
> You have an appointment at the **dentist's** tomorrow morning (dentist's office).
>
> Pumpkins are for sale at my **grocer's** (grocer's store).

In these elliptical constructions the possessive case nouns and pronouns fill in for the omitted subjects, predicate nouns, and objects omitted after the possessives.

The following sentences demonstrate the substitution of a pronoun in the possessive case for another while achieving the kind of ellipsis as described above.

> **Mine** is the faster car.
>
> Hand me **yours**.

In this manner, the first sentence is equivalent to "*My car* is the faster car." The subject *car* has been omitted and the word *mine* substituted for *my*.

The Double Possessive

CCSS.L.9–12.1:
Demonstrate command of the conventions of standard English grammar and usage when writing or speaking.

In this construction the idea of possession is expressed by both a prepositional phrase beginning with *of* and a noun or pronoun in the possessive case used as the object of the preposition.

She is a friend of **mine**.

Needlework is a pastime of my **wife's**.

This type of construction is a well-established idiom.

Exercise 13.5: Identifying Case

Identify the special case forms of the nouns and pronouns.

CCSS.L.9–12.1:

Demonstrate command of the conventions of standard English grammar and usage when writing or speaking.

1. The earplugs are on sale at your druggist's.

2. She will send you some of hers.

3. Let's tell them the whole story.

4. We found him to be a loyal benefactor of the arts.

5. Let her pay for it herself.

6. We believed the embezzler to be him.

7. Oh my! I didn't want to do that.

8. Dear me! What shall we do about it?

9. I am an acquaintance of hers, but not an actual friend.

10. He thought them to be us.

11. The lotion is on sale at your druggist's.

12. He will send you some of his.

13. Let's tell them the whole story.

14. We found him to be a staunch supporter of the cause.

15. No discontent would be theirs.

16. Let him pay for it himself.

17. The world is his who can see through its pretensions.

18. We believed the stranger to be her.

19. Oh my! I didn't mean to do that.

20. He had blue eyes in that old face of his which were amazingly like a boy's.

21. Dear me! What shall we do about it?

22. I am an acquaintance of his, but not a friend.

23. She thought them to be us.

24. He was a man whom I thought to be honest.

25. I like mine better than yours.

26. They considered her to be an artist.

AGREEMENT OF PRONOUN AND ANTECEDENT

A pronoun agrees with its antecedent in person, number, and gender.

"Everybody," "Each"

CCSS.L.9–12.1:
Demonstrate command of the conventions of standard English grammar and usage when writing or speaking.

A singular pronoun is used with an indefinite antecedent: as, *everybody, each, anybody, somebody, neither, either* or a word or phrase preceded by *every* or *each*.

> Everybody must play **his** part (not their part).
>
> Each of the groups will have **its** spokesperson.
>
> Somebody left **his** keys.
>
> Neither of the girls knew what **she** needed.
>
> Every man and woman must do what **he** can to contribute.
>
> Each desk in this classroom must be left where you found **it** (not **them**).

The above rule can create an ambiguous reference when the group of people indicated by the antecedent consists of males and females. No difficulties arise, however, when the group consists of, or is presumed to consist of, males only or females only, in which case the pronoun will be either masculine or feminine respectively.

> Everybody (in the fraternity) took **his** seat.
>
> Everybody (in the sorority) took **her** seat.

Traditional grammar has always recommended that a masculine pronoun refer to groups of people. Despite the ambiguity and sexism of the reference, it is still customary to use the masculine pronouns *his, he,* and *him* since there is no singular, third person pronoun of common gender.

> Everybody at the meeting expressed **his** surprise (**everybody** includes both men and women).

CCSS.L.11–12.1.A:
Apply the understanding that usage is a matter of convention, can change over time, and is sometimes contested.

The use of the masculine pronoun is arbitrary and points out an illogical relation between pronoun and antecedent. Careful writers can avoid the ambiguous reference by using the phrase *his or her:* "Everybody at the meeting expressed *his or her* surprise." This construction is awkward and inelegant and should be used only when a special exactness in the reference of the pronoun is required. Reconstructing the sentence may be the best alternative.

All the members expressed **their** surprise. (Nonsexist "their")

Everybody expressed surprise.

"Either—Or"

CCSS.L.9–12.1:

Demonstrate command of the conventions of standard English grammar and usage when writing or speaking.

When the antecedent consists of two nouns or pronouns connected by the conjunctions *either—or, neither—nor,* or *or,* a singular pronoun is used if the separate parts of the antecedent are singular, a plural pronoun if the parts are plural.

Either the **owner** of the firm or his **son** will give us **his** best advice.

Neither the **supervisors** nor the **clerks** have finished **their** work.

I can ask **him** or his **boss** for **his** key.

When the parts are of different persons, numbers, or genders, the pronoun agrees with the nearer antecedent.

Neither the **father** nor his **sons** are restrained in **their** opinions.

Collective Nouns

CCSS.L.9–12.1:

Demonstrate command of the conventions of standard English grammar and usage when writing or speaking.

A singular or plural pronoun may be used as the antecedent of a collective noun, depending on whether the group represented by the noun is thought of as acting as a unit or as individuals.

The committee agreed on **its** final report.

The congregation was divided in **their** thoughts about the nativity scene.

"One"

CCSS.L.9–12.1:

Demonstrate command of the conventions of standard English grammar and usage when writing or speaking.

When the indefinite pronoun *one* functions as an antecedent, the pronoun referring to it can be *one* or *one's.* More commonly, *he, him,* and *his* are used for such reference. *She, her,* and *hers* are also used.

One will find out that **one's** education is insufficient for what **one** wants to accomplish.

One will find out that **his** education is insufficient for what **he** wants to accomplish (or **her** and **she**).

Both ways are correct.

PRONOUNS WITHOUT DEFINITE ANTECEDENTS

Indefinite Plurals

CCSS.L.9–12.1:
Demonstrate command of the conventions of standard English grammar and usage when writing or speaking.

The plural forms of the personal pronouns can be used indefinitely in the sense of *one, a person, people in general.*

> After further consideration, **we** have decided to pass on your offer.
>
> There are exits on either side of **you**.
>
> **They** say the medicine has many side effects.

Indefinite "Your"

CCSS.L.9–12.1:
Demonstrate command of the conventions of standard English grammar and usage when writing or speaking.

The possessive case *your* is similarly used in a few expressions:

> You have **your** Democrats and **your** Republicans.

Note. It may be better to revise this kind of indefinite construction in formal writing.

Indefinite "It"

CCSS.L.9–12.1:
Demonstrate command of the conventions of standard English grammar and usage when writing or speaking.

The pronoun *it* is used indefinitely in a number of constructions.

- In some statements about the weather, time, etc.

> **It** is hot today.
>
> **It** is snowing.
>
> **It** sounds like rain.
>
> **It** is almost noon.
>
> **It** is time for us to leave.

- As an introductory word used to emphasize a particular word or phrase near the beginning of the sentence.

> **It** is you I want to talk to (emphasizes **you**).
>
> **It** was here that we were married (emphasizes **here**).
>
> **It** is a long wait at the airport.

> **It** is a day's drive to New York.
>
> **It** seems only a short time since we got here.
>
> **It** was in California that I met my wife.
>
> **It** is for this reason that I quit my job.
>
> **It** is what we do that matters most.

The gain in emphasis in the above sentences is obvious, especially when compared with the following:

> I want to talk to **you**.
>
> We were married **here**.

- As an *Expletive*—a filler word with little or no meaning—standing for an infinitive or a clause that follows the verb and is the real subject of the sentence.

  > **It** is rumored that he stole the money (**that he stole the money** is rumored).
  >
  > **It** is difficult to know what to say (**to know what to say** is difficult).

- As an *Expletive* standing for the direct object.

  > The students found **it** difficult to understand (the students found **it,** that is, **to understand (understanding)** difficult).

- As an impersonal object after certain verbs.

  > She held **it** over me.
  >
  > Mark Twain roughed **it** in his youth.
  >
  > They fought **it** out.

- As an introductory pronoun that refers to persons, contrary to the rule that *it* is a neuter pronoun.

  > **It** is **I**.
  >
  > **It** is my **wife**.
  >
  > **It** is **they** I trust.

It may refer indefinitely to words of any person, gender, or number. In the first sentence *I* is in the first person, whereas *it* is in the third person. In the second, *wife* is feminine, whereas *it* is neuter. In the third, *they* is plural, whereas *it* is singular.

Exercise 13.6: Understanding Pronouns and Antecedents

Explain the uses of it *and other indefinite pronouns.*

CCSS.L.9–12.1:
Demonstrate command of the conventions of standard English grammar and usage when writing or speaking.

1. We considered it an honor to be nominated.

2. They say that it takes two to tango.

3. It was thirty miles to the nearest post office.

4. They had been roughing it for a month in the mountains when they ran out of provisions.

5. It was she who made the discovery.

6. At four o'clock we called it a day and went home.

7. It was in April when I first fell in love.

8. It was January, and the weather was beautiful.

9. It is notorious that important elections are decided by votes bought with money.

10. We considered it an honor to be invited.

11. It was twelve miles to the nearest post office.

12. I take it that he had little to fear on that score.

13. It seemed possible to carry out the program within the alloted time.

14. It was I who made the discovery.

15. For if any man was happy, it was surely he.

16. It was dark, but many stars shone now.

17. Now it was distinctly a feat for me to stay in school.

18. At four o'clock we called it a day and went home.

Exercise 13.7: Understanding Pronoun-Antecedent Agreement

Fill in the blanks with the correct pronouns. Each pronoun must agree with its antecedent in person, number, and gender.

CCSS.L.9–12.1:

Demonstrate command of the conventions of standard English grammar and usage when writing or speaking.

1. The members of the jury delivered _____ verdict.

2. Either Mark or Mary will drive _____ car.

3. If you see Brett or his brother, will you tell _____ what just happened?

4. The mutual funds company has prepared a prospectus to be sent to all _____ customers.

5. Everyone felt that the latest change in procedures was directed at _____ personally.

6. Neither the textbooks nor the work folders could be found when the students needed _____.

7. The committee cannot agree on what _____ should do.

8. The company is convinced that _____ analysis paints a more accurate picture of _____ profit margins.

9. The voters have already given _____ verdict.

10. Either Mary or Helen will drive _____ car.

11. If you see John or his brother, will you tell _____ what happened?

12. The company has prepared a prospectus to be sent to all _____ customers.

13. Everybody felt that the new rules were directed at _____ personally.

14. The committee cannot agree on how _____ should vote.

15. The committee is convinced that _____ report presents a true picture of _____ findings.

16. Neither of the countries would admit _____ guilt in beginning the war.

17. One cannot always tell how _____ will conduct _____ in an emergency.

18. Every senator and congressman will be asked to give _____ support to these bills.

19. Each of the candidates will be invited to present _____ views on the proposed law.

Chapter

14

Adjectives

ENGLISH LANGUAGE ARTS STANDARDS

☞ **CCSS.ELA-LITERACY.L.9–10.1.B:** *Use various types of phrases (noun, verb, adjectival, adverbial, participial, prepositional, absolute) and clauses (independent, dependent; noun, relative, adverbial) to convey specific meanings and add variety and interest to writing or presentations.*

ADJECTIVES

CCSS.L.9–10.1.B:
Use various types of phrases (noun, verb, adjectival, adverbial, participial, prepositional, absolute) and clauses (independent, dependent; noun, relative, adverbial) to convey specific meanings and add variety and interest to writing or presentations.

Any word or group of words that modifies a noun is an adjective. The following constructions are commonly used as adjectives.

- Regular adjectives: *loud* people; *ripe* fruit.

- Nouns and Pronouns: *Easter* eggs; *that* house.

- Nouns or Pronouns in the Possessive Case: *Murphy's* Law; *my* car.

- Participles or Participial Phrases: *impending* catastrophe; a woman *pushing a stroller;* a man *caught in too many lies.*

- Infinitives or Infinitive Phrases: cakes *to bake;* an effort *to reverse our bad luck.*

- Prepositional Phrases: the car *in the driveway.*

- Clauses: the girl *who was lost.*

COMMON CORE GRAMMAR

- A Past Participle followed by an Adverb: a *broken-down* truck; a *strung-out* addict; a *messed-up* situation.

- A Noun, equivalent to a Prepositional Phrase, used in the following way: a pair of shoes a *size* too small (of a size); water the *color* of mud (of the color).

- A Preposition with no expressed object: "I'll see you *around* (*around town*).

- Idiomatic Expressions like "a hundred-mile trip" and "a twenty-dollar purchase," consisting of a plural numeral combined with a singular noun to form an adjective phrase.

These types of expressions come only before a noun, and a hyphen is placed between the plural numeral and the singular noun. When a corresponding expression follows the noun it modifies, the plural form—*miles, dollars,* etc.—is used with no hyphen: "the trip is a *hundred miles* long."

NUMBER

CCSS.L.9–10.1.B:
Use various types of phrases (noun, verb, adjectival, adverbial, participial, prepositional, absolute) and clauses (independent, dependent; noun, relative, adverbial) to convey specific meanings and add variety and interest to writing or presentations.

The determiners (demonstrative pronouns) *this* and *that* (plural *these* and *those*) are the only adjectives in the English language that change form before singular and plural nouns.

> **This** computer, **these** computers; **that** girl, **these** girls

Before the nouns *kind* and *sort,* which are singular, the singular forms *this* and *that* are used. The plural forms *these* and *those* precede *kinds* and *sorts.*

> **This** kind of trouble; **these** kinds of troubles

> **This** sort of thing; **those** sorts of things

All other adjectives have the same form when used with singular or plural nouns: *hard* time, *hard* times.

POSITION OF ADJECTIVES, ADJECTIVE PHRASES AND CLAUSES

A pure adjective phrase or clause, or a pure adjective modified by a phrase or clause, generally follows the noun.

> The name **of the game** is Monopoly (phrase).

May be copied for classroom use. Common Core Grammar by Thomas Fasano (Coyote Canyon Press: Claremont, CA); © 2015.

CCSS.L.9–10.1.B:
Use various types of phrases (noun, verb, adjectival, adverbial, participial, prepositional, absolute) and clauses (independent, dependent; noun, relative, adverbial) to convey specific meanings and add variety and interest to writing or presentations.

She sent us an invitation **to attend her wedding.**

The car **belching smoke** was in the shop.

The man **who bought the house** has lived there ever since (clause).

A piece of cheese **black with mold** is in the refrigerator (adjective modified by a phrase).

Note. The above expression "pure adjective" is used to distinguish these constructions from those with both adjective and adverbial meaning. This latter type, when it modifies the subject of a sentence, may be placed either before the subject or after it.

Sensing trouble, the officer called for backup.

The officer, **sensing** trouble, called for backup.

Happy about her promotion, Sally wanted to celebrate.

Sally, **happy** about her promotion, wanted to celebrate.

Some adjective phrases have become idiomatic and often precede the noun they modify.

This is an **out-of-date** model.

This is a **state-of-the-art** stereo system.

PREDICATE ADJECTIVES

CCSS.L.9–10.1.B:
Use various types of phrases (noun, verb, adjectival, adverbial, participial, prepositional, absolute) and clauses (independent, dependent; noun, relative, adverbial) to convey specific meanings and add variety and interest to writing or presentations.

In addition to regular adjectives, there are several constructions that can be used as *Predicate Adjectives*.

- A Participle.

  The movie is **interesting**.

  The gossip was **titillating**.

A participle used as a predicate adjective needs to be distinguished from one used as part of a progressive-tense verb.

Alfred is **entertaining** (predicate adjective).

Alfred **is** currently **entertaining** his colleagues from work (part of a verb).

- An Infinitive.

  The dictionary is **to use**.

The secret is **to wait**.

- Prepositional Phrase.

    The speaker is **in high demand** (popular).

    He is **out of his mind** (crazy).

    The movie is **in black and white** (with no color).

    My nephew is **from the country** (a country boy).

    He is **of small stature** (short).

    Beowulf is **by an unknown poet** (anonymous).

- A Clause.

    He is **what I call innovative**.

    This is **how it's done.**

Uses of Predicate Adjectives

CCSS.L.9–10.1.B:
Use various types of phrases (noun, verb, adjectival, adverbial, participial, prepositional, absolute) and clauses (independent, dependent; noun, relative, adverbial) to convey specific meanings and add variety and interest to writing or presentations.

A predicate adjective may become an objective complement in a passive sentence.

The museum docent was **knowledgeable**.

The museum docent was considered **knowledgeable**.

The girl was **alive**.

The girl was found **alive**.

The barn was **red**.

The barn was painted **red**.

A predicate adjective describes the subject in a simple adjective relation.

The apples are **green**.

Bus service is **unreliable**.

After certain verbs indicating *becoming* or *turning*, the predicate adjective describes the subject as having changed due to the action described by the verb.

The milk turned **sour**.

The situation became **critical**.

Note. In the above sentences, the predicate adjectives show the close relation of adjective and adverb. Thus, in "The milk turned sour" the adjective *sour* both describes the noun *milk* and tells the result produced by the verb *turned*.

A predicate adjective used after a passive verb usually has much the same meaning as an adverbial clause of time.

> The frosting was applied **wet** (while it was wet).

> The coffee was served **hot** (while it was hot).

Distinction Between Predicate Adjective and an Adverb

CCSS.L.9–10.1.B:
Use various types of phrases (noun, verb, adjectival, adverbial, participial, prepositional, absolute) and clauses (independent, dependent; noun, relative, adverbial) to convey specific meanings and add variety and interest to writing or presentations.

After certain verbs, care should be taken to avoid using an adverb when an adjective is called for.

> The patient feels **bad** (not **badly**).

> The drink tastes **awful** (not **awfully**).

> His story rang **true** (not **truly**).

> The flowers smell **sweet** (not **sweetly**).

In the first sentence *bad* describes what the *patient* feels, which is *bad;* the second sentence makes a statement about an *awful* drink; the third, about a *true* story; the fourth, about *sweet* flowers. Yet in all these sentences the **_Predicate Adjectives_** also qualify to some degree the verbs; that is, they are adjectives with adverbial meaning—a dual relationship that may explain why they are often misused.

Here is a test to determine whether an adjective or an adverb should be used: Does the modifier say more about the subject or the verb? If it says more about the subject, then use an adjective; if it says more about the verb, then use an adverb. Compare the following two sentences:

> The man looked **stupid**.

> The man looked **stupidly** at the painting.

In the first sentence, the adjective *stupid* describes the man; in the second, the adverb *stupidly* describes the manner in which the man looked at the painting.

Another test for determining whether an adjective or an adverb should be used is to substitute *is* or *was* (*are* or *were*) for the verb in the sentence, and to place the adjective form after it. If this substitution can be done without altering the intended meaning of the sentence, then an adjective is the proper form; if the meaning changes, then an adverb should be used. Thus, for "The man *looked* stupid," we can substitute "The man *was* stupid"; here the adjective form is correct. In the sentence, "The man looked *stupidly* at the painting," substituting a form of the verb *to be* makes the sentence illogical: "The man *was* stupid at the painting." Therefore, the adverb is required.

ADJECTIVES AS OBJECTIVE COMPLEMENTS

CCSS.L.9–10.1.B:

Use various types of phrases (noun, verb, adjectival, adverbial, participial, prepositional, absolute) and clauses (independent, dependent; noun, relative, adverbial) to convey specific meanings and add variety and interest to writing or presentations.

A present or past participle may be used as an ***Objective Complement***.

> The guards found the prisoner **hanging**.
>
> The police discovered the house **locked**.
>
> The coach kept his players **running**.

A phrase can be used as an objective complement.

> I considered his advice **of value** (valuable).
>
> We found the girls **in a tizzy** (agitated).
>
> The news made me **out of sorts** (irritable).

An infinitive phrase in sentences like the following is usually referred to as an objective complement.

> I know this brand **to be reliable**.
>
> The examination proved the accused **to be sane**.

We may consider these to be objective complements, or we can see the respective expressions *the brand to be reliable* and *the accused to be sane* as infinitive phrases with a subject, each phrase being used as an object of the verb.

An adjective used as an objective complement is sometimes preceded by *as*.

> They regarded him **as efficient**. (They considered him **efficient.**)

Sometimes the adjective used as an objective complement is modified by an infinitive phrase.

> They consider him **slow** to make a decision.
>
> We find her too **quick** to judge people.

Occasionally an impersonal *it* acts as a "stand-in" for the object.

> We thought **it** best to leave.
>
> We thought it **prudent** to invest in mutual funds.

When used after verbs denoting *making* or *causing,* the objective complement describes the object as it is after its nature has been changed by the action of the verb; thus, it shows the result of the action on the object.

> The meal made her **happy**.
>
> I made the door **secure**.
>
> She toweled the dog **dry**.
>
> He painted the fence **brown**.

When used after some verbs, the objective complement describes the object without indicating a change in its nature or appearance.

> I consider my boss **irrational**.
>
> I thought your comment **absurd**.
>
> The nurse found the patient **unconscious** on the floor.

ARTICLES

Articles with Names and Proper Names

CCSS.L.9–10.1.B:
Use various types of phrases (noun, verb, adjectival, adverbial, participial, prepositional, absolute) and clauses (independent, dependent; noun, relative, adverbial) to convey specific meanings and add variety and interest to writing or presentations.

An article is principally used with a noun designating a member of a class. The indefinite articles *a* and *an* indicate any member of a class; the definite article *the* indicates a particular member.

> I want **a** bottle of water.
>
> I want **the** bottle of water on the table.

With proper names, one might expect that the article would be omitted since the proper name itself indicates a particular member of a class. In most instances, it is omitted, but there are a number of exceptions. The following list is, of course, not complete, but it gives an idea of the diversity of usage of proper nouns.

Names Requiring an Article

The article *the* is regularly used when the proper noun consists of *a class name preceded by an adjective,* such as:

- *Nations:* the United States, the Peoples Republic of China, the Soviet Union.

CCSS.L.9–10.1.B:
Use various types of phrases (noun, verb, adjectival, adverbial, participial, prepositional, absolute) and clauses (independent, dependent; noun, relative, adverbial) to convey specific meanings and add variety and interest to writing or presentations.

- *Oceans, Seas, Rivers, and Channels:* the Pacific Ocean, the Dead Sea, the Mississippi River, the English Channel.

- *Mountains (when plural) and Valleys:* the Rocky Mountains, the Berkshire Hills (also elliptical expressions: the Appalachians, the Andes, the Alps, the Berkshires), the San Joaquin Valley, the Hudson Valley. Single mountains regularly do not take an article, with the class name either first or last: Bald Mountain, Lookout Mountain, Bunker Hill, Mt. Rushmore, Mt. Everest, Mt. Baldy.

- *Corporations, Companies, Magazines, Newspapers, Buildings:* the Twin Towers, the Hilton Hotel, the Franklin Trust, the 3M Corporation, the First National Bank, the *New Yorker*, the *Los Angeles Times*, the Fox Theater, the Empire State Building.

- *Any Name containing an "of" Phrase:* the County of Los Angeles, the Commonwealth of Virginia, the Province of Quebec, the District of Colombia, the Gulf of Mexico, the Bay of Pigs, the Strait of Hormuz.

Names Omitting the Article

CCSS.L.9–10.1.B:
Use various types of phrases (noun, verb, adjectival, adverbial, participial, prepositional, absolute) and clauses (independent, dependent; noun, relative, adverbial) to convey specific meanings and add variety and interest to writing or presentations.

The article is regularly omitted in the following names, despite the fact that they contain place names.

- *Counties and Cities:* Cook County, County Cork, Atlantic City.

- *Single Islands:* Long Island, Bikini Island (but *the* Falkland Islands, *the* Bahama Islands (also *the* Bahamas)).

- *Lakes, Creeks, Bays, Sounds:* Salt Lake, Bear Lake (also when the class name precedes: Lake Erie, Lake Ontario), Antietam Creek, Hudson Bay, Puget Sound.

- *Streets, Avenues, etc.:* State Street, Forty-Second Street, Michigan Avenue, Sunset Boulevard (Sunset Strip), Route 66, Interstate 405 (a unique California usage is the placement of the article *the* before highway numbers: as, *the* 405).

- *Any Name having the Qualifying Word in the Possessive Case:* St. George's Channel, Sullivan's Theater, Joe's Bar and Grill.

The article is often omitted with the names of persons and with geographical names that do not contain a class name.

Abraham Lincoln, General Custer, Queen Elizabeth II, North America, Canada, Italy, Germany, Florida, San Francisco.

Note. The is used to distinguish one person, place, or thing from another with the same name.

> **The** Chris Bonk I friended on Facebook is **the** Chris Bonk I knew years ago in Chicago.

ARTICLES WITH COMMON NOUNS

Abstract Nouns and Names of Classes without Units

CCSS.L.9–10.1.B:
Use various types of phrases (noun, verb, adjectival, adverbial, participial, prepositional, absolute) and clauses (independent, dependent; noun, relative, adverbial) to convey specific meanings and add variety and interest to writing or presentations.

With an abstract noun or a noun indicating a class thought of as bulk or not consisting of parts or units, the article is commonly omitted.

> **Courage** is respected.
>
> Americans are guaranteed **freedom** of **speech**.
>
> **Water** when boiled will take the form of **steam**.
>
> **Plastic** is more durable than it used to be.
>
> **History** is a fascinating subject.

Note. Usage might vary in different contexts.

> **Night** is the time I sleep.
>
> At **night,** we must be vigilant.
>
> In **the night,** burglars ply their trade.

Classes Composed of Individual Units

CCSS.L.9–10.1.B:
Use various types of phrases (noun, verb, adjectival, adverbial, participial, prepositional, absolute) and clauses (independent, dependent; noun, relative, adverbial) to convey specific meanings and add variety and interest to writing or presentations.

When the name indicates a class comprising individual members, the following forms are regularly used:

- With plural class names, the article is omitted.

  > **Dogs** are great pets.
  >
  > **Typewriters** are now collectibles.

- With some of the more general class names in the singular number, an indefinite article is called for, not a definite one.

  > **An animal** is one of God's creatures (not **the** animal).

An education is a valuable thing (not **the** education).

A jewel is a precious stone (not **the** jewel).

- With more specific class names in the singular number, either a definite or indefinite article may be used.

    The dog (**a dog**) is a great pet.

    The typewriter (**a typewriter**) is a valuable antique.

It should be noted that in the case of singular class names, the article typically becomes more definite as the class becomes more definite in pointing towards its individual parts. Thus, the classes indicate no individual units. The words *journalism*, *journalist*, and *editorial* illustrate these classifications.

Journalism is a specialized type of writing.

A journalist (not **the journalist**) engages in a specialized type of writing.

The editorial (**an editorial**) is a specialized type of writing.

Keep in mind that the above principles are only general ones. The English article has many subtle distinctions in use. Observation and practice are the best guides.

SPECIAL USES OF ARTICLES

"Such a" and "To"

CCSS.L.9–10.1.B:
Use various types of phrases (noun, verb, adjectival, adverbial, participial, prepositional, absolute) and clauses (independent, dependent; noun, relative, adverbial) to convey specific meanings and add variety and interest to writing or presentations.

In expressions like *such a*, *many a*, and *what a*, the article follows the adjective instead of preceding it.

Such a way, **many** a time, **what** a show

Note. When using too with an adjective preceding a noun used with an indefinite article, do not add "of." Say or write *too big a deal* not *too big "of" a deal*.

Too is not normally used with an adjective in front of a noun although *too* is used in front of the determiners *many, much,* and *few*.

There is **too much** room for error.

Too few people nowadays care about good music.

You ask **too many** questions.

"A Dozen" and "a Few"

CCSS.L.9–10.1.B:
Use various types of phrases (noun, verb, adjectival, adverbial, participial, prepositional, absolute) and clauses (independent, dependent; noun, relative, adverbial) to convey specific meanings and add variety and interest to writing or presentations.

In idiomatic expressions like *a dozen eggs* and *a few books*, the article *a* appears to modify a plural noun.

This construction originates from the dropping of the preposition *of*: as, *a dozen (of) eggs*, in which *a* modifies the singular noun *dozen*, which in turn is modified by the phrase *of eggs*.

Note. Compare the above expressions with *a few of every kind* and *a dozen of each*, in which the *of* is retained.

"As Good A"

CCSS.L.9–10.1.B:
Use various types of phrases (noun, verb, adjectival, adverbial, participial, prepositional, absolute) and clauses (independent, dependent; noun, relative, adverbial) to convey specific meanings and add variety and interest to writing or presentations.

The indefinite article follows an adjective that is preceded by the word *as*.

Often the preposition *of* is mistakenly inserted between the adjective and the article.

Say or write *"as good a time as you,"* not *"as good 'of' a time as you"*; say or write *"as fine a painting* that ever hung in the gallery," not *"as fine 'of' a painting* that ever hung in the gallery."

Emphatic "The" and "The" as an Adverb

CCSS.L.9–10.1.B:
Use various types of phrases (noun, verb, adjectival, adverbial, participial, prepositional, absolute) and clauses (independent, dependent; noun, relative, adverbial) to convey specific meanings and add variety and interest to writing or presentations.

The is used to emphasize a specific object, person, concept, etc.

He was voted Man of **the** Year.

We were the talk of **the** town.

The is sometimes used not as an article but as an adverb of degree.

The harder you try, **the** more progress you make.

The more, **the** merrier.

She sings **the** most beautifully when she has an audience.

Exercise 14.1: Identifying Adjective Constructions

Underline the adjective constructions — words, phrases, and clauses — used as predicate adjectives and objective complements.

WRITING PROMPT:
Describe a favorite hobby of one of your friends, or maybe your hobby. Use correctly the words *good* and *well*, *bad* and *badly*.

1. Farmers found their fields too dry for cultivation.

2. The Virginia colonists regarded the natives as unfriendly and treacherous.

3. He was one of those people who are always out of luck.

4. He imagined himself saving people from sinking ships.

5. His eyes were on fire.

6. She felt a vague fear making her tremble.

CCSS.L.9–10.1.B:
Use various types of phrases (noun, verb, adjectival, adverbial, participial, prepositional, absolute) and clauses (independent, dependent; noun, relative, adverbial) to convey specific meanings and add variety and interest to writing or presentations.

7. I find myself shy in the presence of strangers.

8. He was passionate about his beliefs.

9. The house was ransacked upon our return.

10. She was of a ruddy complexion.

11. He was one of those actors who are always in luck.

12. I found the meadow and the other fields too dry for cultivation.

13. The houses were all in darkness, because evening meals were laid in the kitchens.

14. In the early years the colonists regarded the natives as unfriendly and treacherous.

15. Our growth in wealth and power was without precedent.

16. He saw himself saving people from sinking ships.

17. That silence and brooding obscurity would make a man contrite and willing to learn.

18. He was a man of passionate temper who always kept himself suppressed.

19. Rip now felt a vague apprehension stealing over him.

20. Dick just waked to another morning of blank despair, and his temper was of the shortest kind.

Chapter

Verbs

15

ENGLISH LANGUAGE ARTS STANDARDS

NOTE:
Some of the skills in this chapter were introduced at lower grade levels; yet, due to the recursiveness of the language standards, they require further attention at the high school level.

☞ *CCSS.ELA-LITERACY.L.9–12.1: Demonstrate command of the conventions of standard English grammar and usage when writing or speaking.*

☞ *CCSS.ELA-LITERACY.L.11–12.1.A: Apply the understanding that usage is a matter of convention, can change over time, and is sometimes contested.*

☞ *CCSS.ELA-LITERACY.L.11–12.1.B: Resolve issues of complex or contested usage, consulting references (e.g., Merriam–Webster's Dictionary of English Usage, Garner's Modern American Usage) as needed.*

☞ *CCSS.ELA-LITERACY.L.11–12.2.B: Spell correctly.*

☞ *CCSS.ELA-LITERACY.L.9–10.1.B: Use various types of phrases (noun, verb, adjectival, adverbial, participial, prepositional, absolute) and clauses (independent, dependent; noun, relative, adverbial) to convey specific meanings and add variety and interest to writing or presentations.*

☞ *CCSS.ELA-LITERACY.L.8.1.A: Explain the function of verbals (gerunds, participles, infinitives) in general and their function in particular sentences.*

☞ *CCSS.ELA-LITERACY.L.8.1.C: Form and use verbs in the indicative, imperative, interrogative, conditional, and subjunctive mood.*

PHRASAL VERBS

CCSS.L.9–10.1.B:
Use various types of phrases (noun, verb, adjectival, adverbial, participial, prepositional, absolute) and clauses (independent, dependent; noun, relative, adverbial) to convey specific meanings and add variety and interest to writing or presentations.

Frequently a preposition or an adverb is closely tied to the function of a verb and helps to express the meaning of the verb. The two words together are regarded as a *Phrasal Verb.*

They **wound up** the meeting (ended).

The store **ripped off** its customers (overcharged).

The children's father **set up** the swing set (assembled).

The wrecking ball **knocked down** the building (demolished).

The tour guide **pointed out** important sites (indicated).

In these sentences, *on, up, down,* and *out* are not prepositions introducing phrases, a distinction that can be seen by comparing "pointed out *important sites*" with "pointed *out the window,*" in which the prepositional use is obvious.

Phrasal verbs consist of the following:

- A verb followed by an adverb:

    The plane **took off**.

    He **sat down**.

    Cold weather **set in.**

- A verb followed by a preposition (sometimes known as a *prepositional verb*).

    She **looked after** the children (tended, minded).

    He **sailed through** the examination (passed, aced).

    The author **brooded on** his life (pondered, contemplated).

Note. The nouns at the end of the above example sentences are objects of prepositions and not direct objects of verbs.

- A verb followed by an adverb and a preposition.

    The company **cut back on** spending (reduced).

    The author **followed up on** her success (pursued).

    He **put up with** a lot of aggravation (tolerated).

    She **fell in with** a bad crowd (befriended).

Phrasal verbs can be transitive or intransitive. *The object of a transitive phrasal verb can be placed in several positions.*

When the object is short, it can be placed after the second word of the phrasal verb, or after the first word and before the second.

> He **filled up** his car.
>
> He **filled** his car **up**.
>
> She **handed over** the money.
>
> She **handed** the money **over**.

When the object is a pronoun such as *me, her,* or *it,* it almost always comes before the second word of the phrasal verb.

> He **nailed** it **down**.
>
> She **won** him **back**.
>
> He **tied** her **up**.

When the object is an abstract noun such as *liberty, hope,* or *courage,* it usually comes after the second word of the phrasal verb.

> The candidate **won over** enough support to win.
>
> She **pulled apart** his logic.
>
> The mayor attempted to **stamp out** graft and corruption.

Several phrasal verbs consist of a transitive verb and a preposition. They have an object after the verb and an object after the preposition.

> The man **sicced** his dogs **on** them.
>
> The attorney **laid** the evidence **before** the jury.
>
> The con man **talked** the widows **out** of their life savings.

Here is a list of phrasal verbs which consist of a transitive verb and a preposition.

build into	build on	draw into	drum into
frighten into	hold against	keep to	lay before
leave off	let into	lumber with	make of
put on	put onto	put through	read into
set against	set back	set on	talk into
thrust upon	write into	lay before	talk out

Some phrasal verbs consist of three words: a verb, an adverb, and a preposition. This type of verb is called a ***Phrasal-Prepositional Verb***. Most three-word phrasal verbs are intransitive. The preposition at the end is followed by its own object.

> His wife **walked out on** him.
>
> Teachers have to **put up with** a lot of interruptions.
>
> The police are **cracking down on** texting while driving.

Here is a list of some intransitive three-word phrasal verbs.

break out of	brush up on	bump up against	burst in on
call out for	catch up with	chime in with	clamp down on
clean up after	come across as	come down on	come down to
come up with	crack down on	creep up on	crowd in on
cry out against	cry out for	cut back on	date back to
fall in with	get away with	get down to	get in on
get off with	get on to	get on with	get round to
go down with	go in for	go off with	go over to
go through with	grow out of	keep in with	keep on at
measure up to	miss out on	zero in on	play along with
play around with	put up with	read up on	run away with
snap out of	stick out for	stick up for	suck up to
take up with	talk down to	tie in with	walk away from
walk away with	walk off with	walk out on	wriggle out of

A few three-word phrasal verbs are transitive. The direct object of the verb comes immediately after the verb, and the preposition is followed by its object.

> The movie **frightened** me **out of** my mind.
>
> The boss often **plays** one employee **off against** another.
>
> We tried to **talk** her **out of** quitting.

Here is a list of transitive three-word phrasal verbs:

do out of	frighten out of	let in for	let in on
play off against	put down as	put down to	put up to
take out on	take up on	trick out of	fake out of

Verb Plus Infinitive

A form of *be, have,* or *ought* used with an infinitive (*is to go, have to run, ought to contribute*), or a form of *be* used with *going* or *about* and an infinitive (*are going to pay, were about to shout*), makes a verb group similar to a verb phrase having *will, must, should,* etc., as an auxiliary.

CCSS.L.8.1.A:
Explain the function of verbals (gerunds, participles, infinitives) in general and their function in particular sentences.

She **is to sing** "The Star Spangled Banner" (**will sing**).

You **have to make** the announcement (**must make**).

We **ought to check** his progress (**should check**).

I **am going to write** a book (**will write**).

My grandparents **are about to visit** us (**will soon visit**).

His advice **is to be followed** (**should be followed**).

In a similar manner *used* combined with an infinitive makes a verb phrase equivalent to the past tense of a verb modified by the adverb *formerly*.

She **used to sew** (**formerly sewed**).

Exercise 15.1: Identifying Phrasal Verbs

Underline the phrasal verbs in the following sentences. Write your own translation of what the phrasal verb means.

WRITING PROMPT:
Choose ten phrasal verbs from the previous lists and write sentences with them.

1. They wound up the meeting on time.

2. A bad parent plays one sibling off against the others.

3. The police set up a perimeter around the crime scene.

4. Knowledge can knock down your illusions.

5. She was always afraid that she was missing out on something important.

6. The professor pointed out the key section in the chapter.

7. We were happy that the plane took off in time.

8. You need to let me in on your secret.

9. The police are cracking down on aggressive panhandlers.

10. When fatigue sets in, it's good to get off the computer.

11. She looked after the neighbors' children all summer.

12. I know someone who sailed through the bar exam with no problems.

CCSS.L.9–10.1.B:
Use various types of phrases (noun, verb, adjectival, adverbial, participial, prepositional, absolute) and clauses (independent, dependent; noun, relative, adverbial) to convey specific meanings and add variety and interest to writing or presentations.

13. I spend way too much time brooding on my life.

14. My wife is tired of cleaning up after me.

15. Stephen King is always following up on his previous bestsellers.

16. My parents put up with a lot of nonsense from their children.

17. I hate having to fill my car up with gas.

18. You have to stick up for your friends

19. My brother fell in with a bad crown.

20. The company needs to do better with cutting back on expenses.

21. The kidnappers handed the boy over to the authorities.

22. You'll need to brush up on the subject before trying to be such an expert.

23. I hammered the loose board down with heavy nails.

24. The accident frightened me out of my wits.

25. I hate it when you talk down to me.

26. It's time to turn the lights out.

Exercise 15.2: Writing with Phrasal Verbs

Use the following phrasal verbs in sentences. Change the tense or the person if you want

CCSS.L.9–10.1.B:
Use various types of
phrases (noun, verb, adjectival, adverbial, participial,
prepositional, absolute)
and clauses (independent,
dependent; noun, relative,
adverbial) to convey specific meanings and add variety
and interest to writing or
presentations.

1. put down

2. look into

3. see about.

4. ask after

5. watch for

6. turn into

7. have at

8. think up

9. win over

10. drop over

11. break out of

12. frighten out of

13. stuck up for

14. put down to

15. play along with

16. take up on

17. miss out on

18. brush up on

19. go through with

20. play off against

TENSE

CCSS.L.8.1.C:
Form and use verbs in the indicative, imperative, interrogative, conditional, and subjunctive mood.

The six tenses in English were introduced in Chapter Four. This introduction presented only a rudimentary look at how these tenses are used: it outlined basic principles and presented charts of the simple and perfect tenses.

For a more thorough understanding of how tense works in English, the first step is to distinguish between *grammatical tense* and *actual time*. A closer look at *grammatical tense* will reveal the forms of the verbs and their adherence to definite rules. The future tense makes use of the auxiliary verbs *shall* or *will;* the present perfect tense, *have* or *has;* the past perfect, *had*. The distinction between grammatical tenses, then, is largely a matter of form; that is, the different tenses do not always represent the *actual time* implied by their names. For example, the present tense does not always represent present time, and the future tense is not the only tense that may indicate future time. The following several pages cover the principal uses of the different tenses.

TENSES IN THE INDICATIVE MOOD

Uses of the Present Tense

CCSS.L.8.1.C:
Form and use verbs in the indicative, imperative, interrogative, conditional, and subjunctive mood.

The principal uses of the ***Present Tense*** are:

- To indicate an action happening in actual present time.

    She **is** at work.

    His hair **looks** oily.

    I **am listening** to the radio.

- To express a universal truth.

    The earth **orbits** the sun.

    Heat **rises**.

In this use, the present tense encompasses past, present, and future time.

- To indicate habitual or customary action.

    I **go** to work every morning.

    Robert **eats** doughnuts every day.

She **is working** for a law firm (meaning that this is what she does for a living).

Here the present tense encompasses past and present time and implies continued action in the future.

- To indicate an intended action in the future (the future sense is derived from the context).

    I **leave** for Europe tomorrow.

    The circus **is coming** this weekend.

Combined with an Infinitive

CCSS.L.8.1.A:

Explain the function of verbals (gerunds, participles, infinitives) in general and their function in particular sentences.

The present tense forms of *be* and *be going* are frequently used with an infinitive to indicate future time (*about* is also used with *be* in this construction).

    You **are to be** here at 8am.

    He **is going to do** the landscaping tomorrow.

    The show **is about to begin** (will soon begin).

The Historical Present

CCSS.L.8.1.C:

Form and use verbs in the indicative, imperative, interrogative, conditional, and subjunctive mood.

Writers often use the present tense to add immediacy to a past event.

    He dreamed of his childhood home and the last time everyone in his family was together. It is Thanksgiving, and his mother is taking the turkey out of the oven. His father offers to help and takes the pan from her and sets it on the counter. There he begins carving it. (Notice the change from the past tense to the present tense when the telling of the past event begins.)

The present tense is used in other instances to indicate past time. For example, in the following sentences the present tense gives a past action a definite connection with the present.

    I **hear** he received a promotion.

    I **see** that Johnson has been promoted.

The first sentence does not mean that I am hearing this news *now* for the first time; it indicates rather that I *have heard* the news and am *now* recalling it.

Uses of the Past Tense

CCSS.L.8.1.C:
Form and use verbs in the indicative, imperative, interrogative, conditional, and subjunctive mood.

The **Past Tense** is generally used to place an action wholly in past time, that is, cut off from any connection with present time. Its two regular functions are:

- To indicate an action that occurred at a specific time in the past (a specific time may be expressed or understood from the context).

  She **went** hiking in the mountains on Saturday.

  He **took** his seat, unnoticed by anyone.

  She **was standing** by the car.

- To indicate habitual or customary action in past time.

  The signatories of the Constitution **believed** in liberty.

  Carpetbaggers **were** disgusting people.

  Veteran bores **regaled** Nick Caraway with their stories.

Idiomatic Uses

CCSS.L.8.1.C:
Form and use verbs in the indicative, imperative, interrogative, conditional, and subjunctive mood.

The Past Tense has a few idiomatic uses as illustrated below.

  I was going to say something (meaning that I intended to say something, but I've reconsidered).

  I was leaving tomorrow (meaning that I intended to leave tomorrow, but have reconsidered).

In the sentences above, the past tense indicates a future action was contemplated in the past but is no longer going to happen.

  I knew that you had them (in reply to such a remark as "I found the tickets").

  I thought you looked pale (in reply to such a remark as "I feel sick").

In each of these sentences the verb in both the main and the subordinate clause is in the past tense, despite the fact that the conditions described are still continuing. Thus, the first example means essentially "I *knew* (before you said anything) that you had the tickets," but it also means that I still *know* that you have the tickets. The past tense in the subordinate clause is the result of attracted sequence.

Uses of The Future Tense

CCSS.L.8.1.C:
Form and use verbs in the indicative, imperative, interrogative, conditional, and subjunctive mood.

The *Future Tense* is used:

- To indicate an expected future action.

    We **will be** there Sunday morning.

    My work assignment **will be done** by Friday.

- To indicate customary action—present, past, and future.

    Often Randy's brother **will anger** their parents.

- To indicate that a fact is true at a certain time.

    She **will welcome** you now.

    You **will find** him at home at this time.

    He **won't be** here this early.

The future tense is used in these sentences because there is an implication of future action. Thus, the first sentence, in addition to stating that the woman is in a welcoming mood, suggests that when you encounter her, she will welcome you. The present meaning is carried by the adverb *now*.

Occasionally, this kind of construction expresses the hope or expectation that something might be true in the future.

    The store **will** certainly **be** open by this time.

A verb with *will* as an auxiliary often indicates determination or persistence.

    She **will babysit** the kids, though she can't stand doing so.

Here there is an implication that she has babysat in the past, babysits in the present, and will continue to babysit.

Uses of the Present Perfect Tense

CCSS.L.8.1.C:
Form and use verbs in the indicative, imperative, interrogative, conditional, and subjunctive mood.

In the *Present Perfect* tense the time specified must extend to a present event or state of being that is ongoing in some way.

    John **has worked** in Glasgow for ten years.

    The time specified (ten years) extends to the present (now), for John still works in Glasgow.

John **has run** his own business now for ten years.

The time specified (ten years) extends to the present (now), for John still runs his own business.

My father **has been** dead since 1995.

The time specified (since 1995) extends to the present (now), for the state of my father's death continues.

The two principal characteristics of the present perfect tense are: (a) it refers to an action or situation at some *indefinite* time beginning in the past, and (b) it establishes the present as the time to which the past action or situation leads.

The Present Perfect is used with **Stative Verbs**—which express states or conditions rather than actions or events—to refer to a state that began in the past and extends to the present and will perhaps continue in the future.

We **have lived** in Los Angeles for ten years.

I **have** always **liked** teaching.

The Present Perfect is used with **Dynamic Verbs**—which express actions and events—to refer to one or more events that have occurred at some time within a period leading up to the present.

Obama **has won** every presidential election **he has been** in.

I **have listened** to your nonsense long enough.

The Present Perfect is also used with dynamic verbs to refer to past events that repeatedly occur up to and including the present.

The magazine **has been** published every month since 1887.

Socrates **has influenced** many philosophers.

Uses of the Past Perfect Tense

CCSS.L.8.1.C:
Form and use verbs in the indicative, imperative, interrogative, conditional, and subjunctive mood.

In the **Past Perfect** tense the time specified must extend to a relevant point in the past.

When I met him, John **had worked** for the company for fifteen years.

The time specified (fifteen years) extends to a relevant point in the past (when I met him).

When Martin Luther died in 1546, the Protestant Reformation **had spread** throughout Europe.

> *The time specified (the time of the Protestant Reformation) extends to a relevant point in the past (1546).*

> By the time Mr. Winkler retired, he **had taught** the same classes for twenty years.

> *The time specified (twenty years) extends to a relevant point in the past (when Mr. Winkler retired).*

Some writers make the mistake of using the simple past and the past perfect interchangeably. However, the past perfect should not be used when the simple past will suffice.

> I took out the garbage after my wife **came** (not **had come**) home from work.

Here the adverb *after* is enough indication of past time to make the past perfect redundant.

Note. The past perfect is the past of the present perfect by way of attracted sequence, especially in speech and indirect discourse.

> John tells me that he **hasn't seen** Mary since Friday.

> John told me that he **hadn't seen** Mary since Friday.

> He told the police that he **hadn't heard** any shouting from the house since the last disturbance.

The Past Perfect tense is used in certain *if*-clauses to imply that a situation is *contrary to fact.*

> If car sales **had been** up, morale among the dealership's sales force would have been up as well.

> If I **had known** that you wanted to go, I would have invited you.

> He described the scene as vividly as if he **had been** there.

In Modern English the past perfect tense is often used in reported speech with specific time-indicators (*since, in, for,* etc.)

> He replied that he **hadn't seen** the car **since** it was towed away from the crash scene.

> The police said that the close-knit family **hadn't heard** from her **in** over a week, and that was unusual.

> I told the repairman that I **hadn't smelled** gas **for** several months.

The best advice for writers is not to overuse the past perfect. It should be used only if required for clarity.

I had a feeling when the phone rang that my father **had died**. (The simple past (my father **died**) would indicate that my father died the moment the phone rang.)

Uses of the Future Perfect

In the ***Future Perfect*** tense a future event or state of being must extend to the time specified.

When he shows up, we **will have finished** the job.

The previous event (we finish the job) extends to the time specified (when he shows up).

When a cure for cancer is finally discovered, millions more **will have died** from the disease.

The previous event (millions die from cancer) extends to the time specified (when a cure for cancer is discovered).

Exercise 15.3: Recognizing Verb Tense in the Indicative Mood

Name the grammatical tenses of the verbs and explain the actual time relations that they represent.

WRITING PROMPT:
Write a paragraph describing a scene from one of your favorite movies. Use only dynamic verbs to add vividness to your descriptions.

1. The sun is setting, and I see the shadows lengthening across the yard.

2. We must hurry, for the movie is about to start.

3. We were going home tomorrow, but the roads may be too icy.

4. Sometimes in the evening I will sit for several hours looking at a book but reading nothing.

5. My mother likes to dress in red although that color is unflattering on her.

CCSS.L.8.1.C:
Form and use verbs in the indicative, imperative, interrogative, conditional, and subjunctive mood.

6. He lived in London after his student days at Oxford.

7. He has lived in London since the 1970s.

8. He has been living in London awhile.

9. I hear that you were in Los Angeles for a while last month.

10. My relatives were coming next week, but my wife is ill.

11. He has been the Washington correspondent for the *Times* since 1992.

12. Misers get up early in the morning; and burglars, I am informed, get up the night before.

13. The sun is setting and I see the shadows stealing across the lake.

14. My father liked my poem when he heard me read it at commencement.

15. "I'm going down to the office immediately after breakfast," he said. "What are you going to do with yourself?"

16. The books of an older generation will not fit easily into the curriculum.

17. Character is higher than intellect.

18. You must hurry, for the play is about to begin.

19. These lagoons have long since disappeared, but they were beautiful things in their time.

20. Don't be afraid that I am going to talk of the "romance" of the inn.

Exercise 15.4: Using Proper Verb Tense

Fill in the blanks with the tense form that best expresses the time indicated in the context of each sentence.

CCSS.L.8.1.C:
Form and use verbs in the indicative, imperative, interrogative, conditional, and subjunctive mood.

1. I _____ to the movies every night this week (go).

2. They _____ before we came (leave).

3. When I met him he said that he _____ in the city for the past month (be).

4. We _____ to him on Friday about his work (speak).

5. We _____ to him already about his work (speak).

6. When we finally heard from him, he _____ out of the country for a year (be).

7. They _____ if you ask them (come).

8. We _____ this movie twice since it came to the local cinema (see).

9. We _____ this movie twice after it came to the local cinema (see).

10. She _____ on us twice yesterday (call).

11. They _____ in the city yesterday (visit).

12. The boys _____ every day since New Year's (work).

13. I _____ in Chicago now (live).

14. For the meeting this evening, the committee _____ a long, detailed report (prepare).

15. Yesterday we _____ an order from a firm in Brazil (receive).

16. I _____ to the theater every night this week (go).

17. I _____ to the theater every night so far this week (go).

18. I _____ to the theater every night last week (go).

19. I _____ to the theater every night since last Sunday (go).

20. They _____ before we came (leave).

21. By the time we were ready, the legislature _____ in session for over a week (be).

22. When I met him he said that he _____ in the city for the past month (be).

TENSES OF THE SUBJUNCTIVE MOOD

Time Indicated by the Present Tense

CCSS.L.8.1.C:
Form and use verbs in the indicative, imperative, interrogative, conditional, and subjunctive mood.

The present tense of the subjunctive mood indicates present time. It can also indicate future time if appropriate context is provided.

> If that **be** true, then we don't stand a chance (more commonly **is**).
>
> If the sun **refuse** to shine, then life on Earth will perish (more commonly **refuses**).

Time Indicated by the Past Tense

CCSS.L.8.1.C:
Form and use verbs in the indicative, imperative, interrogative, conditional, and subjunctive mood.

The past tense of the subjunctive mood has no connection to past time. As is the case with the present tense subjunctive, it commonly refers to present time.

> If I **were** a rich man, I would help you out (now).
>
> I wish that she **were** here (now).
>
> He acts as if he **were** in charge (now).

The difference between these two tenses in conditional expressions is that the present subjunctive indicates an expression that *may or may not be true to fact*, whereas the past subjunctive indicates a condition that is *contrary to fact*. The past tense in this context has lost its force as an indicator of time and is now an indicator only of certain conditions.

Note. When the verb in the main clause is in the past tense, the past subjunctive in wishes and after *as if* and *as though* indicates the same time as the main verb—that is, it represents a time contemporaneous with the action indicated by the main verb.

> I wished that she **were** here (at the time of the wishing).
>
> He dressed as if he **were** homeless.

The ***Past Subjunctive*** might refer to actual future time or to time subsequent to that of the main verb if indicated clearly by context.

> If he **were** to ask me tomorrow, he would find me a grave man.
>
> I wish that she **were** vacationing with me next month.
>
> He acted as though his luck **were** about to change.

Time Indicated by the Past Perfect Tense

CCSS.L.8.1.C:

Form and use verbs in the indicative, imperative, interrogative, conditional, and subjunctive mood.

For indicating actual past time in the subjunctive mood, the past perfect form is used.

> If you **had seen** it, you would've known what I was talking about.
>
> If he**'d grabbed** the rope, the rescuers would've been able to pull him out.
>
> I wished you **had told** me of your plans to get married.
>
> He acted as if he**'d been placed** in charge.

Exercise 15.5: Identifying Verb Tense in the Subjunctive

Name the grammatical tenses of the verbs in the subjunctive mood and indicate what actual time they represent.

CCSS.L.8.1.C:
Form and use verbs in the indicative, imperative, interrogative, conditional, and subjunctive mood.

1. If that were true, he would be a genius.

2. If that be true, he should be recognized.

3. I wish that he were here so that you could ask him yourself about why he lost his job.

4. I wish he had been here so that I could have asked him myself.

5. I wish that she were going with us to the next showing.

6. If I knew his name, I would introduce you to him.

7. I wish that she had been less effusive with her praise.

8. I wish that I had time to read the book.

9. She felt as if she were living in a make-believe world.

10. He acted as if he had never heard the story.

11. If that were true, he would be a hero.

12. If that be true, he should be rewarded.

13. I wish that he were here so that you could talk with him.

14. I wish that he had been here so that you could have seen him.

15. I wish that he were going with us to the next convention.

16. If everyone were as kind as Uncle John, how nice the world would be.

17. It makes no difference whether the actors be many or one, a tyrant or a mob.

18. If I knew his name, I would introduce him.

19. Then the sheep began to pant heavily and to shake as if a spasm were upon it.

20. Had they been regular troops, the results would have been most fatal.

SEQUENCE OF TENSES

CCSS.L.8.1.C:
Form and use verbs in the indicative, imperative, interrogative, conditional, and subjunctive mood.

Sequence of Tenses is the principle that governs the tense relations between the time of the main clause and that of any accompanying clause.

The verbs may be in Natural or Attractive Sequence.

Verbs are in *Natural Sequence* when they indicate the natural or logical time relation between the actions they represent.

For example, when the actions in the main clause and the subordinate clause take place in the present time and future time respectively, natural sequence requires that the verbs be in the present tense and the future tense respectively: "She *knows* that I *will make* dinner."

Verbs are in *Attracted Sequence* when the verb in the subordinate clause is "attracted" from the natural form to agree with the tense of the main clause, with no regard to the actual time represented.

For example, if someone says, "I *am* angry," that statement may be immediately repeated by someone else in the form, "He *said* that he *was* angry." Here the verb *am* is attracted into the past tense *was* to make it agree with the past tense *said*, with no regard to the present emotional state of the original speaker.

Attracted Sequence

CCSS.L.8.1.C:
Form and use verbs in the indicative, imperative, interrogative, conditional, and subjunctive mood.

Attracted sequence is the only type of sequence that poses challenges. It is largely restricted to direct discourse and to clauses of purpose following main clauses with verbs in the past and past perfect tenses.

In Indirect Discourse

CCSS.L.8.1.C:
Form and use verbs in the indicative, imperative, interrogative, conditional, and subjunctive mood.

Indirect Discourse is a type of statement in which a speaker's words are repeated but in a different way from that originally used.

He said, "**I will quit**" (direct discourse).

He said **that he would quit** (indirect discourse).

When the verb of the main clause is in the past or past perfect tense, attracted sequence occurs.

- A present tense verb in the original direct statement becomes a past tense verb in the indirect statement.

  He said that you **were** wrong (Direct—"You **are** wrong").

  She told me that he **was watching** TV ("He **is watching** TV").

  I asked whether you **were prepared** (**"Are** you **prepared?"**).

  I said that I **would attend** ("I **will attend**").

Note. The present tense is regularly used in the subordinate clause when a main clause is in the past tense to express a universal truth or general wisdom.

  Copernicus **proved** that the earth **orbits** the sun.

  My mother **told** me that misery **loves** company.

- A present perfect tense becomes a past perfect tense.

  They **said** that she **had finished**. (Direct—"She **has finished.**")

- A future or a future perfect tense takes a form with an auxiliary *would* (*should*) or *would have* (*should have*), respectively.

  They **said** that she **would finish**. (Direct—"She **will finish.**")

  They **said** that she **would have finished** her work by then. ("She **will have finished** her work by then.")

- A past or a past perfect tense, because it already agrees with the tense of the main verb, regularly retains its past or past perfect tense, respectively.

  She **said** that he **got** her mail by mistake. (Direct—"He **got** my mail by mistake.")

  I **knew** that when I walked out of the store, I **had been ripped off**. ("When I walked out of the store, I **had been ripped off**.")

A similar kind of attracted sequence occurs after such verbs as *expect, suppose, think,* and *know,* and certain predicate adjectives like *evident, certain,* and *sure.* Constructions using these verbs and adjectives are similar to indirect discourse although they do not actually state what someone said.

For example, upon flipping the channels on the television and finding a particular show, one might say, "I was certain that this show *was* on." The verb in the subordinate clauses attracted into the past tense, despite the fact that the show is *still* on. Compare also, "I knew that you *would help* me," made in response to the statement, "I *will help* you."

Note. When the verb in the main clause in indirect discourse is in any tense other than the past or past perfect, natural sequence occurs with the verb in the subordinate clause.

> She **says** that he **is** a teacher.
>
> She **says** that he **was** formerly a teacher.
>
> She **says** that he **will be** a teacher.
>
> He **said** that you **will buy** the food.
>
> He **said** that you **bought** the food.
>
> She **will think** that you **are** cheap.

In Clauses of Purpose

CCSS.L.8.1.C:
Form and use verbs in the indicative, imperative, interrogative, conditional, and subjunctive mood.

When the verb of the main clause is in the past or past perfect tense, the past tense of a modal auxiliary like *might, could, would,* or *should* is used in a subordinate clause of purpose in attracted sequence.

> He **bought** a chainsaw in order that he **might clear** the brush on his land.
>
> When I visited him last year, he **had bought** a chainsaw in order that he **might clear** the brush on his land.
>
> He **bought** a chainsaw so that he **could have** a necessary tool for rural living.
>
> He **took** care that he **should** not **invalidate** the warranty on the chainsaw.

Note. When the verb of the main clause is in any tense other than the past or past perfect, the present tense of a modal auxiliary is regularly used in the subordinate clause.

> He **is buying** a chainsaw in order that he **may clear** his land.
>
> He **will buy** (**has bought**) a chainsaw in order that he **may clear** his land.
>
> He **is buying** a chainsaw so that he **can clear** his land.

Natural Sequence

CCSS.L.8.1.C:
Form and use verbs in the indicative, imperative, interrogative, conditional, and subjunctive mood.

The principle controlling the sequence of tenses in these clauses is largely predictable. *Regardless of the tense of the verb in the main clause, the verb in the subordinate clause may be in any tense whatsoever that is essential to the logic of the sentence.*

Years ago I **liked** my job more than I **do** now.

We once **camped** where the new development **will be built**.

I **was** once homeless, although I **am** now a teacher.

Colonial Americans **did** not **eat** as we **do** now.

She **studied** harder than I ever **will** (study).

He **is** happy because he **found** his cell phone.

You **will eat** what I **cooked**.

You **can check** your email after I **have checked** mine.

I **have** always **lived** where the winters **are** hard.

Exercise 15.6: Writing with Sequence of Tenses in Discourse

Rewrite the following sentences, changing them from direct to indirect discourse or from indirect to direct discourse.

WRITING PROMPT:
Write two or three paragraphs to describe a social gathering, meeting, dinner, etc. Use logical time sequence and correct verb tenses.

1. He replied, "I live in California."

2. I said, "We are going to the movies tonight."

3. "Will you visit this weekend?" he asked.

4. "I have found my missing iPhone," she announced.

CCSS.L.8.1.C:
Form and use verbs in the indicative, imperative, interrogative, conditional, and subjunctive mood.

5. "Honesty is the best policy," she declared.

6. "I know that I am getting better," he said.

7. "May I see your supervisor?" he inquired.

8. "I have worked since I got up this morning," I began, "and I am exhausted."

9. They promised that they would pay their bill by the end of the month.

10. I said that I was willing to let your borrow my car.

11. She says that she has the time to help us.

12. She said that she had the time to help us.

Exercise 15.7: Identifying Correct Sequence of Tenses

Underline the verb form in parentheses which best expresses the logical time sequence in the sentence.

CCSS.L.8.1.C:
Form and use verbs in the indicative, imperative, interrogative, conditional, and subjunctive mood.

1. When the president and first lady (hosted, had hosted) a state dinner with a foreign leader, they sent invitations to American citizens and representatives from other countries.

2. All the passengers were glad (to break, to have broken) the monotony of the voyage and gathered around the piano in the companion-house.

3. (Doing, Having done) my best in the interview, I returned home to await the outcome.

4. If the car (would have started, had started), I would have made it to my appointment on time.

5. (Seeing, Having seen) herself in the mirror, Christine admired her new dress.

6. For some time we have wanted (to invite, to have invited) you to have dinner at our house.

7. (Hearing, Having heard) the bell, I knew I was late for my first-period class.

8. After the firemen (put, had put) out the blaze, the supervisor from the fire department immediately began to inspect the premises.

9. When I (saw, had seen) the monoliths on Easter Island, I was amazed at their size and at the ingenuity involved in moving them to their location.

10. The library assistant intended (to reshelve, to have reshelved) the books on her cart.

11. Franklin said that he was sorry (to miss, to have missed) your wedding on Saturday.

12. When the hurricane (ended, had ended) we went outside to survey the damage.

13. (Looking, Having looked) over the stone wall, I could see the farm workers stooped in their labor in the field.

14. The Seven Years' War involved the British colonists against the royal French forces and the various indigenous tribes that (aligned, had aligned) against them.

15. In the account of the raising of Lazarus, Jesus (met, had met) with Lazarus's sisters Martha followed by Mary.

Exercise 15.8: Identifying Correct Sequence of Tenses

Draw a line through the incorrect verb form and write the correct form above it.

CCSS.L.8.1.C:
Form and use verbs in the indicative, imperative, interrogative, conditional, and subjunctive mood.

1. She said that you are wrong.

2. I told you that he is at home.

3. They asked whether we are ready.

4. I remarked that I may be there.

5. He declared that the earth was round.

6. They said that he has gone.

7. She said that she will go.

8. I said that you will have finished the work by that time.

9. I said that you are at home yesterday.

10. He bought the house in order that he may live in comfort.

11. He will buy the house in order that he might live in comfort.

12. He was once stronger than he was now.

13. The general once lived where the new depot would be built.

14. He was once homeless, although he was now wealthy.

15. The Romans did not dress as we did.

16. He worked harder than you ever would.

17. She is unhappy because she found things stressful.

18. They promised that they will send the money.

19. I said that I will be willing to sell the house.

20. I argued that I have a right to present my side of the case.

21. They have always lived where the winters were warm.

22. I will have read the book when I will have finished it.

23. We took care that we shall not be seen.

May be copied for classroom use. Common Core Grammar by Thomas Fasano (Coyote Canyon Press: Claremont, CA); © 2015.

SIMPLE AND PROGRESSIVE VERB-FORMS

General Distinctions

CCSS.L.8.1.C:
Form and use verbs in the indicative, imperative, interrogative, conditional, and subjunctive mood.

In general, the progressive form of the verb, as opposed to the simple form, expresses an action more vividly and emphasizes the fact that the action is *in progress* at a specific time. In the following sentences this is primarily the only consideration that governs the choice of the verb-form.

I **feel** strange.

I **am feeling** strange.

Later in the day it **rained** hard.

Later in the day it **was raining** hard.

She **will address** the audience.

She **will be addressing** the audience.

I **have taught** at the school for twenty years.

I **have been teaching** at the school for twenty years.

In other instances the differences are more specific, such as the following.

Present Tense

CCSS.L.8.1.C:
Form and use verbs in the indicative, imperative, interrogative, conditional, and subjunctive mood.

In the present tense the simple and progressive forms can have vastly different functions.

- With many verbs the simple present indicates only habitual action. The progressive form is used when an action is decidedly in actual present time.

  The professor **writes** on the board (habitual action).

  The boys **play** in the abandoned lot.

  The professor **is writing** on the board (actual present).

  The boys **are playing** in the abandoned lot.

- With some verbs, the simple present alone may indicate actual present time.

  I **know** he broke the window.

  The car **looks** snazzy.

> The milk **smells** sour.
>
> I **hear** someone coming.
>
> I **see** the problem now.
>
> I **understand** your reasoning.

The distinction between the groups above is that the verbs in the first group describe *action or activity* (*write, play, run,* etc.) or sometimes a cessation of activity (*stay, sit, stand,* etc.), whereas those in the second group largely describe a *state or condition* (*know, look, smell, hear, see, understand,* etc.). The progressive aspect expresses continuity of action or time more vividly and is thus better suited to express an action or activity.

Note. Verbs that describe certain states generally do not occur in the progressive (certain exceptions will be found).

- States of being and having: *be, contain, depend, have, resemble.*

- Intellectual states: *believe, know, realize, think, understand.*

- States of emotion or attitude: *agree, disagree; like, dislike; want, wish, love.* (*I'm loving it* is an odd expression, despite its current use in advertising.) *Enjoy* is an exception: "I'm enjoying this book."

- States of perception: *feel, hear, see, smell, taste.*

- States of bodily sensation: *ache, feel, hurt, itch, tickle.*

Some of the verbs above take the progressive form to indicate actual present time when they are used in the sense of definite action.

> I **am thinking** of traveling to Vienna ("I **think** that's a good idea").
>
> He **is realizing** that now for the first time ("He **realizes** what he did wrong").

Tenses Indicating Past Time

CCSS.L.8.1.C:
Form and use verbs in the indicative, imperative, interrogative, conditional, and subjunctive mood.

In the tenses indicating past time (past, present perfect, and past perfect), the progressive form implies that an action or situation is in progress at a particular time but is not necessarily complete.

> He **was painting** the house yesterday (progressive form—he may not have finished painting the house).
>
> He **painted** the house yesterday (simple form—he probably finished painting the house).

She **has been reading** the Bible.

She **has read** the Bible.

John claimed that he **hadn't been dating** Mary all these years.

John claimed that he **hadn't dated** Mary, ever.

In the past tense, when one action of brief duration occurred while another action of longer duration was in progress, the simple past is used for the briefer action, and the past progressive for the longer one.

He **was studying** in the library when I saw him.

The man **was brandishing** a firearm when the police shot him.

The man **was running** in the rain when he slipped.

When two actions are of about the same duration, either the simple past or the past progressive may be used for both actions, the latter being used for special emphasis or vividness.

She **laughed** when I **fell**.

She **was laughing** the whole time they **were tickling** her.

Notice the difference in the next two sentences.

She **laughed** when he **fell**.

She **was laughing** when he **fell**.

In the first sentence, she laughed in reaction to his falling. In the second, she was in the midst of laughing about something when he fell.

Exercise 15.9: Explaining Simple and Progressive Verb Forms

Explain the differences in meaning and time relationships expressed by the simple and progressive verb-forms.

CCSS.L.8.1.C:
Form and use verbs in the indicative, imperative, interrogative, conditional, and subjunctive mood.

1. In the evening we go to the movies or play computer games.

2. You are going over the speed limit.

3. Everyone looks tired.

4. My students are looking at the clock.

5. He reads German easily.

6. He is reading one of Stephen King's novels.

7. I have now read all of Stephen King's novels.

8. I have been reading the latest Stephen King novel.

9. In the evening we go to the theater or play bridge.

10. We are going over sixty miles an hour.

11. Everyone looks sleepy.

12. Everyone is looking at the clock.

13. Night came, and the stars came out.

14. Night was coming, and the coyotes were beginning to yap.

15. They left the square and were passing up Harley Street.

16. They passed the police station on their way home.

17. He climbed to the top of the mountain.

18. He was climbing to the top of the mountain.

19. She smiled when he looked at her.

20. She was smiling when he looked at her.

PARTICIPLES

Uses of the Participle

CCSS.L.8.1.A:
Explain the function of verbals (gerunds, participles, infinitives) in general and their function in particular sentences.

A participle or a participial phrase may be used:

- As an adjective.

  A **singing** bird is a joy.

  The boy **bouncing the ball** is my son.

  I threw away the **burnt** toast.

- As a Predicate Adjective.

  The driving I do is **exhausting**.

  His arm is **broken**.

  The speaker is **interesting**.

- As an Adverb in a Dual Relation.

  Facing larger penalties, the company settled out of court.

  He showed up **whistling a tune**.

  The shooting victim lay on the floor, **writhing in pain**.

- As an Objective Complement.

  I found the story **compelling**.

  We discovered the house **broken into**.

- In the Nominative Absolute Construction.

  The deadline **approaching,** we picked up the pace of our work.

  The blizzard continued overnight, snow **reaching** the windows by morning.

  She told the boys to stop, her voice **raised** in anger.

- Parenthetically.

  All things **considered,** we have made progress.

  Generally **speaking,** there are only two kinds of pet owners.

- As Part of a Verb Phrase.

  I **am planning** my retirement.

The police **have found** the missing boy.

They **have** not **considered** all the evidence.

Tense

CCSS.L.8.1.A:

Explain the function of verbals (gerunds, participles, infinitives) in general and their function in particular sentences.

Contrary to what their names suggest, present and past participles do not indicate actual present or past time. The time they indicate is governed by the time of the verb in the main clause.

The *Present Participle* regularly describes an action occurring at the time represented by the verb.

> Every city official **accepting** bribes **was arrested**.

> Every city official **accepting** bribes **is being arrested**.

> Every city official **accepting** bribes **will be arrested**.

In the sentences, the city officials have been in the continuing process of accepting bribes, and the arrests are placed in the past, present, and future respectively.

Sometimes the Present Participle represents an action taking place at the time the sentence was written or spoken and not at the time indicated by the verb.

> The student **giving** the speech **was awarded** a scholarship.

> The student **giving** the speech **will be awarded** a scholarship.

The *Past Participle* regularly describes an action that occurred before the time represented by the verb in the main clause.

> The car **dented** in the accident **is being** repaired.

> The car **dented** in the accident **was repaired**.

> All orders **received** today **will be fulfilled** tomorrow.

The *Past Participle* may indicate an action that was begun before the time represented by the verb and the effect of which is still perceived at the time of the verb.

> I saw the homeless man **dressed** in a dirty overcoat.

> The branch office **located** in Chicago will be closed.

The *Perfect Participle* describes an action that occurred definitely before the time represented by the verb and emphasizes that the action was completed before that time.

The mathematician, **having solved** a difficult problem, went in search of another problem.

The mail clerk, **having finished** his morning rounds, is on his break.

His morning rounds **having been finished,** the mail clerk is on his break.

Voice

CCSS.L.8.1.A:
Explain the function of verbals (gerunds, participles, infinitives) in general and their function in particular sentences.

The ***Present Participle*** regularly indicates that the person or thing named by the noun that the participle modifies is the performer of the action described by the participle.

The woman **shouting** at everyone is crazy.

The ***Past Participle*** regularly indicates that the person or thing named by the noun that the participle modifies is the receiver of the action described by the participle.

The boy **hit** by the car survived.

In the first example the present participle *shouting* modifies *woman*—and the woman is doing the shouting. In the second sentence the past participle *hit* modifies *boy*—and the boy received the action.

Exercise 15.10: Identifying the Functions of Participles

Underline the participles and participial phrases. Point out those that have a dual function as adjective and adverb.

CCSS.L.8.1.A:
Explain the function of verbals (gerunds, participles, infinitives) in general and their function in particular sentences.

1. This latest advisory by the Department of Homeland Security is alarming and bluntly worded.

2. The door, being locked from the inside, could not be opened.

3. Their citizenship having been established, they were released by border security.

4. Strictly speaking, he was not qualified for the job.

5. The stone steps leading down to it from the level of earth were quite unlighted.

6. These two reports by the Bureau of Fisheries are interesting and well written.

7. I saw them coming back that night.

8. Living at home, I was never absorbed in the life of the university.

9. A few years ago they bought this farm, paying part, mortgaging the remainder in the usual way.

10. The rural population, impoverished and often enslaved, frequently revolted.

11. The next morning they heard the Squire moving about in his room.

12. A few scattering clouds were drifting on the west wind, their shadows sliding down the green and purple slopes.

13. About an hour before sundown, having stowed our water-casks, we commenced getting under way.

14. The door, being bolted on the inside, could not be opened.

15. Toiling and resting and toiling again, we wore away the morning.

16. Their identity having been established, they were released by the customs officials.

17. Colet watched the papers sprawling and scattering.

Exercise 15.11: Using the Correct Tense of Participles

Fill in the blanks with the appropriate tense form of the participles—present, past, or perfect; active or passive—of the verbs indicated in parentheses.

CCSS.L.8.1.A:

Explain the function of verbals (gerunds, participles, infinitives) in general and their function in particular sentences.

1. _____ the movie before, I knew what the ending would be (see).

2. _____ the book aside, I began to write my impressions of it (lay).

3. The latest Taliban attack _____, the battalion waited nervously for the next round of attacks (repulse).

4. The weather _____ cold, we wore layers of clothing (be).

5. The weather _____ cold, we are wearing layers of clothing (be).

6. The weather _____ much colder during the night, we wore layers of clothing the next day (turn).

7. My dog will be at the door, _____ for me (wait).

8. _____ the email the night before, I was concerned because I did not receive a reply (send).

9. A letter _____ by Lincoln is in the collection at the Huntington Library (write).

10. Their identity _____, they were released by the customs officials (establish).

11. I followed him, _____ of answers to each point as he made it (think).

12. He began to pace the room, his head _____ in thought (bow).

13. _____ at home, I was never absorbed in the life of the university (live).

14. About an hour before sundown, _____ our water-casks, we commenced getting under way (stow).

15. The door, _____ on the inside, could not be opened (bolt).

16. _____ her suitcases, Susan ran toward me (drop).

17. _____ to explain anything, Harry was already being his secretive self (refuse).

18. _____ the basic theory of narrative, Aristotle created a way of looking at storytelling that has never gone out of fashion (explain).

INFINITIVES

As a Noun

CCSS.L.8.1.A:
Explain the function of verbals (gerunds, participles, infinitives) in general and their function in particular sentences.

An infinitive or infinitive phrase may be used as a noun.

- Subject of a Verb.

  To hesitate would be a mistake.

  It's not easy **to be poor.**

- Predicate Noun.

  My desire is **to see you succeed**.

- Object of a Verb.

  He agreed **to sell the car**.

  They wanted **to go to the circus**.

- Objective Complement.

  He found a hammer **to be what he needed**.

  They wanted their son **to go to college**.

- Retained Object of a Verb.

  In the 1990s Steve Jobs was forced **to leave Apple Computer**.

- Object of a Preposition.

  You have no option but **to take your medicine**.

- In Apposition with a Noun.

  My first idea, **to threaten them,** was counterproductive.

As an Adjective

CCSS.L.8.1.A:
Explain the function of verbals (gerunds, participles, infinitives) in general and their function in particular sentences.

An infinitive or an infinitive phrase may be used as an adjective.

A need **to be heard** drove him to write.

You have a chance **to win the auction**.

My order is **to go** (predicate adjective).

As an Adverb

CCSS.L.8.1.A:
Explain the function of verbals (gerunds, participles, infinitives) in general and their function in particular sentences.

An infinitive or an infinitive phrase may be used as an adverb, in which case it modifies or completes the meaning of a verb, adjective, or adverb.

I went **to see what the problem was** (modifies the verb).

The crowd stood **to see better**.

He came **to help you out**.

She is certain **to make a name for herself** (modifies an adjective).

The movie wasn't easy **to follow**.

She was indiscreet enough **to say something** (modifies the adverb **enough**).

Some infinitives have a relation to the words they modify that is so general that it is difficult to classify them according to their meanings. These types of infinitives are called "Complementary Infinitives used as Adverbs." In some instances they easily fall into one of the adverbial groups.

The girl was too short **to ride the roller coaster** (degree).

They showed up **to pick up their flowers** (purpose).

In a Verb Phrase

CCSS.L.8.1.A:
Explain the function of verbals (gerunds, participles, infinitives) in general and their function in particular sentences.

An infinitive used with a form of *be* or *have* completes a verb phrase.

The latest issue **is to publish** next week.

They **have to borrow** money.

Commonly the infinitive is combined with *going, about, ought,* or *used*.

I **am going to fly** a kite.

The train **is about to depart**.

I **used to cook** a lot.

Used Parenthetically

CCSS.L.8.1.A:
Explain the function of verbals (gerunds, participles, infinitives) in general and their function in particular sentences.

An infinitive may be used parenthetically.

> Your business plan, **to be honest,** is doomed to failure.
>
> **To state the obvious,** America has a large military.

Used Absolutely with a Noun

CCSS.L.8.1.A:
Explain the function of verbals (gerunds, participles, infinitives) in general and their function in particular sentences.

An infinitive modifying a noun may form a construction similar to a nominative absolute with a participle.

> The contest ends on Friday, **the winner to be announced that night**.
>
> The court issued its ruling yesterday, **the prisoner to be exonerated and released from custody**.

Combined with "How," etc.

CCSS.L.8.1.A:
Explain the function of verbals (gerunds, participles, infinitives) in general and their function in particular sentences.

An infinitive combined with *how, when, where, which,* and *whether* forms a construction equivalent to a noun clause.

> She didn't know **what to say** (object of a verb).
>
> Can you tell me **how to do this?**
>
> The question is **whether to accept the job** (predicate noun).
>
> **Which strategy to use** is our next challenge (subject).

Infinitive with a Subject

CCSS.L.8.1.A:
Explain the function of verbals (gerunds, participles, infinitives) in general and their function in particular sentences.

An infinitive with a subject can also be the object of the preposition *for*.

> We expect **you to fulfill the contract**.
>
> We intend **for you to fulfill the contract**.

Infinitive without "to"

An infinitive with the marker *to* omitted may be used:

CCSS.L.8.1.A:

Explain the function of verbals (gerunds, participles, infinitives) in general and their function in particular sentences.

- After verbs like *dare, see, make, help*.

  I dare not **try** this (to try).

  I saw you **swim** (to swim).

  The smell made me **recoil** (to recoil).

- After auxiliaries to form verb phrases.

  I will **finish**.

  He can't **swim**.

  They should **collaborate**.

- As the object of the preposition *except* or *but*.

  The maid did everything required except **vacuum**.

  The baby has done nothing but **cry** all day.

TENSES OF THE INFINITIVE

CCSS.L.8.1.A:

Explain the function of verbals (gerunds, participles, infinitives) in general and their function in particular sentences.

The infinitive has two tenses: the **Present** and the **Perfect**. Examples are *to go* (present) and *to have gone* (perfect). Infinitives also have **Progressive** and **Passive** forms: as, *to be going, to be gone, to have been going, to have been gone*.

Tenses of an infinitive do not represent actual present or past time; they indicate time relative to the verb with which they are used.

Present Infinitive

CCSS.L.8.1.A:

Explain the function of verbals (gerunds, participles, infinitives) in general and their function in particular sentences.

The present infinitive may be used with any tense of a verb. It represents several types of action:

- An action contemporaneous with the time of the verb that it modifies or accompanies.

  I **like to eat pizza**.

  He **appeared to trip**.

  The agents **will help** you **to find** a house.

  I **agreed to help** them.

  She **seems to be struggling** a lot.

He **likes to be heard**.

- An action occurring after the time of the verb.

    I **want to go** to the beach tomorrow.

    Yesterday he **agreed to call** a meeting for Friday.

    She **will leave** tomorrow **to travel** to Canada.

    They **have invited** us **to attend** their wedding.

Perfect Infinitive

CCSS.L.8.1.A:

Explain the function of verbals (gerunds, participles, infinitives) in general and their function in particular sentences.

The perfect infinitive regularly describes an action that occurred before the time of the verb that it modifies or accompanies. Generally, it is used with a verb in the present tense; occasionally with one in the future tense; less often with one in the past tense.

- With a verb in the present tense.

    I **am** happy **to have helped** you start your business.

    I **am** sorry **to have inconvenienced** you.

    She **is supposed to have been allowed** entrance.

- With a verb in the future tense.

    You **will find** him **to have been lying**.

    As you work on this project, it **will seem** more and more **to have presented** difficulties from the start.

- With a verb in the past tense.

    When the audience filed out, they **seemed to have enjoyed** the concert.

    The soldier was **reported to have been captured** by Al Qaeda.

When using a perfect infinitive with a verb in the past tense, one should be certain that the action expressed by the infinitive actually belongs to a time previous to that of the verb. Frequently a writer will discover that such is not the case and that the present infinitive should be used.

I hoped **to have been** there (incorrect).

I hoped **to be** there (correct).

She would like **to have been** there (incorrect).

She would like **to be** there (correct).

May be copied for classroom use. Common Core Grammar by Thomas Fasano (Coyote Canyon Press: Claremont, CA); © 2015.

Exercise 15.12: Identifying Infinitives

Underline the infinitives and infinitive phrases.

CCSS.L.8.1.A:

Explain the function of verbals (gerunds, participles, infinitives) in general and their function in particular sentences.

1. To do the job properly would require at least a week.

2. A manuscript supposed to have been penned by Shakespeare is on display in the British Museum.

3. She is planning for her family to meet her at the airport.

4. At first the plan seemed achievable but was later discovered to be unworkable.

5. There was no alternative except to take the matter to a higher authority.

6. The baby's weight, to be exact, was eight pounds five ounces.

7. Where to get the funding was the most important question.

8. Under these conditions, for him to go was hard to imagine.

9. It is better to have loved and lost.

10. There is still one possibility—namely, to sell your car and use the subway.

11. To do the work properly would require at least a month.

12. Still the young man would have to be disciplined, to get him back in his place.

13. A house supposed to have been built by Lincoln, has been preserved.

14. I did not know whether to laugh or cry.

15. He is planning for you to meet him in Boston.

16. At first the plan seemed feasible, but later they found it to be impractical.

17. Nobody likes to be asked favors.

18. We have the power, but we have still to learn how to use our power.

19. For a hundred years America was in a position to supply land to all immigrants who cared to till the soil.

20. We intimated that the prairie was hardly the place to enjoy a quiet life.

21. The exiles were forbidden to return at peril to their lives.

22. She lets her clever tongue run away with her sometimes.

Exercise 15.13: Using Tense Forms of Infinitives

Fill in the blanks with the appropriate tense form of the infinitives—present or perfect, active or passive. (Use the infinitive of the verb given in parentheses.)

CCSS.L.8.1.A:

Explain the function of verbals (gerunds, participles, infinitives) in general and their function in particular sentences.

1. In March the company was said to _____ nearly bankrupt (be).

2. The escaped convicts were reported yesterday afternoon to _____ in the Everglades (see).

3. They want to _____ next week (go).

4. He was believed to _____ a cousin of the escaped convicts (be).

5. I am happy to _____ you so cheerful today (find).

6. I am happy to _____ him speak at the last convention (hear).

7. I was happy to _____ so good an opportunity to see the Supreme Court in session (have).

8. He would have been happy to _____ you when he was here (meet).

9. She ought to _____ early enough to be here by this time (rise).

10. She ought to _____ early enough to be here early tomorrow (rise).

11. To _____ wealthy was my primary goal in life (become).

12. To _____ friendly, we invited our new neighbors to dinner (be).

13. To _____ your soul mate, you must be open to all possibilities (find).

14. Some people are unable to _____ in the face of adversity (smile).

15. Everyone was eager to _____ about the new neighbors and what they were like (hear).

16. No one was going to _____ for a favor (ask).

17. Many executives would like to _____ more free time (have).

18. It's possible that the suspect wanted to _____ unrecognizable (appear).

19. The refrigerator that we bought was too big to _____ in the space where the old one was (fit).

20. I longed to _____ the man better (know).

21. I long to _____ the man better (know).

22. I wanted to _____

23. I am happy to _____ you with your little problem (help).

MODAL AUXILIARIES

Verb phrases indicating permission, possibility, probability, ability, obligation, and other similar ideas are regularly formed with the aid of modal auxiliaries: namely, *may, can, must, might, could, would, should,* and *shall.*

Time Indicated by the Modal Auxiliaries

CCSS.L.9–10.1.B:
Use various types of phrases (noun, verb, adjectival, adverbial, participial, prepositional, absolute) and clauses (independent, dependent; noun, relative, adverbial) to convey specific meanings and add variety and interest to writing or presentations.

Might, could, would, and *should,* despite their classification as the past tenses of *may, can, will,* and *shall,* do not usually indicate actual past time. They regularly indicate present or future time, just as the present forms do.

Distinguishing the uses of the present and past tenses is a matter of understanding their different shades of meaning. Mainly the past tense forms express an idea with more doubt and thus with less definiteness.

> I **can** call him today.
>
> I **could** call him tomorrow.
>
> You **may** like it.
>
> You **might** like it.

Often the past tense form is governed by attracted sequence of tenses.

> We thought that he **might** quit. (He may quit.)
>
> She said that Jonathan **would** agree. (Jonathan will agree.)

In order to place an action definitely in past time, the present and past tense forms of a modal are regularly used with the helping verb *have,* the past tense form expressing greater doubt.

> She **may have** left yesterday.
>
> She **might have** left yesterday (more doubtful).
>
> We **could have** visited them.

Note. In some uses *could* and *would* alone may indicate past time: "He *would* cause a fuss" (was determined to cause a fuss). "He *could* play the piano at the age of five."

General Uses

In sentences expressing *condition, necessity, concession,* and *purpose,* the modal auxiliaries have the following uses.

In Main Clauses

CCSS.L.9–10.1.B:
Use various types of phrases (noun, verb, adjectival, adverbial, participial, prepositional, absolute) and clauses (independent, dependent; noun, relative, adverbial) to convey specific meanings and add variety and interest to writing or presentations.

The verb of the main clause generally has *might, could, would,* or *should* as its auxiliary when modified by a conditional clause contrary to fact in the past tense of the subjunctive mood.

If I **were** younger, I **would** have more energy.

If you **knew** web design, you **could** earn some extra money.

If we **had** more savings, we **might** be able to afford a house.

The verb of the main clause has *might have, could have, would have,* or *should have* as its auxiliary when modified by a conditional clause contrary to fact in the past perfect tense of the subjunctive mood.

If I **had been** younger, I **would have** had more energy.

If you **had known** web design, you **could have** earned some extra money.

If we **had had** more savings, we **might have** been able to afford a house.

Note. In sentences expressing a condition that may or may not be true to fact, the verbs in both the main and subordinate clauses may be in any form or tense required by the logic of the sentence. A modal auxiliary may or may not be used.

If you **travel** to Florida, **bring** your bathing suit.

If she **is** unhappy, she **brought** it on herself.

If what you say **is** true, then I **was** wrong.

If you **spend** your money on that, you **will be** sorry.

If you **said** that, I am certain that he **regrets** it.

If he **quits** his job, he **will tell** you.

If they **knew** what happened, they **failed** to say anything.

If you **were** lost, you **should have called** me.

If you **have seen** her play the violin, you **will know** how good she is.

In Subordinates Clauses

CCSS.L.9–10.1.B:
Use various types of phrases (noun, verb, adjectival, adverbial, participial, prepositional, absolute) and clauses (independent, dependent; noun, relative, adverbial) to convey specific meanings and add variety and interest to writing or presentations.

Verb phrases with modal auxiliaries have replaced most of the uses of the former subjunctive mood, but the subjunctive is still in regular use in a number of verb phrases.

- *Should* is used in conditional clauses that *may or may not be true to fact* to indicate doubt about whether the condition will be fulfilled.

   Should he wake up, call me at once.

   If the crowd **should** turn violent, leave at once.

Compare "If the crowd *turns* violent" and "If the crowd *turn* violent." *Turns* (indicative), *turn* (subjunctive), and *should turn* (with the modal auxiliary) indicate increasing degrees of doubt.

- *Should* (or *shall*) is occasionally used instead of the present subjunctive in certain clauses that depend on a verb, noun, or adjective to express some sort of wish, command, or urgency.

   They wished that the protocols **should** be obeyed.

   It is imperative that you **should** clean out your office at once.

   His order was that we **should** be transferred to another base.

   The teacher requires that all homework **should** be done in ink.

- *May, might,* or *should* is used in clauses of concession that admit something as doubtful or possible.

   Although she **may** be right, I haven't changed my opinion about her.

   Even though we **might** go bankrupt, we have each other.

   Even though the ship **should** sway, our gear doesn't have to go overboard.

"Although she *is* right," "Although she *be* right," "Although she *may be* right," "Although she *might be* right" point out increasing degrees of doubt.

- *May* or *might* (sometimes *should* or *would*) is used in clauses of purpose.

   They saved for many years in order that they **may** buy their dream house.

   My mother cooked extra so that she **might** fill up her hungry family.

   I arrived early so that I **would** have time to prepare.

Specific Meanings of the Modal Auxiliaries

CCSS.L.9–10.1.B:

Use various types of phrases (noun, verb, adjectival, adverbial, participial, prepositional, absolute) and clauses (independent, dependent; noun, relative, adverbial) to convey specific meanings and add variety and interest to writing or presentations.

"May" (past tense, *might*) denotes:

- Permission.

  You **may** borrow that (you have my permission).

  May I tell you something?

  She says that you **may** not like the color.

  She says that you **might** not like the color.

- Possibility.

  He **may** know the answer.

  He **might** know the answer (more doubtful).

  I think that I **may** finally understand.

  I think that I **might** finally understand.

- A wish (*may* only).

  May you live long and prosper.

  May that never happen.

"Can" (past tense, *could*) denotes:

- Ability.

  He **can** swim a mile easily.

  He **could** swim a mile easily (if he tried).

  She says that she **could** run a marathon.

- Refusal of permission—in negative statements.

  You **cannot** watch TV now (I forbid you to).

"Must" denotes:

- Necessity or obligation.

  You **must** pay your bill.

  The jury **must** deliberate.

To show necessity or obligation in past time, the verb *had* is used with an infinitive.

May be copied for classroom use. Common Core Grammar by Thomas Fasano (Coyote Canyon Press: Claremont, CA); © 2015.

They **had to speak** with the mayor about an urgent matter.

Must regularly indicates past time when used in sequence with a verb in the past tense.

You told us that we **must** stop bickering.

- Emphasis in a statement of inference.

It **must** be a record high temperature today (judging by how hot it feels, I infer that a record has been broken).

He **must** think that you are stupid (from the way he talks to you, I infer that he considers you to be stupid).

To indicate past time, *must have* is used.

It **must have** been after closing when he left.

"Would" denotes:

- Habitual action in the past.

In those days, I **would** be up all night.

People **would** stand in line overnight.

- Determination.

I **would** go out of my way to avoid her.

He **would** deliberately tease the dog.

- Willingness to do something.

We **would** give you money if you needed it.

I **would** tighten the screws if I had a screwdriver.

You **would** not like prison.

He **would** be singing a different tune if he knew what was waiting for him.

- A Wish.

Would that it were so!

Would that tomorrow were here!

This use of *would* is largely poetical or emphatic. The ordinary form is "I *wish* that it were so."

Note. In sequence with a verb in the past tense, *would* may stand in place of *will* used in direct discourse: "He said that he *would* pay for our dinner" (direct discourse: "I *will* pay for your dinner").

"Should" denotes:

- Duty or obligation—similar meaning as *ought to. Should* expresses a weaker degree of obligation than *must.*

  I **should** go to bed now.

  You **should** keep him company.

  He **should** work fewer hours.

- Inference.

  He **should** have received the delivery by now (considering when we mailed it, I infer that the package has probably been delivered by now).

  We **should** be there on time, if traffic doesn't back up.

- Simple futurity—in the first person

  I'm positive that I **should** have a good time if I went.

  I **should** be glad to spend the day with you.

- In expressions like "I *should say,*" "I *should think,*" etc., *should* softens the statement and makes it less abrupt, more polite, than I *say* and I *think.*

  I **should say** that you are wrong ("I **say** that you are wrong").

  I **should think** that she would have grown tired of it by now.

Note. In sequence with a verb in the past tense, *should* regularly replaces *shall* used in direct discourse: "I said that I *should* be glad to spend the day with you" (direct discourse: "I *shall* be glad to spend the day with you").

Distinction Between "Shall" and "Will"

CCSS.L.11–12.1.A:
Apply the understanding that usage is a matter of convention, can change over time, and is sometimes contested.

The distinctions between *shall* and *will* are no longer closely observed. The modern tendency is to use *will* for *shall* in constructions where *shall* was formerly required. Differences, however, are still observed by careful speakers and writers.

"Shall." In the ***First Person*** *shall* denotes simple futurity—the fact that something is going to happen.

  I **shall return** one day.

In the **Second** and **Third Persons** *shall* expresses determination or denotes a command on the part of the speaker.

> You (he) **shall go** to college (I am determined that you (he) shall go).

Note. *Will* is frequently used in commands to make them more polite.

> You **will** clean the bathrooms today.

"Will." In the **First Person** *will* always indicates willingness, determination, or a promise.

> I **will deliver** the package when told to do so.
>
> I **will attend** despite not wanting to go.

"Will." In the **Second** and **Third Persons** *will* denotes:

- Simple futurity.

> You **will find** the place a mess.
>
> He **will agree** to the offer.

- Willingness or determination on the part of the *doer* of the action.

> They **will help** all they can.
>
> He **will smoke** till the day he dies.

Mistakes in the use of simple futurity commonly occur. Traditional grammars have always emphasized the preceding distinctions: simple futurity is expressed by *shall* in the first person and by *will* in the second and third persons.

> I **shall** drive.
>
> You **will** drive.
>
> She **will** drive.

"Shall" and "Will" in Questions

CCSS.L.11–12.1.A:
Apply the understanding that usage is a matter of convention, can change over time, and is sometimes contested.

In questions the modal auxiliary anticipated in the answer is the one used in all persons.

> **Shall** we go shopping? (We **shall**—futurity)
>
> **Will** I have a second helping? (I **will**—willingness)
>
> **Shall** you have the honor? (I **shall**—futurity)
>
> **Shall** he bring his tools? (He **shall**—command)

"Should" and "Would"

CCSS.L.11–12.1.A:
Apply the understanding that usage is a matter of convention, can change over time, and is sometimes contested.

In expressing simple futurity, *should* and *would* are governed by the same rule for *shall* and *will*.

> I **should** be glad to talk with her.
>
> We **would** be surprised if she said that.
>
> You **would** be welcomed with open arms.
>
> He **would** not like what I said.

May be copied for classroom use. Common Core Grammar by Thomas Fasano (Coyote Canyon Press: Claremont, CA); © 2015.

Exercise 15.14: Explaining the Use of Modal Auxiliaries

Underline the modal auxiliaries and explain their meaning.

CCSS.L.11–12.1.B:
Resolve issues of complex or contested usage, consulting references (e.g., *Merriam–Webster's Dictionary of English Usage, Garner's Modern American Usage*) as needed.

1. Of course, I should attend tomorrow, but I can't leave work.

2. He would often spend the day in the downtown area, collecting bottles and cans.

3. She would buy the car, in spite of all I could do to dissuade her from doing so.

4. He might find the Easter eggs if he would look carefully.

5. You may leave at four o'clock if your work is done.

6. May your life savings never grow smaller.

CCSS.L.9–10.1.B:
Use various types of phrases (noun, verb, adjectival, adverbial, participial, prepositional, absolute) and clauses (independent, dependent; noun, relative, adverbial) to convey specific meanings and add variety and interest to writing or presentations.

7. This form should be filed with the IRS before the deadline.

8. She should like to see the sequel to this movie.

9. She would like to read the sequel to this novel.

10. At such times his thoughts would be full of valorous deeds.

11. Indeed, as a class, I should say that men of science were happier than other men.

12. The long-boat would have taken the lot of us; but the skipper said we must save as much property as possible.

13. He would often spend the day in the mountains, collecting ferns and mosses.

CCSS.L.8.1.C:
Form and use verbs in the indicative, imperative, interrogative, conditional, and subjunctive mood.

14. I would that my tongue could utter the thoughts that arise in me.

15. There may be a reduction in price later in the month.

16. About his internal life we can only speculate.

17. I knew that my visit must be measured by days, almost by hours.

Exercise 15.15: Using Modal Auxiliaries

Use the proper form of shall *and* will, should *and* would.

WRITING PROMPT:
Write declarative sentences, using *will* or *shall* in the first person to express a threat, a promise, resolution, consent, desire, determination, simple futurity.

1. _____ I have time to send a fax?

2. I want to know whether I _____ include my travel expenses.

3. I _____ say that his estimate for the air conditioner repairs is too high.

4. I _____ go if I had the time and money to spend.

5. You _____ be stupid to do that.

CCSS.L.11–12.1.B:
Resolve issues of complex or contested usage, consulting references (e.g., *Merriam–Webster's Dictionary of English Usage, Garner's Modern American Usage*) as needed.

6. You _____ be disloyal to the school if you posted your criticism of the principal on Facebook.

7. They _____ be disloyal if they disobeyed their boss.

8. I _____ like to believe that he is honest.

9. She _____ like to make the trip by plane.

10. We _____ be glad to work with you on this project.

CCSS.L.9–10.1.B:
Use various types of phrases (noun, verb, adjectival, adverbial, participial, prepositional, absolute) and clauses (independent, dependent; noun, relative, adverbial) to convey specific meanings and add variety and interest to writing or presentations.

11. We _____ be too late for the first act of the play.

12. The guide _____ be at the station to meet you.

13. All right, then, I _____ go, since you insist.

14. We _____ be surprised if the plan is successful.

15. I _____ expect a reply by noon tomorrow.

16. He _____ be glad to mail the letter for you.

17. I _____ be glad to help you.

18. We _____ have to hurry, or we _____ be late.

CCSS.L.8.1.C:
Form and use verbs in the indicative, imperative, interrogative, conditional, and subjunctive mood.

19. I _____ find the answer to this problem if I have to work all night.

20. I hope that I _____ find them at home.

21. He _____ be on duty at the main entrance, and I _____ be at the side door.

22. I _____ probably hear from him sometime today.

STRONG AND WEAK VERBS

CCSS.L.11–12.1.B:
Resolve issues of complex or contested usage, consulting references (e.g., *Merriam–Webster's Dictionary of English Usage, Garner's Modern American Usage*) as needed.

Weak Verbs regularly form the past tense and past participle by adding *-ed* or *-d* to the present tense form (base form).

Irregular (Strong) Verbs differ from regular (weak) verbs in the following ways:

The past and past participle are identical, with an identical vowel and the addition of a suffix.

PRESENT	PAST	PAST PARTICIPLE
bend	bent	bent
lend	lent	lent
spend	spent	spent

CCSS.L.9–10.1.B:
Use various types of phrases (noun, verb, adjectival, adverbial, participial, prepositional, absolute) and clauses (independent, dependent; noun, relative, adverbial) to convey specific meanings and add variety and interest to writing or presentations.

The past tense and past participle are identical, with a shift in the base vowel and an addition of a suffix.

PRESENT	PAST	PAST PARTICIPLE
bring	brought	brought
lose	lost	lost
mean	meant	meant
tell	told	told

The past tense and past participle are identical, with no shift in the base vowel and no suffix.

PRESENT	PAST	PAST PARTICIPLE
let	let	let
set	set	set
hit	hit	hit
cost	cost	cost

CCSS.L.8.1.C:
Form and use verbs in the indicative, imperative, interrogative, conditional, and subjunctive mood.

The past tense and past participle are identical, with a change in the base vowel and no suffix.

PRESENT	PAST	PAST PARTICIPLE
bleed	bled	bled
dig	dug	dug
stick	stuck	stuck
win	won	won
sit	sat	sat

The past tense and past participle are not identical, with or without a change in the base vowel and with a suffix.

PRESENT	PAST	PAST PARTICIPLE
break	broke	broken

swear	swore	sworn
bite	bit	bitten
forget	forgot	forgotten
lie	lay	lain
blow	blew	blown
shake	shook	shaken
beat	beat	beaten

The past tense and past participle are not identical, with a change in the base vowel and no suffix.

PRESENT	PAST	PAST PARTICIPLE
begin	began	begun
shrink	shrank	shrunk
swim	swam	swum
run	ran	run
drink	drank	drunk

Forms of the Auxiliaries "Do," "Have," "Be" and the Modal Auxiliaries

CCSS.L.11–12.1.B:
Resolve issues of complex or contested usage, consulting references (e.g., *Merriam–Webster's Dictionary of English Usage, Garner's Modern American Usage*) as needed.

Special attention must be given to the negative and contraction forms of *do* and *have*.

The auxiliary **do** has the following forms.

NON-NEGATIVE	UNCONTRACTED NEGATIVE	CONTRACTED NEGATIVE
do	do not	don't
does	does not	doesn't
did	did not	didn't

AIN'T:
Ain't has a widely established use, especially in popular songs, where it is a euphonious substitute for the strident *isn't, hasn't, doesn't*. As for the future of *ain't*, Yogi Berra said it best: "It ain't over till it's over."

The auxiliary **have** has the following forms.

NON-NEGATIVE	UNCONTRACTED NEGATIVE	CONTRACTED NEGATIVE
have	have not	haven't
has	has not	hasn't
had	had not	hadn't

The verb **be** is unique among English verbs in having eight different forms, including the base form *be*.

NON-NEGATIVE	UNCONTRACTED NEGATIVE	CONTRACTED NEGATIVE
am	am not	(aren't, ain't)
is	is not	isn't

are	are not	aren't
was	was not	wasn't
were	were not	weren't
being	not being	
been	not been	

CCSS.L.8.1.C:

Form and use verbs in the indicative, imperative, interrogative, conditional, and subjunctive mood.

The auxiliary verbs have the following forms.

NON-NEGATIVE	UNCONTRACTED NEGATIVE	CONTRACTED NEGATIVE
can	cannot, can not	can't
could	could not	couldn't
may	may not	mayn't
might	might not	mightn't
shall	shall not	shan't
should	should not	shouldn't
will	will not	won't
would	would not	wouldn't
must	must not	mustn't
ought (to)	ought not (to)	oughtn't (to)
used to	used not to	usedn't to
need	need not	needn't
dare	dare not	didn't dare to (daren't)
do	do not	don't
does	does not	doesn't
did	did not	didn't
doing	not doing	
done	not done	

LIST OF IRREGULAR VERBS

CCSS.L.11–12.1.B:

Resolve issues of complex or contested usage, consulting references (e.g., *Merriam–Webster's Dictionary of English Usage, Garner's Modern American Usage*) as needed.

Among the English irregular verbs are some of the most common and most useful and some of the rarest and most archaic in the language. Their forms are unpredictable as they are surviving members of a highly developed system of verb classes found in Old English.

The following list is drawn up in three columns showing the principal parts of the English verb: the present tense base, the past tense, and the past participle. As for prefixes that do not affect conjugation, I have listed these in the left-hand column next to the verbs to which they attach. I have left out the prefix *re-*, which can attach to numerous verbs in the list. Nor do I include prefixes that produce no more than one form in common usage (participles such as *overgrown* and *underslung*). (R) denotes that the verb also occurs with regular inflections. Some regular verbs that have nonstandard irregular forms are not included: *drag* and *sneak*.

CCSS.L.11–12.2.B:
Spell correctly.

	PRESENT	PAST	PAST PARTICIPLE
	be	was/were	been
for-, over-	bear	bore	borne/born
brow-	beat	beat	beaten
	beget	begot	begotten
	begin	began	begun
un-	bend	bent	bent
	bereave (R)	bereft	bereft
	beseech (R)	besought	besought
	bet (R)	bet	bet
for-	bid (R) "implore"	bade/bid	bidden
out-, over-, under-	bid "bet"	bid	bid
a-	bide (R)	bode	bided
un-	bind	bound	bound
	bite	bit	bitten
	bleed	bled	bled
	blend (R)	blent	blent
	bless (R)	blest	blest
	blow	blew	blown
	break	broke	broken
	breed	bred	bred
	bring	brought	brought
	build	built	built
	burn (R)	burnt	burnt
	burst	burst	burst
	buy	bought	bought
broad-, fore-	cast	cast	cast
	catch	caught	caught
	chide (R)	chid	chidden
	choose	chose	chosen
	cleave "cling" (R)	clove	cleaved
	cleave "split" (R)	cleft/clove	cleft/cloven
	cling	clung	clung
be-, over-	come	came	come
	cost	cost	cost
	creep	crept	crept
	crow (R)	crew	crowed
	cut	cut	cut

CCSS.L.11–12.2.B:
Spell correctly.

mis-	deal	dealt	dealt
	dig	dug	dug
	dight (R)	dight	dight
	dive (R)	dove	dived
out-, over- under-, un-	do	did	done
over-, with-	draw	drew	drawn
	dream (R)	dreamt	dreamt
	drink	drank	drunk
	drive	drove	driven
	dwell (R)	dwelt	dwelt
	eat	ate	eaten
be-	fall	fell	fallen
	feed	fed	fed
	feel	felt	felt
	fight	fought	fought
	find	found	found
	fit (R)	fit	fit
	flee	fled	fled
	fling	flung	flung
	fly	flew	flown
	forget	forgot	forgotten
	forsake	forsook	forsaken
	freeze	froze	frozen
	get	got	got/gotten
	gilt (R)	gilt	gilt
	gird (R)	girt	girt
for-, mis-	give	gave	given
for-, fore- out-, under-	go	went	gone
	grave (R)	graved	graven
	grind	ground	ground
out-	grow	grew	grown
over-	hang	hung	hung/hanged
	have	had	had
over-	hear	heard	heard
	heave (nautical)	hove	hove
	hew (R)	hewed	hewn
	hide	hid	hidden
	hit	hit	hit
be-, with-	hold	held	held
	hurt	hurt	hurt

CCSS.L.11–12.2.B:
Spell correctly.

	keep	kept	kept
	kneel (R)	knelt	knelt
	knit (R)	knit	knit
fore-	know	knew	known
	lade (R)	laded	laden
	lay	laid	laid
mis-	lead	led	led
	lean (R)	leant	leant
over-	leap (R)	leapt	leapt
	learn (R)	learnt	learnt
	leave	left	left
	lend	lent	lent
	let	let	let
over-, under-	lie	lay	lain
	light (R)	lit	lit
	lose	lost	lost
	make	made	made
	mean	meant	meant
	meet	met	met
	mow (R)	mowed	mown
	pay	paid	paid
	pen (R)	pent	pent
	plead (R)	pled	pled
	prove (R)	proved	proven
	put	put	put
	quit (R)	quit	quit
	read	read	read
	reave (R)	reft	reft
	rend (R)	rent	rent
	rid (R)	rid	rid
over-	ride	rode	ridden
	ring	rang	rung
a-	rise	rose	risen
	rive (R)	rived	riven
	rot	rotted	rotten
out-, fore- over-	run	ran	run
	saw (R)	sawed	sawn
	say	said	said
fore-	see	saw	seen
	seek	sought	sought
under-	sell	sold	sold

CCSS.L.11–12.2.B:
Spell correctly.

	send	sent	sent
be-, off-	set	set	set
	sew (R)	sewed	sewn
	shake	shook	shaken
	shave (R)	shaved	shaven
	shear (R)	sheared	shorn
	shed	shed	shed
	shine (R)	shone	shone
	shit	shit/shat	shit/shat
	shoe (R)	shod	shod
over-	shoot	shot	shot
	show (R)	showed	shown
	shred (R)	shred	shred
	shrink	shrank	shrunk
	shut	shut	shut
	sing	sang	sung
	sink	sank	sunk
baby-	sit	sat	sat
	slay	slew	slain
over-	sleep	slept	slept
	slide	slid	slid
	sling	slung	slung
	slink	slunk	slunk
	slit	slit	slit
	smell (R)	smelt	smelt
	smite	smote	smitten
	sow (R)	sowed	sown
be-	speak	spoke	spoken
	speed (R)	sped	sped
mis-	spell (R)	spelt	spelt
	spend	spent	spent
	spill (R)	spilt	spilt
	spin	spun	spun
	spit	spit/spat	spit/spat
	split	split	split
	spoil (R)	spoilt	spoilt
over-	spread	spread	spread
	spring	sprang	sprung
misunder- under-, with-	stand	stood	stood
	stave (R)	stove	stove
	steal	stole	stolen

CCSS.L.11–12.2.B:
Spell correctly.

	stick	stuck	stuck
	sting	stung	stung
	stink	stank	stunk
	strew (R)	strewed	strewn
be-	stride	strode	stridden
	strike	struck	struck/stricken
ham-	string	strung	strung
	strive	strove	striven/strived
for-	swear	swore	sworn
	sweat (R)	sweat	sweat
	sweep	swept	swept
	swell (R)	swelled	swollen
	swim	swam	swum
	swing	swung	swung
be-, mis-, par- over-, under-	take	took	taken
	teach	taught	taught
	tear	tore	torn
fore-	tell	told	told
	think	thought	thought
	thrive (R)	throve	thriven
over-	throw	threw	thrown
	thrust (R)	thrust	thrust
	tread	trod	trodden
a-	wake (R)	woke	woken
	wear	wore	worn
	weave	wove	woven
	wed (R)	wed	wed
	weep	wept	wept
	wet (R)	wet	wet
	win	won	won
	wind	wound	wound
	wont	wont	wont/wonted
	work (R)	wrought	wrought
	wring	wrung	wrung
under-	write	wrote	written

Exercise 15.16: Using the Correct Forms of Irregular Verbs

Write down the proper past form of each verb in parentheses.

WRITING PROMPT:
Write ten sentences with a weak (regular) verb used in the past tense; ten with a strong (irregular) verb used in the past tense.

1. The boys soon (run) out of money.

2. Several burglars (snuck, sneaked) into the art museum in Los Angeles.

3. They (stole, stoled) a painting by Pablo Picasso.

4. According to police, several people (seen, saw) the robbery.

5. The first baseman (threw, throwed) the ball to the catcher.

CCSS.L.11–12.1.B:
Resolve issues of complex or contested usage, consulting references (e.g., *Merriam-Webster's Dictionary of English Usage, Garner's Modern American Usage*) as needed.

6. As the play (begun, began) several latecomers were rudely finding their seats in the theater.

7. The defendant (denyed, denied) that he had anything to do with the crime.

8. When temperatures fell below freezing, the oranges in many of the Florida groves were (froze, frozen).

9. The newspaper reported that at least two people (drownded, drowned) during the flood.

10. When the bell (rang, rung), several students were still in the hallway.

CCSS.L.9–10.1.B:
Use various types of phrases (noun, verb, adjectival, adverbial, participial, prepositional, absolute) and clauses (independent, dependent; noun, relative, adverbial) to convey specific meanings and add variety and interest to writing or presentations.

11. The bloodhounds (lead, led) the police to the fugitive.

12. The lifeguard (dragged, drug) him out of the water and performed CPR on him.

13. In Hugo's novel, Jean Valjean (stoled, stealed, stole) the bishop's candlesticks.

14. They (brung, brought) the SUV into the shop because the radiator was overheating.

15. The bushes in the front yard have (growed, grew, grown) several feet since last year.

16. Since it was about to rain, we (brung, brought) in the clothes from the line.

CCSS.L.8.1.C:
Form and use verbs in the indicative, imperative, interrogative, conditional, and subjunctive mood.

17. I'm angry at the water company and have not (paid, payed) the bill yet.

18. After he finished his chores, he (come, came) in for dinner.

19. While moving, we accidentally (busted, broke) the hutch.

20. He came in and, tired from yard work, (sunk, sank) into a chair.

Exercise 15.17: Writing with Irregular Verb Tenses

Write sentences in which the past tense of each of the following verbs is used. Then write sentences with the past participle of each one.

CCSS.L.11–12.1.B:
Resolve issues of complex or contested usage, consulting references (e.g., *Merriam–Webster's Dictionary of English Usage, Garner's Modern American Usage*) as needed.

1. drink
2. grind
3. sow
4. get
5. wake
6. dwell
7. sing
8. pay
9. bid
10. sneak
11. bereave
12. build
13. ride
14. hang
15. swim
16. run
17. sink
18. split
19. rise
20. raise

21. shrink
22. slay
23. wring
24. weave
25. thrive
26. spin
27. tread
28. shake
29. burst
30. slink
31. dive
32. flee
33. fly
34. swing
35. wet
36. fling
37. kneel
38. drag
39. chide
40. creep

May be copied for classroom use. Common Core Grammar by Thomas Fasano (Coyote Canyon Press: Claremont, CA); © 2015.

Exercise 15.18: Distinguishing between *Sit* and *Set*

Underline the correct verb in parentheses.

CCSS.L.11–12.1.B:
Resolve issues of complex or contested usage, consulting references (e.g., *Merriam–Webster's Dictionary of English Usage, Garner's Modern American Usage*) as needed.

1. To him that overcometh will I grant to (sit, set) with Me in My throne.

2. Thou hast (sit, set) my feet in a large room.

3. The spirits of the wise (sit, set) in the clouds and mock us.

4. (Sit, Set) me as a seal upon thine heart.

5. A statue of Longfellow (sits, sets) in a park in Portland, Maine.

6. "Always seems to me," said Wemmick, "as if he (sat, set) a man-trap and was watching it.

7. We took our seats at the round table, and my guardian kept Drummle on one side of him, while Startop (sat, set) on the other.

NOTE:
To distinguish these words, look them up in a good dictionary or reference text like *Merriam–Webster's Dictionary of English Usage* or *Garner's Modern American Usage*.

8. My mother would draw a glass of cold water and (sit, set) it down where I could get it by reaching for it.

9. He (sat, set) at the piano and played Chopin through the evening.

10. The new sofa will (sit, set) in the living room, in front of the window.

11. He wanted to know where they (sat, set) all his photography equipment.

12. The student (sat, set) at a table in the library with all his laptop and books spread in front of him.

13. In the upstairs hall (sits, sets) a large display case containing all his bowling trophies.

14. Originally, Jamestown (sat, set) at the edge of a low and swampy area.

15. I suddenly realized that I was (sitting, setting) in someone else's seat.

16. The psalmist declares that God has (sat, set) man in dominion over all the beasts of the field.

17. Monticello, Italian for "little mountain," (sits, sets) upon a low rise in the countryside of Virginia.

18. The old grandfather clock (sat, set) in that same place in my family's house for over a hundred years.

19. I (sat, set) my glasses down somewhere and can't find them.

Exercise 15.19: Distinguishing between *Rise* and *Raise*

Underline the correct verb in parentheses.

CCSS.L.11–12.1.B:
Resolve issues of complex or contested usage, consulting references (e.g., *Merriam–Webster's Dictionary of English Usage, Garner's Modern American Usage*) as needed.

1. The thick mist still did not (rise, raise) from the valley.

2. Brandon (rises, raises) his hand whenever the teacher asks for volunteers.

3. The moon, (rising, raising) in clouded majesty, at length apparent queen, unveil'd her peerless light.

4. The couple finally (rose, raised) the money for the down payment.

5. The crowd (rose, raised) every time their team scored a touchdown.

6. Walter (rose, raised) before dawn so he could work on his musical.

7. If you (rise, raise) the window, a pleasant breeze will blow into the room.

NOTE:
To distinguish these words, look them up in a good dictionary or reference text like *Merriam–Webster's Dictionary of English Usage* or *Garner's Modern American Usage.*

8. Their English landlords (rose, raised) the taxes on their land so high that their ancestors could not afford to pay them.

9. Oil from the sunken vessel has continued to (rise, raise) to the surface of the water all these years.

10. King Lear, now quite mad, (rose, raised) his arms and called upon the storm to "strike flat the thick rotundity of the world."

11. As the earth warms, the polar ice will melt and (rise, raise) the level of the earth's oceans.

12. Livingstone said that he could see the smoke of a thousand villages (rising, raising) into the African sky.

13. As bombs continued to fall, the soldiers (rose, raised) the flag.

14. The weather balloon (rose, raised) many miles into the atmosphere to gather necessary meteorological data such as temperature and wind speed.

15. The pressure on the top of a wing is less than the pressure on the bottom, and this difference in pressure creates a force on the wing that (rises, raises) the plane into the air.

16. Working together, the townsmen were able to (rise, raise) the frame for the new barn.

17. John Tyndall in 1860 discovered the Greenhouse Effect and theorized that the Earth's temperature would continue to (rise, raise) with an increase in pollutants.

May be copied for classroom use. Common Core Grammar by Thomas Fasano (Coyote Canyon Press: Claremont, CA); © 2015.

Exercise 15.20: Distinguishing between *Lie* and *Lay*

Underline the correct verb in parentheses.

CCSS.L.11–12.1.B:

Resolve issues of complex or contested usage, consulting references (e.g., *Merriam–Webster's Dictionary of English Usage, Garner's Modern American Usage*) as needed.

1. Hush, my dear, (lie, lay) still and slumber.

2. All the fields are (lying, laying) brown and bare.

3. A soldier of the Legion (lay, laid) dying in Algiers.

4. The original and more potent causes, however, (laid, lay) in the rare perfection of his animal nature.

5. Stretching forth the official staff in his left hand, he (laid, lay) his right upon the shoulder of a young woman.

6. Oh! ye whose dead (lie, lay) buried beneath the green grass; who standing among flowers can say—here, here (lies, lays) my beloved.

7. Listen to what the best and latest authorities have (lain, laid) down.

8. By the time he visited her, she had (lain, laid) in the hospital room for six weeks.

9. His trousers are neatly (lain, laid) on the chair.

10. To the queen's astonishment and joy, she could perceive no token of the child's being injured by the hot fire in which he had (lain, laid).

11. The H.M.S. Titanic has (lain, laid) at the bottom of the North Atlantic since that fateful day in 1912.

12. By the end of World War II, Berlin (lay, laid) in ruins.

13. The woman (lay, laid) her hand lovingly on the young child's head.

14. In your opinion, what is the primary concern that (lies, lays) at the bottom of objections to the Affordable Care Act?

15. Her upper lids were pink, as if she were (lying, laying) in the sun.

16. After the storm, two large trees were (lying, laying) in the yard, one having crushed our car.

17. Bears are clever hunters, often (lying, laying) down parallel or even contradictory tracks in search of their prey.

18. Any person who has (lain, laid) in bed to this hour of the morning deserves a cold glass of water in the face.

NOTE:

To distinguish these words, look them up in a good dictionary or reference text like *Merriam–Webster's Dictionary of English Usage* or *Garner's Modern American Usage.*

COMMON CORE GRAMMAR

SUBJECT–VERB AGREEMENT

A verb must agree with its subject in person and number. The following sections will examine a few special constructions.

Compound Subjects

CCSS.L.9–10.1.B:
Use various types of phrases (noun, verb, adjectival, adverbial, participial, prepositional, absolute) and clauses (independent, dependent; noun, relative, adverbial) to convey specific meanings and add variety and interest to writing or presentations.

A compound subject connected by *and, both—and, not only—but* requires a plural verb.

> The doctor and his patient **were** in the examining room.
>
> San Francisco, Los Angeles, and San Diego **are** large coastal cities.
>
> Both the Senate and the House **are** in gridlock.
>
> Not only the farmhouse but also the barn **have** burned to the ground.

Note. When the two parts of the compound subject refer to the same person or thing, a singular verb is used: "My wife and best friend is here."

A compound subject connected by *or, either—or, neither—nor* requires a singular verb if the individual parts of the subject are singular; a plural verb if the individual parts are plural.

> The principal or the assistant principal **is** always in the office.
>
> Either Chaucer or Shakespeare **was** the greatest English author.
>
> Neither the rides nor the acts **were** any fun at the circus.

When the separate parts of the compound are of different numbers or one of the parts is the pronoun *you*, the verb must agree with the closest part of the subject.

> Neither the pear nor the plums **were** ripe.
>
> Either you or Sidney **is** the one.
>
> Either Sidney or you **are** the one.

A Collective Noun as Subject

A collective noun can take either a singular or a plural verb. In general, when the group named by the collective noun is regarded as a single unit, a singular verb is used; when the members of the group are regarded as individuals, a plural verb is used.

CCSS.L.11–12.1.A:

Apply the understanding that usage is a matter of convention, can change over time, and is sometimes contested.

> My family **wants** to go to Europe on vacation.
>
> My family **are** living in different parts of the country.

The previous usage is not always closely observed. Often in the same sentence a singular or a plural verb can be used interchangeably with no noticeable change in meaning.

> The Senate **is** (**are**) divided.
>
> My family **is** (**are**) gathered here.

The tendency in British English is to use the plural verb. In American English, the choice is determined by the speaker's (writer's) sense of whether the subjects are acting individually or collectively, with a general trend toward the singular.

"With" Phrase

Adding a "with" phrase to a singular subject does not make it plural.

> The motorcycle cop with other officers throughout the city streets **is** awaiting speeders.
>
> My best friend with his many cousins **is** going to be at the party.

"Everybody," "Each," etc.

CCSS.L.9–10.1.B:

Use various types of phrases (noun, verb, adjectival, adverbial, participial, prepositional, absolute) and clauses (independent, dependent; noun, relative, adverbial) to convey specific meanings and add variety and interest to writing or presentations.

The pronouns *everybody, everyone, every one, somebody, someone, some one, anybody, anyone,* and nouns modified by *every* or *each* are always singular. When used as a subject, they require a singular verb.

> Everybody in the class **was** ready for a break.
>
> Anybody **is** capable of doing more.
>
> Every one of the windows **was** shattered.
>
> Every man, woman, and child **was** accounted for.
>
> Each boy and girl **has** a piece of birthday cake.

"Some," "Half," etc.

CCSS.L.9–10.1.B:
Use various types of phrases (noun, verb, adjectival, adverbial, participial, prepositional, absolute) and clauses (independent, dependent; noun, relative, adverbial) to convey specific meanings and add variety and interest to writing or presentations.

Some, half, part, quarter, and similar words take a singular or a plural verb according to whether the words have a singular or a plural meaning.

> Some of the marbles **were** cracked.
>
> Some of the flour **was** caked.
>
> Half of your concerns **were** addressed.
>
> Half of the cake **was** gone.
>
> A part of the regiment **have** been reassigned to other bases.
>
> Part of my body **is** numb.

"None"

CCSS.L.11–12.1.A:
Apply the understanding that usage is a matter of convention, can change over time, and is sometimes contested.

Language purists insist that *none* must be singular: *None of them **is** here,* not *None of them **are** here.* The fact is there's nothing wrong with the plural when used logically. *None but my closest friends **were** invited* (not ***was***); *Almost none of my students **are** doing well in the class* (not ***is***).

None takes a singular or a plural verb according to whether its meaning is singular or plural.

> None of the pizza **was** left.
>
> None of the pizzas **were** left.

Some grammars state that *none* is always singular, but rigid adherence to this rule may result in awkward locutions.

> Almost none of the children **were** (not **was**) well behaved.
>
> None but a few of the boys **were** (not **was**) able to finish the obstacle course.

The above singular verbs are illogical and inelegant.

"Neither"

CCSS.L.11–12.1.A:
Apply the understanding that usage is a matter of convention, can change over time, and is sometimes contested.

Neither regularly takes a singular verb.

> Neither girl **was** having any luck.
>
> Neither **was** having any luck.

Neither of is commonly used with a singular verb although a plural verb is sometimes used.

> Neither of these theories **makes** sense.
>
> Neither of the children **were** there.

"Number"

CCSS.L.9–12.1:
Demonstrate command of the conventions of standard English grammar and usage when writing or speaking.

Number takes a singular verb when used with the article *the;* a plural verb when used with *a.*

> The number of people traveling this summer **is** high.
>
> A number of people **are** traveling this summer.

"There"

CCSS.L.9–12.1:
Demonstrate command of the conventions of standard English grammar and usage when writing or speaking.

The expletive *there* is used with a singular verb or a plural verb, according to whether the "notional" or "actual" subject of the *there*-sentence is singular or plural. (In these kinds of sentences *there* is the "grammatical" subject, not the actual subject.)

> There **are** two bulldozers knocking the place flat.
>
> There **appears** to be something wrong with the engine.

Plural Form, Singular Meaning

CCSS.L.9–10.1.B:
Use various types of phrases (noun, verb, adjectival, adverbial, participial, prepositional, absolute) and clauses (independent, dependent; noun, relative, adverbial) to convey specific meanings and add variety and interest to writing or presentations.

Usage varies when the subject is plural in form but can be construed as singular in meaning.

- Expressions indicating distance, amount, etc. can take either a singular or a plural verb.

> A hundred bushels of apples **is** (**are**) a lot.
>
> A thousand dollars **is** (**are**) missing from the account.
>
> Ten miles of pavement **needs** (**need**) to be replaced.
>
> Fifty yards of rope **is** (**are**) wound onto the spool.

- The titles of books, movies, plays, etc. take a singular verb.

> **Into the Wild is** a great book.
>
> "Blueberries" **is** a famous poem by Robert Frost.

- When a plural noun is used as a word, not as a name of something, it takes a singular verb.

  > **Heroes** is a word one hears often nowadays.

- Certain words that are plural in form have an unpredictable use of either a singular or a plural verb (the following list, of course, is not complete).

  - A singular verb is used with *news, physics, economics, mathematics, metaphysics.*

  - A plural verb is used with *proceeds, riches, tongs, pincers, scissors, trousers, goods, athletics, nuptials, obsequies.*

Note. Modern usage appears to be divided in the case of *athletics*. But most careful writers prefer the plural verb-form.

- Either a singular or a plural verb is used with *means, series, species,* and *statistics,* according to their meaning.

  > this means **is,** these means **are;** this series **is,** these series **are;** this species **is,** these **species are**; statistics **is** a science, these statistics **are** misleading.

Exercise 15.21: Using Correct Subject-Verb Agreement

Fill in the blanks with the correct form of the verb that agrees with the subject.

WRITING PROMPT:
Make a list of ten collective nouns. Use them in sentences (1) with a singular verb, (2) with a plural verb. Explain the difference in meaning.

1. The city, with its suburbs, _____ a population of over two million (have, has).

2. The farmhouse and the vineyards _____ to be sold by the owner's heirs (is, are).

3. Neither Walter nor Rebecca _____ where you have been (know, knows).

4. The English class _____ reading Shakespeare (is, are).

5. Each of the presidential candidates _____ confident of winning (feel, feels).

6. There _____ a number of reasons for his behavior (is, are).

CCSS.L.9–10.1.B:
Use various types of phrases (noun, verb, adjectival, adverbial, participial, prepositional, absolute) and clauses (independent, dependent; noun, relative, adverbial) to convey specific meanings and add variety and interest to writing or presentations.

7. In the last analysis there _____ only two factors involved (is, are).

8. None of the existing procedures _____ this particular case (fit, fits).

9. We found that none of the property _____ vandalized (was, were).

10. Last year, the number of employees _____ decreased (has, have).

11. The city, with its suburbs, _____ a population of over two million (have, has).

12. Every home, office, and shop _____ visited (was, were).

13. Neither Mary nor Alice _____ where you have been (know, knows).

14. The class in second-year Latin _____ reading Caesar (is, are).

CCSS.L.8.1.C:
Form and use verbs in the indicative, imperative, interrogative, conditional, and subjunctive mood.

15. There _____ a number of exceptions to the rule (is, are).

16. In the last analysis there _____ only two questions involved (is, are).

17. The company _____ agreed to pay half of the damages (has, have).

18. Mathematics _____ required of all freshmen (is, are).

Exercise 15.22: Identifying Correct Subject-Verb Agreement

Circle the verb that agrees with its subject.

CCSS.L.9–10.1.B:

Use various types of phrases (noun, verb, adjectival, adverbial, participial, prepositional, absolute) and clauses (independent, dependent; noun, relative, adverbial) to convey specific meanings and add variety and interest to writing or presentations.

1. In the attic, as I recall, there (was, were) many loose boards.

2. The filmed version of the story (don't, doesn't) bring Ambrose Bierce to life.

3. My interest in language perhaps (goes, go) back to my childhood experiments with fiction.

4. The results of this endeavor (was, were) amazing.

5. July or August (are, is) my least favorite time of year.

6. Every one of these memories (brings, bring) a different feeling about my past life.

7. A scratch or a small cut sometimes (cause, causes) serious infection.

8. The rules for this stupid game (doesn't, don't) make sense to me.

9. The old transmission (needs, need) fixing.

CCSS.L.8.1.C:

Form and use verbs in the indicative, imperative, interrogative, conditional, and subjunctive mood.

10. Here (is, are) the names of everyone I do business with.

11. Each one of my colleagues (has, have) an interesting hobby.

12. There (weren't, wasn't) any ice cream left for us.

13. The long skid marks on the pavement (shows, show) how long it took the car to brake.

14. The number of servings (were, was) printed on the package.

15. Either of these hats (looks, look) good on you.

16. The size and the price of the container of pepper (has, have) increased.

17. This light bulb (don't, doesn't) give enough light.

18. The gems in this wristwatch (are, is) genuine.

19. Where (is, are) the saucers for these cups?

20. Every one of these tomato plants (needs, need) watering.

21. One of my friends (knows, know) the owner of the business.

22. A man who had too much to drink (leads, lead) the singing.

23. Too many of your sentences (contain, contains) an *and*.

24. Either of these mutual funds (are, is) a good investment.

Chapter

Adverbs

16

ENGLISH LANGUAGE ARTS STANDARDS

☞ *CCSS.ELA-LITERACY.L.9–12.1: Demonstrate command of the conventions of standard English grammar and usage when writing or speaking.*

☞ *CCSS.ELA-LITERACY.L.11–12.1.A: Apply the understanding that usage is a matter of convention, can change over time, and is sometimes contested.*

☞ *CCSS.ELA-LITERACY.L.11–12.1.B: Resolve issues of complex or contested usage, consulting references (e.g., Merriam–Webster's Dictionary of English Usage, Garner's Modern American Usage) as needed.*

☞ *CCSS.ELA-LITERACY.L.9–10.1.B: Use various types of phrases (noun, verb, adjectival, adverbial, participial, prepositional, absolute) and clauses (independent, dependent; noun, relative, adverbial) to convey specific meanings and add variety and interest to writing or presentations.*

PRINCIPAL CONSTRUCTIONS USED AS ADVERBS

CCSS.L.9–12.1:
Demonstrate command of the conventions of standard English grammar and usage when writing or speaking.

Any word or group of words that modifies a verb, an adjective, or another adverb is an adverb.

The principal constructions used as adverbs are:

- Regular Adverbs: "He ran *quickly*." "The pie was *very* good."

- Prepositions without Objects: "Drink *up*." "I've seen the movie *before*."

CCSS.L.9–10.1.B:
Use various types of phrases (noun, verb, adjectival, adverbial, participial, prepositional, absolute) and clauses (independent, dependent; noun, relative, adverbial) to convey specific meanings and add variety and interest to writing or presentations.

- Nouns denoting Time, Distance, Weight, etc.: "She walked *a mile.*"

- Participial Phrases in a Dual Relation: "*Realizing he was headed the wrong way,* Frank turned the car around."

- Infinitives and Infinitive Phrases: "She came *to help.*" "My friends and I went *to see the play.*"

- Prepositional Phrases: "She sat the cup *on the table.*"

- Clauses: "I could not pay the tax *because it was too high.*"

- Elliptical Clauses: "*While stationed in Germany,* he learned the language" (*while he was stationed in Germany*).

Nouns Ending in -s

CCSS.L.9–10.1.B:
Use various types of phrases (noun, verb, adjectival, adverbial, participial, prepositional, absolute) and clauses (independent, dependent; noun, relative, adverbial) to convey specific meanings and add variety and interest to writing or presentations.

Some nouns that end in *-s* but are not actually plural in number are used as adverbs.

> I work **nights**.
>
> I attend church **Sundays**.

Note. In modern usage, a singular noun naming a day of the week is often used as an adverb: "I will be there *Monday.*"

From a historical point of view, these nouns are not plural. They derive from Old English possessive forms used in an adverbial sense to indicate time. A vestige of the older forms can be seen today in words like *always* and *nowadays,* which are true adverbs.

Pronouns with Adjectives

CCSS.L.9–10.1.B:
Use various types of phrases (noun, verb, adjectival, adverbial, participial, prepositional, absolute) and clauses (independent, dependent; noun, relative, adverbial) to convey specific meanings and add variety and interest to writing or presentations.

In the following sentences the expressions *his best* and *our hardest* act as adverbs of degree or manner.

> He did **his best** to finish on time.
>
> We worked **our hardest to** satisfy our boss.

These expressions appear to be elliptical constructions resulting from the omission of cognate objects: "We worked our hardest *work,*" in which *our* and *hardest* are adjectives modifying the cognate object.

PRINCIPAL USES OF ADVERBS

Modifying a Phrase or a Clause

CCSS.L.9–10.1.B:
Use various types of phrases (noun, verb, adjectival, adverbial, participial, prepositional, absolute) and clauses (independent, dependent; noun, relative, adverbial) to convey specific meanings and add variety and interest to writing or presentations.

An adverb may modify an adverbial or an adjective phrase or clause.

- Adverbial phrase or clause:

    I got there **almost** at closing time.

    I was teaching **long** before you were born.

    She pointed the camera **exactly** at the squirrel.

    The students left school **soon** after the final bell.

    He gave me the money **only** because he trusts me.

- Adjective phrases and clauses:

    A woman **almost** in tears is at the door.

    He lives **right** across the street from us.

    I especially like the time **just** before the sun sets.

Some grammars regard these adverbs as modifiers of the preposition or conjunction rather than of the whole phrase or clause.

    I got there **almost at** closing time.

    The students left school **soon after** the final bell.

Sentence Adverbials

CCSS.L.9–10.1.B:
Use various types of phrases (noun, verb, adjectival, adverbial, participial, prepositional, absolute) and clauses (independent, dependent; noun, relative, adverbial) to convey specific meanings and add variety and interest to writing or presentations.

Sentence adverbials modify the thought of entire sentences, not any single verb, adjective, or adverb. They commonly are used at the beginning of a sentence or clause and can be either single words or phrases.

    Surprisingly, I found myself enjoying the opera.

    Fortunately, I had enough money to pay for the tickets.

    Luckily, our house was spared the fire.

    Oddly enough, she has never been to Europe.

    The doctor **wisely** sent her straight to the hospital.

To this class of adverbials belong *yes* and *no* (and words like *perhaps* and *maybe*) when used as in the following sentences.

> **Yes,** I see you.
>
> **No,** I won't help you.
>
> **Perhaps** you might be right.
>
> **Maybe** with some help we'll finish.

A sentence adverb can, through ellipsis, stand as a complete sentence. This construction is more common in answers to direct questions.

> Will you be here today? **Yes.** (**Yes,** I will be.)
>
> Will the book be of help? **Perhaps.** (**Perhaps** it will be.)

"Not"

CCSS.L.9–10.1.B:

Use various types of phrases (noun, verb, adjectival, adverbial, participial, prepositional, absolute) and clauses (independent, dependent; noun, relative, adverbial) to convey specific meanings and add variety and interest to writing or presentations.

The adverb *not* has a peculiar use in certain kinds of questions.

> The wine is great, is it **not?** (**isn't** it?)
>
> She has been difficult, has she **not?** (**hasn't** she?)
>
> Will you **not** participate? (**won't** you?)

What's peculiar about *not* in this type of construction is that it has no negative meaning. It actually anticipates an affirmative answer in approval of the statement that precedes it. When the *not* is omitted, the question is neutral; the answer may be either affirmative or negative: "She's been difficult, has she?"

Occasionally, *not* is employed to express surprise that some expected outcome or occurrence has not come to pass: "*Hasn't* he done that yet?" Here the expected answer is "No," but an affirmative quality is nevertheless present because there is an implication that the answer should be "Yes."

"Here" and "There" and the Expletive "There"

A peculiar use of *here* and *there* is seen in the following sentences.

> My job **here** at the office is boring.
>
> The book's place **there** on the shelf is appropriate.

Here and *there* are adverbs of place. For example, in the first sentence *here* modifies the noun *job*, thus acting as an adjective. The deeper structure of the

CCSS.L.9–10.1.B:

Use various types of phrases (noun, verb, adjec- tival, adverbial, participial, prepositional, absolute) and clauses (independent, dependent; noun, relative, adverbial) to convey specif- ic meanings and add variety and interest to writing or presentations.

sentence indicates that *here* is the remains of an adjective clause, *which I have here at the office*, in which *here* is a pure adverb modifying the verb *have*. The rest of the clause was dropped through ellipsis, with the adverb *here* remaining to modify the noun *job*.

The use of ***there*** as an adverb of place should be easily distinguished from its use as an expletive.

> **There's** the intruder over there (adverb).

> **There** is an intruder in the house (expletive).

In the first sentence, *there* is an adverb of place. In the second, it is an exple- tive, a word used to leave the subject position vacant of content; used this way, *there* is an empty "slot-filler."

Short Adverbs

CCSS.L.11–12.1.A:

Apply the understanding that usage is a matter of convention, can change over time, and is some- times contested.

In brief commands and exhortations, a short form of the adverb may be used without the *-ly* suffix. These adverbs are identical in form with their correspond- ing adjectives.

> Walk **slow** (instead of **slowly**).

> Speak **louder,** please (instead of **more loudly**).

These short adverbs are used to give emphasis to the commands. In other sen- tences, where there is no such emphasis required, the regular form of the adverb is used: "She spoke *loudly* in order to be heard."

"Very"

CCSS.L.9–10.1.B:

Use various types of phrases (noun, verb, adjec- tival, adverbial, participial, prepositional, absolute) and clauses (independent, dependent; noun, relative, adverbial) to convey specif- ic meanings and add variety and interest to writing or presentations.

Very regularly modifies ordinary adjectives and present participles; as, *very hap- py, very sick, very lucky, very hot; very interesting, very annoying*.

> He is **very lucky**.

> She is **very annoying**.

With past participles, *very much* is regularly used, not *very:* as, *very much an- ticipated, very much excited, very much annoyed*.

> I was **very much annoyed** by her behavior (not **very annoyed**).

With some past participles commonly used as regular adjectives, *much* is omitted: as, *very tired, very drunk*.

He was **very drunk** when he left the bar.

Exercise 16.1: Identifying Adverbial Constructions

Underline the special adverbial forms and uses described in the preceding sections.

CCSS.L.9–10.1.B:
Use various types of phrases (noun, verb, adjectival, adverbial, participial, prepositional, absolute) and clauses (independent, dependent; noun, relative, adverbial) to convey specific meanings and add variety and interest to writing or presentations.

1. You saw the article in the *New York Times*, didn't you?

2. There is the man who was formerly the mayor.

3. That month we worked nights and weekends and tried our best to finish the project.

4. Come quick, and see the moon rise.

5. Her time here was hurried and disappointing.

6. Naturally, he was not expecting a decision today.

7. He was surely expecting a decision today, wasn't he?

8. He always eats quick.

9. He could now walk almost without pain.

10. I was interested in it long before I was suspected of being a politician.

11. He left the house with his briefcase conspicuously under his arm.

12. The world will never be the better for it.

13. There is the man who was formerly the alderman from the fourth ward.

14. There is no need for secrecy any longer.

15. That month we worked Sundays and holidays, and tried our best to finish our assignments.

16. The more he disliked him, the kinder he would be to him.

17. Besides, there was something engaging in his countrified simplicity.

18. But he woke even before the bugle sounded.

CLASSIFICATION OF ADVERBIAL ELEMENTS

CCSS.L.9–10.1.B:
Use various types of phrases (noun, verb, adjectival, adverbial, participial, prepositional, absolute) and clauses (independent, dependent; noun, relative, adverbial) to convey specific meanings and add variety and interest to writing or presentations.

Classifying adverbial elements by use is difficult primarily for two reasons.

The range of meanings they cover is varied and wide and potentially mixed. The meaning of an adverbial element may vary according to context—especially the verb or adjective that it modifies; and since the context is capable of such a wide range of variation, the shades of meaning expressed by adverbial elements are correspondingly numerous.

The adverbial meaning they express may be varied or have the dual nature of an adverb and adjective.

Mixed Adverbial Meanings

CCSS.L.9–10.1.B:
Use various types of phrases (noun, verb, adjectival, adverbial, participial, prepositional, absolute) and clauses (independent, dependent; noun, relative, adverbial) to convey specific meanings and add variety and interest to writing or presentations.

In some of these uses only a suggestion of the secondary meaning is apparent; in others it is clearly pronounced. The following are typical examples:

It is unwise to drive fast **when motorcycle cops appear to be at every intersection** (time and reason).

It is hotter now **than it was this morning** (degree and comparison).

The book was so good **that I stayed up all night reading it** (degree and result).

The tornado raced across the state of Kansas, **leaving a path of destruction in its wake** (accompanying circumstances and result).

The boys rode the sled down the hill, **laughing and screaming and then piling off to push it back up the hill** (accompanying circumstances and manner).

He used a microphone **so as to be heard** (manner and result).

Dual Adverbial and Adjectival Meanings

Often a construction has the dual nature of an adverb and an adjective.

Hearing the sirens, the driver pulled over. (The participle **hearing,** as an adjective, modifies **driver;** the whole phrase, as an adverb, modifies **pulled over**—it tells why the driver pulled over.)

May be copied for classroom use. Common Core Grammar by Thomas Fasano (Coyote Canyon Press: Claremont, CA); © 2015.

CCSS.L.9–10.1.B:
Use various types of phrases (noun, verb, adjectival, adverbial, participial, prepositional, absolute) and clauses (independent, dependent; noun, relative, adverbial) to convey specific meanings and add variety and interest to writing or presentations.

Alert from drinking coffee, Nancy could not fall asleep. (As an adjective, **alert** modifies **Nancy;** as an adverb, it tells why she could not fall asleep.)

The iron bar was pounded **straight**. (**Straight** is a predicate adjective modifying **bar,** but it is also similar in meaning to an adverbial clause of result: "until it was **straight.**" In this type of sentence, **straight** can also be considered an objective complement in the passive voice.)

These overlapping meanings and uses will be found often in the major adverbial elements that are discussed in the rest of this chapter.

Adverbial Elements of Time

CCSS.L.9–10.1.B:
Use various types of phrases (noun, verb, adjectival, adverbial, participial, prepositional, absolute) and clauses (independent, dependent; noun, relative, adverbial) to convey specific meanings and add variety and interest to writing or presentations.

Usual forms of adverbial elements indicating time are shown in the following examples.

They will pick the grapes **today** (single adverb).

I am leaving **now**.

My brother will arrive **Saturday**.

She used to work **at night** (phrase).

I have not flown **since 9/11**.

The commencement being finished, the graduates threw their caps in the air (nominative absolute).

Summer over, it was time to go back to school (elliptical—**summer being over**).

He will call his grandmother **as soon as he arrives at the airport** (clause).

While I was napping, the telephone rang.

Now that he has passed the bar exam, he can get a job as a lawyer.

Once you understand the basic concept, the rest is easy.

While in town, he visited his old hangouts (elliptical—**while he was in town**).

When last heard from, Chris McCandless was walking into the wild.

Note. Some of these sentences carry a suggestion of *reason* or *condition* in addition to *time*.

The most commonly used conjunctions that introduce clauses of time are *when, since, while, before, after, until, as soon as, as long as, once, now that,* etc.

Modifications of the Time Relation

CCSS.L.9–10.1.B:
Use various types of phrases (noun, verb, adjectival, adverbial, participial, prepositional, absolute) and clauses (independent, dependent; noun, relative, adverbial) to convey specific meanings and add variety and interest to writing or presentations.

Adverbial elements largely answer the question *when?* and indicate the definite time an action occurs. Sometimes they answer the question *how long?* and indicate the duration or extent of the action.

> They practiced **until the sun went down**.

> He had been a smoker **since he was a teenager**.

The following sentence shows the duration of the effect or result of the action (*for how long?*).

> She kept her children home **for the day**.

Note. A modifier of time used as an adverb should not be confused with one used as an adjective to modify a noun that in itself indicates time.

> The show was scheduled for a time **when more people would be watching** (adjective clause modifying the noun **time**).

Adverbial Elements of Place

CCSS.L.9–10.1.B:
Use various types of phrases (noun, verb, adjectival, adverbial, participial, prepositional, absolute) and clauses (independent, dependent; noun, relative, adverbial) to convey specific meanings and add variety and interest to writing or presentations.

The following sentences show various elements indicating place.

> I live **here** (single adverb).

> She went **home**.

> Tim drives a cab **in Tampa** (prepositional phrase).

> I live **by the railroad tracks**.

> I saw her **going to the store** (participial phrase).

> We found the dog **hiding in his doghouse**.

> The police found the car **where the thieves left it** (clause).

> I will travel **wherever my employer sends me**.

Adverbs of place may indicate *where* as well as *whence* (place from which).

> My neighbors come **from outer space**.

Note. Adverbial elements of place need to be distinguished from adjectival elements modifying nouns that indicate place.

> This is the town **where my father grew up** (adjective clause).

Adverbial Elements of Manner

CCSS.L.9–10.1.B:

Use various types of phrases (noun, verb, adjectival, adverbial, participial, prepositional, absolute) and clauses (independent, dependent; noun, relative, adverbial) to convey specific meanings and add variety and interest to writing or presentations.

Manner may be shown as follows.

She danced **gracefully** (single adverb).

He worked **alone** in a cubicle.

She spoke **with disrespect** (phrase).

I make money **by writing books**.

The sergeant counted the cadets, **left to right** (elliptical—**from left to right**).

He came **running** (participle in a dual relation).

He drives his car **as if he's in a hurry** (clause).

She eats **as though she can't get enough**.

I do **as I am directed**.

I take care of my family **as a good husband** (elliptical—**as a good husband should**).

Some participial and prepositional phrases indicating "accompanying circumstances" function somewhat as adverbs of manner.

The most common conjunctions used in clauses of manner are *as, as if, as though, just as, like, much as.*

Adverbial Elements of Degree

CCSS.L.9–10.1.B:

Use various types of phrases (noun, verb, adjectival, adverbial, participial, prepositional, absolute) and clauses (independent, dependent; noun, relative, adverbial) to convey specific meanings and add variety and interest to writing or presentations.

Adverbial elements of degree cover a wide range of meanings, but what distinguishes them is that they tell *how much, how little, how far*, or some other *how* relation (except for manner). They include various phrases and clauses indicating degree as well as comparison or result. The distinction between degree, comparison, and result is frequently so difficult to distinguish that in Part I of this book they were all included in one general group. In the present section they are treated separately even though in some of the examples there are overlapping meanings. They generally qualify verbs in addition to adjectives and adverbs.

Degree can be indicated as follows.

I walked a **mile** (single adverb).

The book weighed a **pound**.

She was **very** angry.

My wife was **almost** finished.

He was **thoroughly** fed up.

I have enough wood **for a good fire** (prepositional phrase).

The speaker was limited **to only ten minutes**.

I am too old **for this job**.

The portion is large enough **to fill me up** (infinitive phrase).

She is too fat **to fit in the seat**.

We have enough wood **to build a huge fire**.

The situation is more **than I can handle** (clause).

I help as much **as I can**.

I will be there as soon **as possible** (elliptical—**as soon as it is possible for me to be there**).

Clauses and phrases of degree are often used after *so, so much, too, enough,* and *so that.*

Adverbial Elements of Comparison

LESS / FEWER

Despite the "rule" that one must use *fewer*, not *less*, to refer to count nouns, *less* naturally applies to singular count nouns, as in *one less mouth to feed* and *one less thing to worry about.* It is also used in certain expressions like *He made no less than ten mistakes* and *Describe yourself in fifty words or less.*

An adverbial element can indicate comparison between two actions, conditions, etc.

He claimed that life in the military had been hard for him **ever since he served in combat** (clause).

He writes with a fountain pen, **just as people did in the nineteenth century**.

There were fewer contributions **than we expected**.

He was not as strong **as we believed**.

She sings better **than she dances**.

I am taller **than my brother** (elliptical clause).

There is nothing worse **than a liar**.

He was the least engaged **of all those in attendance** (phrase).

CCSS.L.11–12.1.A:

Apply the understanding that usage is a matter of convention, can change over time, and is sometimes contested.

Some expressions that indicate comparison show extreme ellipsis.

The sooner, the better.

The more, the merrier.

Adverbial Elements of Result

CCSS.L.9–10.1.B:
Use various types of phrases (noun, verb, adjectival, adverbial, participial, prepositional, absolute) and clauses (independent, dependent; noun, relative, adverbial) to convey specific meanings and add variety and interest to writing or presentations.

An adverbial element may indicate the result of an action.

> The roads have been improved **so that it is possible to drive without hitting potholes** (clause).

> The table tipped over, **the result being that the food for the picnic went all over the grass** (phrase—with a clause adjunct).

> The plane lost cabin pressure, **with the result that it had to make an emergency landing**.

The indication of result is common in participial phrases.

> He tripped on the steps and fell, **breaking his arm**.

> The bus came to a sudden stop, **jolting the passengers hard**.

These constructions are sometimes difficult to distinguish from participles indicating accompanying circumstances.

An adverbial element often indicates result and degree.

> The car is so quiet **that it is hard to hear it coming**.

> I woke up early enough **to see the sun rise**.

> She was so kind **as to pay for lunch**.

A subordinate clause of result introduced by *so that* must not be confused with a coordinate clause of consequence or a subordinate clause of purpose introduced by the same conjunction.

Adverbial Elements of Cause or Reason

CCSS.L.9–10.1.B:
Use various types of phrases (noun, verb, adjectival, adverbial, participial, prepositional, absolute) and clauses (independent, dependent; noun, relative, adverbial) to convey specific meanings and add variety and interest to writing or presentations.

Reason or cause may be indicated as follows.

> He received attention **for breaking the scoring record** (prepositional phrase).

> My wife suffers **from headaches**.

> **Because of his bad eyesight,** he could not get a drivers license.

> **Spotting the oncoming car,** the driver came to a stop (participial phrase).

> The cat, frightened by the firecracker, took off running.

> **The day being hot,** the air conditioning was on (nominative absolute).

He was kicked out of college **because he was caught cheating** (clause).

As I was starving, I looked for a place to eat.

Since we have no other offers, we must accept or reject the only one we have.

A clause of reason introduced by *that* regularly modifies an adjective.

We are **happy** that you found your cat.

The primary conjunctions used with clauses of cause or reason are *because, as, since, for, for the reason that, on the grounds that, in that, seeing that, considering that, in case, just in case.*

Some adverbial clauses give the reason for our knowledge of a fact instead of the reason for the fact itself; in other words, they tell the reasoning for thinking that a statement is true.

My neighbor must be home from his trip, **for his car is parked in his driveway**.

The party must have been over, **for most of the guests had left**.

In the first sentence, for example, the fact that I can see my neighbor's car in his driveway is not the reason why he returned; it is the reason for my thinking that he has returned.

The thought expressed by a complex sentence containing a subordinate clause of reason may also be expressed by a compound sentence with a coordinate clause of consequence or inference.

As he was not even close to finishing the project, he left off for the day (subordinate clause of reason).

We had driven for twelve hours when we arrived in Tulsa early that evening, and were tired; **therefore, we rented a hotel room for the night** (coordinate clause of consequence).

Adverbial Elements of Purpose

Purpose may be indicated in the following ways.

They are here **for the money** (prepositional phrase).

I became a teacher **with the idea of having a positive impact on young people**.

The police questioned her **for details of the incident**.

CCSS.L.9–10.1.B:

Use various types of phrases (noun, verb, adjectival, adverbial, participial, prepositional, absolute) and clauses (independent, dependent; noun, relative, adverbial) to convey specific meanings and add variety and interest to writing or presentations.

They came **to get their belongings** (infinitive phrase).

We had to hurry **to make it to the movie in time**.

I was careful **to align the holes**.

He worked in the garden all spring **so that he would have vegetables that summer** (clause).

We bought a house in a nice neighborhood **in order that we might live comfortably**.

They took care **that no one found out about their business failure**.

People gamble **that they might win**.

Guard your property **lest someone take it** (**lest** means **that—not** and introduces a clause in the subjunctive mood).

The most common conjunctions used in purpose clauses are *in order that, in order to, so, so as to, so that,* and *to.*

Adverbial Elements of Condition

CCSS.L.9–10.1.B:

Use various types of phrases (noun, verb, adjectival, adverbial, participial, prepositional, absolute) and clauses (independent, dependent; noun, relative, adverbial) to convey specific meanings and add variety and interest to writing or presentations.

Condition may be indicated as follows.

Without a computer nowadays, you can barely communicate with others (prepositional phrase, equivalent to **if you do not have a computer nowadays**).

With a little more money, we can buy a new car.

His ideas, **based on years of reading and thinking,** are well articulated (participial phrase—equivalent to **since they are based on years of reading and thinking**).

I will finish the lesson plans, **time permitting** (nominative absolute—equivalent to **if time permits**).

If what you're telling me is true, then we have nothing more to say (clause).

Whether a Republican or a Democrat, you must support the troops (**if you are a Republican or if you are a Democrat**).

He will help build the fence, **provided we pay him** (**if we pay him**).

You will not graduate **unless you pass all your classes** (**if you do not pass all your classes**).

If possible, I will speak with her this morning (elliptical clause—equivalent to **if it is possible**) .

They will deliver the mail, **rain or shine** (**if it rain or if it shine**).

The principal introductory words are *if, unless* (means *if—not*), *supposing that, whether—or, provided, provided that, on condition that, in case that.*

The clause might not have a conjunction or introductory word. If so, the order of the subject and verb is inverted.

> **Had you seen the accident,** you would have been horrified (**if you had seen the accident**).

> **Should you need our help,** we will lend you a hand.

Occasionally, the conditional clause is used alone as an exclamatory sentence, the main clause being omitted.

> **If you had only said so! (If you had only said so,** I would have been pleased.)

A conditional element may give the condition under which a statement is made, not under which an action is performed.

> The argument, **as I recall,** started over money.

> I was feeling a bit down, **as it were**.

Thus, the first sentence means "The argument, *if I recall it correctly,* started over money." The second sentence is equivalent to "I was feeling a bit down, *if I may be permitted to use the expression.*"

Note. These kinds of clauses are frequently classified as parenthetical expressions.

Condition can also be expressed by a coordinate clause with a verb in the imperative mood (this construction can be classed as a main clause and not as an adverbial clause).

> **Do that again,** and see what happens (**if you do that again**).

Adverbial Elements of Concession

Concession may be indicated in the following ways.

> **With all his mistakes,** he still does a good job (phrase—equivalent to **although he makes many mistakes**).

> I would not trade places with him **for all the money in the world**.

> **Notwithstanding her obvious hatred and disrespect,** we were forced to work with her.

CCSS.L.9–10.1.B:
Use various types of
phrases (noun, verb, adjectival, adverbial, participial,
prepositional, absolute)
and clauses (independent,
dependent; noun, relative,
adverbial) to convey specific meanings and add variety
and interest to writing or
presentations.

In spite of his claims of riches, he filed for bankruptcy.

Though he was his parents' favorite, he was treated no better than his siblings.

Although he was very ill, he still attended the family gathering.

Even if he is popular, I don't like him.

The car, **though old,** runs well (elliptical clause—**though it is old**).

Occasionally the word order in a clause is inverted with the result that the conjunction might be omitted.

Odd though he may be, he's good at getting his point across.

Drunk as he was, he was able to back the car out of the driveway.

Try as we could, we were unable to pick up the log.

Be that as it may, you still have to do your homework.

Clauses of concession may be introduced by compound relative pronouns or various other words ending in -*ever*.

Whatever he wanted, they didn't have it.

However hard we try, it still won't be enough.

Wherever he is hiding, the police will find him.

Whichever road you take in life, you will need to be prepared.

Sometimes, because of ellipsis, only a conjunction remains.

Any effort **whatsoever** will be appreciated (**whatsoever it may be**).

Any excuse **whatever** won't be believed (**whatever it may be**).

The idea of concession is sometimes very similar to the idea expressed by coordinate clauses showing contrast. For example compare:

Although he was bright, he was a poor student (concession—subordinate) .

He was bright, **but** he was a poor student (contrast—coordinate).

The most common clauses used in concession clauses are *although, despite, even if, even though, except that, in spite of, much as, not that, though, whereas, while, whilst.*

Adverbial Elements of Accompanying Circumstances

CCSS.L.9–10.1.B:

Use various types of phrases (noun, verb, adjectival, adverbial, participial, prepositional, absolute) and clauses (independent, dependent; noun, relative, adverbial) to convey specific meanings and add variety and interest to writing or presentations.

An adverbial element may indicate accompanying circumstances: that is, actions or circumstances that occur at the same time as the action represented by the verb.

> They drove across the country, **doing odd jobs for money**.
>
> Emily lived in the family home, **never leaving the last years of her life**.
>
> Her parents, **with much pride and delight,** saw her graduate from medical school.

A nominative absolute phrase may indicate accompanying circumstances.

> The car sat parked in the yard, **its axles resting on cinder blocks**.

Note. These constructions often carry a strong adjectival sense.

Adverbial Complements of Adjectives

CCSS.L.9–10.1.B:

Use various types of phrases (noun, verb, adjectival, adverbial, participial, prepositional, absolute) and clauses (independent, dependent; noun, relative, adverbial) to convey specific meanings and add variety and interest to writing or presentations.

The majority of the preceding adverbial elements are used to modify verbs, the exception being adverbs of degree, which generally qualify verbs as well as adjectives and adverbs. In addition to these, a large number of adverbial phrases and clauses modify adjectives. Some of them even approximate the meaning of the classes of adverbials discussed above; but because they demonstrate such a wide and varied range of meanings, it is difficult to place them into convenient categories. They are therefore brought together under one general category called "Adverbial Complements of Adjectives." What follows are some typical examples.

- Prepositional Phrases.

> The book is dense **with theory**.
>
> She was friendly **to her coworkers**.
>
> You are not worthy **of our attention**.
>
> The neighborhood is convenient **to shopping**.
>
> Are the poor really dependent **on handouts?**
>
> He is sanguine **by nature**.
>
> Henry was angry **at his family**.
>
> The gang members, eager **for revenge,** shot a rival gang member.
>
> The candidate, confident **of victory,** gave a rousing speech.

The firefighters were overcome **with smoke inhalation**.

- Infinitives or Infinitive Phrases.

    The book is easy **to read**.

    I am happy **to be of service**.

    The show was ready **to begin**.

    Someone able **to lift heavy packages** would be useful.

- Clauses.

    I am confident **that she is innocent**.

    We feel disappointed **that he stole the money**.

    The family, happy **because they found their missing cat,** fed it a plate of fresh fish.

Exercise 16.2: Noting Functions of Adverb Classes

Underline the adverb clauses, noting their grammatical functions.

WRITING PROMPT:
Form an adverb of manner from each of the following adjectives. Use each adverb in a sentence. Tell what it modifies—*proud, careless, vehement, tender, vigorous, dainty, brave, formal, courteous, blunt, sharp, keen, weary, heavy, true, skillful, legible.*

1. Its colorful collage of musical images coheres largely because of the work's persistent overall theme of death.

2. Although compromises were now necessary, he remained a man of principle and the Fourteen Points a contract absolutely binding upon him.

3. Both sides have promised to abide by Friday's ruling, but Mr. MacKinnon, the *Globe* reporter in Kiev, noted that a new vote cannot go ahead unless the parliament passes a slate of laws allowing another election.

CCSS.L.9–10.1.B:
Use various types of phrases (noun, verb, adjectival, adverbial, participial, prepositional, absolute) and clauses (independent, dependent; noun, relative, adverbial) to convey specific meanings and add variety and interest to writing or presentations.

4. He could not be sad because his son died for America, died for freedom.

5. It's not unthinkable, even if it's not likely.

6. We believe we responded as well as we reasonably could given the unique and demanding circumstances.

7. The finding of a new writer gave him as much pleasure as if he had been the fiction editor who accepted the first story by the literary genius.

8. Since this article was written, Sir Andrew Lloyd Webber as been knighted by Queen Elizabeth II of England and has released a compact disc of music composed by his late father.

9. Such lies are commonplace as shaken parents try to shield young children from the reality of deportation, counselors said.

10. Lower courts said the former students would have to sue individually because their complaints are different.

Exercise 16.3: Classifying Adverbial Elements

Point out the words, phrases, and clauses used adverbially.

CCSS.L.9–10.1.B:
Use various types of phrases (noun, verb, adjectival, adverbial, participial, prepositional, absolute) and clauses (independent, dependent; noun, relative, adverbial) to convey specific meanings and add variety and interest to writing or presentations.

1. Be it ever so humble, there's no place like home.

2. Tired and discouraged, they were ready to pack it in for the day before anything unfortunate happened.

3. The second attempt having failed, we decided to call it quits.

4. To ensure the fastest service, you should fill out the paperwork ahead of time.

5. Tired as he was, he could not ignore the work he had to do.

6. This done, he pulled the car into the garage and shut the door.

7. One must be a mathematician to understand the performance evaluation matrix.

8. He is almost sure to be promoted by the end of the summer.

9. Sick or well, he will be there.

10. This time I did not acquiesce, as on previous occasions, but defended my position on the matter.

11. They were all very joyful because, barring accidents, they would be home for Christmas.

12. Once inside, the sightseer stands in the heart of utter desolation.

13. He stared at the house, thinking that there he was at last, after all these years.

14. A Democrat in politics, Bancroft displayed a natural pride in the growth of American democracy.

15. The congregation returned to the hotel, to put down their impressions in note books and diaries.

16. With true Indian craft he always befriended the whites, well knowing that he might thus reap great advantages for himself.

17. In a few minutes a heavier sea was raised than I had ever seen.

18. He is almost sure to be nominated after the primaries are over.

SOME TROUBLESOME ADVERBS

CCSS.L.11–12.1.A:
Apply the understanding that usage is a matter of convention, can change over time, and is sometimes contested.

Many adverbs end in **-ly,** and have no other form (***intensely***). Others have the same form as adjectives (***fast***). Still others have both a short form and one in **-ly** (***late, lately***). A final group of adverbs consists of those that don't end in **-ly** and have no adjective form.

Here is a list of adverbs that have the same form as adjectives.

alike	all right	fine	first	just	kindly
off-hand	only	solo	still	alone	clean
deep	direct	even	extra	far	fast
free	freelance	full	full-time	further	hard
high	jolly	last	late	little	long
loud	low	next	non-stop	outright	overall
part-time	past	pretty	quick	right	slow
straight	tight	well	wide	wrong	

CCSS.L.11–12.1.B:
Resolve issues of complex or contested usage, consulting references (e.g., *Merriam–Webster's Dictionary of English Usage, Garner's Modern American Usage*) as needed.

With some of these words, there are also forms ending in *-ly.*

cleanly	directly	deeply	evenly	finely
firstly	freely	fully	hardly	highly
justly	lastly	lately	loudly	quickly
rightly	slowly	tightly	widely	wrongly

Note that these **-ly** forms sometimes have the same meaning as the non-*ly* form.

Here is a list of adverbs that have no adjective forms.

afresh	alas	alike	almost	aloud
also	altogether	anyhow	anyway	apart
besides	doubtless	either	enough	forthwith
furthermore	half	hence	hereby	however
indeed	instead	likewise	maybe	meanwhile
more	moreover	much	nevertheless	nonetheless
otherwise	perhaps	quite	rather	regardless
so	somehow	somewhat	therefore	thereupon
though	thus	together	too	very
whatsoever				

Exercise 16.4: Using Troublesome Adverbs

In the following sentences use the correct forms. Consult a dictionary, if necessary.

CCSS.L.11–12.1.A:

Apply the understanding that usage is a matter of convention, can change over time, and is sometimes contested.

1. He could learn to write _____ if he tried (good, well).

2. He treats his employees _____, and pays them next to nothing (bad, badly).

3. He _____ makes the trip to the city on Saturday (regular, regularly).

4. She comes to the office _____ every day (almost, most).

5. Living conditions now seem to be _____ better (some, somewhat).

6. In those early days horses ran _____ on the prairies (wild, wildly).

7. The frightened child ran _____ down the street (wild, wildly).

8. They finished the work as _____ as they could (quick, quickly).

9. The room was furnished quite _____ in the modernistic manner (artistic, artistically).

10. You can finish all this work _____ in half a day (easy, easily).

11. The judges were interested in the boy's picture and commented very _____ on it (favorable, favorably).

12. The mayor was _____ surprised at this new criticism (very, very much).

13. Surely the law was passed more _____ than that (recent, recently).

14. He must live _____, or he wouldn't be so healthy (right, rightly).

15. The trail up the mountain was steep and we were _____ exhausted when we _____ reached the top (real, really; near, nearly).

16. Talk _____, and don't mumble your words (louder, more loudly).

17. He needs the money and the house will be sold _____ (cheap, cheaply).

18. The audience was not _____ interested in the speech (very, very much).

19. The Wrights have _____ more money than the Smiths (considerable, considerably).

20. The car runs very _____ and needs but little oil (smooth, smoothly).

21. He is working _____ now at the post office (steady, steadily).

22. The chairman remained _____ (firm, firmly).

Fragments, Run-Ons, and Other Errors

ENGLISH LANGUAGE ARTS STANDARDS

NOTE:
Some of the skills in this chapter were introduced at lower grade levels; yet, due to the recursiveness of the language standards, they require further attention at the high school level.

☞ ***CCSS.ELA-LITERACY.L.9–12.1:*** *Demonstrate command of the conventions of standard English grammar and usage when writing or speaking.*

☞ ***CCSS.ELA-LITERACY.L.9–10.1.A:*** *Use parallel structure.*

☞ ***CCSS.ELA-LITERACY.L.7.1.C:*** *Place phrases and clauses within a sentence, recognizing and correcting misplaced and dangling modifiers.*

SENTENCES, FRAGMENTS, AND RUN-ONS

CCSS.L.7.1.C:

Place phrases and clauses within a sentence, recognizing and correcting misplaced and dangling modifiers.

In traditional grammar a **Sentence** is a group of words that expresses a complete thought and can stand alone. A sentence will have a subject (either expressed or understood) and a predicate and may have complements. It may contain phrases or clauses which modify the verb, subject, or complements or which are used as subjects or complement themselves.

A **Fragment**, however, is only part of a sentence or a clause that has been punctuated to look like a sentence. Fragments are commonly used by professional writers but should be avoided by student writers. Your teacher will likely mark you down for using them.

> Ophelia did not know what to think. **Because Hamlet's behavior was strange.** (adverbial clause)

> Chaucer's Wife of Bath is traveling to Canterbury. **To find herself another husband.** (infinitive phrase)

Ishmael narrates Ahab's quest. **For revenge on Moby Dick, a white whale that destroyed Ahab's ship and severed his leg.** (prepositional phrase)

In William Faulkner's *The Sound and the Fury,* Benjy is mentally disabled. **A constant source of shame to the Compson family.** (absolute phrase)

Romeo and Juliet being members of feuding families. Their love was forbidden. (nominative absolute)

A fragment may only need to be reconnected to a sentence from which it has become separated.

Because Hamlet's behavior was strange, Ophelia did not know what to think.

Chaucer's Wife of Bath is traveling to Canterbury **to find herself another husband.**

Ishmael narrates Ahab's quest for **revenge on Moby Dick, a white whale that destroyed Ahab's ship and severed his leg.**

In William Faulkner's *The Sound and the Fury,* Benjy is mentally disabled, a **constant source of shame to the Compson family.**

Romeo and Juliet being members of feuding families, their love was forbidden.

Sometimes the fragment needs to be rewritten. Words may need to be added or deleted to make the fragment into a complete sentence.

The modern piano, which is a descendant of the harpsichord. (fragment)

The modern piano is a descendant of the harpsichord. (sentence)

A **Run-On Sentence** is the opposite of a fragment. It is two or more sentences which have been joined together and written as one sentence. Two independent clauses form a **Fused Sentence** when joined together with no punctuation at all. They form a **Run-on** when joined together with only a comma, a construction sometimes called a "comma splice." Two different ways independent clauses can be correctly joined together are (1) by means of a comma and a coordinating conjunction (*and, but, or, nor, for, yet, so*) and (2) by means of a semicolon.

The American Civil War began at Fort Sumter, South Carolina, in 1861, it ended at Appomattox, Virginia, in 1865. (incorrect—a comma splice)

The American Civil War began at Fort Sumter, South Carolina, in 1861 it ended at Appomattox, Virginia, in 1865. (incorrect—no comma and coordinating conjunction)

A run-on sentence can be corrected several ways.

You may separate the two parts into separate sentences.

> The American Civil War began at Fort Sumter, South Carolina, in 1861. It ended at Appomattox, Virginia, in 1865.

You may correct it through coordination, using either a comma and a coordinating conjunction or a semicolon.

> The American Civil War began at Fort Sumter, South Carolina, in 1861, and it ended at Appomattox, Virginia, in 1865.

> The American Civil War began at Fort Sumter, South Carolina, in 1861; it ended at Appomattox, Virginia, in 1865.

You may correct it through subordination. Turn one of the clauses into a phrase or a dependent clause.

> The American Civil War, begun at Fort Sumter, South Carolina, in 1861, finally came to an end at Appomattox, Virginia, in 1865. (participial phrase)

> The American Civil War, which began at Fort Sumter, South Carolina, in 1861, finally came to an end at Appomattox, Virginia, in 1865. (adjective clause)

Exercise 17.1: Identifying Fragments and Run-ons

Correct the fragments and run-ons by writing complete sentences for them. Mark C for those that are correct.

CCSS.L.7.1.C:

Place phrases and clauses within a sentence, recognizing and correcting misplaced and dangling modifiers.

1. I gave the presentation, which the committee agreed to, then I addressed their concerns.

2. Climate change increases in global temperature over the last century.

3. Graduating from college with a degree in English, my life spiraled down into homelessness.

4. The computer system is being updated this weekend therefore the database will be unavailable until Monday morning.

5. I like my job as an English teacher is to instruct students in the proper use of language.

6. During the long, hot days of an Arizona summer, in the land of desert and cacti.

7. I try to do all my work in the mornings I find that I have more energy then.

8. First you roll a piece of paper in the typewriter, next you start typing away.

9. It snowed last night our car is buried today.

10. *Moby Dick* is more than just a novel, it is the centerpiece of American literature.

11. *Me and Earl and the Dying Girl*, a movie set in Pittsburgh and based on a popular YA novel.

12. The Secretary of State and the Foreign Minister of Russia read prepared statements, then they answered questions from the press corps.

13. Penny and Chloe cooked and cleaned Mango and Dango ate and enjoyed.

14. A detailed study of ravens in winter with drawings by the author.

15. Friday is payday so let's go out somewhere.

16. It rained last night so there are puddles everywhere.

 17. You're brave and successful so I admire you.

18. Our garage roof leaks, however it hasn't caused much of a problem yet.

19. It was mating season and the mockingbird sang all night.

20. Last night I couldn't sleep so I read a book and almost finished it.

Exercise 17.2: Correcting Run-ons and Comma Splices

Combine these sentences by using one of the four methods to avoid run-on sentences and comma splices.
    semicolon
    comma + FANBOYS
    subordinating word
    period
Use more than one of these four methods.

> **Example:** Museums are wonderful; they are beautiful and quiet.

CCSS.L.7.1.C:

Place phrases and clauses within a sentence, recognizing and correcting misplaced and dangling modifiers.

1. Johann Sebastian Bach is known for his beautiful church music he composed hundreds of sacred cantatas for the Lutheran Church.

2. Jose lives in Los Angeles, however, he manages to get out into the country on the weekends.

3. The old man visits Starbucks often, it's just down the street from his house.

4. Most days, after he puts in a long day teaching, he's too tired he doesn't want to go out.

5. It's important to do what you love for a living about this he is certain.

6. He's always glad he went wine country is one of his favorite places.

7. What he loves about his wife is her sense of humor she can brighten anyone's day.

8. His name, she thinks, is Andrew, she's never found the right time to ask him.

9. She doesn't know her professor from previous classes therefore she doesn't know the best way to approach him with questions about the course.

10. Today when he's cycling he wonders what would happen if he got run over by a car then he would be in the hospital or worse.

11. My brother drives a cab and spends a lot of time imagining what might happen to his business should ride-sharing companies take over, they would destroy the traditional taxi industry.

12. He'd sit in his cab at the taxi stand with no fares, he would be unable to pay his rental fees to the cab company.

13. Then maybe he would become an Uber driver, he would still be friends with his fellow cabbies, he would just be making money in a different way.

14. At this point in his life he realizes how limited his options are he has begun to panic.

    May be copied for classroom use. Common Core Grammar by Thomas Fasano (Coyote Canyon Press: Claremont, CA); © 2015.

EXCESSIVE COORDINATION

CCSS.L.9–12.1:
Demonstrate command
of the conventions of
standard English grammar
and usage when writing or
speaking.

Excessive coordination leads to two problems. A chain of main clauses joined by *and* or *so* can be tedious and boring to the reader. Coordination also does not adequately express the exact relationship of ideas. To eliminate excessive coordination, break the sentence up into separate sentences or turn some of the independent clauses into phrases or dependent clauses.

> The paintings are fragile and festering, and they are slowly disintegrating.
> Because the paintings are fragile and festering, they are slowly disintegrating.

> Emily hardly noticed that her son wasn't feeling well, so the boy became sicker.
> Since Emily hardly noticed that her son wasn't feeling well, the boy became sicker.

COORDINATION IN FICTION:
Some writers are very skilled at coordination. For example, see the opening of Ernest Hemingway's *A Farewell to Arms*. After reading that novel, you will never forget its artful cadences.

Subordinating conjunctions are the workhorses of sentence construction, helping writers eliminate excessive coordination and clarify the relationships between ideas.

Consider the following independent clauses and how they might be joined by subordinating conjunctions.

The car was in bad shape.   •   Bryon refused to spend money on it.

Did Byron refuse to spend money on the car because it was in bad shape, or was the car in bad shape because Byron refused to spend money on it?

> **Because** the car was in bad shape, Byron refused to spend money on it.

> **Because** Byron refused to spend money on it, the car was in bad shape.

> **Although** the car was in bad shape, Byron refused to spend money on it.

> **As long as** Byron refused to spend money on it, the car was in bad shape.

The relationship between Byron and the car is established by the choice of subordinating conjunctions. Combining the two independent clauses with coordination would not express the subtle relationship.

> Byron hesitated to spend money on it, **and** the car was in bad shape.

> The car was in bad shape, **but** Byron refused to spend money on it. (*But* in this sentence is better than *and*, but it doesn't quite express the subtleties involved.)

Exercise 17.3: Writing with Coordination

Edit these sentences, eliminating any errors in the use of coordination. Rewrite them in the spaces provided.

CCSS.L.9–12.1:
Demonstrate command of the conventions of standard English grammar and usage when writing or speaking.

1. What he sees when he comes out on the steps is beyond anything he has ever imagined, and the memory tumbles him back into childhood again, and for a moment he freezes there on the steps, and he thinks it's like the biggest, most intense thunderstorm anyone ever saw.

2. There'd never been a KEEP OUT sign on the door, and she'd stayed here in the house lots of times when her husband was alive, and maybe she should post a sign on the gate, but the hunters would probably keep marching through her property anyway.

3. The important thing is how memory affects the stories you write, and I wanted to delve into those memories, and I got excited all over again, and I started writing stories again in the old way, and it felt good.

4. She finished her cycle of treatments for the rabid dog bites with a great deal of pain, but she had no serious problems, but the potential seriousness of the disease was always present, and she was feeling depressed, but she was closely watched.

5. Frank knocked out the partitions to make one big garage, and there the summer cars waited out the long months of autumn and winter in the dank shadows, and their bright surfaces were dulled by the steady drift of hay chaff from the loft, and the cars were parked bumper to bumper and side to side.

MISPLACED MODIFIERS

CCSS.L.7.1.C:

Place phrases and clauses within a sentence, recognizing and correcting misplaced and dangling modifiers.

A misplaced modifier is a word, phrase, or clause that has not been placed in proper relation to the word it modifies. The modifier ends up modifying a different word in the sentence, with the result that the sentence doesn't say exactly what the writer intended.

Words that are commonly misplaced are *only, merely,* and *just,* and other similar words like *practically, still, often, even, almost, nearly, usually, not, frequently.*

A good rule is to position *only* (and similar modifiers) directly before the word it is intended to modify, as in *I have only five dollars to my name.* (Here, *only* modifies *five,* the positioning of *only* emphasizing the limited cash flow of the writer.)

> My garage has room for **only** my car.
> My garage **only** has room for my car.
> My garage has **only** room for my car.

> My software works **only** with older Macs.
> My software **only** works with older Macs.

> The movie is available **only** on Blu-ray.
> The movie is **only** available on Blu-ray.

Placement of a modifier in a faulty position can cause confusion. Sentences such as the following are ambiguous and require careful revision.

> The police discovered an incendiary device inside the theater **that was underneath a seat**. (The sentence states that the theater was under the seat.)

> **No matter how stupid**, most moviegoers will be entertained by this screwball comedy. (The sentence states that most moviegoers are stupid.)

> He realized how many people are murdered **through his work as a police officer**. (The sentence states that the officer's work results in many homicides.)

> The court ruled that the school district failed to provide an adequate education to disadvantaged children **in violation of the law**. (The sentence states that the children are in violation of the law.)

Expressions like *all do not* and *everyone does not* can cause confusion by the misplacement of *not,* unless your intent is *not a single one* or *none.*

> **Everyone** in America **does not** use ObamaCare. (Faulty)
> **Not everyone** in America uses ObamaCare

All the money **hasn't** been spent. (Faulty)
Not all the money **has** been spent.

All the homeless **are not** substance abusers. (Faulty)
Not all the homeless **are** substance abusers.

Another area of confusion involves two-way adverbs.

People who interrupt **constantly** annoy me.

Which word does the adverb *constantly* modify? Is it *interrupt* or *annoy?* Does the sentence mean that *people who constantly interrupt me annoy me,* or does it mean that *people who interrupt all the time out of habit annoy me constantly?*

In your writing try to be precise and place your adverbs carefully.

Exercise 17.4: Eliminating Misplaced Modifiers

Edit these sentences, eliminating any misplaced modifiers. Rewrite them in the spaces provided.

CCSS.L.7.1.C:
Place phrases and clauses within a sentence, recognizing and correcting misplaced and dangling modifiers.

1. Hanging on a hook in the garage, he found his father's old rake.

2. The paramedics took the shooting victim to the hospital with the gunshot wound to the head.

3. The clown kissed the little girl with the big rubber nose.

4. They imagined a trip to Mars in their classroom.

5. I spotted the neighbor's girl riding her tricycle in the middle of the street on the way to work.

6. As a baby my mother sang lullabies to me.

7. Lumpy and sour, my father didn't bake the bread right.

8. Molly the dog only hides underneath the bed during a thunderstorm.

9. Loud and shrill, Dianne turned off the car alarm.

10. One morning I spotted a squirrel in my pajamas.

11. My brother writes about his efforts to find Bigfoot on his blog.

12. We do not have any books about killers in our house.

Exercise 17.5: Correcting Misplaced Modifiers

In the following sentences, the misplaced modifying word has been highlighted. Draw an arrow to where it should be placed. Sometimes more than one place is possible.

CCSS.L.7.1.C:

Place phrases and clauses within a sentence, recognizing and correcting misplaced and dangling modifiers.

1. Florence is the girl in the car **with red hair**.

2. Johnny sat thinking about yelling at his neighbor **in his room at night**.

3. The commercial drove home the point that smoking can kill you **last night**.

4. We prepared a meal for our guests **low in fat**.

5. The manager screamed at the umpire **in the dugout**.

6. **Both modern and traditional**, we loved the staging of Mozart's *The Marriage of Figaro*.

7. A valuable coin was found by a taxi driver **with two heads**.

8. The philanthropist died in the house in which she was born **at the age of ninety-seven**.

9. **Starving and abused**, the newspaper reported that the puppies were adopted by good families.

10. The boys gave a present to their mother **wrapped in newspaper**.

11. Grandma gave ice cream to the children **covered in chocolate syrup**.

12. The man tripped over the kitten **with work boots on**.

13. Ham was served by the chef **that was glazed with pineapple**.

14. In my street this morning I saw two coyotes **on the way to work**.

DANGLING MODIFIERS

CCSS.L.7.1.C:

Place phrases and clauses within a sentence, recognizing and correcting misplaced and dangling modifiers.

A participial phrase that is not related grammatically to any noun in the sentence is said to be a ***Dangling Modifier***.

A participial phrase contains no subject, but if it is placed near the subject of the sentence it is "understood" to refer to it.

> **Speaking to her yesterday**, her attitude could not have been worse. (dangling)
> **Speaking to her yesterday**, I thought her attitude could not have been worse. (correct)
>
> **Covered in leaves during the autumn**, I always enjoy my yard in the months leading up to winter. (hanging)
> **Covered in leaves during the autumn**, my yard is a joy in the months leading up to winter. (correct)

CCSS.L.11–12.1.A:

Apply the understanding that usage is a matter of convention, can change over time, and is sometimes contested.

The "hanging participle" is commonly condemned as ungrammatical although it has been used for centuries by great writers, most famously by Shakespeare:

> **Sleeping in mine orchard**, a serpent stung me.

The same rule that a participle must refer to the subject applies when the participle is introduced by a conjunction or a preposition.

> **When buying a new computer**, your budget is a consideration. (dangling)
> **When buying a new computer**, you must consider your budget. (correct)
>
> **When asked about this**, no answer was given. (dangling)
> **When asked about this**, the attorney general gave no answer. (correct)
>
> **Instead of sleeping all day**, there are chores to do. (dangling)
> **Instead of sleeping all day**, you could do some chores. (correct)

Some phrases, though technically dangling, have become so commonly used that they are clearly understood and accepted.

> **Considering his poor education,** he was remarkably well read.
> The project should proceed, **provided there is sufficient funding available.**

Some danglers are not errors at all. Many participles have evolved into prepositions, such as *according, barring, concerning, considering, excepting, excluding, failing, following, given, granted, including, owing, regarding,* and *respecting*. And these prepositions do not require a subject corresponding to the subject of the sentence.

Exercise 17.6: Eliminating Dangling Modifiers

Edit these sentences, eliminating any dangling modifiers. Rewrite them in the spaces provided.

CCSS.L.11–12.1.A:
Apply the understanding that usage is a matter of convention, can change over time, and is some-times contested.

1. Walking up the stairs of his grandmother's house, the sound of his soles could be heard on the polished wood.

2. Looking out the windows of the airplane, the Rocky Mountains sparkled in the distance.

3. Getting the best performance from your engine, it needs regular maintenance.

4. When quitting your job, the time most convenient and beneficial to you is paramount.

5. Having listened to the same Beethoven symphony repeatedly all day, the sound of the music was stuck in his head.

6. Hiking ten miles this morning, his legs felt as if they were going to give out.

7. Going to the movies during the summer to while away the time, my fun money was running out.

8. Obsessed with washing his car, his anger boiled over when the neighborhood kids egged it last night.

9. Speaking endlessly at the podium, the disgust of the audience for the speaker's positions became increasingly obvious.

10. Having gotten sand kicked in his face, his eyes were irritated and red.

Exercise 17.7: Correcting Misplaced and Dangling Modifiers

Correct each of the misplaced and dangling modifiers by placing it elsewhere in the sentence, adding words to the phrase, or changing some of the words in the main clause.

CCSS.L.11–12.1.A:
Apply the understanding that usage is a matter of convention, can change over time, and is sometimes contested.

1. Not being taught as a system in any school, no special importance has ever been placed on punctuation.

2. In answering my students' questions, it has always been my aim to seize teachable moments.

3. Being a weekend golfer and not a professional, my interest has always been on enjoying the game and nothing else.

4. When speaking to students about their behavior, it is usual for me to take them aside out of earshot of other students.

5. Even admitting that a relaxed writing style takes years of hard work, much academic writing is too abstruse for its own good.

6. Applying the principles of fairness to the situation, it is obvious that participants need to be reimbursed.

7. I saw the Statue of Liberty flying into JFK.

8. The Illinois law requires a teenager's doctor to notify a parent before undergoing an abortion.

9. A noted expert in the field of animal behavior, his opinion mattered a lot.

10. Jones was the school bus driver in which the injured students were riding.

11. The man has lived with the virus that causes AIDS for twenty years.

12. Both boys passed out in the summer home their mother rented after doing drugs.

PARALLELISM

CCSS.L.9–10.1.A:
Use parallel structure.

Parallelism is the logical matching of sentence parts, a balancing which satisfies every reader's desire for cadence and rhythm in language. For example, in a sentence one might have noun + noun + noun, or verb + verb + verb, or infinitive phrase + infinitive phrase. By using these parallel grammatical structures, ideas flow and relate and connect in a satisfying rhythm.

Parallelism is the mark of a good, clear, and precise writer. All good writers have a clear grasp of words, phrases, verb-forms, and other parts of speech. A lack of parallelism can be very annoying and confusing to readers. Readers lose patience when they have to cope with something like the following:

My twin brother lives in Tampa, drives a cab, and camping in the woods.

Parallelism can be achieved in a number of ways.

- Parts of Speech

  The poem is **elegiac, incantatory, and prayerful**.

  Mozart was a composer of **symphonies, concertos, and operas**.

  Time of day, amount of light, and distance from the subject are all factors involved in taking good photographs.

  A good mate would be **kind, patient, and funny**.

- Phrases and Clauses

  Our accountants urged **that we raise prices** and **that we lower costs**.

  Tolkien's novels contain characters **who are fantastic** but **who have realistic human emotions**.

  Orthopedic surgeons study for **four years in a college or university** and **four years in an orthopedic residency program**.

  Kansas City suffered especially **when the Depression happened, when the drought hit,** and **when the war started**.

- Elliptical Constructions

Be especially careful to achieve parallelism when you are using correlative conjunctions (conjunctions which come in pairs): *either . . . or, neither . . . nor, both . . . and, not only . . . but also*. Each part of these sets should come immediately in front of the parallel elements.

He is **not only our leader but also our chaplain**.

He is responsible **not only for leading us but also for feeding our souls**.

The day was **both hot and humid**.

I want to explain **both who I am and what I believe**.

COMMON CORE GRAMMAR

Exercise 17.8: Writing with Parallel Structure

Rewrite the sentences below so that they contain correct parallel structure.

CCSS.L.9–10.1.A:
Use parallel structure.

1. Cross-country travel in 1870 was tiring, uncomfortable, and cost a lot of money.

2. In the summertime, I love swimming, hiking, or to relax.

3. My best friend is small, quick, and an athlete.

4. Going to the movies is more fun than to watch videos at home.

5. My boss praised me for being conscientious and promptness.

6. The new software is inexpensive, user-friendly, and can be shipped to your home address overnight.

7. He faces a maximum ten years in prison, half a million in fines and must pay back the money he stole.

8. My brother promised to clean his room and that he would take out the trash.

9. I was more interested in the exhibit than in what Martha said.

10. Riding the bus is less expensive than to drive a car.

11. I enjoy beef, chicken, and eating fish.

12. It was both a hot day and humid.

13. The old house needs new wiring, new insulation, and to be given a new coat of paint.

14. I want to explain both who I am and my beliefs.

15. The teacher said that I should write more and to talk less.

16. Food at the ballpark is greasy, doesn't taste very good, and I spend a lot of money on it.

Exercise 17.9: Correcting Errors in Parallelism

Edit these sentences, correcting any errors in parallelism. Rewrite them in the spaces provided.

CCSS.L.9–10.1.A:
Use parallel structure.

1. The agriculture professor presented some techniques for composting, planting, and how to prevent weed growth.

2. By spending a year in Germany, you will not only enjoy living among a different culture, but also to be able to travel easily to different parts of Europe.

3. This book is useful for practicing language skills, learning grammar, and to understand basic writing.

4. The state university is relatively close to his hometown, less expensive than most private schools, and its biology program, which he wants to major in, has a stellar reputation.

5. The dialogues of Plato include situations from Socrates' life and which raise important philosophical questions.

6. Upon completing your semester-long research project, you will both prepare a formal research paper and an oral class presentation.

7. The Basque Country is a region located throughout the Pyrenees, both in Spain and France.

8. Not only did the Vikings establish settlements in Greenland but also on the North American mainland.

Chapter

Punctuation

18

ENGLISH LANGUAGE ARTS STANDARDS

NOTE:
Some of the skills in this chapter were introduced at lower grade levels; yet, due to the recursiveness of the language standards, they require further attention at the high school level.

☞ ***CCSS.ELA-LITERACY.L.11–12.1.A:*** *Apply the understanding that usage is a matter of convention, can change over time, and is sometimes contested.*

☞ ***CCSS.ELA-LITERACY.L.11–12.2.A:*** *Observe hyphenation conventions.*

☞ ***CCSS.ELA-LITERACY.L.9–12.2:*** *Demonstrate command of the conventions of standard English capitalization, punctuation, and spelling when writing.*

☞ ***CCSS.ELA-LITERACY.L.9–10.2.A:*** *Use a semicolon (and perhaps a conjunctive adverb) to link two or more closely related independent clauses.*

☞ ***CCSS.ELA-LITERACY.L.9–10.2.B:*** *Use a colon to introduce a list or quotation.*

☞ ***CCSS.ELA-LITERACY.L.8.2.A:*** *Use punctuation (comma, ellipsis, dash) to indicate a pause or break.*

PUNCTUATION

CCSS.L.9–12.2:
Demonstrate command of the conventions of standard English capitalization, punctuation, and spelling when writing.

This chapter considers two factors that determine the ***Punctuation*** used in a sentence: the kind of relationship between words, and the position of grammatical elements in the sentence.

Groups of words are *placed in a particular order* so that the thought flows naturally from one idea to the next. The issue here is to indicate the kind of relationship that exists between these groups.

Groups of words are *separated* by other elements that interrupt the natural flow of thought. In this case the issue is to set off the interpolated element so that the reader can easily see where the thought is interrupted and where it resumes.

The general characteristics of the marks of punctuation need to be kept in mind. A *semicolon* is stronger than a *comma* and indicates that the connection in thought is more remote. A *colon* indicates that a specific list or enumeration, or an explanation, is to follow. A *dash* marks a break in thought or adds emphasis to what follows.

In the following discussion, note the reasoning behind the classifications. In *Series of Equal Elements* related groups go together; in *Main and Subordinate Elements,* some groups go together while others are separated; in *Interrupters* the related groups are separated; in *Enumerations and Explanations* and in *Direct Quotations* the relationships are of various specific types.

SERIES OF EQUAL ELEMENTS

Main Clauses in Series

CCSS.L.9–12.2:

Demonstrate command of the conventions of standard English capitalization, punctuation, and spelling when writing.

Note two types of main clauses:

- those that are connected by the coordinate conjunctions: *for, and, nor, but, or, yet,* and *so.*

- those that have no conjunction or may use a conjunctive adverb, such as *therefore, however, nonetheless.*

Main Clauses Connected by Coordinate Conjunctions

CCSS.L.8.2.A:

Use punctuation (comma, ellipsis, dash) to indicate a pause or break.

With these clauses, the punctuation may vary, depending on the length of the clauses and the closeness of the relation between them.

A **Comma** is regularly used between clauses of short or moderate length with a fairly close connection.

> Then she jumped to her feet and slipped her hand into his, and they tiptoed across the fields, jumping and swinging from dry spot to dry spot. (F. Scott Fitzgerald.)

> The blazing matches fell sizzling into the snow, but the birch bark was alight. (Jack London.)

You have to fill out these forms now, or you will have to come back later.

I did not want to go to a movie, nor did I want to go out at all.

CCSS.L.9–10.2.A:

Use a semicolon (and perhaps a conjunctive adverb) to link two or more closely related independent clauses.

A *Semicolon* is regularly used between long clauses, especially if the clauses contain commas and have the same subject.

He attended university in Europe, was in the Peace Corps in Tunisia, and traveled extensively in Africa; and now he was coming back to California to teach in the public schools.

The sheriff did not attempt his retention; but being at least as prudent as he was valiant, he succumbed, leaving Slade the master of the situation and the conqueror and ruler of the courts, law and law-makers. (Mark Twain.)

If the clauses are short and have a close logical connection, *No Punctuation* is required.

It was Monday and I didn't want to go to work.

Main Clauses Not Connected by Coordinate Conjunctions

CCSS.L.9–10.2.A:

Use a semicolon (and perhaps a conjunctive adverb) to link two or more closely related independent clauses.

These clauses may have no conjunction, or they may employ a connective such as *therefore, nevertheless, however, in fact,* or other conjunctive adverbs.

A *Semicolon* is used with this group, no matter the length of the clauses.

The journalist details life; the novelist interprets life.

By nature he is an introvert; by avocation he is a public speaker.

There is no need to worry about the wealthy in this country; in fact, their wealth outstrips the economy.

Life can at times be difficult; however, that is no reason to despair.

Exercise 18.1: Punctuating Series of Equal Elements

Punctuate the main clauses and indicate why you use each mark of punctuation.

CCSS.L.9–12.2:
Demonstrate command of the conventions of standard English capitalization, punctuation, and spelling when writing.

1. He lived for many years in Florida but he never thought of it as his home.

2. The book is enlightening moreover it is entertaining.

3. The moon was in total eclipse and the planet Mars was in proximity.

4. Many of the buildings were not retrofitted for earthquakes and inadequately prepared and in other respects as well they were not modernized.

5. Lauren is a freshman her brother is a junior.

6. He never had any experience with financial problems nevertheless he was confident that he could deal with it.

CCSS.L.9–10.2.A:
Use a semicolon (and perhaps a conjunctive adverb) to link two or more closely related independent clauses.

7. We were now about a mile from the place where we had access to the river and the trail was becoming steeper and more difficult with every step.

8. Homicide detectives may work for months on a case or if they get a few breaks they may quickly solve the crime.

9. Today the secretary of state may be in Tel Aviv or in Paris and tomorrow she may find herself in Moscow or Beijing.

10. He was the last of a long line of scholars and writers and as might be expected he was proud of his lineage.

CCSS.L.8.2.A:
Use punctuation (comma, ellipsis, dash) to indicate a pause or break.

11. A few of the suicide bombers were from Europe and the others were radicalized citizens of Middle-Eastern countries.

12. He promised to be at the conference therefore he must go.

13. At Albany you can continue your trip to Buffalo by boat or you have the option of finishing the journey by rail.

14. The new law will correct some of the problems with ObamaCare but it does not resolve the issue of subsidies.

SERIES OF WORDS, PHRASES, OR SUBORDINATE CLAUSES

CCSS.L.8.2.A:

Use punctuation (comma, ellipsis, dash) to indicate a pause or break.

A *Comma* is regularly used to separate a series of three or more words, phrases, or clauses of equal rank or importance.

> Most of the cab drivers are from **the Middle East, Central Asia, or Africa**.
>
> The movie takes a **light, funny, and ironic** look at life on Wall Street.
>
> In the garden she **dug the soil, planted the seeds, and harvested the vegetables**.
>
> The store accepts **cash, checks, and credit cards**.
>
> The article detailed **how the killer found his victims, how he killed them, and what his motivations were**.

CCSS.L.11–12.1.A:

Apply the understanding that usage is a matter of convention, can change over time, and is sometimes contested.

The final comma in a series is known as the *Oxford Comma* (sometimes called a *serial comma*) and is often omitted in modern journalism but should always be used when needed for clarity, as when there are other *ands* in the series.

> I shop at J.C. Penney, Barnes & Noble, and Macy's.
>
> I shop at J.C. Penney, Barnes & Noble and Macy's.

In academic writing, the comma is preferred.

CCSS.L.9–10.2.A:

Use a semicolon (and perhaps a conjunctive adverb) to link two or more closely related independent clauses.

A *Semicolon* is used if the members of a series are long or if they contain elements set off by commas.

> On the street in front of us were **a sodden, bedraggled homeless man with a garbage bag full of cans and bottles; a toothless woman, distempered and screaming at all who passed; and a street busker, singing and playing a guitar**.

SERIES OF VARIOUS TYPES

CCSS.L.8.2.A:

Use punctuation (comma, ellipsis, dash) to indicate a pause or break.

Commas are used to separate the members of the following groups, which are miscellaneous series.

- A long compound predicate.

  > I **poured** a cup of coffee brewed from the finest South American beans**,** and **sat** in my favorite chair to do some reading.

- A declarative sentence followed by a short question.

You will be there, **won't you?**

Contrasted elements, positive or negative.

I was talking to him, **not you**.

The secret lies, **not in the effort,** but in innovation.

- Parts of addresses, dates, names, titles, and similar word groups.

Abraham Lincoln was born on **February 12, 1809, in Kentucky**.

By **August 2011,** there was ample intelligence concerning a terrorist attack against the United States.

My family moved to **92 Basswood Drive, Newport News, Virginia,** when I was a small child.

For the best information about L.B.J.'s life in the senate, you should read Robert Caro's **Master of the Senate, Vol. III of "The Years of Lyndon Johnson."**

The valedictory speech was given by **Dr. Robert Zimmerman, Ph.D., president of Florida Southern College**.

- Words in apposition.

The campus of Florida Southern College, **one of the most beautiful in the country,** was designed by Frank Lloyd Wright.

His partner in crime, **a teenage boy,** was under his control.

I will be visiting my twin brother, **Tim,** in Tampa next week.

Exercise 18.2: Punctuating Series of Various Types

Punctuate the following sentences and give your reasons.

CCSS.L.9–12.2:
Demonstrate command of the conventions of standard English capitalization, punctuation, and spelling when writing.

1. In San Francisco California the plan continues to be tried with marked success.

2. The union hoped for a settlement of the labor dispute not by striking but by arbitration.

3. Chris Bonk a prominent Chicago artist had his own exhibit at a downtown gallery.

4. The Treaty of Versailles was signed on June 28 1919 by Germany the United States England France Italy and Japan.

5. The villagers chased Frankenstein's monster through the countryside on foot with torches screaming for vengeance.

CCSS.L.9–10.2.A:
Use a semicolon (and perhaps a conjunctive adverb) to link two or more closely related independent clauses.

6. You see now how much we value your opinion don't you?

7. The main building a six-story modern earthquake-proof structure is located at 4929 Wilshire Boulevard Los Angeles California in the Miracle Mile.

8. He claimed that he'd often read about the intelligence of ravens and was pleased to observe them at close range.

9. Early January the candidates for president made their first appearance in Iowa City Iowa a college town and home to the University of Iowa.

10. He found a long straight sturdy branch of an oak tree and made a walking stick out of it.

11. The first three places in the contest were won by Robert Fletcher of Yorktown Virginia Frank Mercer of Phoenix Arizona and Carol Berger of Dallas Texas.

CCSS.L.8.2.A:
Use punctuation (comma, ellipsis, dash) to indicate a pause or break.

12. In November 1963 President Kennedy made a visit to Dallas Texas a city seething in anti-Kennedy sentiment

13. His companion a younger woman by several years took him by the arm and hurried him up the stair.

14. The stevedores already finished unloading the cargo of the first steamer and were lounging on the dock until the next boat arrived.

15. The chief wealth of the country lies in its mines of lead iron and gold its agricultural products such as wheat and barley and its great forests of rare woods suitable for the finest cabinet work.

MAIN AND SUBORDINATE ELEMENTS

Punctuation is needed if the main and subordinate clauses are not closely related, or if the subordinate clause is placed so that it delays or interrupts the normal flow of thought.

ADVERBIAL CLAUSES AND PHRASES

Interruption of the Thought in a Sentence

CCSS.L.8.2.A:
Use punctuation (comma, ellipsis, dash) to indicate a pause or break.

A *Comma* is regularly used to set off a clause or phrase preceding a main clause; coming between the subject and the verb in the main clause; or coming between the verb and its object or predicate noun.

In the first instance, the subordinate clause delays the expression of the main thought; in the next two instances, the subordinate element interrupts the regular flow of thought in the sentence, from subject—to verb—to object or predicate noun.

- Before the *Main Clause*.

  If I believed in that for a second, I would not be a teacher.

  While working hard at our careers, we must be sure to spend time with our families.

  Having little regard for the latest government mandates, I will run my classroom as usual.

  When the subordinate element is short and closely related in thought to the main clause, the comma is often omitted.

  Late last week the stock market plummeted.

  Where there is smoke there is fire.

- Between the *Subject and the Verb*.

  The house, **when we first moved in ten years ago,** had a leaky roof.

  Karen, **stretching after a workout,** gave the appearance of a fit athlete.

- Between the *Verb and the Object or the Predicate Noun*.

She had, **even at the beginning of her journey,** a sense that her life was never going to be the same.

She was, **by all accounts,** an excellent pianist.

No Interruption of the Thought

CCSS.L.9–12.2:
Demonstrate command of the conventions of standard English capitalization, punctuation, and spelling when writing.

An adverbial element that comes after the verb and does not separate the verb from its object or predicate noun is not regularly punctuated since there is no interruption of the thought in the sentence.

You would not like to drive **if you had a long commute.**

He walked for miles through the woods **until he came to a highway.**

No one noticed **when he fell overboard.**

Exceptions

CCSS.L.8.2.A:
Use punctuation (comma, ellipsis, dash) to indicate a pause or break.

Certain types of adverbial elements are regularly punctuated when they follow the verb.

A clause of reason introduced by *for* or *as,* and a clause of concession introduced by *though* or *although.*

We had little time to think, **for the fire was racing toward the house.**

He has managed the old farm for years, **though he is letting it go back to forest.**

Additionally, any adverbial element following the verb may be set off with punctuation if the writer wants to give it special emphasis: for example, a participial phrase that modifies the subject but is removed from it; or a nominative absolute phrase.

Hawthorne lived for many years in the house, **writing in seclusion and honing his craft.**

The old hag screamed at the children, **her dentures flopping out of her mouth.**

Both of the above constructions perform the dual function of adverb and adjective.

Exercise 18.3: Punctuating Main and Subordinate Elements

Punctuate the adverbial clauses and phrases when punctuation is needed, and give your reasons.

CCSS.L.9–12.2:
Demonstrate command of the conventions of standard English capitalization, punctuation, and spelling when writing.

1. If what your employer requires of you seems to be a violation of your contract then the union should get involved.

2. English has become an international language a *lingua franca* for many people throughout the world have learned the language.

3. Each applicant as he entered the waiting room of the recruiting office was given a pile of forms to fill out.

4. He belonged to the aristocracy of the old South his family being former plantation owners.

5. The other driver filled with road rage swung sharply to the right cutting off everyone in that lane.

CCSS.L.8.2.A:
Use punctuation (comma, ellipsis, dash) to indicate a pause or break.

6. Measuring off fifty yards from the beginning of the skid marks the investigator came to an understanding of what contributed to the accident.

7. Whether he writes about the African diaspora or Russian hegemony he shows the same grace and attention to detail.

8. Although they left before sunrise it was well after sunset when they arrived at the hotel.

9. He was well qualified for the teaching position having been a teacher in another district for twenty years.

10. I have always felt when my boss talks that he is not entirely forthcoming.

11. Pedestrians were hurried to places of safety as no one knew when the next attacker would strike.

12. Disturbed by the continued decrease in sales the directors increased their advertising budget.

13. She was well qualified for the position having been an assistant in the department for twenty years.

14. I always felt when the president was speaking that he was never telling the truth.

15. The motion having been seconded the issue was brought before the committee.

ADJECTIVE CLAUSES AND PHRASES

Restrictive Elements

CCSS.L.9–12.2:
Demonstrate command of the conventions of standard English capitalization, punctuation, and spelling when writing.

Restrictive clauses and phrases are not punctuated.

Everyone **who lived there** was affected by the drought.

The bank **that was robbed last week** now has an armed guard outside.

The dog **digging a hole in my garden** is my neighbor's.

Nonrestrictive Elements

CCSS.L.8.2.A:
Use punctuation (comma, ellipsis, dash) to indicate a pause or break.

Nonrestrictive adjective clauses and phrases are set off by commas.

The year I spent in Europe, **living in Vienna,** was the happiest of my life.

The newspaper article, **which ran on three pages,** detailed the latest thinking about climate change.

Westminster Abbey, **completed in 1066,** is the final resting place of England's finest poets and writers.

Note. A restrictive clause or phrase is one that indicates what particular person or thing is meant: in other words, it restricts the statement to that person or thing. If omitted, the meaning of the sentence changes.

Coffee **that is cold** is nasty.

CCSS.L.9–12.2:
Demonstrate command of the conventions of standard English capitalization, punctuation, and spelling when writing.

A nonrestrictive clause or phrase may be omitted without changing the meaning of the sentence.

The tire, **which has barely any tread,** is dangerous.

Notice that even when a restrictive element comes between the subject and the verb, it is so closely connected with the main clause that it is not set off by punctuation. Occasionally, a long restrictive clause so placed may be followed by a comma but not preceded by one, the better to indicate where the resumption of the main thought occurs.

Economic plans **that do not take into consideration defaulted mortgages, the banking crisis of the past few years, and the widespread disruption to international markets,** have not been carefully considered.

Exercise 18.4: Punctuating Adjective Clauses and Phrases

Punctuate the adjective clauses and phrases when punctuation is needed, and give your reasons.

CCSS.L.8.2.A:
Use punctuation (comma, ellipsis, dash) to indicate a pause or break.

1. Most of the trees that were leveled in the hurricane have been cleared.

2. The driver of the wrong-way car who was drunk and responsible for the head-on collision was the only survivor.

3. John le Carré who once worked for the British intelligence services is an important author of espionage fiction.

4. The panhandler smiling his best smile asked the passersby for spare change.

5. Apollo 11 which was the first spaceflight that landed humans on the moon stands as the crowning achievement of the American space program.

CCSS.L.9–12.2:
Demonstrate command of the conventions of standard English capitalization, punctuation, and spelling when writing.

6. We could find no one whom we could trust to carry the suitcase of money for us.

7. *Huckleberry Finn* was written by Samuel Clemens whom we know better as Mark Twain.

8. It was a story that was told to me in a bar by an man who spent many years working for the CIA.

9. Rowan Oak where William Faulkner lived and wrote most of his novels has been preserved by the University of Mississippi which owns and operates it.

10. The mayor dressed in casual clothing came to the festival to congratulate the volunteers who helped at the food bank.

11. A skyscraper constructed of steel and concrete cannot withstand a terrorist's airplane.

12. His uncle who was a director of the corporation insisted on his promotion.

13. The Telford Inn where Washington once had his headquarters will be restored by the local historical society which is collecting funds for that purpose.

14. The city where I was raised and the people whom I went to school with have long since vanished from my life which now is disconnected from my childhood.

NOUN CLAUSES

CCSS.L.9–12.2:

Demonstrate command of the conventions of standard English capitalization, punctuation, and spelling when writing.

Ordinarily, noun clauses and phrases are not punctuated.

> We could see **that he was struggling with something** (object of the verb).
>
> She is **what is commonly referred to as a prima donna** (predicate noun).
>
> **How well you do in the wilderness** is related to how prepared you are (subject of the verb).

A comma is regularly used to set off a clause that is the object of the verb when it is placed at the beginning of the sentence, or a clause that is the subject of the verb but ends with a verb in awkward juxtaposition with the main verb.

> **Whatever you need,** we will provide (direct object of the verb).
>
> **What he needs,** needs to be looked at (subject of the verb).

INTERRUPTERS

CCSS.L.9–12.2:

Demonstrate command of the conventions of standard English capitalization, punctuation, and spelling when writing.

Such elements as **Parenthetical** and **Independent Elements** and words in **Direct Address** interrupt and delay the normal flow of thought in a sentence. For this reason, punctuation is needed to set them off from the rest of the sentence.

The following elements are regularly punctuated with *Commas*.

- Parenthetical and Independent Elements.

> His entire life, **one might suppose,** was one long struggle to rise above poverty.
>
> The tree, **it seems,** is dying from blight.
>
> The initial medical tests, **of course,** are not conclusive.
>
> **Thankfully,** the building inspector discovered the termite infestation.
>
> I did not become a teacher, **believe it or not,** to teach to a test.
>
> The early pioneers had, **also,** something of the Puritan work ethic.
>
> **Nevertheless,** we are going to have to begin afresh.
>
> I, **alas,** am free of my nemesis.

Note. Sometimes an interjection can be emphatic, in which case it is set off by an exclamation point.

Rubbish! he doesn't know what he's talking about.

- Direct Address.

You know what I mean, **my dear friend**.

Mr. Meriwether, please take a seat.

Listen to me, **pal,** when I'm talking to you.

Complete Breaks in Thought

A **Dash** is often used to indicate a more emphatic interruption in a sentence, or a complete break in thought.

A transient named Flash—**we called him that because his car looked like Flash Gordon's**—was actually living in his car.

When I lived in Florida—**a time when I was unemployed**—I had many interesting friends.

I washed my hands of him, and—**but why waste my time talking about him?**

We pay enough money already to live here, and now they are going to raise the—**why they surely must be joking**.

"Four score and seven years ago—" the famous speech begins.

"He told me—**promised me**—that he would pay his share," she said.

- **Parentheses** may be used in place of dashes to set off parenthetical expressions.

Flash **(we called him that because his car was like something out of Flash Gordon)** was actually living in his car.

Parentheses are regularly used to enclose various minor or routine details.

Three recent presidents have been left-handed: George H. W. Bush **(Republican)**, Bill Clinton **(Democrat)**, and Barack Obama **(Democrat)**.

In an upcoming chapter **(see p. 327)** this concept is explained more thoroughly.

In the following table **(Fig. 7)** the rate of inflation is indicated.

CHAPTER
18

Exercise 18.5: Punctuating Noun Clauses and Interrupters

Punctuate the parenthetical and independent elements, and the words in direct address.

CCSS.L.8.2.A:
Use punctuation (comma, ellipsis, dash) to indicate a pause or break.

1. The same kind of thing we are pretty sure exists in many American cities.

2. The graphics in case you weren't aware have to be completed at least a day before the paper goes to press.

3. The president was annoyed too by the Republican Party's criticism of his policies.

4. His wife she was a farmer's daughter from South Dakota was active in the Audubon Society of Southern California.

5. Oddly enough he was never on an airplane before his trip to Europe.

CCSS.L.9–12.2:
Demonstrate command of the conventions of standard English capitalization, punctuation, and spelling when writing.

6. This in fact has been the subject of much chatter in social media.

7. The Texas governor's stupidity yes my friends it was stupidity was responsible for his disastrous presidential candidacy.

8. His success in the company was largely due of course to his dedication.

9. Unfortunately sir your remark was misinterpreted as insensitive and racist.

10. Nonetheless the apartment will have to be vacated.

11. A. C. Fabri spelled with an *i* instead of a *y* is their representative in this country.

12. No yes well I suppose so he stammered.

13. Nevertheless the project will have to be abandoned.

14. No doubt you are right Mr. Dutwin but there are you must admit some arguments on the other side.

ENUMERATIONS AND EXPLANATIONS

CCSS.L.9–10.2.B:
Use a colon to introduce a list or quotation.

A *Colon* is regularly used before a list or formal enumeration of details following an introductory statement, or before a specific example or explanation.

The enumeration, example, or explanation may be introduced by words like *namely, as, for example, that is, in other words;* or may follow the phrases *the following* or *as follows;* or may have no introductory element whatsoever.

- Enumerations.

  The book about the history of Western Civilization has several helpful maps: **namely, Ancient Near East, Early Greece, Alexander's Empire, Germanic Migrations, and Carolingian Empire**.

  Retirement income can come from **the following sources: pensions, IRAs, 401k's, savings, stocks, social security, home equity, etc.**

  The things in my study are important to me: **a desk I built myself, a Mac computer, a collection of favorite pens, a typewriter, an old barometer from my childhood, a dictionary stand, and a bookcase**.

- Specific Explanations

  President Kennedy had a visionary goal for space travel: **America would be dedicated to"landing a man on the moon and returning him safely to the earth," and she would do so by the end of the 1960s**.

  His morning routine was predictable: **that is, he awoke at the same hour, showered, ate his cereal, read the paper, and drove to work**.

Note that a comma is used after introducing words like *for example, that is, namely, as, in other words,* etc.

CCSS.L.9–12.2:
Demonstrate command of the conventions of standard English capitalization, punctuation, and spelling when writing.

Enumerations, examples, and explanations in the middle of a sentence may be punctuated with dashes for special emphasis or clarity.

  Three officials in the mayor's office—**his secretary, treasurer, and office manager**—were taken away in handcuffs.

  The whistle blower's revelation—**that the government was spying on its citizens**—was widely condemned.

  The accident—**the result of a drunk driver**—held up traffic for hours.

Exercise 18.6: Punctuating Enumerations and Explanations

Punctuate the following sentences, and give your reasons.

CCSS.L.9–10.2.B:
Use a colon to introduce a list or quotation.

1. There were four men in the hunting party a plumber a teacher a businessman and a banker.

2. Three levels on the scoring rubric namely Proficient Adequate and Deficient are used in grading the essays.

3. Mozart was the composer of several great operas namely *Le nozze di Figaro The Magic Flute* and *Don Giovanni.*

4. Some cancers can be cured that is their progress can be forced into remission if they are caught in the early stages.

5. Hitler had one undeniable gift the ability to make great speeches.

CCSS.L.8.2.A:
Use punctuation (comma, ellipsis, dash) to indicate a pause or break.

6. Often a rewording of a sentence gives a more courteous phrasing for example as you request I will pay the bill rather than I will pay the bill because you request it.

7. The following cities were included in our itinerary Glasgow Edinburgh Aberdeen and Dundee.

8. Johann Sebastian Bach is regarded as the composer of some of the greatest masterpieces of all time the Brandenburg Concertos The Well-Tempered Clavier the Mass in B Minor and numerous other compositions of church and instrumental music.

9. His excuse for not completing his assignment was a fabrication he was sitting in the emergency room because of his asthma.

10. The text message read as follows your article is accepted email with confirmation details to follow.

11. Two books an Oxford paperback dictionary and a rhyming dictionary are always on my desk.

12. On my desk I always have two books namely an Oxford paperback dictionary and a rhyming dictionary.

13. William Faulkner was one of the greatest writers of the 20th century for several reasons his unmatched stylistic resourcefulness the depth of his characterization and his persistence in exploring fundamental human issues.

14. I have several reasons to retire I'm old enough I have the money and I'm sick of the day-to-day grind of working.

DIRECT QUOTATIONS

CCSS.L.9–12.2:
Demonstrate command of the conventions of standard English capitalization, punctuation, and spelling when writing.

A *Comma* or a *Colon* is used before a formal direct quotation. The modern tendency is towards the use of a comma unless the quotation is long.

> He said**, "Oh no, I've got another one here,"** and he produced another couple of inches of tallow candle. (Mark Twain.)

> Finally, during a lull caused by a new deal, the Swede suddenly addressed Johnnie**: "I suppose there have been a good many men killed in this room."** (Stephen Crane.)

With expressions such as *he said*, a direct quotation is followed by a comma, except when the quote is a question or exclamation.

> **"You're handsomer than you used to be,"** she said thoughtfully. (F. Scott Fitzgerald.)

> **"Are you very tired?"** she asked.

> **"Who could help from laughing!"** I said.

CCSS.L.8.2.A:
Use punctuation (comma, ellipsis, dash) to indicate a pause or break.

When *he said, she said*, etc., come within the quotation, the punctuation following these expressions may be a comma or a period. The choice depends upon the closeness of the connection between the two parts of the quotation, or whether they can stand alone as complete sentences.

> "I don't believe," **she said,** "that he is responsible."

> "Yes," **I said,** "pasta would be perfect."

> "We can't go," **she said.** "We don't have the time."

> "What's his complaint?" **she asked.** "We've given him more than enough money."

A quoted word or phrase inserted informally into a sentence does not require a comma to set it off.

> Turning to others online for help or money is known as "crowdsourcing."

(See also the examples in the following section.)

Miscellaneous Use of Quotation Marks

CCSS.L.9–12.2:

Demonstrate command of the conventions of standard English capitalization, punctuation, and spelling when writing.

Slang and words or phrases used in a special sense; translations of foreign words or phrases; the titles of poems, short stories, and periodical articles are enclosed in quotation marks.

> His **"little friend"** got him into trouble.

> One of the first Latin expressions I learned was **In Hoc Signo Vinces** ("In this sign you will conquer").

> **"The Waste Land"** is one of my favorite poems.

Many newspapers and magazines prefer the use of quotation marks for all titles, including books.

When the name of a magazine or newspaper and the title of a book or an article occur together, the former is italicized and the latter is enclosed in quotation marks.

> This week's ***New Yorker*** features John Updike's last article, "Museum Hours."

Quotations Within a Quotation. A quotation within a quotation is enclosed by single quotation marks.

> "When he said, **'You won't believe this,'** we had no idea what he meant," replied John.

Exercise 18.7: Punctuating Just About Everything

Insert quotation marks and make any other changes that are needed.

WRITING PROMPT:
Relate an interesting conversation you have had. Include both direct and indirect quotations.

1. But why did you choose this river out of all the rivers they asked him

2. Take these for a week the doctor said blandly and fixed his eyes steadily on his patient's face

3. After a moment's hesitation she replied I understand without my explaining further

4. It's right here he said to the taxi driver as she saw her building ahead

5. In his football articles he's always using words like pigskin and gridiron

CCSS.L.9–12.2:
Demonstrate command of the conventions of standard English capitalization, punctuation, and spelling when writing.

6. When I received your text message to come at once I lost no time in heading out

7. For ninth grade students Romeo and Juliet is easy peasy compared to Shakespeare's other plays.

8. Then we read Whitman's Song of Myself and compared it with Wordsworth's The Prelude

9. Well he replied this is what I want to eat

10. The word occasionally is often misspelled.

11. On the contrary however there is excellent reason to hold that a man of thirty forty or even fifty can learn nearly anything better than he could when he was fifteen.

CCSS.L.8.2.A:
Use punctuation (comma, ellipsis, dash) to indicate a pause or break.

12. He is not really wise he is only intelligent.

13. Wherever Mrs. Good turned in protest she met the scornful opposition of aldermen, clergymen, statesmen.

14. And there are only three qualifications for tenants that they own good implements be reasonably free from debt and have interest in ultimate farm ownership.

15. Adventure would come and for the moment he was at ease lingering on its threshold.

16. In their pioneer days only a scant few years ago news broadcasters who were mostly ex-newspapermen tried using city-room methods.

17. Moreover they have been on the whole poor linguists and so they have dragged their language with them and forced it upon the human race.

HYPHENS

CCSS.L.11–12.2.A:
Observe hyphenation conventions.

Hyphenation is full of pitfalls and not at all an exact science. The rules vary between academic disciplines and publishing styles, leaving little room for personal preferences. Often it's up to an editor to make a decision about how to hyphenate. The choices are often beguiling.

For example, the word *water-ski* is hyphenated when it's a verb, according to most major dictionaries. But *water ski* takes no hyphen when it's a noun. No rules can help you understand these differences. Students and writers must look them up in a dictionary.

What follows are the major instances in which hyphenation is called for.

Compound Modifiers

CCSS.L.11–12.2.A:
Observe hyphenation conventions.

A compound modifier consists of two or more words modifying another word. They can act as adjectives or adverbs. Some of these are in the dictionary, many are not.

- Permanent compound modifier before a noun.

The compounds found in most major dictionaries retain the hyphen when placed before a noun.

> I hate dealing with **ill-informed** bureaucrats.

> It was a **no-holds-barred** fight.

MLA suggests not using the hyphen when placed after the noun.

> The bureaucrat was **ill informed**.

> The fight was **no holds barred**.

CCSS.L.11–12.1.A:
Apply the understanding that usage is a matter of convention, can change over time, and is sometimes contested.

- *-ly* Adverbs.

An exception to the compound modifier rules is that *-ly* adverbs are not hyphenated.

> My neighbors are a **happily married** couple.

> My neighbors are **happily married**.

> He has **surprisingly helpful** ideas.

> His ideas are **surprisingly helpful**.

Compound Adjectives Containing Specific Words

CCSS.L.11–12.2.A:
Observe hyphenation
conventions.

Compounds with specific words are hyphenated (or not) as follows.

- Compound adjective with **better**.

    His is a **better known** book.

    His book is **better known**.

- Compound adjective with **elect**.

    President-elect Obama.

- Compound adjective with **ever**.

    My **ever-important** business partner.

    My business partner is **ever important**

- Compound adjective with **half**.

    A **half-baked** idea

    His idea was **half-baked**.

- Compound adjective with **ill**.

    An **ill-conceived** idea.

    The idea was **ill conceived**

- Compound adjective with **less** or **least**.

    The **least known** fact.

    His ideas are **less known**.

- Compound adjective with **little**

    A **little-known** song.

    The song was **little known**.

- Compound adjective with **lower**.

    Lower-level employees.

    Everyone under him is considered **lower level**.

- Compound adjective with **much**.

    It was a **much-needed** break

The break was **much needed**.

- Compound adjective with *near*.

  A **near-death** experience.

  I had an experience that was **near-death**.

- Compound adjective with *self*.

  He was a **self-proclaimed** genius.

  His genius was **self-proclaimed**.

- Compound adjective with *too*.

  A **too-difficult** class.

  The class was **too difficult**.

- Compound adjective with *well*.

  My grandfather was a **well-loved** man.

  My grandfather was **well loved**.

Compound Adjectives of Specific Types and Forms

CCSS.L.11–12.2.A:
Observe hyphenation conventions.

Compounds of certain specific types are hyphenated as explained below.

- Compound adjective with a comparative or superlative.

  A **slower moving** cancer.

  His cancer is **slower moving**.

  The **longest lasting** battery.

  The battery is the **longest lasting**.

- Compound adjective indicating age with *year* and *old*.

  A **five-year-old** child.

  The child is **five years old**.

- Compound adjective formed with a past participle.

  A **well-known** fact.

  The fact is **well known**.

A **moth-eaten** garment.

The garment was **moth eaten**.

- Compound adjective using a common multi-word phrase.

    A **best-of-all-possible-worlds** experience.

    Carpe diem is a **live-for-today** philosophy.

- Compound adjective of two or more colors.

    A **brownish-gray** swamp.

    The swamp was **brownish gray**.

    An **orange-red** sunset.

    The sunset was **orange-red**.

- Compound adjectives containing a number.

    A **thousand-mile** road trip.

    A **third-rate** plumber.

    A **two-thirds** majority.

    The **second-largest** city.

    A **half-hour** program.

    A **two-thirty** appointment.

    A **ten percent** majority. (no hyphen)

Prefixes

CCSS.L.11–12.2.A:
Observe hyphenation conventions.

The general rule is not to hyphenate a prefix unless it precedes a capital letter (*pre-Christian*) or number (*post-9/11*), the hyphen prevents confusion (*re-create* vs. *recreate*), or the hyphen ends with the same letter of the word it precedes. (*anti-industrial, ultra-adversary*).

- **anti-**

    Hyphenate most words with *anti-*, with a few exceptions: *antibiotic, antidepressant, antidote, antifreeze, antihistamine, antipasto, antiperspirant, antithesis, antitrust.*

- **co-**

  When *co-* indicates an occupation, position, or status, hyphenate the word: *co-author, co-chair, co-host, co-owner, co-pilot, so-sponsor, co-star, co-worker.*

- **in-**

  Don't confuse the prefix *in-* ("not") with the preposition *in*. Compounds with *in-* are not hyphenated: *insufferable, inaccurate, indecisive, intolerable, indiscreet, indirect, infallible.*

  Compounds formed with the preposition *in* are hyphenated: *an in-depth study, an in-house investigation.*

CCSS.L.11–12.1.A:
Apply the understanding that usage is a matter of convention, can change over time, and is sometimes contested.

- **non-**

  Hyphenate only when necessary to avoid confusion or awkwardness: *non-nuclear, non-party-goers, non-Beatles fan.*

- **pre-**

  American newspapers hyphenate this prefix if the word that follows begins with an *e: pre-election, pre-eminent, pre-empt, pre-establish, pre-exist.*

Suffixes

CCSS.L.11–12.2.A:
Observe hyphenation conventions.

Most compounds with suffixes are not hyphenated. However, there are some exceptions.

- **-fold**

  Hyphenate if this suffix follows a numeral: (*10-fold*) or follows another hyphenated word (*thirty-two-fold*).

- **-in-law**

  This suffix is always hyphenated: *father-in-law, mother-in-law, sister-in-law, brothers-in-law.*

- **-like**

  Hyphenate all words with this suffix unless listed differently in the dictionary: *stupid-like, crazy-like, expert-like, Arizona-like.*

- **-wide**

  If not found in the dictionary, hyphenate these compounds: *institution-wide, company-wide, neighborhood-wide*

Chapter

19

Spelling and Confusing Words

COMMON CORE STATE STANDARDS

NOTE:
Some of the skills in this chapter were introduced at lower grade levels; yet, due to the recursiveness of the language standards, they require further attention at the high school level.

☞ *CCSS.ELA-LITERACY.L.11–12.1.B: Resolve issues of complex or contested usage, consulting references (e.g., Merriam–Webster's Dictionary of English Usage, Garner's Modern American Usage) as needed.*

☞ *CCSS.ELA-LITERACY.L.11–12.2.B: Spell correctly.*

☞ *CCSS.ELA-LITERACY.L.4.1.G: Correctly use frequently confused words (e.g., to, too, two; there, their).*

Even in the digital age spelling is important. Learn to apply the ***Spelling Patterns*** given below, and guard against repeatedly making the same spelling errors.

Pattern 1: IE and EI

CCSS.L.11–12.2.B:
Spell correctly.

The following old rhyme might be helpful.

> Put *i* before *e*,
> Except after *c*,
> Or when sounded like *a*,
> As in *neighbor* and *weigh*;
> And except *seize* and *seizure*
> And also *leisure*,
> *Weird, height,* and *either,*
> *Forfeit* and *neither.*

Examine the following list of common words spelled with *IE*.

ach**ie**ve	bel**ie**f	f**ie**nd	gr**ie**f	interv**ie**w
aggr**ie**ve	bel**ie**ve	misch**ie**vous	f**ie**rce	gr**ie**vance

alien	besiege	fiery	grieve	piece
chief	brief	friend	mischief	piety
niece	lieu	mien	pierce	priest
quiet	piebald	pied	reprieve	retrieve
review	relief	relieve	shriek	thievery
view	wield	sieve	handkerchief	befriend
field	frontier	hygiene	thieve	fief
efficient	conscience	prescient	ancient	deficient

Examine the list below of common words spelled with *EI*.

deceit	freight	either	ceiling	deceitful
perceive	veil	height	conceit	deceive
receive	neigh	leisure	seizure	receipt
forfeit	counterfeit	seize	conceive	receive
surfeit	height	neither	seize	weird

Pattern 2: -SEDE, -CEED, -CEDE

CCSS.L.11–12.2.B:
Spell correctly.

Examine the list below of the words that end in -*sede, ceed,* and *cede.*

supersede	proceed	exceed	succeed	accede
precede	secede	concede	intercede	accede

Pattern 3: -ABLE, -IBLE

CCSS.L.11–12.2.B:
Spell correctly.

The suffix -*able* is used to form adjectives.

comfortable	drinkable	laughable	readable	unthinkable
adjustable	affable	conceivable	degradable	educable
executable	honorable	impermeable	measurable	immutable
intractable	irrefutable	laughable	navigable	knowledgeable

Words ending in -*ible* are often preceded by a double *ss* before the -*ible.*

accessible	permissible	admissible	transmissible	compressible

Words ending in -*ible* often have a noun form ending in -*ion.* Drop the -*ion* and add -*ible*: for example, *permission* ⇒ *permissible.*

admissible	reversible	extensible	compressible	reversible
corruptible	coercible	divisible	transmissible	comprehensible
perceptible	combustible	digestible	reprehensible	destructible

| collect**ible** | convert**ible** | deduct**ible** | access**ible** | expans**ible** |

The suffix -*ible* is used following the soft sound of *g* or *c*.

| dedu**cible** | produ**cible** | incorri**gible** | invin**cible** | iras**cible** |
| eli**gible** | le**gible** | intelli**gible** | negli**gible** | tan**gible** |

Pattern 4: -OUS

CCSS.L.11–12.2.B:
Spell correctly.

Nouns ending in -*f* change the *f* to *v* when adding -*ous*.

grief ⇒ grie**vous**   mischief ⇒ mischie**vous**

Nouns ending in -*y* drop the *y* and add *e* before -*ous*.

beauty ⇒ beaut**eous**   pity ⇒ pit**eous**   joy ⇒ joy**ous** (exception)

When adding -*ous* to a noun ending in -*e*, drop the *e*.

adventure ⇒ adventur**ous**   analogue ⇒ analog**ous**   desire ⇒ desir**ous**

Exceptions are the following:

courag**eous**   advantag**eous**   outrag**eous**

Pattern 5: -AL

CCSS.L.11–12.2.B:
Spell correctly.

addition**al**	gener**al**	origin**al**	acquitt**al**	propos**al**
adverbi**al**	jovi**al**	ov**al**	arriv**al**	recit**al**
annu**al**	leg**al**	pen**al**	betray**al**	refus**al**
brut**al**	logic**al**	person**al**	capit**al**	reviv**al**
classic**al**	magic**al**	reg**al**	deni**al**	sign**al**
cleric**al**	medic**al**	trivi**al**	fat**al**	neutr**al**

Pattern 6: -EL

CCSS.L.11–12.2.B:
Spell correctly.

bush**el**	jew**el**	nov**el**	satch**el**	canc**el**
kenn**el**	nick**el**	shov**el**	chann**el**	kern**el**
pan**el**	swiv**el**	flann**el**	mod**el**	parc**el**
trav**el**	funn**el**	mors**el**	quarr**el**	trow**el**
ang**el**	barr**el**	duff**el**	mors**el**	past**el**
runn**el**	snork**el**	yod**el**	bag**el**	gosp**el**

Pattern 7: -LE

CCSS.L.11–12.2.B:
Spell correctly.

sample	dribble	muscle	settle	battle
ample	drizzle	muzzle	shuffle	gable
angle	fable	myrtle	shackle	nuzzle
article	fickle	needle	sizzle	sprinkle
ankle	fiddle	nestle	shuttle	beetle
baffle	frizzle	nibble	sparkle	gentle

Pattern 8: -ER or OR

CCSS.L.11–12.2.B:
Spell correctly.

actor	counselor	operator	advertiser	manager
administrator	editor	radiator	beginner	manufacturer
aviator	elevator	senator	computer	printer
bachelor	escalator	spectator	consumer	purchaser
collector	governor	sponsor	employer	receiver
commentator	indicator	supervisor	farmer	scanner
conductor	inventor	interpreter	treasurer	contractor

Pattern 9: L -AR

CCSS.L.11–12.2.B:
Spell correctly.

Only a small number of words end in -ar.

beggar	dollar	grammar	familiar	calendar
regular	peculiar	liar	collar	singular

Pattern 10: AL- and -FUL

CCSS.L.11–12.2.B:
Spell correctly.

Al- is a prefix written with one *l* when preceding another syllable.

almost   **al**so   **al**ways   **al**though

-Ful is a suffix written with one *l* when added to another syllable.

truth**ful**   regret**ful**   event**ful**   use**ful**

Single vowel *y* changes to *i* when adding any ending unless the ending begins with *i*. Notice adding the suffix -*ful* causes a single vowel *y* to change to *i*.

beauty + **ful** = beaut**iful**   bounty + **ful** = bount**iful**   mercy + **ful** = merc**iful**

Pattern 11: -ANCE, -ANT, -ANCY

CCSS.L.11–12.2.B:
Spell correctly.

abund**ant**	descend**ant**	import**ant**	malign**ancy**	abund**ance**
eleg**ance**	inherit**ance**	f**ancy**	ten**ancy**	remembr**ance**
hesit**ancy**	milit**ancy**	relev**ancy**	vagr**ancy**	preponder**ant**

Pattern 12: -ENCE, -ENT, -ENCY

CCSS.L.11–12.2.B:
Spell correctly.

abs**ence**	dilig**ence**	occurr**ence**	abs**ent**	dilig**ent**
oppon**ent**	abstin**ence**	diverg**ence**	pat**ent**	abstin**ent**
diverg**ent**	pati**ence**	tend**ency**	viol**ence**	transpar**ency**

Pattern 13: -ENSE

CCSS.L.11–12.2.B:
Spell correctly.

def**ense**	exp**ense**	imm**ense**	off**ense**	pret**ense**
susp**ense**	d**ense**	inc**ense**	nons**ense**	s**ense**
cond**ense**	def**ense**	t**ense**	disp**ense**	lic**ense**

Pattern 14: -ARY, -ERY

CCSS.L.11–12.2.B:
Spell correctly.

More than three hundred words end in *-ary*; fewer end in *-ery*.

auxili**ary**	honor**ary**	secret**ary**	bound**ary**	imagin**ary**
second**ary**	diction**ary**	volunt**ary**	tribut**ary**	element**ary**
vocabul**ary**	evolution**ary**	tempor**ary**	sedent**ary**	ancill**ary**
adult**ery**	slav**ery**	bak**ery**	batt**ery**	glitt**ery**
groc**ery**	jitt**ery**	liv**ery**	orn**ery**	sorc**ery**
scull**ery**	slith**ery**	tann**ery**	wat**ery**	witch**ery**

Pattern 15: -ISE, -IZE, -YZE

CCSS.L.11–12.2.B:
Spell correctly.

There are no hard and fast rules for distinguishing between these two endings.

advert**ise**	enterpr**ise**	adv**ise**	exerc**ise**	ar**ise**
franch**ise**	chast**ise**	merchand**ise**	comprom**ise**	superv**ise**
agon**ize**	item**ize**	antagon**ize**	local**ize**	caps**ize**
modern**ize**	central**ize**	familiar**ize**	hypnot**ize**	visual**ize**

Note. There are only two common words that end in *-yze*.

analy**ze**   paraly**ze**

Pattern 16: -IC

CCSS.L.11–12.2.B:
Spell correctly.

Sometimes a *-k* is added before a suffix beginning with *e, i,* or *y*. This is done in order to preserve the hard consonant sound.

coli**cky**	froli**cking**	froli**cked**	picni**cked**	picni**cking**
gimmi**cked**	gimmi**cking**	mimi**cked**	mimi**cking**	traffi**cked**
traffi**cking**	si**cked**	si**cking**	politi**cked**	politi**cking**

Pattern 17: Final -Y after a Vowel

CCSS.L.11–12.2.B:
Spell correctly.

A final -y after a vowel is retained with the addition of a suffix.

attorne**ys**	chimne**ys**	donke**ys**	medle**ys**	pulle**ys**
trolle**ys**	valle**ys**	volle**ys**	alla**yed**	alla**ying**
anno**yed**	anno**ying**	bu**ying**	swa**yed**	portra**yal**
bu**yer**	emplo**yer**	conve**yance**	anno**yance**	destro**yer**

Exceptions are the following:

da**ily**	pa**id**	ga**iety**	sla**in**	la**id**	sa**id**

Pattern 18: Final -Y after a Consonant

CCSS.L.11–12.2.B:
Spell correctly.

When a consonant precedes the -y, the y changes to *i* with the addition of a suffix. Note that when adding -ing, the y is always retained:

carr**ied**	cop**ied**	hurr**ied**	mudd**ied**	accompan**ied**
carr**ying**	cop**ying**	hurr**ying**	mudd**ying**	accompan**ying**

Pattern 19: Final -Y in a Plural of a Noun Formed with -ES

CCSS.L.11–12.2.B:
Spell correctly.

Change the -y to *i* and add *-es*.

all**ies**	enem**ies**	salar**ies**	traged**ies**	dictionar**ies**

Pattern 20: Third-Person Singular Verb Form

CCSS.L.11–12.2.B:
Spell correctly.

To make a verb third person singular, add the ending -s.

| reads | walks | falls | plays | jumps |

If the word *hisses*—after -ch, -s, -sh, -x, and z—then add -es.

| boxes | marches | buzzes | hisses | washes |

For verbs with *y's* that change to *i*, add -es.

| harries | dignifies | marries | miscarries | classifies |
| ferries | flurries | carries | worries | tarries |

For verbs that drop the final silent *e*, add -es.

| lives | arrives | approves | improves | shoves |

For verbs that end with *f* that changes to *v*, add -es.

| shelves | elves | calves | halves | wolves |

Pattern 21: Final -Y in Adverbs Formed by Adding -LY

CCSS.L.11–12.2.B:
Spell correctly.

Change the -y to *i*.

| airily | angrily | busily | clumsily | easily |
| bodily | daily | easily | gaily | hastily |

Pattern 22: Final -Y in Nouns Formed by Adding -NESS, -LESS

CCSS.L.11–12.2.B:
Spell correctly.

Change the -y to *i*.

| business | coziness | iciness | merciless | earthiness |
| blurriness | bossiness | craziness | fatherliness | happiness |

Pattern 23: Drop a Final -E Before a Vowel Suffix

CCSS.L.11–12.2.B:
Spell correctly.

Drop the final -*e* before a suffix beginning with a vowel.

guidance	plumage	usable	grievance	observance
larger	bravest	movable	lovable	imaginable
receiving	aching	bridal	definable	lovable
noticing	servicing	encouraging	charging	owing

Exceptions are the following:

to**eing**	sho**eing**	dy**eing**	sing**eing**	ting**eing**
chang**eable**	notic**eable**	manag**eable**	outrag**eous**.	servic**eable**

When -*ing* is added to words ending in -*ie*, the -*e* is dropped and the *i* changed to *y* to prevent a double *i*: *dying, lying, vying, tying.*

Pattern 24: Retain a Final -E Before a Consonant Suffix

CCSS.L.11–12.2.B:
Spell correctly.

complete**ness**	genuine**ness**	acute**ness**	like**ness**	polite**ness**
amuse**ment**	enforce**ment**	advance**ment**	arrange**ment**	engage**ment**
advertise**ment**	move**ment**	require**ment**	manage**ment**	discourage**ment**
age**less**	taste**less**	care**less**	noise**less**	voice**less**
blame**less**	clue**less**	base**less**	use**less**	price**less**

Exceptions are the following:

abridg**ment**	acknowledg**ment**	judg**ment**	misjudg**ment**	abridg**ment**
care**ful**	grace**ful**	remorse**ful**	revenge**ful**	disgrace**ful**
hate**ful**	taste**ful**	resource**ful**	shame**ful**	revenge**ful**

Pattern 25: Doubling a Final Consonant

CCSS.L.11–12.2.B:
Spell correctly.

Words formed by adding a suffix beginning with a vowel to single-syllable words or words accented on the last syllable, when these words end in a single consonant preceded by a single vowel, the consonant is doubled.

cla**nn**ish	pla**nn**ed	ba**gg**age	wi**tt**y	abe**tt**ed
infe**rr**ed	prefe**rr**ed	refe**rr**ed	defe**rr**ed	gri**nn**ed
nu**nn**ish	cha**tt**y	fa**tt**y	cru**dd**y	da**dd**y

Chief exceptions to this rule are words in which the accent is thrown back to another syllable:

pref**er**ence	ref**er**ence	def**er**ence	conf**er**ence	indiff**er**ence

Pattern 26: Adding a Vowel to a Double Vowel Ending

CCSS.L.11–12.2.B:
Spell correctly.

Words formed by appending a vowel suffix to a word ending with two vowels generally retain the double vowels.

agree**able**	disagree**able**	woo**er**	tattoo**er**	unforesee**able**

COMMONLY MISSPELLED WORDS

The following words are frequently misspelled. Pick out those which give you trouble, and learn how to spell them. Perhaps you have been misspelling some of them regularly for years. A little concentration and practice should help.

CCSS.L.11–12.2.B:
Spell correctly.

abnormal	apparently	boycott
abolition	appraisal	brief
abscess	appreciation	bulletin
absence	argument	bureau
accede	assent	burglaries
accommodate	assessment	business
accumulate	assistance	
acknowledge	athletic	cafeteria
acquaintance	attendance	calendar
acquiesce	attendants	campaign
acquire	attorneys	canceled
actually	attribute	cancellation
adaption	auditor	candor
adequate	authentic	census
adjacent	autumn	certainty
affix	auxiliary	challenger
ageless		chameleon
aggravate	bachelor	changeable
aggressive	bacteria	chief
aging	bankruptcy	chronological
agitation	barely	classification
agreeable	basically	classified
all right	believe	coincidence
already	belligerent	collaborator
amateur	benefited	collateral
amplification	biased	colonization
analogous	bimonthly	colossal
analysis	biographer	column
analyze	bisect	commentator
answer	bombard	communal
anticipate	bondage	computerized
anxious	bookkeeper	concede
apparatus	boundary	conceive

CCSS.L.11–12.2.B:

Spell correctly.

concession
conflagration
congenial
congruent
connoisseur
connotation
conscience
conscientious
conscious
consensus
consistent
consultant
continually
controller
corporal
correspondence
courtesies
courtesy
credentials
criticism
cross-reference
crucial
currency
custody

debtor
deceive
decision
deductible
deemphasize
defective
defendant
deferred
deficit
definite
deliberate
delicious
dependent
derogatory
descendant

desert
desperately
dessert
develop
development
dilemma
disappear
discipline
disinterest
dispensable
dissatisfied
dissimilar
distasteful
documentary
dossier
drastically
durable
dyeing

economical
economy
effects
efficient
elaborate
embarrass
emergency
emigrant
eminent
emphasis
emphasize
endorse
endurance
enormous
enthusiastic
entrepreneur
envious
enzyme
equipped
erroneous
error

evasive
exaggerate
exceed
excel
excitable
exhaustible
exhibition
exhibitor
exhilarate
existence
exonerate
exorbitant
external
extraordinary
extravagant

facilitation
facsimile
faculties
falsify
familiarity
fascinating
fastener
fiendish
fiery
filament
filmstrip
finalist
finally
financial
financier
fissure
flecks
flexible
fluorescent
foliage
foreign
foresee
forfeit
forty

CCSS.L.11–12.2.B:
Spell correctly.

fourteen
function

gallery
galvanized
gauge
generalization
geographic
geological
ghetto
glamorous
glamour
glucose
gnash
government
graft
grammar
grateful
gravitational
grieve
grievous
gruesome
guarantee
guardian
guidance
guild
gymnast

handicapped
handkerchief
happily
harass
harassment
height
helium
hemoglobin
hemorrhage
heterogeneous
hindrance
homage

hors d'oeuvre
hosiery
hostage
humorous
hygiene
hygienic
hypocrisy

idiomatic
ignorant
illegitimate
illustrator
imminent
immovable
impasse
impenetrable
imprisonment
inasmuch as
incidentally
indict
indispensable
individual
inference
inflammatory
influential
infraction
ingenuity
inhuman
innocuous
innuendo
innumerable
inoculate
input
insurance
integrity
intelligent
intercede
interim
intermission
interpretive

interruption
intuition
inverted
involuntary
irrelevant
irreparably
irrigation
irritable
itemized
itinerary

jealous
jeopardy
journal
jovial
judgment
judiciary
jurisdiction
justice

khaki
kidney
kindergarten
kinsman

labeled
laboratory
ladies
latter
league
leased
legion
legitimate
leisure
liable
liaison
libel
liberal
liberate
license

CCSS.L.11–12.2.B:
Spell correctly.

lien	neither	plagiarism
likeness	nickel	planned
likewise	niece	playwright
linguist	ninety	pneumonia
liquefy'	ninth	politician
literally	noticeable	portable
logical	nuclear	possession
loose	nuisance	possibilities
lose	numerous	potato
losing		potatoes
lovable	oceanography	practically
lucrative	offense	preceding
	omission	preferable
maintain	omitted	preferably
maintenance	optional	preference
maneuver	ordinary	preparation
manual	outdated	prerogative
marital	overview	presume
mechanical	overweight	presumptuous
medieval		pretense
mediocre	pamphlet	previous
memento	panicky	principal
merely	paradigm	privilege
mileage	parallel	probably
milieu	parasite	procedure
millennium	pastime	proceed
miniature	patience	profit
minuscule	patient	programmed
miscellaneous	peculiar	promissory
mischievous	people's	pronunciation
mislaid	permissible	promissory
misspell	perseverance	pronunciation
monkeys	persistent	pseudonym
mortgage	persuade	psychiatric
movable	phenomenal	publicly
muscle	phony	pursue
	physical	
naturally	physician	quandary
necessary	picnicking	quantities
neighbor	pitiful	quartet

CCSS.L.11–12.2.B:

Spell correctly.

questionnaire	seize	thoroughly
queue	separate	though
quizzes	siege	thought
	sieve	threshold
raisin	similar	totaled
rarefy	sincerely	tragedy
realize	skeptic	traveler
reasonable	skillful	
receipt	souvenir	unanimous
receive	specialized	unauthorized
recognizable	specifically	unbearable
recommend	sponsor	unconscious
reconcile	stationary (fixed)	undoubtedly
regrettable	stationery (paper)	unfortunately
reinforce	statistics	uniform
relevant	strength	unify
rendezvous	subtlety	unique
repetitious	subtly	unmanageable
rescind	succeed	unnecessary
resemblance	successor	unwieldy
resilience	summarize	usage
resistance	supersede	
resources	surprise	vacancy
responsibility	surreptitious	vaccinate
restaurant	surveillance	vacillate
rhapsody	symmetrical	vacuum
rhetorical		vague
rhyme	tariff	valuing
rhythm	taunt	vegetable
rhythmic	taxiing	vengeance
	teammate	verbal
sacrifice	technical	villain
sacrilegious	technique	vinyl
salable	temperament	visible
salaries	tempt	volume
salient	tendency	voluntary
satellite	theater	voucher
scenes	theory	
schedule	thesis	warrant
scissors	thorough	weather

CCSS.L.11–12.2.B:
Spell correctly.

Wednesday

weird

welfare

whether

wholly

width

wield

wiring

withhold

witnesses

woeful

woman's

women's

woolly

wrapped

wretched

yacht

yield

yoke

COMMONLY CONFUSED WORDS

CCSS.L.11–12.1.B:
Resolve issues of complex or contested usage, consulting references (e.g., *Merriam–Webster's Dictionary of English Usage, Garner's Modern American Usage*) as needed.

English has a large number of words often confused in writing because the same sound in English can be spelled in a number of different ways.

Some of the words are pronounced alike but are different in meaning or spelling(*coarse, course; throne, thrown; their, there, they're*). These are known as homophones.

Some words look alike or almost alike (*affect, effect; accept, except*). Some words are sometimes written as one word and sometimes as two words (*all ready, already; any way, anyway; some times, sometimes*). Some words look entirely different but their meanings are confused (*amount of, number of; fewer, less*).

CCSS.L.4.1.G:
Correctly use frequently confused words (e.g., *to, too, two; there, their*).

The following exercises contain the most commonly confused words in the English language. Look them up in a good dictionary or usage guide to distinguish the differences in meaning. Be prepared to use them in sentences.

Exercise 19.1: Writing with Commonly Confused Words

Look up the meanings of the following words, write down the definitions, and write a sentence for each of the words. Be sure you understand why these words are often confused.

CCSS.L.11–12.1.B: Resolve issues of complex or contested usage, consulting references (e.g., *Merriam–Webster's Dictionary of English Usage, Garner's Modern American Usage*) as needed.

1. ability, capability, capacity

2. abjure, adjure

3. accept, except

CCSS.L.4.1.G: Correctly use frequently confused words (e.g., *to, too, two; there, their*).

4. accident, mishap

5. acknowledge, admit

6. adduce, deduce, induce

7. adequate, sufficient, enough

8. adverse, averse

9. advice, advise

10. aesthetics, ascetics

Exercise 19.2: Writing with Commonly Confused Words

Look up the meanings of the following words, write down the definitions, and write a sentence for each of the words. Be sure you understand why these words are often confused.

CCSS.L.11–12.1.B:
Resolve issues of complex or contested usage, consulting references (e.g., *Merriam–Webster's Dictionary of English Usage, Garner's Modern American Usage*) as needed.

CCSS.L.4.1.G:
Correctly use frequently confused words (e.g., *to, too, two; there, their*).

1. affect, effect

2. aid, aide

3. allude, elude

4. allusion, illusion

5. already, all ready

6. altar, alter

7. alternate, alternative

8. although, though

9. altogether, all together

10. ambiguous, equivocal

Exercise 19.3: Writing with Commonly Confused Words

Look up the meanings of the following words, write down the definitions, and write a sentence for each of the words. Be sure you understand why these words are often confused.

CCSS.L.11–12.1.B: Resolve issues of complex or contested usage, consulting references (e.g., *Merriam–Webster's Dictionary of English Usage, Garner's Modern American Usage*) as needed.

1. amend, emend

2. amiable, amicable

3. amoral, immoral, unmoral

CCSS.L.4.1.G: Correctly use frequently confused words (e.g., *to, too, two; there, their*).

4. amount, number

5. antidote, anecdote

6. anxious, eager

7. appraise, apprise

8. apt, liable, likely

9. assent, consent

10. assume, presume

Exercise 19.3: Writing with Commonly Confused Words

Look up the meanings of the following words, write down the definitions, and write a sentence for each of the words. Be sure you understand why these words are often confused.

CCSS.L.11–12.1.B:
Resolve issues of complex or contested usage, consulting references (e.g., *Merriam–Webster's Dictionary of English Usage, Garner's Modern American Usage*) as needed.

1. assumption, presumption

2. assure, ensure, insure

3. astrologer, astronomer

CCSS.L.4.1.G:
Correctly use frequently confused words (e.g., *to, too, two; there, their*).

4. attain, obtain

5. attend, attend to, tend to

6. augment, supplement

7. avenge, revenge

8. avert, divert

9. awhile, a while

10. bad, badly

Exercise 19.4: Writing with Commonly Confused Words

Look up the meanings of the following words, write down the definitions, and write a sentence for each of the words. Be sure you understand why these words are often confused.

CCSS.L.11–12.1.B:
Resolve issues of complex or contested usage, consulting references (e.g., *Merriam–Webster's Dictionary of English Usage, Garner's Modern American Usage*) as needed.

1. baited, bated

2. bale, bail

3. bare, bear

CCSS.L.4.1.G:
Correctly use frequently confused words (e.g., *to, too, two; there, their*).

4. bath, bathe

5. because of, due to

6. better, had better

7. between, among, amid

8. blatant, flagrant

9. born, borne

10. brake, break

May be copied for classroom use. Common Core Grammar by Thomas Fasano (Coyote Canyon Press: Claremont, CA); © 2015.

Exercise 19.5: Writing with Commonly Confused Words

Look up the meanings of the following words, write down the definitions, and write a sentence for each of the words. Be sure you understand why these words are often confused.

CCSS.L.11–12.1.B:
Resolve issues of complex or contested usage, consulting references (e.g., *Merriam–Webster's Dictionary of English Usage, Garner's Modern American Usage*) as needed.

1. breach, breech

2. breath, breathe

3. cache, cachet

CCSS.L.4.1.G:
Correctly use frequently confused words (e.g., *to, too, two; there, their*).

4. canvas, canvass

5. capital, capitol

6. carat, caret, carrot, karat

7. career, careen

8. censer, censor, censure, sensor

9. cite, site, sight

10. claim, maintain

Exercise 19.6: Writing with Commonly Confused Words

Look up the meanings of the following words, write down the definitions, and write a sentence for each of the words. Be sure you understand why these words are often confused.

CCSS.L.11–12.1.B:
Resolve issues of complex or contested usage, consulting references (e.g., *Merriam–Webster's Dictionary of English Usage, Garner's Modern American Usage*) as needed.

1. clench, clinch

2. coarse, course

3. common, mutual

CCSS.L.4.1.G:
Correctly use frequently confused words (e.g., *to, too, two; there, their*).

4. compelled, impelled

5. compliment, complement; complimentary, complementary

6. comprise, compose

7. concept, conception

8. condole, console

9. confidant, confidante, confident

10. congruous, congruent

Exercise 19.7: Writing with Commonly Confused Words

Look up the meanings of the following words, write down the definitions, and write a sentence for each of the words. Be sure you understand why these words are often confused.

CCSS.L.11–12.1.B:
Resolve issues of complex or contested usage, consulting references (e.g., *Merriam–Webster's Dictionary of English Usage, Garner's Modern American Usage*) as needed.

1. connive, conspire

2. connotation, denotation

3. conscience, conscious

CCSS.L.4.1.G:
Correctly use frequently confused words (e.g., *to, too, two; there, their*).

4. consequent, subsequent

5. contagious, infectious

6. consist, compose

7. contemporary, contemporaneous

8. contemptuous, contemptible

9. continual, continuous

10. converse, obverse, inverse, reverse

Exercise 19.8: Writing with Commonly Confused Words

Look up the meanings of the following words, write down the definitions, and write a sentence for each of the words. Be sure you understand why these words are often confused.

CCSS.L.11–12.1.B:
Resolve issues of complex or contested usage, consulting references (e.g., *Merriam–Webster's Dictionary of English Usage, Garner's Modern American Usage*) as needed.

1. convince, persuade

2. corollary, correlation

3. corporal, corporeal

CCSS.L.4.1.G:
Correctly use frequently confused words (e.g., *to, too, two; there, their*).

4. council, consul, counsel

5. councilor, counselor

6. credible, creditable, credulous

7. criterion, criteria

8. currant, current

9. deductive, inductive

10. definite, definitive

Exercise 19.9: Writing with Commonly Confused Words

Look up the meanings of the following words, write down the definitions, and write a sentence for each of the words. Be sure you understand why these words are often confused.

CCSS.L.11–12.1.B:
Resolve issues of complex or contested usage, consulting references (e.g., *Merriam–Webster's Dictionary of English Usage, Garner's Modern American Usage*) as needed.

1. defuse, diffuse

2. desert, dessert

3. deviant, deviate

CCSS.L.4.1.G:
Correctly use frequently confused words (e.g., *to, too, two; there, their*).

4. die, dye

5. differentiate, distinguish

6. discreet, discrete

7. disinterested, uninterested

8. distinct, distinctive, distinguished

9. dual, duel

10. e.g., i.e.

Exercise 19.10: Writing with Commonly Confused Words

Look up the meanings of the following words, write down the definitions, and write a sentence for each of the words. Be sure you understand why these words are often confused.

CCSS.L.11–12.1.B:
Resolve issues of complex or contested usage, consulting references (e.g., *Merriam–Webster's Dictionary of English Usage, Garner's Modern American Usage*) as needed.

1. each other, one another

2. elicit, illicit

3. empathy, sympathy

CCSS.L.4.1.G:
Correctly use frequently confused words (e.g., *to, too, two; there, their*).

4. enervate, innervate

5. enough, sufficient

6. especially, specially

7. evoke, invoke

8. explicit, implicit

9. extemporaneous, impromptu

10. fair, fare

Exercise 19.11: Writing with Commonly Confused Words

Look up the meanings of the following words, write down the definitions, and write a sentence for each of the words. Be sure you understand why these words are often confused.

CCSS.L.11–12.1.B:
Resolve issues of complex or contested usage, consulting references (e.g., *Merriam–Webster's Dictionary of English Usage, Garner's Modern American Usage*) as needed.

1. farther, further

2. faze, phase

3. feasible, possible

CCSS.L.4.1.G:
Correctly use frequently confused words (e.g., *to, too, two; there, their*).

4. fictional, fictitious

5. flack, flak

6. flare, flair

7. flaunt, flout

8. flesh out, flush out

9. flounder, founder

10. fluctuate, vacillate

Exercise 19.12: Writing with Commonly Confused Words

Look up the meanings of the following words, write down the definitions, and write a sentence for each of the words. Be sure you understand why these words are often confused.

CCSS.L.11–12.1.B:
Resolve issues of complex or contested usage, consulting references (e.g., *Merriam–Webster's Dictionary of English Usage, Garner's Modern American Usage*) as needed.

1. forbear, forebear

2. forego, forgo

3. foreword, forward

CCSS.L.4.1.G:
Correctly use frequently confused words (e.g., *to, too, two; there, their*).

4. former, latter

5. fortuitous, fortunate

6. fortuitous, fortunate

7. friar, fryer

8. gantlet, gauntlet, gamut

9. grisly, grizzly

10. groan, grown

Exercise 19.13: Writing with Commonly Confused Words

Look up the meanings of the following words, write down the definitions, and write a sentence for each of the words. Be sure you understand why these words are often confused.

CCSS.L.11–12.1.B:
Resolve issues of complex or contested usage, consulting references (e.g., *Merriam–Webster's Dictionary of English Usage, Garner's Modern American Usage*) as needed.

1. guild, gild

2. handle, manage

3. hangar, hanger

CCSS.L.4.1.G:
Correctly use frequently confused words (e.g., *to, too, two; there, their*).

4. hanged, hung

5. happen, transpire, occur

6. heroin, heroine

7. hilarious, hysterical

8. historic, historical

9. hoard, horde

10. hurdle, hurtle

Exercise 19.14: Writing with Commonly Confused Words

Look up the meanings of the following words, write down the definitions, and write a sentence for each of the words. Be sure you understand why these words are often confused.

CCSS.L.11–12.1.B:
Resolve issues of complex or contested usage, consulting references (e.g., *Merriam–Webster's Dictionary of English Usage, Garner's Modern American Usage*) as needed.

1. idle, idol, idyll

2. immigrate, emigrate

3. imminent, eminent, immanent

CCSS.L.4.1.G:
Correctly use frequently confused words (e.g., *to, too, two; there, their*).

4. imply, infer

5. inculcate, indoctrinate

6. infamous, notorious

7. inflammable, flammable

8. inflict, afflict

9. ingenious, ingenuous

10. innate, inherent

May be copied for classroom use. Common Core Grammar by Thomas Fasano (Coyote Canyon Press: Claremont, CA); © 2015.

Exercise 19.15: Writing with Commonly Confused Words

Look up the meanings of the following words, write down the definitions, and write a sentence for each of the words. Be sure you understand why these words are often confused.

CCSS.L.11–12.1.B:
Resolve issues of complex or contested usage, consulting references (e.g., *Merriam–Webster's Dictionary of English Usage, Garner's Modern American Usage*) as needed.

1. invaluable, valuable

2. irregardless, regardless

3. its, it's

CCSS.L.4.1.G:
Correctly use frequently confused words (e.g., *to, too, two; there, their*).

4. judicial, judicious

5. ladder, latter

6. lay, lie, lye

7. lead, led

8. leave, let

9. lend, loan

10. less, fewer

Exercise 19.16: Writing with Commonly Confused Words

Look up the meanings of the following words, write down the definitions, and write a sentence for each of the words. Be sure you understand why these words are often confused.

CCSS.L.11–12.1.B:
Resolve issues of complex or contested usage, consulting references (e.g., *Merriam–Webster's Dictionary of English Usage, Garner's Modern American Usage*) as needed.

1. lightening, lightning

2. loathe, loath

3. lose, loose, loosen

CCSS.L.4.1.G:
Correctly use frequently confused words (e.g., *to, too, two; there, their*).

4. luxuriant, luxurious

5. mantle, mantel

6. moral, morale

7. nauseous, nauseated

8. oblige, obligate

9. obtuse, abstruse

10. occur, transpire

Exercise 19.17: Writing with Commonly Confused Words

Look up the meanings of the following words, write down the definitions, and write a sentence for each of the words. Be sure you understand why these words are often confused.

CCSS.L.11–12.1.B:
Resolve issues of complex or contested usage, consulting references (e.g., *Merriam–Webster's Dictionary of English Usage, Garner's Modern American Usage*) as needed.

1. oral, verbal, aural

2. ordnance, ordinance

3. partly, partially

CCSS.L.4.1.G:
Correctly use frequently confused words (e.g., *to, too, two; there, their*).

4. patience, patients

5. peak, peek, pique

6. peal, peel, peeled

7. peer, pier

8. people, persons

9. persuade, convince

10. pitiable, pitiful

Exercise 19.18: Writing with Commonly Confused Words

Look up the meanings of the following words, write down the definitions, and write a sentence for each of the words. Be sure you understand why these words are often confused.

CCSS.L.11–12.1.B:
Resolve issues of complex or contested usage, consulting references (e.g., *Merriam–Webster's Dictionary of English Usage, Garner's Modern American Usage*) as needed.

1. pore, pour, poor

2. precede, proceed

3. principal, principle

CCSS.L.4.1.G:
Correctly use frequently confused words (e.g., *to, too, two; there, their*).

4. prophesy, prophecy

5. proscribe, prescribe

6. prostate, prostrate

7. proved, proven

8. provided, providing

9. rack, wrack

10. raise, rear, rise, raze

May be copied for classroom use. Common Core Grammar by Thomas Fasano (Coyote Canyon Press: Claremont, CA); © 2015.

Exercise 19.19: Writing with Commonly Confused Words

Look up the meanings of the following words, write down the definitions, and write a sentence for each of the words. Be sure you understand why these words are often confused.

CCSS.L.11–12.1.B:
Resolve issues of complex or contested usage, consulting references (e.g., *Merriam–Webster's Dictionary of English Usage, Garner's Modern American Usage*) as needed.

1. regrettable, regretful

2. rein, reign, rain

3. relegate, delegate

CCSS.L.4.1.G:
Correctly use frequently confused words (e.g., *to, too, two; there, their*).

4. repel, repulse, repellent, repulsive

5. riffle, rifle

6. right, write, rite, wright

7. rout, route

8. sail, sale, sell

9. seasonal, seasonable

10. sensual, sensuous

Exercise 19.20: Writing with Commonly Confused Words

Look up the meanings of the following words, write down the definitions, and write a sentence for each of the words. Be sure you understand why these words are often confused.

CCSS.L.11–12.1.B:
Resolve issues of complex or contested usage, consulting references (e.g., *Merriam–Webster's Dictionary of English Usage, Garner's Modern American Usage*) as needed.

1. silicon, silicone

2. simple, simplistic

3. slay, sleigh

CCSS.L.4.1.G:
Correctly use frequently confused words (e.g., *to, too, two; there, their*).

4. slew, slough, slue

5. sneaked, snuck

6. so, sow, sew

7. soar, sore

8. stake, steak

9. stare, stair

10. stationary, stationery

Exercise 19.21: Writing with Commonly Confused Words

Look up the meanings of the following words, write down the definitions, and write a sentence for each of the words. Be sure you understand why these words are often confused.

CCSS.L.11–12.1.B:
Resolve issues of complex or contested usage, consulting references (e.g., *Merriam–Webster's Dictionary of English Usage, Garner's Modern American Usage*) as needed.

1. staunch, stanch

2. steal, steel

3. straight, strait

CCSS.L.4.1.G:
Correctly use frequently confused words (e.g., *to, too, two; there, their*).

4. subsequent, consequent

5. systematic, systemic

6. tack, tact

7. than, then

8. there, their, they're

9. threw, through, thorough

10. throne, thrown

Exercise 19.22: Writing with Commonly Confused Words

Look up the meanings of the following words, write down the definitions, and write a sentence for each of the words. Be sure you understand why these words are often confused.

CCSS.L.11–12.1.B:
Resolve issues of complex or contested usage, consulting references (e.g., *Merriam–Webster's Dictionary of English Usage, Garner's Modern American Usage*) as needed.

1. till, until, 'til

2. to, too, two

3. tore, tour

CCSS.L.4.1.G:
Correctly use frequently confused words (e.g., *to, too, two; there, their*).

4. toward, towards

5. troop, troupe, trooper, trouper

6. use, usage

7. vain, vane, vein

8. vale, veil

9. venal, venial

10. way, weigh, whey

May be copied for classroom use. Common Core Grammar by Thomas Fasano (Coyote Canyon Press: Claremont, CA); © 2015.

Exercise 19.23: Writing with Commonly Confused Words

Look up the meanings of the following words, write down the definitions, and write a sentence for each of the words. Be sure you understand why these words are often confused.

CCSS.L.11–12.1.B:
Resolve issues of complex or contested usage, consulting references (e.g., *Merriam–Webster's Dictionary of English Usage, Garner's Modern American Usage*) as needed.

1. weak, week

2. weather, whether

3. which, witch

CCSS.L.4.1.G:
Correctly use frequently confused words (e.g., *to, too, two; there, their*).

4. who's, whose

5. whole, hole

6. wreak, reek

7. yoke, yolk

8. your, you're

INDEX

COMMON CORE GRAMMAR

Printed in Great Britain
by Amazon

83294340R00255